W9-DAO-560

STAND

A Memoir on Activism. A Manual for Progress.
What really happens when we stand on the front lines of change.

by Kathryn Bertine

NEW SHELF PRESS

Hardcover ISBN: 9781735901404
Paperback ISBN: 9798694588775
eBook ISBN: 9781735901411

Library of Congress: TXu 2-223-983

First paperback edition February 2021.

Cover art by Jennifer Vasko
Interior design by Thorsten Radde
Spine photo by Flaviano Ossola
Author photo by Kris Hanning

This is a work of nonfiction. All people portrayed are real. Some names have been changed.

Printed by New Shelf Press in the USA.

www.kathrynbertine.com

OTHER BOOKS & FILMS
BY KATHRYN BERTINE

All the Sundays Yet to Come

As Good As Gold

The Road Less Taken

Fathers & Daughters & Sports (anthology)

Half the Road:
The passion, pitfalls and power of women's pro cycling.

Fresh from the Homestretch

Praise for *STAND*

"On and off the bicycle, Kathryn Bertine has always chosen the challenging road. Whether it was her tenacious battle for equal road at the Tour de France, or her soul-searching comeback from a traumatic crash, Bertine's career as an athlete and advocate has been marked by courage, determinedness and an unshakeable sense of humor. As a slowpoke on two wheels, I hate that a talented cyclist can also be a great writer, but STAND is an inspiring testament to the power of choosing the challenging road, and it demonstrates how lucky all of sports – not just cycling – is to have Kathryn Bertine." **–Jason Gay, *The Wall Street Journal*. Author of *Little Victories*.**

"In *STAND*, Kathryn Bertine delivers more than a memoir – she presents a bold, honest blueprint for achieving change. All women who've had to work harder, stronger, and smarter to be recognized will identify with Kathryn's fight for women's inclusion at the Tour de France – a journey that was both painful and joyful (sometimes at the same time), and during which she met entrenched resistance at every step. Kathryn's story will inspire all readers – men and women, athletes or not – with strategies supporting a simple premise: when you want to achieve something, you set your goal, and you go out and make it happen no matter the obstacles. For anyone who doubts Kathryn's – or his or her own – ability to affect change, *STAND* dares you to ditch your doubts and get to work." **–Kyrsten Sinema, first female U.S. Senator for Arizona and IRONMAN triathlete.**

"No one takes a stand like Kathryn Bertine. Rider, writer and above all activist she has fought long and hard for everyone to share the road. As a collaborator and interviewee she's warm, witty and above all wise, as a writer she has the rare talent of infusing activism with humour and it's her intelligence and humanity that makes STAND such a compelling, honest and kick ass (could substitute inspiring but you're a kick ass) read." **–Suze Clemitson, *The Guardian* (UK).**

"I remember the first bike race I watched after retiring from seven years of pro cycling. Looking at the mob of flesh and carbon fiber flying around the European countryside, I couldn't believe I ever did that. How hard I worked to barely eke out a living... I still feel lucky that I survived. Reading *STAND*, I realize I had it easy. Kathryn Bertine is a force of a human, a great athlete and a brilliant, funny author. Men and women alike will find *STAND* inspires, entertains, and educates."
–Phil Gaimon, professional cyclist. Author of *Draft Animals.*

"Candid, raw, insightful, honest. As a four-time Olympian in ice hockey, I'm no stranger to the barriers women face in male-dominated sports. Bertine's story goes far beyond sports. Her memoir is unique, her manual is necessary. *STAND* will resonate with anyone who wonders what it takes to create change and move the dial forward." **–Angela Ruggiero, Olympic Gold Medalist. Author of *Breaking the Ice.***

"Great. Another book by a chick. Completely missed the mark. Didn't have any recipes or life-hacks for vacuuming. Just relentless optimism, indefatigable kindness and delusional visions of justice. I want a refund. But if you like this equality bullshit, Bertine's a fucking good writer and STAND is pretty good for a girl."
–Doug Stanhope, comedian. Author of *Digging Up Mother.*

"I don't have time for a blurb, but congratulations on your book!"
–Malcolm Gladwell. Author of *The Tipping Point, Blink, Outliers, What the Dog Saw* and *David and Goliath.*

DEDICATION

For my father, Peter K. Bertine.
Always there.

"Anyone willing to think like a Freak will occasionally end up on the sharp end of someone else's stick. Perhaps you'll raise an uncomfortable question, challenge an unorthodoxy or simply touch upon a subject that should have been left untouched. As a result, people will call you names. They may accuse you of consorting with witches or communists or even economists.
You may be heading toward a bruising fight. What happens next?"

-Stephen J. Dubner and Steven D. Levitt.
Authors of *Freakonomics* and *Think Like A Freak*.

"No matter what people tell you,
words and ideas can change the world."

-Robin Williams.

TABLE OF CONTENTS

Preface   xiii

1. Pauses, Silence & Cerberus   1
2. The Women's Tour that Used to Be   9
3. Love and Balance   22
4. St. Kitts and Nevis and Spearmint Gum   28
5. Couch Surfing is for Queens   34
6. Hope Hides in Tragedy   38
7. Back on Staff at ESPN   43
8. UCI Dinosaurs and Belgian Broomwagons   46
9. Censorship & Sisterblocking   48
10. Presidential Jesters, Kings of Norway & Queens of Persistence   55
11. Dreams, Realities and Documentaries   60
12. IndieGogo-ing the Distance   66
13. No One Climbs Hills Smiling   74
14. Mastering Almost and U-turns   78
15. Driving the Bus of Progress   82
16. List of Names   89
17. Paradox of Tradition   97
18. Dog Days and Broken Arms   104
19. Let's Get Excessive   107
20. Roll Camera, Roll Costa Rica   112
21. Team Camp and Water Buffalo Horns   118
22. Normal Kathryn   126
23. Inching Toward the Comma   129
24. Building the Sisterhood   140
25. Spacedust Sendoff   149
26. The World Responds (Except ASO)   157
27. Dinosaurs Love Silence   169
28. Crickets Be Damned   177

29.	The Meeting	188
30.	Adding Amy	199
31.	Broken Things	204
32.	Secret Mistress Activists	212
33.	World Premiere	218
34.	Try, Try, Try	224
35.	No More Sidelines	237
36.	Unraveling	247
37.	Universal Sports	254
38.	La Course by Tour de France	261
39.	Leaving Home	275
40.	Exits	281
41.	Camels in Dubai and Other Places Where I Lost My Shit	288
42.	Beginning of the Homestretch	295
43.	El Grupo and Moving Forward	299
44.	Crashes, Craters and Silence	307
45.	"Major" Changes	315
46.	Learning to Trust, Learning to Lose	328
47.	The Crash	336
48.	Rage and Remembering	344
49.	Back in the Saddle	352
50.	The Importance of Turning Left	355
51.	Together We All Move Forward	362
Epilogue/Spillogy		365
An Activist's Manual		371
Photo Insert		379
Bibliography & References		387
Acknowledgements		389
About the Author		391

PREFACE

The most pivotal day of my journey in activism went by way too fast, no matter how hard I try to slow the incalculable speed of memory. July 27, 2014. *Flashes of color, noise and blurry people as crowds pressed against the cycling barriers lining the Champs-Élysées. Wind in my ears and the whir of gears as we encircled the Arc d' Triomphe. Pounding heart and burning lungs in sync with the peloton of women around me.* We were racing at the Tour de France. A race that once banned women. For the last five years, I'd taken up arms—alongside fellow athletes and supporters around the world—against the discriminatory regulations and the bureaucratic dinosaurs that barred us from the roadways of France while men competed in the most iconic cycling race in the world. Finally, on this momentous day, here we were. 125 female professional cyclists in the heart of Paris, racing down the cobblestones of the Champs-Élysées. I reveled in every moment of our prodigious, triumphant day. Inside, though, I was cracking.

A photographer snapped a picture of me on my bike that day—appearing invincible, victorious, joyful and as though I had my shit together as I rolled toward the start line of the inaugural La Course by Tour de France. *All smiles! All strength! All confidence!* All lies.

What cannot be seen in that photograph are the tears streaming down behind my glasses. Beneath my glove, the wedding ring I cannot bear to take off. The fractures and fissures deep within. My body, strong. My soul, lost. I am weak, empty, scared, scarred, scripted, rehearsed and acting triumphant, fulfilled, confident, collected. In the fleeting pause between each cobblestone, despair seeps through the cracks of stillness and movement. On the outside, I am a warrior for justice. Inside, stone-cold fucking broken. That day, the weight of worthlessness consumed me. Hiding it seemed better. So I wore the historic victory of our presence at the Tour de France like mask over the private, ugly pain of advocacy.

When I sat down to write this story—about what we achieved for women's equality that day—I thought: People don't want to read about worthlessness. The

Brokenness. The Empties. Better to skip that stuff. Vulnerability isn't important. Took me five years to find the courage to disagree.

To write about creating change takes data, and I had plenty of that. But to write about activism requires a mirror. And a steel gut. And a box of tissues. And a reckoning with Vulnerability. In 2019 I taped the photograph of myself, on the bike in Paris, above my computer. As I sat down to write, the woman in the photograph whispered from under her mask:

You want to talk about what it takes to make change happen? You want to stop throwing away shitty first drafts? Fine. Then start writing about what really happens when we stand up and fight for what we believe. All of it. What happened in public. What happened in private. About your plan to walk in the woods and not come out. Write about what we need to talk about in our culture, our society, right now, today. That's how change happens. Facts, schmacts. That's not enough. Remember what Quixote said? "Facts get in the way of truth." You've got plenty of facts. Now bring in the truth. If you want to write anything worthwhile and meaningful about activism, then you're going to need to step onto that terrifyingly thin tightrope of vulnerability strung across the abyss of truth and authenticity. Ready?

No.

Ready?

Nope.

Ready?

Ooof.

Okay, Voice. Here we go...

We need to talk about what really happens when we stand up and fight for what we believe. We need to talk about the nasty underbelly of activism. And its beautiful, beautiful wings. We need to talk about the myth of strength, the truth of masks and the dark side of progress. We need to talk about being broken. Because the universal truth of adulthood is that we're all a little bit broken. We need to look closely at photographs and wonder about what isn't there, and shine a light into the cracks and caves of all the things we cannot see. We don't all need to be activists. But all do need to talk about how to support those who are out there standing on the frontlines of Change.

We need to stop thinking that happy people don't carry the weight of despair. We need to check in on our strongest friends and ask how they're really doing. We need to tell those who have their Shit Together that it's okay to Come Undone. We need to talk about demons; ours and others. We need to talk about suicide. We need to ask *Why* and embrace *How,* so we can be the Who, What and Where if someone needs us. Even if they don't ask. We need to talk about the frailty of strength and the armor of vulnerability. No, I don't have those mixed up.

We need to talk about divorce. We need to talk about divorce. We need to talk about it twice because there are two. The one we go through in public, the one we go through in private. We need to talk about pain. And how to channel it. We need to talk about sensitivity. And how to unchain it. We need to talk about the wardrobe of Masks, and when to wear them. Or not. We need to talk about depression until we cry tears of laugher from the sweet release of authenticity when we say, out loud, how truly fucking bad it is. We need to laugh. Not just because it feels good, but because Humor is the golden chariot of activism and laughter is how we hail a cab through the ugly, gridlocked traffic on the road to Progress.

We need to talk about demons, again. Not just talk about them, but *to* them. We need to talk to our inner beasts until we can look them straight in the eyes, pet their scaly hides, throw a saddle across their razored spines, grab tight the reins, and ride those crazy ogres wherever we so choose. Because we can choose. We need to stop trying to slay our demons and start building stables. We need to talk about how Activism just might be the great big barn where beasts and demons grow into Change and Progress. We need to understand the reality and consequence of what happens when we stand, lead and fight. We need to talk about it all.

At least I do. How activism bore me, broke me, re-built me and became my cornerstone of Self. Stepping onto the tightrope of vulnerability, I wrote this book because standing up and speaking out matters. And also, this: I was lost for a long time and I needed to write myself home. To figure stuff out. To find peace and clarity. To lock eyes with authenticity. To snuggle with my demons. To confront truth. To help others plot their route into the wilds of activism. To maybe help us all rise. To finally answer the question... Yes, our struggles are worth the journey. At least I've got that much figured out.

–Kathryn Bertine, Tucson, AZ. February 2021

NOTE: INTERACTIVE READER GUIDE

Dear curious, knowledge-craving readers, I've included footnotes throughout the book. Some are labeled **"Interactive Reader Guide."** These will provide more info on certain topics. For those using an eBook, just click the link. For those reading paperbacks or hardcovers of STAND, head over to www.kathrynbertine.com/irg and there will be a chronological list of weblinks to all Interactive Reader Guide footnotes. Happy learning and thank you for reading.

1

PAUSES, SILENCE & CERBERUS

O n a warm spring Arizona afternoon in 2009, I sat at my ancient desktop computer, with my index finger hovering over the send button. Then, paused. Hesitated. Waited. The weary fan in the hard drive wheezed and whirred with fatigue, in then out, one yogic cycle of mechanical breath. I eagerly wanted this email to fly through the data cables between Tucson and Paris, marking my first attempt to lobby the Tour de France for the equal inclusion of women. Still, I paused with my finger hovering over the button.

A whiff of the pungent scent of fresh paint hung in the air, as the deep red pigment labeled Scarlet Dragon exhaled its drying breath from the wall behind my desk. A wall I painted yesterday for no other reason than simply because I could. Such were the joys of first-time home ownership. The ties of an apron dug into my waist. I was a 34-year-old lunch waitress and my shift was about to start. Best to send the email now, I rationalized, since after the lunch shift I went directly to my second job as an adjunct professor of journalism at Pima Community College. Early mornings were spent cycling, middays spent working, evenings spent job searching. And researching women, history, sports and equal opportunity. I had worked on the contents of this email to Christian Prudhomme, race director of the Tour de France, for months. It was time. Send, I whispered. Now.

Every fiber of my being believed in this mission for gender equity. I didn't understand the wait—and weight—of the pause. Not then. I do, now. A decade later.

Something deep inside my soul grabbed onto that pause and held tight. Telling my gut, mind and heart that—should my finger press *send*—things would be different. *Oh please, it's just an email. Enough.* I brought my finger down upon *send* with gusto.

Hitting *send* was the moment my life in activism began, even though I didn't know it at the time. What I did know for certain was this: I wanted to be a professional cyclist. Because of a strange and wonderful turn I'd taken in my early thirties. After spending my twenties striving to be a professional figure skater then professional triathlete, my obstinate determinism had somehow caught the eyes of ESPN. From 2006 to 2008, ESPN hired me as a columnist/gonzo journalist/author as I attempted to qualify for the 2008 Beijing Summer Olympics.

The catch? Not in figure skating. Or triathlon. It had to be any other summer sport. After six months of trying just about every sport on the planet, road cycling became my chosen path for the remaining eighteen months of the assignment.

What started out as ESPN's idea of a "set-up-to-fail" foray into investigative journalism then blossomed into something else: a life-changing personal quest. From 31 to 33, my life as an athlete and a writer merged into one as my public and private lives strove toward the same finish line; an improbable Olympic dream. Hinging delicately on the border of sanity, I dove into this two-year assignment with equal parts personal and professional fervor. I wrote a book about the quest: *As Good As Gold.*

Spoiler alert: I did not qualify for the Beijing Olympics. But something wild happened. I *almost* did. The "almost" changed me. Sometimes, it is not the victories or losses that define our paths in life but the Wonder and What Ifs that lie between. When the ESPN assignment ended, my cycling did not. I was head over heels in love with this crazy sport.

I wanted to race bikes professionally. Not for ESPN, not for journalism. For myself. To fix some of this weirdly archaic stuff in the sport, like the fact only men could race the Tour de France. My love of road bike racing and equal rights for women took root. The ESPN assignment was over, but my passion was redirected. *Game over* morphed to *game on.*

During the 2008 Olympic qualification journey, I gained enough internal strength and power to rise to Category 1, the highest rank of amateur cycling. My position with ESPN literally afforded me the ability to try: all training and racing was covered during those two years. What wasn't automatically covered, however, was the key ingredient to athletic success: experience. To be strong and powerful is one thing. To know what to do with one's strength and power is an entirely different element. One that takes a lot of time. Making it to cycling's pro ranks wasn't going to be any easier than trying to get to the Olympics. The United States had about five top-tier pro women's teams where athletes received salaries and landing a contract was preciously rare.

The physical goal of being a pro bike racer was half my motivation. The other half stemmed from that same internal spring that fueled my inner journalist; exposing truths and solving problems. After nearly two years competing on the Olympic circuit of elite bicycle racing, I saw so many things that didn't make sense in our modern world.

Why were women's bike races shorter than the men's? Why fewer opportunities for women to race? Why were the smaller, poorer nations unable to enter or host races? Why do the women have fewer qualifying spots at the Olympics than the men? Why were the men of pro cycling earning thousands of dollars in prize money and the pro women just a few hundred? At the world's biggest, most famous bike race—The Tour de France—why is there no women's race? Those were my biggest Whys. But from 2006-2008 those Whys remained in the periphery of my own ESPN/Olympic quest. Now that the assignment was over, the Whys bubbled forth. Loudly. Requesting answers that I did not have. (Journalists hate not finding answers. Especially when there aren't any good ones.) On the heels of *Why* came my old friend, *What If*.

What if we could make this sport equal? None of this was really about racing bicycles. It was about challenging—and changing—*any* system where equal opportunity isn't present. Cycling was the medium, not the mission. Had I not qualified for the Knitting World Championships because women from St. Kitts and Nevis weren't granted access to the Yarn Making Preliminaries then I would fight just as hard for knitting equity. But it was cycling that grabbed my soul and didn't let go.

Perhaps, I thought, if I can become a pro cyclist and use my voice as a journalist, then we can truly create change in this weirdly archaic sport. And world. A new quest began.

A few months before sending the email to Christian Prudhomme in France, I began 2009 by ignoring the pit in my stomach slowly being gnawed away by reality. My dreams of becoming a pro cyclist were great, but food, shelter and bills took precedence. When my Olympic quest ended, I held hope my columnist position at ESPN would continue. There were promises of a new assignment. My two-year column *So You Wanna Be an Olympian?* had over two million hits per installment, which is none too shabby for a female amateur athlete writing for the male-dominated audience of professional sports on ESPN. Editors, executives and I engaged in discussions and promises of my next role with ESPN. I put three ideas on the table: A documentary installment profiling the amazing athletes of lesser-known sports. A column about the growth of sports/athletes in underdeveloped nations. And—my personal passion—a column on what exactly it would take for women to race the Tour de France.

See, I explained, all three of these ideas came from the experiences I encountered during As Good As Gold, so it's a natural connection to the original subject, and all the ESPN readers keep asking what's next, so hell, we could cover all three topics over the next few yea—

"Kathryn," ESPN said. "The economy's bad. We're on a hiring freeze."

"Right," my optimism answered. "But that'll thaw soon!"

Unfortunately, my optimism was not in charge at ESPN. They did not renew my contract.

The U.S. economic crash of 2008, as we know, did not thaw soon. Unemployment soared to 10 percent in 2009, nearly double the pre-recession percentage. In addition to my own unemployment, my nerves kicked into full gear when my humble, little condo—a non-luxurious, rectangularly cozy, 800 square-foot palace of independence knighting me into adulthood upon purchase—was suddenly slashed to half its value. I quickly evaluated my prospects. *As Good As Gold* would not be published until 2010. Living off royalties wasn't a reality. Unless Steven Spielberg bought the rights. I treasured this fantasy. The improbable odds of Steven Spielberg buying my life story actually made the odds of becoming a pro cyclist in my thirties seem much more attainable. Until then, reality harkened. To train, race and travel toward the goal of securing a pro contract, I'd need to do what most athletes do: work several other jobs while rising through the ranks.

I found a "new" 1999 Volvo station wagon with 150K miles for $4999 and purchased it with a credit card. I felt exceedingly affluent driving a car with little plastic windshield wipers on the headlights. One of them even worked. I took a job waitressing and landed an adjunct teaching position at Pima Community College. Combined, those careers brought in about $1000/month. Which happened to be the same price of my mortgage. I took in a roommate to cut that expense in half. Then I picked up a $250/month sponsorship from a local benefactor who sponsored athletes. The budget left about $50 a week to spend on groceries. I already mastered the art of discount shopping at Grocery Outlet during my grad student days. God, I loved that place. There were fruit flies in the produce section and boxes of Christmas-themed Rice Krispies in July and weirdly exhilarating foreign foods with pretty pictures that I devoured without actually knowing what they were.

Ok, I could do this again. After all, it was just a hiring freeze at ESPN. I believed everything would be fine. I also believed in unicorns. Going from a livable salary with ESPN to an annual income of $15,000 was terrifying.

"At least you won't have to pay taxes since you're below the poverty line!" my internal optimist chirped. She's annoying as hell. Some days I want to punch her in the face. Lucky for her she was also correct. The poverty line in 2009 hovered at $17,500.

As 2009 rolled underway and I settled into waitressing and adjunct-ing, I sought out all pro cycling prospects. I applied to every professional team, citing the results of my 2008 races during my ESPN quest. As I naively bumbled my way through the Olympic qualification journey, I was fortunate to garner some decent UCI results.[1] From Uruguay to China to Venezuela to El Salvador, in the midst of my fledgling rise through the ranks, I somehow garnered a few top twenty finishes in fields stacked with Olympians and national champions. Locally, I was the Arizona state champion. Also, the national champion of St. Kitts and Nevis,[2] which I vowed to represent for the remainder of my cycling career.

Surely, I thought, these were enough accolades to get noticed by the professional teams. Perhaps I wouldn't be the team leader, but the role of domestique—the French term for "servant" aka workhorse—was the role I wanted. Neither a sprinter nor a climber, the steady grind of endurance was my physiological diesel engine. Taking long pulls at the front of the peloton,[3] fetching bottles, attacking, chasing, blocking the wind… these were my skills. At 34, my mental and physical stamina were stronger than ever. With a background in print and web media, I could also offer teams something off the bike, too: journalism exposure. Perhaps these might be considered a bonus! Confidently, I sent my race resume out to every pro cycling team in the U.S., Canada and Europe. There had to be *one* team would consider a workhorse with experience and media perks.

Nope. Not one. I received nine rejections. Half of which were outright Nos, half of which were ghosted silence. No professional team wanted anything to do

---

[1] UCI; Union Cycliste Internationale, the governing body of cycling.
[2] When St. Kitts and Nevis granted me dual citizenship, I willingly raced under their flag for the permanence of my cycling career. The whole story is a book in itself! Interactive Reader Guide: *As Good As Gold.*
[3] "Peloton" is the term used for the large group of cyclists riding in an amoeba-shaped cluster, from which the winners hope to break away.

with me. Where I saw my enthusiasm, confidence, experience and results as pluses, the reality of pro cycling saw the minuses: Top-twenty results aren't wins. My race experience was less than two years. Worse, my experience as a human being was greater than 28 years. I thought 34 was a good thing until a fellow pro cyclist I admired, Alisha Welsh, explained otherwise.

"The UCI has a rule," Alisha explained, "that women's professional teams must have a median age under 28 years old."

"What?! That's insane!" I balked. "Kristin Armstrong[4] just won her *second* Olympic gold medal in time trial cycling at 39!" This archaic rule made no sense. "*Why* is this rule still around?"

Alisha shook her head. No idea. I did a little digging. As if the UCI couldn't be any more backward in their antediluvian rules stating women must race shorter distances, earn less prize money and receive no base salary, UCI hit the quadfecta of outdated idiocy. Indeed, there it was: All UCI women's pro teams had to average less than 28 years of age. This rule was established not in 1909 but *2009*... when the UCI merged men's and women's pro teams into the same chapter of UCI regulations. What sounded like progress—treating the men's and women's pro teams the same—came with a subtle loophole of inequity.

In 2009, there were *two* levels of pro ranks for the men: Pro Continental and World Tour. Minor league and major league, respectively, as exist in most men's professional sports. The UCI minor league men had an age median, the major league did not. Where women got screwed was the fact there was no major and minor league system. Just one professional league with an age median placed in effect for *every* women's pro team. Worse still, was the idiocy of an age median at all, men or women. But especially women: physiologists discovered women in endurance sports hit their peak in their mid-30s to early 40s,[5] finally helping erase the errant history where, in 1966, doctors actually believed ovaries would fall out if women exercised. The rule for women's pro cycling teams being below age 28 made absolutely no sense. But there it stood, smackdab in the in the middle of the UCI rulebook. Archaic, uniformed and unchallenged.

---

[4] Interactive Reader Guide: Kristin Armstrong. (Reminder! All "Interactive Reader Guide" links are on my website: www.kathrynbertine.com/irg)

[5] Interactive Reader Guide: Endurance cycling peak years. This women's age-limit nonsense went on in other professions, too. Flight attendants weren't allowed to work past age 30, had to be single, not pregnant and maintain weight restrictions. These rules were not lifted until the 1980s. I often wonder if UCI and FAA were BFFs.

Puzzled by the UCI's ignorance of modern data, I sifted through the rosters of the top-tiered women's pro teams. Sure enough, the majority of athletes were younger than 28 because of this rule. But not *all* of them. Some were older than me, and thriving. There was seven-time U.S. national champion Dotsie Bausch on Team Tibco, six-time U.S. national champ Tina Pic on Colavita Pro Cycling, two-time Olympian Ina Teutenberg of Germany on Team T-Mobile … all of whom were in their mid-to-late thirties. I spent the past two years idolizing these badass pro cyclists not for their age but for their incredible performances. Bausch, Pic and Teutenberg were the Gretzkys, Jordans and Favres of women's pro cycling in the mid-2000s, all of them older than the ridiculous age median and still kicking ass.

Despite my two functioning ovaries still hangin' where they're supposed to, my chances of signing a pro contract in my mid-30s wasn't looking good. I had a choice: view the age rule as odds stacked against me, or to see the presence of Bausch, Pic and Teutenberg as the possibility of opportunity. I chose the latter and kept applying to pro teams.

While my pro team hopes fizzled for the 2009 season, I sought out amateur teams who raced events where pro teams also competed. A bicycle shop in Phoenix partnered with Specialized Bicycles and created an elite domestic team in Arizona: Specialized-Bicycle House, which offered me a spot. There would be no salary and no free bicycle. I'd need to pay my way to just about every race. I would receive two free kits (cycling outfits) and a couple water-bottles. Maybe even a paid race entry here and there.

As I teetered on the cliff of financial struggle, free water bottles and clothing felt like gold and platinum. I took the offer and deposited it in the Bank of Progress. Now I could hopefully work my way up the ranks. Maybe catch the eye of a pro team for 2010. These were the dues every athlete pays in any sport: Show up. Do well. People notice. Move up. I joined Specialized-Bicycle House with my closest Tucson friend, Marilyn Chychota. Unlike professional teams where athletes are given bikes for the year, most elite teams lend out loaner bikes. This team did not. If we wanted to ride a Specialized bicycle, we had to buy one. Neither Marilyn nor I were able to afford a new bike so we rode the old bikes of our previous sponsors, Wilier and Trek, respectively. To race on a Trek and wear a Specialized jersey was the equivalent to showing up in a Chevrolet to a Ford event. Still, we had free clothing and energy gels, so we held our heads high and happily deflected the quizzical looks and questions from our competitors.

"Why doesn't your bike match your sponsor?" they'd ask.

"We're just happy our shorts match our shirts," we'd smile.

––––––––––––––––

On the way to the Tucson Bicycle Classic, Marilyn and I carpooled in my Volvo wagon. Somewhere on Interstate 19 around 5am, my car decided it no longer needed the plastic splash shield protecting the undercarriage. It dropped off and flew away, despite the fact I'd double-knotted the rope holding it together. A daily practice that had become quite tiresome.

"Good riddance," I muttered.

"Shouldn't we go back and get that?!" Marilyn yelped.

"No," I surmised. "Sometimes we must let go of the things that weigh us down."

We laughed the rest of the way to the race, neither of us knowing that letting go of things that weigh us down was a lesson I wouldn't truly grasp for many, many years. But in the pre-dawn darkness of a desert morning en route to a bike race, everything was great and the Volvo remained wonderfully faithful for years.

2

THE WOMEN'S TOUR THAT USED TO BE

During the spring of 2009, I started doing some research. The age median rule burrowed under my skin and irked me to no end, as did all the other inequities like race distance, prize money and zero women's fields at the major events, like the Tour de France. Had this extreme lack of parity *always* been this way in cycling?

Turns out, no, women were not always considered a novelty in cycling. In fact, there was an incredible boom of women's racing at the turn of the 20th century. In 1879, Madison Square Garden was erected in New York City and served as the nation's first velodrome; a wildly popular indoor cycling track. Track cycling originated in England in the mid 1800s and made its way to the States soon after. The world fell in love with the fast-paced, spectator-friendly, speed-frenzied racing. Women were saddling up and by 1896, the world paid attention. In Europe and North America, five women—Tillie Anderson, Lizzie Glaw, Dottie Farnsworth, Helen Baldwin and May Allen—became legendary racers, earning sponsorships, salaries and prize money that soared into the six-figure range. Millionaires, at the time. The crowds loved the excitement of the fast-paced laps and the newness of female cyclists, and they placed bets accordingly.[6]

By the mid-1890s feminists and suffragettes embraced the bicycle's transformative powers when Susan B. Anthony famously said, "Let me tell you what I think of bicycling… it has done more to emancipate women than anything else in the world. It gives women a feeling of freedom and self-reliance. I stand and rejoice every time I see a woman ride by on a wheel...the picture of free, untrammeled

---

[6] Interactive Reader Guide: Women on the Move

womanhood." Not just metaphorically untrammeled, but physically too. The bicycle movement brought the concept of "rational dress" to the frontlines, which did away with corsets and long skirts. Bloomers were all the rage, shocking conservatives everywhere.

In addition to the track cycling and the local commuters, women took to the roads worldwide. Annie Londonderry, a Latvian immigrant to the U.S., became the first endurance cyclist. Paving the way toward bike touring culture, Londonderry became the first woman to bicycle around the world in 1895.

The early 1920s were filled with female cycling gamechangers. In Italy, Alfonsina Strada became the only woman to smash the gender barrier and officially ride a men's grand tour event; the 1924 Giro d'Italia. Marguerite Wilson of England raced 100-mile time trials, often besting the male competitors. In 1937, the first female U.S. national champion was crowned; 15-year-old Doris Kopsky from Belleville, New Jersey. Her father Joseph Kopsky, a 1912 Olympic bronze medalist in the men's team time trial, ran a bicycle shop and challenged his male customers to race his daughter, promising everyone she would beat them. She did. Here's to the dads of daughters encouraging girls in sport.

Of course, not every man fancied this new trend of women and bicycles. *There goes the devil in a skirt*, Italian villagers said of Alfonsina Strada's historic achievement. In 1897, male undergrads of Cambridge University showed their opposition to women's admission by hanging an effigy of a woman on a bicycle. By that point, the bike became synonymous with women's liberation, not just in sports but everyday life. By comparison, women weren't granted full equity in matriculation and degrees at Cambridge University until 1947—sixty years later!

Hooked on the history of women's cycling, I made a beeline to researching the Tour de France, looking for women's involvement in the early years. Sure enough, the iconic race that began in 1900 was male dominated and remained so for over half a century until 1955. That year, race director Jean Leulliot added a five-stage women's event. (The men raced—and still race—21 stages). Unfortunately, it wasn't because Leulliot was a progressive visionary, but rather because he sought to prove women *can't* possibly complete such a task of racing five days at the Tour de France. But the forty-one women invited to race proved him wrong, and Millie Robinson of Great Britain became the first official winner of The Tour Feminin. The problem? The public—and the press—of 1955 weren't ready for such progressiveness, and the event was dismissed as a "stunt race." No sponsors were secured for the following year, and the first official women's Tour de France was discontinued for another thirty years.

The UCI was no better in terms of progression. The deep roots of bias, traditionalism and antiquated patriarchy began in 1900, when five countries—Belgium, France, Italy, Switzerland and the United States—banded together to create a governing body for amateur and professional cycling. The headquarters remained in Paris for the first 69 years, then relocated to Geneva. From the get-go, UCI was a slow-moving organization. It took 21 years for them to create World Championships for men, and 58 years until women were allowed to officially compete. *It took 84 years until women were allowed to race at the Olympic Games*! Slower still was the development within the UCI. In 120 years, there have only been 11 presidents, some of whom served terms as long as 21 years. All presidents were white, European men hailing from just eight different countries… despite the fact there are 196 cycling federations today. For smaller countries wanting to speak up and create change, fat chance. UCI congress only doles out votes to 42 countries in their political system. 154 cycling federations without a vote is a lot of unheard voices. When presidencies repeat patterns devoid of adaptation and growth, traditionalism yields a dangerous minefield of ignorance, apathy and laziness.[7]

When a motion to include women in the annual UCI World Championships was introduced in 1957, it was shot down immediately. The major newspaper of France declared: "Good sense has triumphed. Women should be content with existing races and cyclotourism, which corresponds much better to their muscular abilities." (Pardon me while I barf over this quote and pretty much the entirety of the 1950s.) Luckily, British athlete Eileen Gray and Belgian racer Jos de Stobbeleire formed the Women's Cycle Racing Association and lobbied hard for women's inclusion at World Championships. In 1958, they succeeded. Pressing onward, Gray became head of the British Cycling Federation and persuaded the Olympic Committee to finally include women in 1984 Los Angeles Games. Thank you, Eileen.[8]

That same year, Tour de France co-director Felix Levitan created an 18-day course for the women, just three days shy of the men's 21 days.

---

[7] Interactive Reader Guide: Hey UCI, your sexism is showing.
[8] More badass women of early cycling awesomeness: Interactive Reader Guide: History of Women's Racing

"Woman is the equal of man,"[9] Levitan told the press. "She is ready to contend with the hardest challenges in sport. With the Tour, we bring her an audience." The women rode the same routes on the same day as the men, with stages shortened just enough to allow for both pelotons to roll through without impeding or delaying the entire event. It worked, and the crowds loved it! Especially in the mountain stages, where cycling fans hiked for miles to watch the action unfold. Now, instead of watching one group of athletes race by so fleetingly, they got to enjoy twice the action. Victory went to Marianne Martin of the U.S. in 1984 and cycling greats like Maria Canins, Jeannie Longo, Inga Thompson and Connie Carpenter became household names in the cycling world.[10]

Levitan watched the public response to the women's race. People loved it. Well, except for the men who weren't on the bandwagon of progress, like men's Tour de France winner-turned-commentator, Jacques Anquetil. "Cycling is much too difficult for a woman. They are not made for sport," Anquetil said. "I prefer to see a woman in a short white skirt, not racing shorts… I am sorry to see them suffer. On a bicycle, there always a lot of suffering." Lordy! French sexism wasn't on its way out anytime soon, but counterbalancing Anquetil, Levitan pressed on and sought to create a fully equal Tour de France for men and women.

The UCI thwarted his vision by passing a rule in 1985 that no women's race could be longer than 12 days, still holding onto the false ideals that women couldn't physically do long events. Which was just plain wrong. Not to mention, unproven. Crafty Levitan got around this rule by creating two ten-day races with one rest day in between. The women's Tour de France continued for another four years. During that time, the Amaury family—owners of the Tour de France—hired new race directors and Levitan was let go. After 1989, the women's Tour de France was discontinued.

Some race organizers attempted to save and relocate the women's Tour de France by moving it from July to August. Separate from the men's race. Amaury Sports Organization shot it down, claiming copyright infringement on the name "Tour de France." The race directors changed the name to "Grand Boucle" but sponsorship didn't stick. It wasn't the Tour de France. There were no TV media packages offered. Women were considered second-rate, not worth the investment.

---

[9] Well, not exactly equal. The women received a tenth the prize money per day, and raced a quarter of the overall distance. For the 80s, that was progress. Equal-ish.

[10] More history on the women of the '80s Tour de France: Interactive Reader Guide: 1984 Women's TdF

My inner journalist fumed. There was just no reason for women not to have the same opportunity as men. Especially at the Tour de France, which I fixated on because it was the one professional bicycle race the whole world new about. Tennis has Wimbledon, soccer has the World Cup, running has the Boston Marathon, cycling has the Tour de France. Even non-sports fans knew these pinnacle events. *Come on, this is 2009. This has to change,* I harrumphed to myself. *Someone needs to start communicating with ASO and UCI. Surely they've evolved by now.* It didn't immediately occur to me that perhaps I could be that communicator. Not yet.

———————————

In the midst of researching and fuming at my computer, I had races to train for. The thrill of racing was satisfying, but the gazillion miles of training was where my mind sifted through the flotsam and jetsam of my thoughts. I could hear my inner voice whispering *yes, this is what you're supposed to be doing right now.*[11]

My brain, body and heart kept coming back to two topics while I rode. One was very simple: *How far I can push myself as an athlete?* The other wasn't so cut-and-dry: *Why are women still treated so unequally in sport?* This thought lingered long after every workout and long after the story of my Olympic bid had been published in *As Good As Gold.* The inequity of women in sport wrapped its grip around my heartstrings, plucking and pointing, *this way.* Perhaps this is why I'm drawn to endurance sports. There is ample time for wondering.

And for healing. Here's the stone-cold honest truth about endurance athletes: we're either running from something or toward something. Only when we're truthful with ourselves will we figure out whether our joy comes from the Journey Toward or the Escape From. Those who fall into the latter category are doomed to an unhappy experience in endurance sports. Those who embrace the former will find some joy and peace in the weirdness of it all.

Cycling soothed a lot of my personal demons, but it didn't eradicate them. I was well aware of my inclination toward sensitivity, loneliness and self-doubt, but these things were very human conditions. For the most part, I was doing ok. There was a time in my early twenties where food neuroses were in full swing. There was a time in my early thirties where a broken engagement took me down quite a few pegs of worthiness. But by my mid-thirties I felt quite confident that my demons

---

[11] Science proves moving forward—by bike or on foot—physiologically opens and alters our minds in the best way possible. Interactive Reader Guide: Cycling and brain health.

and I were running toward something, not away. That obstacles were surmountable, experience was a gift and persistence was the way through just about anything.

The indignation I'd felt from my glimpse into the history of women's cycling and my very own foray into racing had pointed a way forward. It wasn't only time to do something about the issues—it was time for *me* to do something about it. If change were going to happen in our sport, it had to start with the athletes. And since I got my start in cycling with ESPN, perhaps my old colleagues might be interested in what I had in mind.

I composed a new proposal for ESPN. The idea was this: With ESPN on board, I could approach ASO and ask to work with them to include a women's professional field at Tour de France—not to compete *against* the men, but to have a simultaneous event. Just like Le Tour did in the 80s and 50s. But that was only half the column. In addition to creating the event with ASO, I'd compile an ESPN Women's Professional Racing Team, too. Double the exposure! Maybe I'd even be lucky enough to race for that team, but whatever. The big goal was making a permanent women's race at the Tour de France. With a sustainable infrastructure. After all, it had been twenty years since the women's race had been quashed. About time for a cultural revolution.

I prepared for the reality that ASO would likely say *no thanks, Kathryn, we prefer women in short white skirts*. Or that women were incapable of completing the grueling three-week, 1,100 mile distance. To thwart that, I included an alternative Plan B possibility: If ASO doubted women can even complete the race, I proposed we—a team of 8-12 pro cycling women—could ride the route to prove otherwise, and publicize our ride through ESPN. Even though the 1984 Tour de France Feminin debunked that myth of physical inability, the races back then were a) slightly shorter and b) predated the internet and social media. The women's races in the 1980s were buried in history. This column would bring both the history and the present to life.

Plan B was risky. If ESPN said yes, but ASO said no and continued to ban women from racing Le Tour, we would show up anyway and start each day before the crack of dawn, hours ahead of the men's race. Sports fans could follow us online, keeping track of our data, our challenges while physiologists could monitor our progress, and ESPN could broadcast it all online. Together we would thwart the archaic idea that women couldn't possibly race the Tour de France in this modern day and age! To have the financial backing and media platform of ESPN leading the charge, this could change 100 years of the Tour de France and make history.

My proposal was 22 pages long; outlining all the logistics, challenges and financial needs to pull off such an assignment. During my 2006-2008 ESPN column, the company invested over $100k that included everything from expenses, logistics and monthly stipends. I appropriated the Tour de France budget so it would be similar. If they needed to cut that in half, ok fine. If my fellow cyclists and I had to sleep in a tent and survive on Ramen, so be it. Whatever it takes to get eyes on women in the Tour de France.

Before sending the proposal to ESPN, I ran it past my literary agent, asking whether he saw potential in the book market. Absolutely, he agreed. If inclusion of women in the Tour de France happens, there is a book there. My confidence skyrocketed. I sent the proposal to ESPN. When no one returned my emails, I squeaky-wheeled and asked my former boss for a phone call.

"Ok. Tell me straight. What would it take to make this work?" I asked him.

"We don't have the budget for this kind of project," he responded.

"You did last time," I countered.

"Look, if you find a separate sponsor to back the expenses of racing or riding a Tour de France," he said, "we'll hire you to write the column."

Weird, but interesting! ESPN clearly had the money, but didn't want to spend it without a partnership. *Hmm,* I wondered. *Who do I know with a six-figure budget and a sense of justice?* Perhaps my best chance in finding financial resources was to enlist the help of my university alumni connections. Maybe there were alumni with successful businesses looking to invest in the right sponsorships and opportunities for equality.

Using my Colgate University connections, I was introduced to the owner of one of the world's most prominent cable TV providers of all time: COO of NewsCorp and CEO of DirecTV, Chase Carey. *Yes, yes!* We scheduled a call. The possibility of such a sponsorship was a perfect win-win; media coverage with ESPN but also foreign broadcast networks. Not only could this be a written column, but there could be airtime possibilities as well. More eyes on ESPN, more eyes on the cable network's direct involvement, more eyes on equal opportunities for women... Not only could this work, but everyone would gain—

"I love it," Chase interrupted, adding, "But I have a better idea..."

Pins and needles tingled through me. *He loves it! He's got an idea!* I pressed my ear against to phone, eager to absorb all thoughts of how we could make the most of a business plan from such a successful CEO. "… why don't you find a rich husband?" he said.

At first, I thought he was joking. Alas, Chase was serious. Wishing me luck with the project, that was the end of our call. Crestfallen, I hung up the phone. To have a business proposal turned down is one thing. To suggest women's progress hinges on wealthy spouses was another. The 1950s were still alive and well. *Golly, what a swell idea, Mr. Fancy Cable Baron! Better take my short, white skirt to the dry cleaners!*

I also started to understand the chicken-and-egg deflection between media and sponsorship. *Find a sponsor, and we'll give you media,* says the media. *Give us media, and we'll be a sponsor,* says the sponsors. *Prove your worth.* Top male athletes do not have to fight for the opportunity (or venue) to showcase their talents. They just have to literally play the game. But our less-than-modern society has a subtle, sneaky way of skirting the issue. *Show me the data that proves it's worthwhile to invest in women.* Hogwash. Show me the data that proves it *isn't*. "Prove to us that investing in men is a good idea!" said no one ever.

Stewing on the conundrum, I went out for a ride to have a think. What was I doing wrong? I mean, geez, if only the Tour de France race director could see—

Oh. Wait. I hadn't even shown the Tour de France my proposal yet. Maybe that's what I was doing wrong! Trying to connect with too many outliers before going directly to the source. Ok, then. Of course. Go right to the source and knock on the door. Forget ESPN, forget sponsors, forget the middle man approach. Hiring freezes and the absence of rich husbands were not going to stand in the way of inclusion of women. It was time to approach ASO directly.

On a warm day in March 2009, between my lunch-shift waitressing and my evening classes teaching Journalism 101 and the peaceful ache of athletic exhaustion in my legs, I sat down at my computer. As the still-drying paint of Scarlet Dragon breathed over my shoulder, I paused, exhaled and pressed send.

———————

There was no reason for Christian Prudhomme, race director of the Tour de France, not to respond to my email. Or so thought my fledgling lil' ego. After months of research and multiple drafts, my 22-page presentation on the inclusion of women in the Tour de France covered all the necessities. The race infrastructure, corporate data, the return of investment for ASO and Tour de France. Win-win on all parts. After all, I was an experienced journalist with the accolades of ESPN and two published books. I was highly educated. I mean, I *knew* stuff.

And, I was a legitimate cyclist, with two whole years of experience. Maybe I didn't have an Olympic medal, but I was the Arizona state champion and I had a really cool men's extra small jersey to prove it. Maybe I didn't have the sponsors lined up or the official nod from ESPN yet, but ASO would be nuts not to listen to me, right? After all, this wasn't a business proposal about a bicycle race, this was about common sense: Include women. Not because it's right, but because it's smart. From return of investment stats to visibility demographics, I laid everything out. No brainer. All I had to do was wait for ASO's reply, so we could proceed with a meeting to solidify the details.

There was no response. Not that week. Or month. Or year. Years. Resend, resend, resend. Silence, silence, silence. Crickets, crickets, crickets. Stone-cold quiet. So quiet, I almost missed the first lesson of activism hiding in the stillness: Silence isn't quiet. It's deafening. If we choose to listen closely, we can hear as silence screams, *What now*?

To be an activist is to seek answers. To let silence and pauses not deter us, but guide us toward our path. Of course, that didn't strike me quite so profoundly as I sat there in my waitress apron in my newly painted apartment, late mortgage payment, dwindling savings account, two part-time jobs, one mission for equality and zero responses in my AOL inbox from Christian Prudhomme. But I was aware something within me truly shifted. I paid attention to the silence, which forced me to ask more questions. Not just of ASO, but of myself. Questions that would shape the next decade of my life after embracing the Pause and the Silence and walking through the door of activism. I put the Silence on the backburner and let it simmer, listening and watching as three answers emerged in what to do next: Strive, help and love.

As the emails to ASO continued to go unanswered, I took a good, hard look at why I was being ignored. First, the technical: perhaps they were not actually receiving my email. While the majority of the planet transferred from AOL to Gmail, I stubbornly held fast to tradition and still remained on AOL in 2009. Perhaps I was landing in Christian's spam folder. I created a new email account and tried again. *Grillons, grillons.* (Crickets, in French). Second, I considered the reality that ASO simply wasn't interested in connecting. Despite the solid proposal constructed on evidence, data and common sense, they had zero interest in listening to some unknown lady on a bike in Arizona. I'm not famous. I'm not wealthy. I don't have an Olympic medal. *What now*? Silence asked.

There seemed to be only one answer: Turn professional. Land a pro contract. Win races. Then ASO will pay attention. From that moment on in mid-2009, my motivation to turn pro was fueled by leverage to a Tour de France for women.

Also, I was motivated by the fact that professional cyclists earned a salary. At the time, I was in a state of blissful ignorance on how low the salaries were. I knew female pro cyclists probably weren't wealthy, but surely they earned a salary above the poverty line. The men did. How different could it be? Heck, some men even made millions. No matter how low, it had to be better than waitressing and adjunct professoring, at least. Either way, the silence from ASO solidified my commitment to turning professional. ASO would *have* to listen to me when I turned pro. I would matter then.

Mattering. I wasn't ready to admit it in 2009, but my demons were getting a little growly. Perhaps it was the combination of financial struggle, no longer being part of ESPN, being turned down by so many employers and feeling a little bit lonely on the personal front. My demons were a Cerberus of Worthlessness and Not Enough, a two-headed beast who lived deep, deep within. While I was 100 percent confident in fighting for a Tour de France and equal rights for women, my confidence teetered on a wobbly foundation of inner-acceptance. When our ideas, hearts and efforts are used as instruments for change, it's hard to put a boundary between who we are and what we believe.

How odd this demon began breathing fire just as I finally began to exhale confidence. At 33, adulthood felt glorious. I owned a home. My office chair was an exercise ball, my window opened to a palm tree, fashionable curtains framed the view of my 6-by-6 foot yard, my serious-looking desk was neat and tidy, and each newly painted wall in my small condo bellowed forth color, empowerment and the triumphant cries that, after years of struggle, I finally had my shit together. *I have a home and a desk and a chair! I picked out wall paint all by myself! I am officially adulting and I can do anything!* Anything except slay heads of my Cerberus. Years would pass before I understood "slaying" was neither the correct verb nor answer for how to deal with demons.

The correct verb, I started to realize, was *listening*. I started to check in with myself, with the Not-Mattering and the Not-Enoughness, with the endless waiting and the loneliness, and I began to brainstorm what exactly it was I wanted out of life. I even emailed it to myself:

What I want: I want to make history for women's cycling, I want to get us into the TDF. I want to be a pro cyclist. I want to be able to do the two things I am supposed to be doing: writing and making a difference in the world. I want someone to share this with. I want to come home to someone. I want to give them love and touch and sex and understanding and support. I want to receive these things too, in the same capacity as given. I want to be loved/valued. I want to earn enough money to have food and mortgage payments. I want to not worry about whether or not I will lose my house. I want to be able to go into a grocery store and buy whatever the hell I want. I want one man to not be freaked out by my drive, passion and love of life. I want to stop feeling like I'm less of a person when I'm single. I have so much love to give.

Apparently, I was quite talented at wanting. Receiving, of course, was another matter. It was time. I was finally ready to meet someone and meld this crazy journey of life with another, but I wasn't quite ready to float such personal sentiments into the universe. At least I was slowly gaining the courage to look within.

During the summer of 2009, I discovered Kathrine Switzer's book, *Marathon Woman*, marveling at how the sport of marathon had successfully crossed over the boundaries of sexism thanks to Kathrine. During my human existence on the planet since 1975, watching women and men run marathons was totally normal. Switzer's book ushered me into the realm of Wokeness when I learned marathon parity had only been around for a few short decades.

In 1967 a college freshman at Syracuse University entered the male-only Boston Marathon using her initials on the registration form: K.V. Switzer. Dressed in sweatpants and a hoodie, the event began with typical normalcy. Until mile four, when race director Jock Semple saw Kathrine and lunged toward her, attempting to physically pull her out of the race. Semple was promptly cross-checked by K.V.'s boyfriend, Thomas Miller, running along beside her. The image, the story and the accomplishment gained Switzer the recognition she so greatly deserved and opened the door for women to run. And for the running industry to double their profits. Today, no one bats an eye to see a woman out for a run. 50 years ago they did. It was a non-famous, non-wealthy college kid who changed the perception of what a woman can do.[12] *Call her*, Silence whispered.

---

[12] It's a worthy footnote to include that Semple and Switzer became close friends in the following years. Semple passed in 1988, but his legacy lives on in this important quote: "I still have a postcard from Kathy

On a humid, summer afternoon in New Paltz, New York I made my way to the home of my "shero," Kathrine, and her husband Roger. After reaching out on email, Kathrine kindly responded and invited me to lunch at their lovely home in the rolling, green hills of the beautiful Catskills. I told her I wanted to do for cycling what she did for marathon.

Business proposal in hand, I picked Kathrine's brain on the strategies of a women's Tour de France, and revisited the topic of sponsorship connections. We bonded over the no-brainerness of having a women's Tour de France and discussed ideas and solutions on how we could get ASO to listen. I brought her into the folds of a secret: That if ASO kept ignoring the proposal, I could do what Kathrine did. I could show up, and start the race. The flaw with this tactic was it may work for individual sports, but in a team atmosphere, we weren't there to compete against the men. We would go to show that women are capable of racing the distance. Showing up would likely garner attention and get eyes on the issue—and possibly get myself arrested. I didn't have a problem with potential arrest, but I did have a problem with being dismissed as a stunt that wouldn't move women forward. When Kathrine ran the marathon, she didn't need equipment and teammates. Her job was to show up and run. But at the Tour de France, the team logistics and ability to ride unsupported for three weeks left me vulnerable to danger and sabotage. Kathrine agreed.

"Look," Kathrine said. "A Tour de France for women can happen. But you're up against Goliath and you'll need to be David. It will take a while." We discussed valuable connections to possible sponsors, but the two most important lessons of activism bubbled forth that day: *Ask, ask, ask, collaborate, collaborate, collaborate* and *Be the David.* Look to those who paved the way in their fields, and ask for guidance. Ask about the pitfalls, ask about the unknowns and the risks. But, never ask others for help before we do our own work and research. Value their time. And remember: Patriarchy, tradition and giant corporations are enormous Goliaths. But at the heart of every Goliath is a human with a pulse. Find them. Ask, ask, ask. Always remember that David wins in the end.

---

thanking me after they got the women's marathon, because I was the catalyst that started focusing attention on women's long-distance running… I always say that by doing that I made Kathy famous and I made myself infamous." Switzer added: "Jock gave the world one of the most galvanizing photos in the women's rights movement. 'The Great Shove' on the Boston course in 1967 was the spark that ignited the women's running revolution. Jock was a complex mix of irascible, funny, hot-tempered and lovable. He changed my life in an instant and as a consequence changed millions of women's lives." Moral: When push comes to shove, men and women move society forward together.

Not just David, but *Davids*. From Kathrine Switzer to Billie Jean King to the women of soccer and ice hockey who fight for equal opportunity and equal pay… there is one common thread: They were athletes currently playing the game and speaking out. Not a bunch of retired athletes, but current pros at the highest rank. That's what got the world's attention. Hmmm. *All the more reason to chase this pro dream!* I thought. As 2009 turned the corner into 2010, there was something else that helped me grow stronger, too. Love.

3

LOVE AND BALANCE

In 2010, I fell in love with something other than justice and bicycles. As a fellow cyclist in the Tucson community, I knew George for years. I also knew his wife, Colleen, a strong amateur cyclist and inspiring woman who had beaten breast cancer and got back on the bike to race local events during her remission. Until the wretched disease returned and claimed her life at the age of 31. The cycling community rallied around George, bolstering him with love and support. I dropped off meals and reached out, letting him know I was there to go for a bike ride should he need company during this challenging time. He took me up on the offer one day.

George asked if I wanted to go mountain biking, to which I smiled and said, "Sure!" but grimaced internally. I'm a terrible mountain biker. Rocks are not my thing. But I wasn't going to say no, especially to someone in mourning. We hit the dirt. Myself, literally. Often. With much cursing. Which made George laugh. I fell and cursed for a few hours, offering him a bouquet of dust, dirt, profanities and distraction. Because that's what we do when we want to make our friends smile and laugh during the toughest times in life. Bikes, rocks, blood and laughter. This was our beginning. "Road bikes next time, please!" I smiled (okay, begged). He agreed and asked me to ride again the following week.

On bikes and in coffee shops, conversation grew deep and profound. He not only tolerated my constant questions of curiosity—on life, death, widowhood, pain, desires, dreams, fears—but answered with depth and honesty. I found within this man the one thing I was seeking: Someone with an unhindered ability to communicate through all the unfiltered subjects of life. To think and wonder and discuss… and think and wonder and discuss some more. To embrace questions and freely articulate answers. My soul found peace in his presence like I never experienced before with a man. Many months went by. One day my heart whispered,

George. That's your person. My gut and brain agreed. *Just wait. No rush. See what happens.*

By my mid-thirties, I had enough tumultuous relationship experiences to be wary of placing my heart yet again into the abyss of trust and love. In my late twenties, I was engaged to a closeted alcoholic, whose kindness and stability were tethered to the puppet strings of addiction. When I gained the courage to leave, I rested my heart for a few years. Then came a two-year relationship with the most dashingly handsome, foreign, intriguing, financially prosperous businessman in New York City who had it all. Except joy. While I had none of his aforementioned qualities, I carried a wealth of inner happiness. To this light he was attracted. At first. Then came a resentment so engrained, he could no longer endure the joy of another person when he silently wrestled with his own burden of sadness.

By that point, I believed my due diligence was done in the research of love. I wizened up and steered clear from men carrying all the red flags I'd been warned about or experienced: addiction, corruption, theft, meanness, verbal abuse, physical abuse, control, manipulation, infidelity, etc. I could spot that stuff a mile away and felt empowered that I knew exactly what to avoid in a partner. I had this Red Flag thing down!

I began dating again, happy to wait as long as it took to find an inner-happy man with whom I could communicate, trust and let loose my authentic self of strange, flawed, joyful, driven, silly, persistent, weirdness. (There were many times during the dating span where I believed a Tour de France for women might actually be easier to find.) Two years later, I met George.

In our thirteen-month courtship, George and I faced just about every possible human emotion and fielded infinite interrogations. From our closest confidants to the busybody acquaintances lurking in the cheap seats of the friendship balcony, people had questions about love and widowhood.

"Well, surely George has some emotional baggage because his wife passed away. Is dating a widower weird? Are you okay with the baggage? And, you know, being… second?" friends asked. *Of course* it was weird dating, but not because George was a widower. Because dating anyone is weird. It is impossible for a single person to reach age 35 and not experience dating weird people (self-included). What was so weird about dating George was there was no weirdness. He was incredibly communicative. Supportive. Caring. He was on board with my pro cycling dream and my activism goals. We spoke openly and honestly about everything. About his first wife, about love, death and life. From the intricacies of chemotherapy to learning one's preference for salad dressing, no subject was untouchable or trivial. The depths of our communication secured my heart.

While I knew my friends were being wonderfully protective, what they couldn't see from the outside was something George and I understood and agreed upon: Baggage is not synonymous with loss and grief. Loss and grief are loss and grief. When embraced, processed and dealt with, loss and grief are not baggage. Baggage comes from the *inability* to deal with experiences. Death doesn't produce baggage, it's the failure to live that packs a mental suitcase.

George and his wife were a couple who truly lived. When the diagnosis of breast cancer first entered their lives, she was 26. The cancer went away. Then it came back at 29. Viciously. When the unthinkable loomed before them and the words *Stage 4* and *terminal* surfaced, Colleen gave George an enormous, selfless gift which came in the form of communication.

"I want you to be happy. I want you to find someone. To re-marry," she told her husband. Of course, George wanted nothing to do with this "gift" at the time. He didn't want to think about what loomed. Too hard, too much. But later, when grief and loss knocked on his door and George bravely allowed them to enter, he also let in love. I brought the second round of love, but his first wife helped him open the door to that possibility. This beautiful gift of Colleen's wish for George to move forward brought tears to my eyes and comforted me with knowing our togetherness was ok. I was eternally grateful this incredible woman left her husband with memories of a wonderful marriage, the knowledge of what it means to be loved, the permission to embrace joy and the ability to move forward. Baggage was neither packed nor carried nor shelved between us.

But what about, you know, being second? friends asked. Second fiddle. Second best. Second wife. I thought about it for many months until the answer seemed so obvious: Embrace it. I *am* second. But this wasn't a competition. I wasn't "second place." I was the second chapter. Was life not a book? Was life not filled with characters, situations and plot twists, somehow tied together through unpredictable chapters? We live our lives in chapters. This chapter of love, marriage and life with George was a chapter I wanted to write, read and live all the way to the very end. Every damn word. Devouring it all. Epilogue, notes and bibliography included.

Not all of George's friends and family saw our relationship that way. Some were uncomfortable with George moving forward and cast their judgment upon me. *Who is this woman? What are her ulterior motives?* Some, whom I never met, carried enough anger to call me a gold-digger, to which George and I both laughed. Neither of us were wealthy.

George worked as a sales representative for a pharmaceutical company. Long gone were the days of enormous salaries and extreme bonuses that danced through the Viagra Nineties before the government cracked down on big pharma lavishness. George sold mild pain medications, like muscle patches with aspirin, which most other countries sell over-the-counter. Still, to give George and his antagonists' peace of mind, I assured him I would be happy to sign any agreement or prenup so he could rest assured I wasn't after any of his assets. Knowing we would have a house together was all the peace I needed about tangibles. To have love, marriage and a home together was a beautiful sense of enough. When the doubters came knocking, we had answers for it all.

Five months before the wedding, we moved into a house on the northeast side of Tucson. With the economy still in shreds, renting my condo became impossible and I had to put it up for short sale. I was devastated to lose my first investment of adulthood.

"Don't worry," George consoled. "We have our own home now. It's twice the size of your condo, for almost the same price." Good point. We had the shitty economy to thank for that one. Also, we had a garage, which seemed like a luxurious perk. However, we had three cars between us. "Look," said George. "I don't need two cars. Get rid of that old Volvo wagon and you can have my Prius." I was touched by the generosity. While the ol' Volvo still worked great, I gave her away to a relative in need. (Nothing else ever flew away from the undercarriage).

Everything was coming together… home, car, food, shelter, love. But even more, the deep peace of emotional support. George was thrilled about my goals in cycling and understood the short window of time humans have to be a professional athlete. Before we married, I made sure to lay out the goals and timelines of my mission. I would continue to work as adjunct faculty, while squeaky-wheeling ESPN, pitching my Tour de France proposal, and working my way toward the pro ranks of cycling. None of this surprised George. It was the same life I'd lead while we dated. But there was something important I wanted him to know: Marriage comes first. What gave me the greatest joy was the equilibrium of love, goals and marriage. Days spent chasing large, lofty goals were great, but greater still was coming home to the person I loved. Being with someone who encouraged my dreams and saw the big picture of women's equality brought me an incredible sense of peace.

I gave myself a two-year goal to make it to the pro ranks of cycling. Also two years away: 2012 Olympic Games. Since some races also served as Olympic qualifiers, I decided to go for both long shots. Pro cycling status *and* qualifying for London 2012.

"You got this," George said. Finally, I started to believe he may be right. My Cerberus stopped barking.

Love is not void of prophecies and ironies. The wealthy cable executive who turned down my Tour de France proposal and suggested, *Why don't you find a rich husband?* turned out to be the messenger of a metaphor. I did find a husband with an abundance of wealth. George was rich in kindness, communication, generosity and love. Money, schmoney. In November of 2010, I became the richest woman in the world.[13]

In addition to the wedding, 2010 also brought another milestone. The publication of my book, *As Good As Gold* by ESPN/RandomHouse came out in May. I was thrilled, ecstatic. To see the release of my second memoir with a major publishing company just before my 35th birthday was exhilarating. More exhilarating was the physical entity: I now had boxes of hardcover books, which I saw as tiny bricks I could use to build the house of awareness on women's cycling. Tiny bricks, tiny weapons of information I could send to ASO and the UCI! Perhaps they would listen to me now.

When I emailed my assigned publicist at Random House to ask about our next step for book publicity, the email bounced back. *Glitch*, I thought. I emailed the other woman at Random House copied on our previous thread. That too bounced back. *Weird*, said my brain. *Shit*, said my gut.

Calls to my literary agent and editors at ESPN revealed the truth. ESPN Books pulled the plug on their publishing department. *As Good As Gold* was the last book through ESPN's system. Technically, Random House published and distributed ESPN Books as an imprint of their company. But with the severance of their

---

[13] *The New York Times* covered our marriage for their Vows column, drawn to the element of the story that indeed, widow/ers can find love again. And so too can weird, atypical women in their mid-thirties who take the path less traveled.

partnership, there was zero initiative for Random House to further endorse or promote ESPN Books. My first book in 2003, a memoir on my figure skating career titled *All the Sundays Yet to Come* (Little Brown) garnered some stellar media attention. Positive reviews in *People Magazine, Entertainment Weekly, Publishing Weekly*, numerous newspaper features and a coveted second-edition printing... in the infancy of the internet and years before social media, that was huge! But this time, there was nothing for book number two. Zip. Zilch. Not one ounce of media even acknowledging *As Good As Gold* existed. Stranger still was the fact my ESPN column had over two million hits per installment... so for ESPN to *not* promote to book was a financial loss for them. Unbelievable. *As Good As Gold* fell into publishers no man's land, and took my confidence along into the void. The universe of writing and publishing swings freely on the cruel pendulum of Rewarding and Soul-Crushing.

Through Twitter, Facebook, emails and websites, I tried everything to get word out about the book. My hope was the book might add a bit more clout toward my push for change in women's cycling. I squeaky-wheeled ESPN over and over again about the Tour de France. Maybe now, with the book out, we could talk about the next column? Still, no response. I channeled my frustrations into my professional cycling goals. I wasn't ready to fall into the abyss of impossibility just yet.

4

St. Kitts and Nevis and Spearmint Gum

B ack in 2008, in my quest to qualify for the Olympics, I'd graciously been granted dual citizenship by St. Kitts and Nevis (SKN). I made a promise to myself to represent SKN for the rest of my cycling career. This great nation had taken a chance on me. No way was I going to use SKN for my Olympic dreams and then just throw them away when it was all over. I vowed to fly their colors and help them gain more exposure and representation.[14]

The SKN cycling federation had *zero* funds. Smaller countries and poorer nations do not have financial allocations for most sports. Travel, accommodations, race entries… I covered all these expenses myself. In fact, I even had to physically make my own racing license by printing out the authorized form from SKN and running it through the laminator at Kinko's. I even had to make my own cycling kits and team apparel. While SKN absolutely had my back in emotional support, there was no financial assistance whatsoever. That came from teaching, waitressing and airline mileage affiliated credit card usage.

My adjunct income was meager and my waitressing was less, but I had one perk: I got to keep the airline miles accrued during my ESPN years. There were just enough left to get me to the Eastern Caribbean Championships in St. Lucia and the UCI World Championships in Melbourne, Australia. In September, I traveled to St. Lucia to meet my St. Kitts and Nevis teammates: Reggie Douglas and James

---

[14] Dual citizenship does not grant anyone an Olympic berth, which is a very good thing. Every athlete must earn their way to the top. Some sports, however, have ridiculous hurdles. Olympic cycling qualification is covered in *As Good As Gold*, but I'll summarize the process in three sentences: UCI points system is skewed so smaller/poorer countries have less representation. UCI does not offer equal spots for women and men at the Olympics. Corruption is everywhere and the system is wackadoo.

Weekes. We would take part in the 63km road race among the 11 Eastern Caribbean nations.[15] But upon arrival, we were told there was no women's field at the race.

"Unacceptable," said Winston Crooke, our SKN team manager. He told the race director, "If you don't create a women's field tomorrow, our women will race with the men." The Good ol' Boys of the St. Lucia Cycling Federation did not create a women's field, promptly telling Winston we were not allowed to race. But wonderful, winsome Winston didn't listen and neither did we. The next day, I lined up on the start line with 36 men. Having spent the past three years training and occasionally racing with men, the surroundings felt comfortable to me. None of our male competitors made any complaints, nor did they seem disgruntled. Only the race director, Cyril Mangal, a cantankerous man in his late forties, showed pure annoyance by our presence. Still, we rode. Thirty minutes into the event, I made the break in the men's race and held fast until the finish, crossing the line 11th in the final sprint. Afterward, each male athlete looked me in the eye, shook my hand, and said "great race." Male competition wasn't the problem. Dinosaur directors were.

Cyril refused to publish the results with my name included. For three more subsequent Caribbean Championships, Cyril sought to have me removed altogether from race registration. Even when there *was* a women's field! Despite having all the necessary paperwork, documentation and permission to race for St. Kitts and Nevis since 2008, Cyril badgered the UCI officials to stop my entries because I was a dual-citizen and not purely Caribbean. He did not succeed. Except for fanning the flames of my inner activist, which began burning brighter every time I met resistance simply for being a female cyclist of any country. There was a lot of burning going on.

The term *activist* wasn't something I identified as yet, but all of us on SKN were indeed just that. My teammates and director stood up that day for what was right: to include women.

Sexism issues aside, the race experience at the Eastern Caribbean Championships was a perfect tune up for World Championships in Melbourne.

---

[15] Antigua and Barbuda, Commonwealth of Dominica, Grenada, Montserrat, St Kitts and Nevis, Saint Lucia, St Vincent and the Grenadines, British Virgin Islands, Anguilla, Martinique and Guadeloupe comprise the Order of Eastern Caribbean States. The entire Caribbean is comprised of 26 nations.

Unlike most of my trips revolving around pro cycling goals, this time I didn't have to go alone. My husband accompanied me, and it was glorious to have George's hands-on help. Also, my two compatriots from St. Kitts and Nevis— Reggie and James—earned a spot in the men's time trial. We had bonded as siblings of sport over the previous two years, calling each other bro and sis. Nothing gave me more joy than seeing two Black athletes infiltrate cycling; one of the most non-diverse sports in the world. Though I'd only been on a bike for three years, it was enough time to see cycling was whiter than a wealthy American suburb. The 2010 World Championship time trial roster had 42 male riders: 38 white, 2 Black, 2 Hispanic. In the road race, there were 179 athletes in the men's field: 169 white, 3 Asian, 7 Hispanic. 0 Black athletes. Reggie and James placed as the final two in the time trial, but their presence at Worlds was the win.

The day before the time trial at 2010 UCI World Championships, I brought my Specialized Transition TT bike to UCI for a regulation check. UCI recently announced all handlebars on time trial bikes had to have an aerodynamic measurement of a 3-to-1 height verses width ratio. Now, all handlebars on TT bikes are long and skinny. They often run 20 to 24 inches in length, with flat, sleek height-width ratio similar to a modern smartphone. Perhaps in sports like swimming, track and luge, where nanoseconds can be saved by such a height/width discrepancy, such a rule makes sense. But in a cycling time trial event that lasts from 45 to 60 minutes and competitors often finish many, many seconds—even minutes—apart, this 3-to-1 ratio of a bicycle handlebar is just plain silly. Here's a comparison. Imagine telling one kindergartener with Velcro sneakers that she can't play tag with kids who have string shoelaces, because clearly the Velcro provides an aerodynamic advantage and she'd win tag every time and children everywhere would suffer from such inequity and the world would fall apart.

No matter how incompetent or ridiculous this handlebar issue, rules were rules. I took my bike to pre-check the day before the race to ensure there would be no issues at the start line. This wasn't just some local race. This was *Worlds*. I flew halfway around the world to get here. Handlebars and dumbass rules were not about to take me down.

"All ok," said the UCI official, after whipping out his spiffy, special, sanctioned tape measurer at pre-check. "You're good to go."

"Thank you!" I chirped, as my worries flew away.

The next day, I rolled up to the start of the race and went through mandatory bike check. A different UCI official whipped out his tape measurer and decreed:

"Illegal. This is not a 3-to-1 ratio."

"No, sir," I explained. "I had it checked yesterday. It *is* 3-to-1!"

"No. This is 3-to-.5 of an inch." *Ohforfuckssakeyougottabekiddingme.*

I asked the official to check it again. He refused.

"You're telling me my handlebar height is one *centimeter* off your new rule?"

"Yes."

"Are you saying I can't race?"

"No, not unless the handlebars can somehow magically increase in height." His tinge of his sarcasm wasn't helpful.

Panic and anger battled it out for mind control. The clock was ticking. It was impossible to replace a set of handlebars in less than ten minutes. Cyclists carry around spare handlebars like drivers carry around spare steering wheels. Not a thing. Didn't have any. I looked at my husband. He was as gobsmacked as I was. He was also chewing gum. In that moment, panic gave way to innovation. Just as necessity is the mother of invention, MacGuyver-ism is the step-brother of jerry-rigging. There in my husband's mouth, I saw the way. Replaying the official's words in my head *No, not unless the handlebars can somehow magically increase in height,* I eliminated the *no* and focused on *magic.* I looked at my husband and put out my hand. "Give me your gum."

George kept the gum in his mouth, but handed over the pack of Trident in his pocket. I ran-hobbled in my cycling cleats to the tent with my backpack and pulled out a role of electrical tape. Unlike spare steering wheels, all cyclists have electrical tape stashed somewhere in their giant bags of stuff. I ran back to my bike sidelined in the time trial start house… five riders to go until my departure… and removed the unchewed rectangular pieces of Trident. Stacking them side-by-side, then adding another row on top of the first row, then fastening them together by winding the black electrical tape over and over the layers of gum, my handlebars magically grew a centimeter in height…two riders to go…Ditching the tape, leftover gum and most of my sanity, I ran the bike back through regulatory check-in, less than two minutes to spare…

The UCI official opened his tape measurer, held it vertically along the stacked gum hiding under the electrical tape, then snapped it shut. *Ohgodohgodohgod.* Bringing his curious index finger to the padded mound of unchewed rectangles, he pressed down, yielding a tiny saucer of indentation. We watched as the fingerprint slowly lifted, eroded and vanished. My breath, along with it. Turning to look at me, he paused. Seconds ticked by. Seasons, maybe. Perhaps a year. Finally, he nodded, "Go."

I grabbed the bike, waddled up the platform, clipped into the pedals and with 30 seconds to spare, rolled down the start ramp into the streets of Geelong. I remember very little of that race, except for the rush of adrenaline, the defeat of impossibility and the magical, triumphant scent of spearmint wafting from my handlebars.

In the first few years of my cycling career, my decision to represent St. Kitts and Nevis came with a significant hurdle: overcoming judgment in the peloton. When I began bike racing in 2007 during my ESPN assignment, I was an absolute beginner. A Category Four—"Cat 4"— cyclist. Imagine showing up at races with an ESPN photographer and cameraman following a 31-year-old novice who didn't know her ass from her elbow about bike racing? This brought a bemused interest and occasional discourse from others. Some women in the peloton approached me, asking and wondering why in the world ESPN would pay attention to a fledgling cyclist who often pinned her numbers on upside-down. Others surmised I must be a spotlight lovin' raging egomaniac.

I overcompensated for this misjudgment by being over-friendly and super-chatty and way-too-smiley, hoping to disarm my peloton sisters that I didn't think I was anything special at all. I thought *they* were the special ones! Probably overdoing it, I resembled a human puppy, just hoping one of these badass women in the sport might pick up the ball and play fetch with me for a few minutes or scratch my noggin and tell me I'm a gooooood doggie. Alas. For most of the women in the sport, it appeared safer to ignore me than to include me.

I figured the best way to thwart this "special" stereotype was to bring other women into the fold. To let them know the ESPN assignment was over. I didn't want the media paying attention to *me*. I wanted the media to pay attention to women's cycling. To equal opportunity. To the Tour de France. If racing for St. Kitts and Nevis helped me get to more races and get more exposure for the sport, then I was going to do it despite any misinterpretations along the way. Still, two years later, I was a bit of an anomaly. But there was improvement. I was no longer the strange lady with an ESPN cameraman following her around. Now I was just a strange lady. *Progress!*

Getting pro teams to notice me, though, was still a huge challenge. Maybe it wasn't just my aging ovaries and my St. Kitts & Nevis connection that pro cycling teams found bizarre, but also my voice and opinions. While I believed my ESPN connections, books and journalism was a good thing—More press! More media exposure for the team!—it slowly occurred to me that being opinionated isn't always viewed as an asset. Teams weren't always thrilled about riders who might speak their mind. Later I would find out some women's teams had clauses in their contracts that riders were not allowed to talk to reporters about topics like equality.

However, despite my "old" age, allegiance to SKN and opinionated disposition, there was a tiny hope that surfaced in my pro cycling dreams. The more races I attended, some of my competitors let their guard down and began to see the truth: Yes, I was weird... but also benevolent, kind and trying to do my best for our advancement. Some of them even let me babble on and on about my quest for the inclusion of women at the Tour de France. Slowly, trust took root. Friendships started to blossom.

5

COUCH SURFING IS FOR QUEENS

In January of 2011, my local friend and pro rider, Alisha Welsh, reached out to me asking if I had a spare bedroom to take in a cyclist for a couple months.

"She lives in Colorado," Alisha said, "but it's freezing right now and she needs a place to train. Do you have an extra bed or couch?" I was very familiar with the drill. I'd lent out my old condo couch to lots of my amateur cycling and triathlon friends over the years, when they came to train in Tucson's fantastic winter climate. Now, George and I had a wonderful spare bedroom. Internally, I beamed with pride as through I'd won an Adulthood Badge of Honor. *I. Have. A. Guestroom!*

"Yes!" I said. "We have a bedroom! With a bookshelf! And a lamp! Who's in need?"

"Lauren Hall," Alisha replied.

"Wait… Lauren Hall, the pro cyclist and current U.S. national track cycling champion?"

"Yes, *that* Lauren Hall. Total badass."

Whoa. *The* Lauren Hall? Just like all amateur cyclists, I was an avid follower of the women's pro peloton. Racers who made their way to the professional ranks were my idols. I studied the rosters and watched the results. I even had the good fortune of racing alongside many amazing pro women in my attempt to get to the 2008 Olympics; Marianne Vos, Emma Pooley, Dotsie Bausch. Had there been trading cards, I would have collected them all. Paying close attention to the U.S. athletes, I knew *exactly* who Lauren Hall was, having recently won two national titles in track cycling and currently racing for Colavita Pro Cycling, one of the most esteemed teams in the country. *Lauren Hall is going to stay with us! Wheeee!* That's like being a football fan and getting a call saying, *Hey, can you house Tom Brady?*

What I didn't understand, though, was *why* Lauren was looking for a spare couch or bed... I mean, she's a professional athlete. She has a salary. Why would a professional cyclist not able to rent, lease or sublet their own place to train? That's what all the highest-level pro men do when they go to places like Tucson or Girona, the two hotbeds of pro cycling.

I posed the question to Alisha and was met with a loud laugh, which served to pierce the eardrums of my ignorance.

"Kathryn, do you have any idea what female professional cyclists make?" she chuckled. Well, I wasn't completely stupid. *Of course*, women pro cyclists weren't millionaires. There was no media initiative, no access to the Tour de France, and no lucrative endorsement bonuses (yet). *Of course* I knew they didn't make millions. But come on. The sport was thriving globally and the majority of the women's pro teams were backed by lucrative companies like Lipton, Vera Bradley, Tibco, Colavita, Cervelo, Rabobank. Even if the riders didn't make seven figures, or even six figures, or even upper-five figures... fine, but there's no way they didn't have enough to cover basic human needs like food and shelter. Right? Again, the Laugh of Ignorance.

"Most female pros I know are lucky if they make $10,000 per year," Alisha said. "Why do you think Lauren's looking for a couch?"

"That's insane," I laughed back. "Please have Lauren call me."

In February, Lauren and her big, old, happy yellow lab, Miller, moved in for six weeks. My husband and I were delighted to have them with us. On a personal level, simply helping someone do what they do resonated deeply with me. I wasn't quite ready to articulate my personal relationship to house, home and helping, so I kept it to myself at the time. Now I'm ready.

The concept of home runs through my soul like a fault line. In the past, I fell hard through the cracks of life's intimate earthquakes, twice losing a house to relationships and once to the economy. Before I married, there were two poignant relationships built on the stability of Home. Both relationships fell to rubble when these men struggled with their own demons. In 2005, I slept on 17 beds and couches of friends as I pieced my life back together following a devastating broken engagement. In 2007, my then-boyfriend and I got a home together, until he craftily took my name off the title. Then in 2009, my very own home went belly up. While I was able to sift my way through tangible loss of walls, ceilings and shelter—finite things can be replaced—my body, mind and soul struggled deeply with the displacement of trust, hope, and togetherness. To be without a house was one thing, but the crumbled foundation of losing three trusted senses of home truly crushed me.

Before marrying George, the three years in my small condo bolstered my independence, blossomed my sense of home, and steadied my trembling fault line. Then marrying a man who understood me and creating a home together gave me unfaltering confidence. Nothing could tear down this sense of home. Nothing could leave me houseless or homeless again. Lauren and Miller didn't know it at the time, but giving them a place to call home and a place to be who they are…that helped and healed me. To share, to provide a sense of home to others quieted the tremors along my fault lines and brought me an inner peace of great depth.

Except for that salary discrepancy thing. I found zero inner peace knowing women at the highest level of pro cycling had a miserable wage below the poverty line, and jumped into research mode. The governing body of the cycling federation—the UCI—mandated an annual base salary for professional men at the World Tour of pro racing: €37,000. (About $43,500 USD). Plenty of contracts were much higher but €37,000 was the bare minimum guaranteed. But for the female pro cyclists, there was no base salary in place. A study by the Women's Cycling Association found a few top-tier women's pro teams did pay proper salaries above the poverty line… but only a very, very small handful. The majority of pro women earned less than €8,500/$10,000 a year. And, without UCI's base wage rule—or any union for women's rights—team managers knew they could get away with signing riders for almost nothing. If an athlete balked, management would just hire someone else. Thus, 80 percent of pro women cyclists had to work at least two jobs just to get by. The men did not.

In 2011, it got uglier. UCI President Pat McQuaid was asked by a journalist if it wasn't high time the pro women also deserved a base salary. "I am not so sure," McQuaid responded, "…women's cycling has not developed enough that we are at that level yet." Push back started immediately. A few of the sports' top women like Vos and Teutenberg issued polished responses, but 21-year-old Aussie Chloe Hosking spoke from the heart.

"Pat McQuaid is a dick," she said, at the finish line after winning the Jayco Bay Classic. Hosking then had to pay a fine and issue an apology, as per UCI rules of conduct. The young woman stuck to her guns, responding, "Women's cycling every year is getting stronger and stronger. It needs to get more recognition and I'm not going to apologize for what I said, but I do apologize for how I said it."

Kudos, Chloe. I grabbed a notebook and wrote down McQuaid's crazy dinosaur-esque quote. As I searched for more responses to the base salary predicament, I found very few remarks from the women in the pro peloton. *Why aren't more women speaking out*? I wondered. Ignorance kept me behind the curtain, not yet revealing the fact many of pro women had contracts telling them to keep quiet about pay, equity and anything "controversial." *Wait... discussing equality is controversial? That's weird.* All I knew at the time was someone had to do something about this pay gap and equality stuff.

6

HOPE HIDES IN TRAGEDY

As I rode my bike back from Tucson's highly-acclaimed Saturday cycling group ride, known with ol' southwestern affection as "The Shootout"—a truly unthinkable horrendous event unfolded on the Northwest side of town. An actual shootout. Our beloved congresswoman Gabby Giffords and her constituents were gunned down in front of a neighborhood grocery store, where she held monthly meetings called "Congress on your Corner." What should have been a routine get-together where locals gathered to talk openly with Giffords about their hopes and concerns for the community, became a horrific mass shooting. Six people—from children to senior citizens—lost their lives as random targets of gun violence. 15 more were injured. Yet Giffords, the intended target of the madman's angst, miraculously survived a bullet to the brain.

By the time I rode home, the story unfolded and the victims were identified. Dot Morris, Phyllis Schneck and Dorwan Stoddard were retirees in their 70s. Gabe Zimmerman, 30, was Gifford's community outreach director. John Roll, 63, was a chief judge of the U.S. District Court for Arizona, named to the federal bench by George H.W. Bush in 1991. And then, there was Christina-Taylor Green. A nine-year-old girl who went with her neighbor to hear Giffords speak.

My heart broke for the victims. For our city. Our future. My mind raced with the close connections of my beloved community. I served jury duty for the presiding Judge Roll just a week before the shooting. I had mutual friends with Gabe Zimmerman. I voted for Gabby Giffords in 2007, inspired by how cool it was we finally had more women in Arizona politics. Cooler still, Gabby Giffords loved road cycling! I saw her on the bike a few times. But it was the youngest victim, Christina-Taylor Green, whose story reached into my heart pulled every string. This little girl played on a boy's baseball team.

"I need to write about her," I told my husband.

I hadn't written for nearly two years. The countless freelances pitches and rejections, the non-publicity of *As Good As Gold*, the constant silence on my business proposal to get a women's Tour de France off the ground… knocking on so many unanswered doors took a toll on my confidence. The beast of worthlessness tamped my desire to ever write another word. But Christina-Taylor Green woke me up and hushed the Cerberus.

In the midst of this tragedy there were two glimmers of hope. Gabby Giffords was still alive, and Christina-Taylor's life was a ray of light and progress. People needed to know that this nine-year-old girl who played baseball with boys wasn't just an athlete. She was the embodiment of change. She was progress. She was hope. Hope that girls can do anything they want, like picking up a baseball instead of a softball. People needed to see that we didn't just lose a little girl who was a ballplayer, we lost a tiny activist. And we must celebrate her life. As the grief of this shooting coursed through our collective Tucson soul, I sat down and started writing.

As a female athlete and a resident of Tucson, Arizona, the tragedy of the massacre that took place on Jan. 8, 2011 hit close to home in many aspects. Tucson likes to pretend it's a big city, but those of us who live here know the truth. We're a guppy of a metropolis, and we like it that way. We're a small yet sprawling town of involved citizens, often interconnected to other residents by just one degree of separation. Or fewer.

Six days before that fateful Saturday, I was called to jury duty under the Honorable John Roll, the federal judge killed in the shooting. His demeanor removed any sense of unease or tension from the courtroom, and he seemed a kind and caring man. I teach journalism classes at Pima Community College, where the gunman attended school. Unlike that troubled soul, my students are thoughtful, diligent and eager to learn. I am on Congresswoman Gabrielle Giffords' e-mail Listserv, through which she has regularly asked her constituents how she can make our city better. Her concern and love for Tucson is evident; it transcends partisan lines.

And then there is Christina-Taylor Green, the youngest victim in the shooting, a 9-year-old child with whom I've never crossed paths, yet with whom I feel a deep connection. This little girl was an athlete, and the bond between female athletes is a quiet, connective thread of respect that ties all its participants together. When I learned Christina was both a dancer and a baseball player, I saw in her a shadow of myself as a young athlete (and, frankly, as an older one). I'm currently an elite cyclist, shooting for one last chance at Olympic possibility. But I never would have gotten to this level if my love of sports hadn't taken root in childhood, at around Christina's age. Her smile in her Little

League team photo portrays the soul of an athlete: Here was a little girl who simply loved to play.

According to her coaches at the Canyon del Oro Little League organization, Christina was not just a participant. She was a baseball enthusiast, a leader on the field and off, and a competitor who held her own against the physicality that comes with playing on a boys' team. She was also born into the game, the daughter of Los Angeles Dodgers scout John Green and the granddaughter of Dallas Green, who managed the 1980 Philadelphia Phillies to the World Series title.

"What Christina exemplified in the baseball arena were the core characteristics we all hope our players will gain from Little League Baseball; character, courage and loyalty," read a statement by the Canyon Del Oro Little League.

Christina's father coached her Little League team, and that of her 11-year-old brother, Dallas. But it was another coach of Christina's team, the Pirates, who, through the Canyon del Oro Little League website, shared a memory of Christina's tenacity as an athlete.

"Christina was not short on courage," he wrote. "She played in a baseball league with boys who were strong and fast, but she never once was fazed about being the only girl on the team in 2010. Nor did a hard-hit ball or a whizzing fastball intimidate her. She had the courage to play every position on the field.

"In one particular game, Christina was having a quality at-bat, seeing the ball well and fouling several balls off. After six or seven pitches, the pitcher accidentally let a fastball go that plunked her pretty good. After picking herself up and dusting herself off, Christina was given the choice to take first base or to finish her at-bat, based on loose instructional league rules. With a slight grimace on her face, but without hesitation, she replied, 'I want to hit.' And hit she did. Her tenacious spirit was pumped up, and she drove a hard-hit ball on the next pitch. Courage was just part of who she was."

As is the case with most exceptional athletes, a life in balance was the key to Christina's happiness. "She was so engaged in everything," her coach wrote. "She was always giving her best and excelling, but she still was capable of being a little girl ... wanting to play for the sake of play, climbing the mesquite tree at the park with the rest of the team after practice while parents and coaches talked, laughing at silly jokes ... she was a rock star in so many ways, but also a beautiful little girl."

On Saturday morning, at the time the tragedy was unfolding on the northwest side of Tucson, I was with a small herd of elite cyclists on a training ride we call "The Shootout." The name is a reference to the tough old ways of the Wild West, as well as an accurate portrayal of how hard the training ride feels, physically. Once the group rolls out to the outskirts of Tucson, it is every man for himself, as the pace revs up to a most incredibly challenging speed. We lose cyclists along the way;

as the pace increases, many drop back. I hold on for as long as I can through the 60-mile test across the rural landscape of southwest Tucson. This ride is essential to my training for a shot at the 2012 Olympics.

On Saturday, I was one of two or three women out of 120 total cyclists who show up on The Shootout. The male cyclists accept my presence, and I'm grateful for how far we've come in society. Thirty or forty years ago, this might not have been the case. I'm grateful to the Billie Jean Kings, the Kathrine Switzers, the "Tubby" Johnstons (the first woman to play Little League) and the Title IX-ers who helped pave the way for the acceptance of female athletes in sports once dominated by men. I often wondered what it was like for kids in the current generation coming up through the sports world, and whether they felt the prejudices of the past.

As it turns out, girls like Christina-Taylor Green are a new generation of ambassadors in sport. They not only participate in sports with withering boundaries of gender bias (like baseball), but they're setting newer, bigger goals. In 2010, the registered number of Little League participants in America was 2.7 million children under the age of 18. Of that total, 1,617,000 were 5- to 9-year-olds. And 163,000 were little girls like Christina-Taylor Green, who played mostly on teams comprised of boys. Shortly before her death, Christina told her father she wanted to be the first woman to play in Major League Baseball.

While Christina was robbed of this dream for herself, there is comfort to be found in the immortality of the athletic spirit. She has helped lay the groundwork for other little girls to carry on her dream. Such is the beauty of being a female athlete. Generation by generation, we shape our sports, our games and our competition to rise to a new level of excellence. In her brief nine years, Christina-Taylor Green both upheld and continued an athletic legacy, whether she knew it or not. The members of her Little League baseball team are boys who will grow up to believe girls playing baseball is as normal as guys playing baseball. Those boys will become men who teach their children the same values. Someday there will be a woman in the majors—it's a question of when, not if—and Christina's dream will come full circle for a different female Little League player.

On the way home from my Saturday slugfest of a cycling workout, a friend pulled out his phone. There was a text message advising everyone to avoid Oracle Road. A congresswoman has been shot; several people were dead; chaos reigned. By the time we arrived back at our homes, news of the day's events was all over the television. As Christina's story was unfolding, I couldn't help wondering if our paths had ever crossed. I have cycled past her northwest Tucson ball field hundreds of times. Surely she had seen cyclists pass by the windows of her parents' car en route to Little League practice.

Despite a nearly 30-year age gap and the fact we've never met, Christina's death hit me hard. We were two athletes going about our lives, with very different sports goals stemming from exactly the same foundation. We were playing for the sake of play, and to see if maybe, just maybe, we could make the big leagues of our sport. Though she can no longer chase her dream, she's given me a newfound strength and inspiration to chase mine. And as all female athletes know, inspiration is how we leave our mark on the world.

While the loss of Christina-Taylor Green is an unfathomable tragedy for our country and our small city of Tucson, her legacy as an athlete does not have to end with the end of her short life. We can honor her life by encouraging girls to play sports, to get involved in class politics, to volunteer their time, to dream of major league debuts and local dance recitals. And when faced with society's equivalent of wild pitches, we can give these girls the courage to swing for the fences. Just like Christina did.

I sent the finished piece to my former editor at ESPN. "Look, I know you're not hiring, and you've said no to every pitch I've sent the past two years. But please, publish this one. Somewhere. Anywhere. I don't care. You don't have to pay me. But people need to read about Christina-Taylor Green."

"I'm forwarding this to W," Gary Hoenig replied.

"Who's W?" I asked.

"ESPN's latest venture. Our new website focused on women's sports. It's called espnW."

Three days later, espnW ran the piece on Christina-Taylor Green. Three weeks later, I was hired as Senior Editor of espnW. Three years later, women would stand on the start line of the Tour de France. All of this, from a devastating day in our beautiful Tucson, where the following years would teach me a most incredible lesson: Hope hides in tragedy.

Gabby Giffords amazingly survived being shot in the head, and now she is thriving and leading our nation as the imminent lobbyist for gun control. Christina-Taylor's untimely death made me aware of her existence, but it was her life that opened a door for so many women. I might not ever have known about her had we not experienced January 8 nor had the courage to write about what happened that day, until the door of inspiration was cracked open by Christina-Taylor's life. *Thank you, tiny activist. You've been with me ever since.*

Little did I know the presence of Gabby Giffords in my life was just beginning. Time would unfold her relevance in my journey three more times in the next nine years. 2011 was but the start.

7

Back on Staff at ESPN

enior editor, senior editor. Hello, I'm Kathryn Bertine, former waitress struggling athlete senior editor… I repeated the title over and over as my confidence soared and creativity flourished. I joyfully sat down at my desk in Tucson and dove head first into forty-hour work weeks of content production and editorial bliss.

ESPN, headquartered in Bristol, Connecticut, was in start-up mode with their newly-created espnW so our staff was spread across the country. Long before Zoom, we worked via phone conferences, email and copious amounts of writing. There were three senior editors on staff, covering Breaking News, Features and Profile, Lifestyle and Training. Mine was the middle one, and I was thrilled. Creating storylines focusing on strong, innovative, unique women was a rush of empowerment. Finally, I was in a decision-making position and could shine a light on badass women.

I told my editor-in-chief, Tanya Samson, how the most web hits on my previous ESPN column came from features not about mainstream sports, but about athletes no one's heard of yet. Even more hits on sports the public knew little about, ranging from open-water swimming to team handball and track cycling. Topics like these had brought in 2.1 million new readers. Readers are *hungry* for new material. It was a no-brainer to include new—

"Well, Kathryn, we need to remember that familiarity sells. People love to read about Venus and Serena, Mia Hamm and Abby Wambach, so it's important we feature stars," Tanya reasoned.

I countered with benevolence, agreeing that of course we must include the victories of the current stars, but if we want to move sports journalism forward, we need to cast a wider net into the galaxy of incredible athletes who are not yet household names. We need to prove hijab-wearing female pro skateboarders in Afghanistan are just as important as bikini-clad beach volleyball Olympic gold medalists. Good sports journalism isn't just about sports. It's a tool for shattering stereotypes of what women can do.

"We need to profile as many athletes as possible who are breaking barriers," I added, carefully checking my enthusiasm levels for Human Puppy syndrome. No boss wants to be excitedly slobbered on by a new employee in her first week on the job. *Down, Kathryn. Sit.*

The following months were a writer-editor's dream. My assistant editor and I assigned unique, original, terrific pieces to freelance journalists across the world. South American rock climber record-breakers. Skateboarders in Afghanistan. Olympians suffering from mental illnesses. The rise of females in mixed martial arts. The fall of gender barriers in endurance sports. The unknown women pioneering ski mountaineering and open water swimming. Jockeys, wrestlers, boxers, race car drivers... the pieces were powerful, the talent endless. We didn't stop with athletes.

We created a Power Play series on women who were on the business side of sports management. The doers, shakers, movers and makers quietly stepping up to roles that were traditionally held by men. We let the world know women lived there, too.

Tanya supported most of my pitch ideas, so I let go of the vibe that something felt a little off. She came not from sports journalism, but from "traditional" women's magazines on health, fitness. The kind where sports articles were about what color nail polish looks best in the gym. Occasionally during phone conferences, Tanya would talk over other women as if to establish her place in the pecking order. It became clear to us she didn't feel at ease in her knowledge of sports and athletes, catering to stories about sports celebrities. She steered away from uncomfortable topics or anything controversial. I, on the other hand, dove right in.

The greatest perk of my espnW position was not having to move. Working from home was a gift; get up early, train, work and be fully present in my married life. George was thrilled, as our two-income salary allowed us a new financial game plan. He would pay the mortgage, I would start a savings account for our future. We also divided the home tasks. I chose groceries, dinner and laundry. He vacuumed, did dishes and conquered the kitty litter. The equality of our marriage felt wonderful. We had a home, two cars, two jobs, five cats and ample joy.

About the cats. It would be remiss not to acknowledge the details of marrying a 38-year-old widower with five cats. George and his first wife, Colleen, originally had two cats, which scores relatively low on the Crazy Cat Person scale. However, the unplanned addition of three more felines arrived one day when Colleen went out for bike ride and came across an abandoned litter of six newborn kittens in a dry, desert riverbed. An avid animal lover and kindhearted human, she brought all six home. Three friends adopted half the litter. She and George kept the remainder. While nursing three tiny fur-babies is not an easy task, it gave Colleen great comfort during the throes of her chemotherapy. Four years later, all five cats surrounded her bed with comfort and love when she took her last breath.

"*ThatsthesweetestcatstoryIveeverheardGAAAHHHH*," I sniffle-bawled, when George first told me. I welcomed the five furballs into my heart and home, bonding very closely with Grizzly Bear, the gentlest, gray-and-brown tortoise-patterned kitty who climbed into my lap and parked herself there for hours. Polar Bear, too, the energetic white sassypants who, judging by the time she spent walking on my keyboard, may have been a writer in her past-life. The other three were equally great and I eventually passed their test for an acceptable human specimen.

Explaining the history of five cats to inquiring visitors meant sharing the details of my husband's past. Conversations about life, death, cancer, cats and remarriage garnered a variety of responses and emotions, especially with new acquaintances. In an attempt to thwart awkwardness, I usually kept the cat story short and the tone light, often diverting the topic by picking up Polar Bear and showing guests her special trick: Swinging around in a wicker basket and meowing with glee as I sang made-up songs to her.[16] This quickly solidified my rank of Admiral on the Crazy Cat Person scale. Sometimes it was easier than discussing personal stuff.

Working from home and cat-basket-swingin' was great, but the best perk came in the quiet rhythm of peace and stability. There was a roof over my head, food in the fridge, love in my heart and purpose to my day. Nothing could stop me from chasing my dreams. Nothing.

---

[16] *Polar, Polar the wondercat / loves flying round n' round like that / glad you're having such fun, wheeee! / Time to get back to work for meeee.* At the time, I thought Polar's meow was glee. Perhaps it was the howling of ruptured eardrums. I'm a terrible singer.

8

UCI DINOSAURS AND BELGIAN BROOMWAGONS

W ith the majority of 2012 qualification races in Europe, my best shot for success would be to race there in 2011. Knowing the courses, strategies and competition ahead of time bettered my chances. As for my espnW career, no problem. Have laptop, will travel. If I could find a Dutch or Belgian team to guest ride with in February and March, this could work. George was fantastically supportive. Seven weeks apart was nothing in the long run of marriage. My local elite team *Trisports.com Cycling*, gave me permission to take a temporary leave. Finding a European team, though, wasn't gonna be easy.

I didn't know a soul in Belgium, but I knew I had to get there. That was the epicenter of UCI spring classics. I began drafting emails to the race directors of every UCI event in Belgium and Holland, asking if they knew of any local teams that might need a spare rider. And, if possible, did they know anyone with a spare couch that some random, weird woman from Arizona could occupy for seven weeks? I crossed my fingers and hit send. Much to my unexpected delight, there are no *krekels*[17] in Belgium.

The wonderful Roger Nolmans, race director of UCI Tielt-Winge event in Belgium, responded with kindness. Roger connected me with Peter Despriet, manager of an elite amateur women's team who gave me a temporary spot on the squad. Roger then set me up to stay with his brother and sister-in-law, Wilfried and Els, whose lovely house was just down the street from the start line of Tielt-Winge and within driving distance to just about every race over the next seven weeks.

My team, Gaverzeicht-Matexi, was comprised of lovely, strong, young Dutch and Belgian athletes. I quickly claimed the title of the oldest and shortest. At 5'9,

---

[17] Crickets!

that's quite a feat. Dutch ladies have some fabulous height swimming through their DNA. I was proud to be their foreign shrimp.

The intensity and skill of European bike racers lived up to the legendary stories I'd heard. Dutch and Belgian cyclists often start racing as young as six, and by their twenties they are goddesses of strength, skill and power. Quite a contrast to my roots in road cycling, which began at age 31. The odds of turning pro at 36 weren't in my favor. Neither were my results in Belgium.

I was broomwagoned from five of seven Belgian UCI races, which were harder than any event I'd done outside World Championships. Intense, aggressive and just beyond the reach of my three-year experience. European UCI races had little tolerance for riders dropped from the main peloton. When the chase group falls more than two minutes behind the lead peloton, we are swept away by the broomwagon: the official car—often decorated with a broom—that politely tells riders to leave the course because they have zero chance of winning. The broomwagon is the most humbling, soul-crushing, vulnerability-wielding, crystal-ball-of-inner-reckoning. To hear the slow approach of the broomwagon's motor is a haunting death knell of dread. Sometimes, athletes will try to outride the car. Poor souls. If I ever become president of the UCI, I will mandate all brooms replaced with a shark fins and external loudspeakers blaring the *Jaws* theme, because humor before death would be so much more fun for both athletes and fans.

Despite not finishing five races, something better happened: Clarity. I finally understood just how much work it was going to take if I wanted to turn pro. There was hope, too. Races I did finish were benchmarks of progress. Indications I could get there.

9

CENSORSHIP & SISTERBLOCKING

While in Belgium, my position at espnW was a perfect blend of work and balance. Winter mornings were frigid, damp and cold, so I wrote, researched and edited until the afternoon temperatures rose just enough to head outside and train with slightly less discomfort. I was hitting my stride at espnW, uncovering more and more incredible, talented, unique female athletes across the globe. That March, I crossed paths with one such unforgettable woman.

At one of the most prestigious UCI races in the Netherlands, the Energiewacht Tour, I raced with Natalie van Gogh, an athlete who underwent male-to-female gender reassignment surgery in 2005.[18] Having never competed with a cyclist who transitioned, I was fascinated. Skeptical, even. Would she have an advantage? Be faster and stronger than all of the women? There simply wasn't a lot of public knowledge about athletes who had transitioned, especially back in 2011. While people with a variance in gender were not new to society, their presence in sports was a rarely-discussed topic. My curiosity overrode any fear about Natalie having an unfair advantage. I looked forward to sharing the start line with her and seeing what the race would bring. The next day, I got a first-hand education in the awesomeness of athletes who had transitioned and their need for inclusion.

During a mid-peloton crash in the second stage of Energiewacht Tour, the pack splintered immediately. The leaders surged ahead and the rest of us picked through the detritus of entanglement, trying to chase back to the leaders. Unhurt in the melee, I found myself chasing with two other women and we quickly jumped into a rotating

---

[18] *So, you mean a transgender athlete?* I originally used "transgender" throughout this book, until the knowledgeable Kristen Worley, activist for diversity and inclusion, kindly educated me that "athlete who transitioned" is a more accepted term. *Oh! I see it now*. Less about the label (transgender), more about the fact/action (athlete who transitioned). Thanks Kristen. Interactive Reader Guide: Kristen Worley.

paceline—cycling-speak for working together to conserve energy, draft and escape the dreaded broom/sharkwagon. One of those women was Natalie. As the three of us worked our asses off, I paid close attention. Would some sort of superhuman strength launch Natalie into a different realm of competition? If so, would it matter? In the fifteen minutes it took us to work our way back to the peloton, the three of us were equally snot-faced, eyeball-popping, quad-aching, lung-burning glorious messes of effort and pain. We made it back to the peloton, together. As we grunted exhales of relief, I could see, hear and feel the truth of this athlete: Natalie was no different than me.

I needed to write about her. Natalie's presence in the women's peloton was important. There would be more transitioned athletes in the future and debunking stereotypes had to start now. Besides, I was senior editor. We were already writing about women breaking boundaries. The founding creed of espnW was to "elevate women's sports by providing relevant coverage" and the subject of transitioned athletes in women's sports was exactly that. Relevant. I penned an essay.

The piece was set to run on ESPN's calendar for May 3, 2011. I eagerly refreshed the tab on the webpage, looking forward to sharing it publicly and feeling proud espnW was progressive enough to tackle topics like transitioned athletes.

May 3 came and went. The piece wasn't on the website. Despite seeing it listed for publication three weeks in advance. *Glitch*, I thought and reached out to Tanya. My boss responded not by email but phone call, explaining the topic was "just too controversial" for a website on women athletes.

"But Natalie *is* a female athlete," I said. "She is 100% woman. Operations and all."

"Well…" Tanya said, trailing off.

"We need to publish this, Tanya. It isn't right to label transitioned athletes as 'controversial.' They exist. They're not going away. If we don't write about their presence and their accomplishments, then we're failing as journalists. Come on, this is ESPN. It's our job to let the public know what's happening. It's our job to tell the truth about women's spor—"

"We're not running it," Tanya repeated, ending the call. Took me a while to put the pieces together. ESPN, owned by Disney, one of the most conservative groups in America. After a quick search through the records, no articles on male-to-female transitioned athletes had yet been published.[19]

Silence asked, "*What now?*" through the empty dial tone of our phone call. *Here's what*, I answered, *this piece will be published someday. If not through espnW, then in a future book.*[20] For every no, for every silence, for every illogical rule and regulation of women, sports and progress, my passion for change grew stronger. I kept my cool with Tanya so as to keep my job, but I was growing disillusioned with espnW. If we couldn't write about athletes like Natalie, what other topics would be silenced?

———

As the year progressed, my interest in espnW pieces gravitated toward women who created change, like Kathryn "Tubby" Johnston (Little League), Kathrine Switzer (marathon) and Katie Hnida (football) respectively who batted, ran and punted their way into history and paved the way for women's equality in sport. I implemented an espnW column called *Pioneer, Present, Future* where we shared the history of women in sport as well as the present champions and rising elites. Diane Van Deren, Lindsay Van, Justine Siegal... there were so many incredible gamechangers.[21] Researching these women who were considered "ahead of their time," I silently learned one of my first lessons of activism: When we think of athletes and activists being ahead of their time, let's pause. They are usually right on time. It's society who is late to the game.

While the majority of pieces we ran at espnW were assigned and published without issue, still the silencing continued. One of our freelancers pitched a story about Becky Gibbs-Lavelle, a pro triathlete who founded a nonprofit—Jenny's Light—to raise awareness and assistance on post-partum depression.[22] Becky's twin sister, Jenny, was a vibrant, happy, kind woman who sadly took her own life, and the life of her son, during a tragic struggle in the throes of undiagnosed, severe post-partum depression. Becky used her platform as a successful, well-known professional athlete to bring attention to the issues of mental health and pregnancy. I assigned the article immediately. Absolutely, yes, we need to write about female

---

[19] An article about female-to-male basketball player Kye Allums was added to ESPN's website via Associated Press in 2011, but no ESPN article was written on a male-to-female transitioned athlete until 2018.

[20] My essay on Natalie Van Gogh, *In It With All Her Heart,* was published in my book: *The Road Less Taken.*

[21] Interactive Reader Guides: Katie Hnida, Diane Van Deren, Lindsey Van, Justine Siegal, Kathryn "Tubby" Johnston.

[22] Interactive Reader Guide: Jenny's Light.

athletes who shine a light on mental health. Not enough media outlets were talking about mental health. Once again, espnW's editor in chief cut the piece from publication.

"Depression, suicide… no, too dark," Tanya said. "We can't run that."

"Information like this can help educate and save others," I countered. "Give me one good reason why we can't run this."

"Sponsors don't want to see depression and suicide. They want strong, happy, smiling women who win titles and set records. That's what sells."

Sells what? I thought to myself. *An inaccurate portrayal of reality? Falsehood? Partiality?* I shook my head. Tanya was missing the crucial point of journalism. What sells, above all else, is truth. It's our job, as journalists, to put it out there. Tanya wasn't getting it.

Later that year, I interviewed Marion Jones, the infamous track and field sprinter entwined with the 2004 BALCO doping scandal. The piece was not to rehash her doping violations, but to explore her rehabilitation. In 2011, Jones became an ambassador with U.S. State Department, to share her "Take a Break" story. The mission was for Jones to openly and honestly share her journey with kids, so they could see the reality of wrongdoings and choose a better path.

Jones's lawyer agreed to the interview, as long as ESPN promised not to dredge up Marion's past and to stay focused on the present. Otherwise she wouldn't do the interview.

"Right," I told her lawyer. "No problem." I didn't want to cover the stale, repetitive questions about drugs and cheating, anyway. Clearing the assignment with Tanya, she agreed.

"Good idea," Tanya said. "Focus on what Marion's doing now, not the doping." After writing the piece, ESPN decided to run it on their main site, not espnW. Fantastic, I thought. More exposure.

"But before we do that," said JJ, the editor-in-chief at ESPN, while on a conference call with Tanya and me. "I need you to go back and ask Marion why she lied about the drugs. That's what people want to know. That's what sells. This article is incomplete."

"No, her lawyer said—" I began.

"Yeah, Kathryn," Tanya interrupted. "Your piece is incomplete. Why didn't you ask Marion about the doping?"

Tanya threw me under the bus. Rather than clarifying her approval of the article, she took JJ's side. (He was her superior.) The piece went unpublished, on both ESPN and espnW. Sadly, yet another glimpse into the reality that not all women support other women. Especially not when they feel it threatens their pecking order.

There were more than a few instances of such behavior. Since I couldn't find a word to describe women who hold women back, I made up my own term: Sisterblocking.

Sisterblock : *SIS-ter-blok.* (verb.) To stop other women from rising. When one woman deliberately or passive-aggressively holds another woman back from progress and/or opportunity. ex. *Jane's proposal on eliminating the gender pay gap was sisterblocked when her co-worker Susan threw it in the trash.* Sisterblocker : *SIS-ter-blok-er* (noun.) *Susan is a sisterblocker. Bad Susan.*

Despite my differences with Tanya, I still held hope espnW could have a sustainable impact in the male-dominated sports industry. By June of 2011, the stats were promising. espnW garnered over 500,000 unique monthly visitors. We were growing. Articles were getting noticed and creating change. As more and more hits came through on the pieces featuring new, interesting, strong, fascinating women, I grew more comfortable voicing my thoughts and opinions during our employee meetings and phone conferences.

At our in-house meeting in ESPN's New York City office, I brought up the logo issue. The "espnW" thing gnawed at me from the beginning.

"Look, we need to talk about the font. The all-caps ESPN for men and lowercase espnW for women—that's not great," I pointed out. "Denotes inferiority, like we're smaller. Less than. Diminutive."

"It looks more feminine," Tanya countered.

"No, it looks like we're whispering," I countered back. "THIS IS YELLING, this is whispering. When *The New York Times* writes about female athletes, they don't print it in the new york times. Let's make it ESPNW. Visibility matters." At least it did to me. Then I spoke the words that may have sealed my fate.

"The truth is," I continued, "We shouldn't even have espnW." Slowly, the heads in the meeting turned toward me. Sports media was one of the last bastions of journalism inequity. Do we have a men's and women's section of Breaking News? No. Separate business and finance sections? Arts, travel, books? No. But sports? Sports was stuck in a rut of tradition so deep, so ingrained, that women barely made it into the news at all. When we did we were regulated to espnW rather than ESPN.

To break this outdated pattern of segregation in sports journalism, I suggested we work toward eliminating espnW and feature/combine all articles on women's sports right alongside the men.

"By doing away with gender segregation at ESPN, we'd set a new standard as leaders in sports journalism," my inner activist piped up.

"But people aren't following women's sports," Tanya said. "Readers aren't asking for women."

"People can't ask for what they don't know exists," I said. "As ESPN, we have the power to change this. We can show women's sports exist *equally* to men. It's our job—as news and media—to publish the truth. Creating equal visibility *is* truth. We can make it hap—"

"Well, if sponsors invest, then we can do more..." Tanya said. "Investment comes first."

"Sponsors don't invest in what they can't see," I shot back. "It's our job to show people what's out there. If ESPN wants a return on investment, first we must invest in ourselves. Equal media exposure on men and women yields twice the return."

Tanya smiled with a tinge of condescension, none too thrilled with my idea of merging espnW and ESPN. *Don't believe me? Fine, I'll prove that we can bring more eyeballs and investors to women's sports.* I set up a meeting with the vice president of espnW, to ask if I could have an official ESPN email address. That'll help me reach out to investors. Since I was hired as a contractor, using my personal email address to engage with investors looked ridiculously unprofessional. I was not given an ESPN email. Undeterred, I still tried engaging sponsors on espnW's behalf. By this point, I'm quite sure I won the rank of Most-Ignored Email World Champion.

What we really needed at espnW (and ESPN) was a Katharine Graham at the helm. In 1971, Katharine Graham—owner of *The Washington Post*—made a decision that effectively changed the course of journalism in the United States. Up to that point, most newspapers catered to stories and topics that painted a sunnier picture of America. In the early seventies, the Vietnam war was going very, very badly. But U.S. residents didn't know just *how* bad. A classified government document exposing the truth was mailed to *The Washington Post*. Graham understood the consequences. Publishing classified information was illegal. If her newspaper published the truth, they ran an insurmountable risk of being sued, held in contempt of court, prison sentences, debilitating fines and possible shutdown of the newspaper. *Forget this story*, her all-male governing board urged Katharine. *It will be the end of The Post. It will be the end of newspapers and media as we know it.*

In the middle of the night, two hours before the deadline for printing, Katharine shushed the men who had shushed her for the previous three decades.

"Publish it," she commanded. "The world needs to know the truth." The article woke the public to the false truths of Robert McNamara, Richard Nixon and the Watergate scandal. Indeed a lawsuit was filed. The Supreme Court ruled 6-3 in favor of *The Washington Post*, supporting the media's right to print the news and tell the truth. Katharine's board members were technically right: It *was* the end of newspapers and media as they knew it. A higher standard of reporting and publishing was now finally in place.

The most important part was the ripple effect Katharine Graham created. Every national newspaper and small-town local paper followed the lead of *The Washington Post*, adapting the ideology that truth must be told no matter the consequences. Newspapers thrived. The reality of Vietnam sunk in. Society woke up. All because Katharine went against the norm, listened to her gut, stood up and said, *publish the truth.* [23]

Tanya was no Katharine. Still, I refused to give up hope. Someday sports journalism will put the right woman at the helm of decision making, and the industry will change forever.

---

[23] Interactive Reader Guide: More about Katharine Graham

10

PRESIDENTIAL JESTERS, KINGS OF NORWAY & QUEENS OF PERSISTENCE

In my 2011 season on the bike, chasing Olympic qualification points, I fared quite well in three South American races. Then, at the national championships of St. Kitts and Nevis, I earned enough points to move into 125th on the UCI rankings. To get to the 2012 London Games I needed to be in the top 100. A shudder of excitement coursed through me… moving up 25 places was possible. One race could get me those points! The Olympics were finally within striking distance. As I awaited my national championship points to be tallied and distributed online, I glued myself to the refresh button on the UCI site, waiting for my name to jump from 267th to 125th. Nothing happened. Not that week, or the next. Or the next. My gut quivered. Something was wrong. I reached out to the UCI, inquiring about my national championship points.

"I'm sorry, but your federation sent the race results in after the 48-hour time limit," the UCI responded. "You will be given no points for your national championship." *What?!*

"Wait a minute," I shook my head. "Surely this is a misunderstanding," I explained.

"The results were due Monday, your federation sent them on Tuesday," the UCI official stated.

I argued with UCI about time zones, new federation presidents, and island time. Surely they would not withhold points from an athlete's victory because of some clerical office error in a small country with a federation staff very new to cycling. Those points were *mine*.

The UCI disagreed. Late is late. I was not given any points for my national championship win. Angry and panicked, I couldn't let this go. The fact that Olympic dreams hang in the balance of office errors? No. No way. Instead of emailing UCI secretaries and assistants, it made more sense to reach out to the highest rank; Mr. Pat McQuaid, president of the UCI. This issue of national championship points, rules and rankings could affect all smaller, newer federations and athletes in their attempt to gain Olympic qualification. Surely the president of the UCI would understand how vital it is to develop a better communication system—and ranking system—within the growing sport of cycling. Better still, my cycling coach, two-time Olympian and Tour de France rider Gord Fraser, knew McQuaid personally and had his contact info. I reached out directly via email.

Miraculously, McQuaid emailed back and invited me to meet with him when we would both be in Copenhagen for the World Championships, putting my name on the guest list for the UCI's VIP lounge.

Change, points, progress, rules, helping small-country development and women's pro cycling… even if the president only had five minutes, I could get the ball rolling. Arriving informed was also key. I did a deep dive on McQuaid. With a history in the sport spanning decades as a race director, head of the Irish Cycling Federation and sitting on boards from the International Olympic Committee (IOC) to WADA (World Anti-Doping Agency) to UCI, McQuaid got around. Hints of corruption tinged more than a few of his positions, but his most unscrupulous role was as an athlete.

In 1975, McQuaid flew to Cape Town to race the 14-day Rapport Tour in preparation for the 1976 Montreal Olympic Games. South Africa was in the tumultuous throes of apartheid. IOC took action by protesting apartheid and banning all international athletes from competing in South Africa. McQuaid didn't listen. Neither did his brother, Keiron, and Ireland's famed cyclist Sean Kelly. Whatever their reasons, be it apartheid views or athletic glory, all three quietly went to South Africa and entered the race under false names. The 26-year-old Pat McQuaid chose "Jim Burns" believing no one would ever find out. A freelance photographer for the London Daily Mail working the race noticed "Jim" looked a whole lot like Great Britain's team captain, Pat McQuaid. *Foiled, Jim-Pat*! No lucky charms for you. The story ran the next day in London. The IOC suspended all three riders with a six month ban from general racing and a *lifetime ban* from the Olympic Games.

Thirty years later, Pat McQuaid was elected President of the UCI. There was—and still is—no mention of Jim Burns in UCI archives.

After the road race at Worlds in Copenhagen, I wiped off the snot/residue of physical effort, changed into non-chamois pants and attempted to look as professional as possible in my post-race disheveled state of unkempt funk. I walked to the VIP tent alongside the finish line, where the men's race was in progress. With nearly six hours of racing on tap, there was plenty of time to steal a moment of McQuaid's attention. Approaching the hostess stand outside the tent, I informed her of my meeting with McQuaid and gave her my name. She scoured the guestlist.

"I'm sorry, you're not on the list."

"Please check again," I assured, showing her the email McQuaid sent to me. Not there. I then gave her every possible spelling variation of Kathryn. And Bertine. As she looked again, shaking her head, I glanced into the tent and saw McQuaid.

"PAT!" I called over the hostess's shoulder, waving with enthusiastic confidence toward this man I didn't actually know. "Hello..." I continued, and began walking in.

"Wait here," the hostess barked, halting me. She entered the tent, sidled up to McQuaid, who, in mid-conversation with cocktail in hand looked disgruntled to be interrupted. McQuaid followed her back to the entrance. Looking him square in the eye, I extended my hand and introduced myself.

"Hello, Mr. McQuaid. Wonderful to meet you! Following up on our appointment for a quick chat... thank you so much for your invitation to the VIP te—"

"Right. What's this about again?"

What my brain said, internally: I need my UCI points back, dude. This administration error shit is not right, cycling's small nations are being compromised, and my Olympic dreams are in dangerous jeopardy, yo. Fix this, boss man.

What my voice said, externally, was a lighthearted reminder of the topics in our email correspondence. I smiled wide and dialed down my intensity to convey I was not here to disrupt his glorified lawn party.

"Oh, right, yes. Ok, wait here," McQuaid says, retreating back into the tent without inviting me in. Peeking through the windowed tent flaps, everyone was dressed to the nines. Sponsors, donors, politicians, members of the UCI. There were no other female pro cyclists in the VIP tent. McQuaid returned with a woman dressed in business casual.

"This is Jacqueline. She can help you. I'm busy speaking to the King of Norway," McQuaid said, disappearing into the crowd.

Masking my disappointment, I introduced myself to McQuaid's secretary, thanking her for meeting with me. Stepping toward the tent opening, she stopped me.

"We can talk here," she said, barring my entrance. Couldn't help but smirk at the contradiction. I'm wasn't allowed in the tent set up to watch World Championships in which I just competed. I quickly stifled my forfuckssake grin. Giving Jacqueline the Cliff Notes version, I cut right to the chase. Can you please return my rescinded national championships points?

"No, we can't do that," she decided. "But you can always race again next year!"

"But next year's race is *after* the Olympic qualification date. Only national championship points count *this* year."

"Yes, that is too bad."

"Can next year's championships be moved up before the cut-off date?" I asked.

"In special circumstances, yes."

"Terrific! May we make this a special circumstance?"

"I will put you in touch with someone."

A ray of hope! said my inner optimist. *Fuck!* said reality. *There is no Someone, dummy.* After saying goodbye, I walked away from the tent, then remembered the book in my hand. I brought a copy of *As Good As Gold* to give McQuaid. To make an impression. To thank him for his time. To use as a coaster. Whatever. Turning back toward the tent, I noticed the absence of the hostess. Without hesitation, I walked right in. I, Queen of The Most Ignored, snuck into the Court of Royalty and Jesters of Affluence, and made my way to the King of the UCI chatting with the King of Norway, handing him the book. "It was wonderful to meet you," I smiled. "Looking forward to keeping in touch."

"Thanks Karen," he said, setting it on the table next to him. Took every ounce of human restraint to keep from responding, *You're welcome, Jim*! Exiting the tent, I cast one last look through the plastic windows. McQuaid had moved to the far side of the pavilion. The book did not go with him. *This isn't our last interaction, McQuaid. Go ahead and rule your party of Kings. But I'll have the last word on your reign in cycling.*

———————

Returning from Denmark, a victory appeared in my inbox in the form of an email from a newly formed UCI Dutch pro cycling team, Unovelo, co-sponsored a small, boutique cycling manufacturer in Canada. They had followed my results and cycling media exposure. Paying no attention to my aging ovaries, Unovelo offered me a professional cycling contract in November of 2011. My spirits soared. My gut rejoiced. My ovaries high-fived each other. *I am going to be a pro cyclist!* I signed the contract immediately, but was told to keep quiet until the team announced its official launch in January 2012. Oh, and salaries would be determined later, so don't worry about that now.

I floated downstairs from my office and embraced George in the kitchen. After four years of sending resumes to professional teams, the crickets of silence finally give way to the noisy war-whoops of victory, as I danced in booty-shaking celebration with tears of joy streaming down. My husband joined me, celebrating the moment. I was 36 years old. Eight years past the ridiculous age median required of UCI pro teams. *Geez,* I thought to myself, *they must've signed a middle-schooler to balance out the median.*

As an activist, I felt an internal sea change take place that day. What I set out to do in 2009—create a Tour de France for women—became one step closer. Now that I was a going to be a pro cyclist *and* held senior rank at ESPN, I had to try again contacting ASO again. Maybe now they would listen. I fired off yet another email to Prudhomme. Crickets, but still. Change was afoot!

11

DREAMS, REALITIES AND DOCUMENTARIES

Shortly after signing the Dutch team contract, I received an email from John Profaci, head of marketing for Colavita. The U.S.-based olive oil and pasta/gourmet food company had sponsored a women's—and men's—professional cycling team for over 15 years. With dazzling rosters of legendary Olympians and National Champions, Colavita was one of the best pro teams in North America. Colavita was my dream team. Profaci, a recreational cyclist, was drawn to sponsoring a cycling team after studying the weak sponsorship returns in auto racing.

In 1997, a NASCAR promoter pitched Colavita on getting involved with stock car racing; where a ten-inch bumper sticker cost sponsors $350,000. Profaci was blown away. $350,000 for a bumper sticker on a car going 200mph that fans couldn't even see from the grandstands or TV? *I could fund an entire pro cycling team for that amount*, Profaci thought. So he did. Colavita Pro Cycling was born in 1998.

Every woman aspiring to the pro ranks sent their resumes to Colavita Pro Cycling, following and idolizing their athletes. Behind the scenes, the team was in trouble. At the end of 2011, Colavita's co-sponsor, Fuji Bikes, pulled out fifty-percent of the budget funding. Profaci faced no choice but to fold the team, releasing all riders signed for 2012. Yet, in a last-ditch effort trying to save the program, Profaci reached out to me after seeing many of his athletes I profiled for espnW. Maybe, he thought, there's a way this team could continue with espnW as a co-sponsor.

I eagerly took the call. Profaci explained his model of sponsorship. Colavita would pay espnW for advertising. The revenue generated by ESPN exposure would cover team expenses. Jerseys would be emblazoned with Colavita-espnW.

"EspnW's viewership and fan base are perfect for our company," Profaci said. "We seek communication with the active, healthy, young women in this country. Colavita can help get espnW's name on the streets—literally! It's a win-win situation."

I wanted nothing more than to see the best women's pro team in the U.S. succeed. I assisted Profaci with the sponsor proposal and set up the introduction to espnW's vice president of marketing, Marly Ellis. While not a road cyclist, Marly was a spin class devotee. I was quickly learning one of the most important lessons about doing business with corporate giants like ESPN. Companies aren't untouchable, goliath entities. Companies are made of human beings. People who have interests outside the workplace. When we find common ground of interests, brands and goals, anything is possible. Companies don't make things happen. People do.

If this corporate partnership was going to happen, it wouldn't be espnW saving Colavita. It would be a middle-aged woman who likes spin class and a recreational roadie who makes pasta sitting down together at the table of collaboration.

Arranging the meeting, I briefed Marly about Colavita, letting them know how much I was looking forward to sitting down with them and—

"Thanks Kathryn, we'll take it from here!" Marly informed. Oh, ok. Apparently senior editors are not invited to businessy, financy, discussiony stuff. Even if they bring the actual sponsor to the table. Still, I was thrilled. Two months later, Colavita-espnW Pro Cycling officially partnered up for 2012. Pride coursed through me. Even better, I—a newly minted pro cyclist on a Dutch team—would finally race against the many women I looked up to on Colavita.

Not only was I thrilled, but empowered. Now I had the perfect opportunity to leverage my Tour de France mission. Video journalism was on the rise. ESPN's *30 for 30* documentary series was thriving, viewership was skyrocketing. But there were so few visual pieces on female pro athletes.[24] It was definitely the right time to introduce a documentary on women's pro cycling. To see faces, hear the stories. To expose the corruption, seek solutions, show the public why there is no Tour de France for women…and why there needs to be one.

Seemed an absolute no-brainer ESPN would stand behind such a documentary pitch, especially now that espnW co-sponsored a professional women's team. More

---

[24] ESPN's *30 for 30* film count on athletes profiled as of 2020: 157 men, 9 women. (3 of which are short videos not full documentaries.)

publicity, more branding. Especially now that I had direct access to the athletes, as a journalist and racer. Bringing a documentary crew to interview international superstars was totally doable! Adding to my confidence was the fact ESPN ran three short documentary videos during my Olympic quest which were well-received by the ESPN fanbase. We had proof ESPN fans loved this stuff. With the perfect trifecta in place—experience, originality and new material—I created a documentary proposal and on our next team conference call, delivered the pitch. The key details. The high points. The inequities. The champions. The corruptors. The need for change. All of it, but most important, this: the documentary wasn't really about cycling.

"Tanya," I closed, "it's about women being held back. And rising up for change. Everyone loves an underdog. There are barely any 30 for 30s on female athletes. Let's do this!" After a brief pause, Tanya spoke.

"Well, it's just women's bike racing. Does anyone even watch that?" she said, with a laugh. "You might want to cover your ears, Kathryn, but no one's going to watch a film on women's cycling." Shutting down the proposal, Tanya droned on as the conference call shifted to new topics. My brain stayed right where it was, silently answering her rhetorical question.

Correct, Tanya. No one watches women's pro cycling on TV... because no one can see it! You can't watch what isn't there. For Crissakes, woman, we're ESPN. It's our job to put sports on TV. We. Have. The. Power. To. Create. What. People. Watch. You dingbat sisterblocker.

Disappointment set in. Overwhelming me. My emotions ran the gamut. The dismissive tone of her voice burned in my soul and as it burned, the switch flipped. Now more than ever, I wanted to make this film. To be the change, to create the *see*. Wasn't quite ready to say the words out loud just yet, but something was churning within.

After the documentary-shutdown call, I received an email from Tanya. "Let's schedule a private call on Friday, I have some thoughts."

Ooooh. Maybe something about my film pitch got through to her! I eagerly awaited our call. Or, maybe this was about a bonus, since it was December. Or a promotion! My *London Calling* column, portraying female pro cyclists and their bids for Olympic qualification, had brought a six-figure Colavita sponsorship to espnW. We surpassed the one-million mark of new viewers, and I wrote nearly 40 articles during the year in addition to my editorial and freelance-hiring duties. Nowhere to go but up. There's still more work to do, more strides to make...

especially with all that censoring bullshit of "controversial" topics. Still, I loved this job. On Friday, I picked up the phone, ready to hear Tanya's ideas and make another run at the documentary project.

"We'd like you to write more," Tanya said. "We're going to switch our editorial duties, Kathryn, so now you'll be able to focus on writing full time." Ok. Terrific. I'm in. I asked for the details regarding my salary increase. More writing, more money. *Ka-ching*!

"We're thinking 200…"

My jaw dropped to the floor. Oh my god, a six-figure salary.

"…dollars per piece. And you can write for us twice a month!"

Oh. Ok. Well, math was never my strong suit, but I was able to quickly decipher writing a couple extra pieces each month would total an additional $4,800 per year. Now my total salary would be in the $60,000 range. Fine with me. Then, suddenly, it was not fine at all. Tanya explained this was no salary bump. I would not make an extra $4,800 per year. I would make *only* $4,800 a year.

"Tanya, that's an impossible salary. No thanks. I'll stick with the senior editor role."

"Sorry. We moved that position in-house. It's filled." Tanya had reassigned my editor position to an in-house staff employee at ESPN's Bristol compound.

"I didn't think you'd want the Bristol job," she said, "Since you live in Arizona and you're married." Because of this reasoning, she did not even present me with the opportunity to relocate. *Sisterblocked.* The writing was on the wall. She didn't want me at ESPN. I was being let go. And it didn't stop there.

Weeks after signing the Dutch team pro contract, the sponsor pulled out. There would be no team. Baffled, I didn't understand. Weren't contracts legally binding? My ignorance had a field day with that one. The team was just plain gone. I wouldn't be a pro cyclist. Dream, poof.

In addition to the loss of espnW and the Dutch pro team, my literary agent of ten years ended our relationship. *As Good As Gold* didn't land on bestseller's list, and his agency needed to make room for new authors. My agent loved the idea of women racing at the Tour de France. But since I hadn't made it happen, there was no story.

My demons started puttering about. The Cerberus barked through most of December and clear into the middle of January 2012. I wallowed in the swamps of negativity, deflecting the questions of friends and strangers asking, "How's ESPN?

What are you working on now? Any new book deals?" I had no yeses, just a plethora of nos.

By the end of January, I'd racked up enough job, team and agent rejections that my weight of NotEnoughness grew so heavy I began to fear its load. What I didn't realize then was the power of despair, and how it often hides in the shadows of striving. All I knew was this: I was tired of being sad about all the closing doors. *Yeah, yeah, I know. Go knock on new doors, open new windows.* Slowly, my sadness turned to anger, then anger to motivation, motivation to wonder, wonder to possibility, and finally the switch flipped and I knew what I had to do: Not let ESPN have the last word on what we watch, write or publish. Not give up the pro cycling dream. Not give in till women raced at the Tour de France. Apparently this internal concoction of asking, trying and vying was the kibble that quieted my Cerberus. For now.

———————

In February, I emailed John Profaci and told him of the Dutch team collapse, drew in a deep breath and asked if there was any space left on the Colavita-espnW Pro Cycling roster for 2012.

"I'd love to have you ride for us," John responded. "I also need some help. All the riders we released last month have found new teams. Can you assist me in securing the best riders and finding a new director?" *Uh, you want me to help you find awesome, strong women to comprise the team I've always dreamed of racing for, and also ride for said team at the age of thirty-fucking-seven!? Hang on, let me think about tha—*

"YES, ABSOLUTELY," I bellowed, as professionally as possible, while a chorus of angels sang *Aaaaahhh!* and poured confidence into the cracks of my broken dream. Holy shit. I was going to be a pro cyclist after all.

"Right now, we can only pay our athletes $1000 for the year," John said. Well, after the way things were going, that felt like a million bucks.

I called espnW and told them I was officially racing on Colavita-espnW Pro Cycling, and would continue writing my monthly column, *London Calling*. I didn't ask, but told. Also told the head of marketing that espnW's logo on the jersey needs to be ESPNW for optimal visibility. No more of this lowercase bullshit.[25] Despite being completely undervalued and earning $400 a month to write a couple freelance

———————

[25] Eventually, ESPN listened. They did away with the lowercase on both the website and the team jersey.

pieces, I now had a team and access to the best races and athletes. *Undervalued, my ass. Fuck it. I'll show them.* The switch was flipped. I would make the film ESPN said no one would watch, and prove them wrong. Very wrong. And no one was going to stop me.

12

INDIEGOGO-ING THE DISTANCE

I am going to make a documentary! I am going to make a documentary! Before breathing these words out loud, I dove into research-mode. Other than my 1980s childhood passion of using our family VHS camcorder to film skits usually starring our beloved dog, Taffy, I knew very little about filmmaking. But I did know this: Making a documentary film needs a plan, a script, a cinematographer and a budget otherwise we'd get nowhere. The most important part of that sentence was the "we." Sure, I could write the narrative script and provide the structure and direction of the film. But the videography and editing? That had to be a separate job done by a professional. *Find a video/cinematographer,* I scribbled in my notebook.

The budget however, had to come first. I had no idea how to set about constructing the parameters and expenses of making a documentary film. Travel, fees, whoknowswhatelse… there was so much to learn. One thing I knew for sure, making a film was going to be expensive. My projected income for 2012, combining my pro cycling salary and my measly espnW column pittance yielded a grand total of $5,800. That made waitressing and adjuncting look lucrative. Making a documentary sure as hell wasn't going to come from my pocket. *Find investors*, I wrote. Immediately followed by, *How?*

In February of 2012, I sat down with my husband and gained the courage to share my vision out loud. "I want to make a documentary film," I told George, with my vocal chords, finally releasing the words to the universe. My heart was brimming of equal parts strength and vulnerability. Strength came from knowing, without a doubt, making this film on women, sport and equal opportunity was something I wanted to do with every ember in my soul. My vulnerability, though, was palpable. Without my husband willing to take the role of sole breadwinner in our marriage, this film probably wouldn't happen. Making this documentary meant I'd be an unpaid, fulltime, first-time filmmaker. For a year. Maybe two, even.

"Honey," I quickly clarified, "I'll never ask you to put one dime of yours into this film. But are you ok with me earning below the poverty line for a little while?" That would mean he'd have to cover our household groceries, gas and mortgage. For my entire adulthood, I'd never relied on anyone else, even during the struggling years. Privately, I also struggled with my self-worth. That if I made less, I was less. Didn't occur to me at the time that many marriages have one spouse who supports both, or that one spouse making less money was actually normal and okay. Instead, I felt anxious. Was I doing the right thing? Would it really be okay with my partner? What if the film doesn't fly? What if standing up and speaking out for equal opportunity falls on deaf ears? What if what it really *doesn't* matter after all? *Good lord, if this filmmaking and pro cycling thing doesn't work out, I could always pursue a career in professional overthinking.*

"I believe in what you're doing," George said, likening our circumstance to those where one spouse helps the other through med school knowing there's a better situation on the other side. "Hey, I bet this documentary leads to bigger things. Don't worry, we'll be ok." My heart soared. My husband believed in me even when I didn't.

———

That March, I went to Best Buy and picked up a portable camcorder for $99 called the Sony Bloggie. It was purple. And plastic. And pocket-sized. Perfect. Memories flooded back from the first time I ever held filmmaking equipment in my hands.

In 1984, my childhood friend Kerry and I wrote, directed and starred in our homemade 10-minute movie, *Murder in the Mansion*. We played all the parts; the heiress, the maid, the burglar, the detective, the villain, the victim. I don't remember the theme or the outcome, other than this: we spoke in British accents, the bad guy was eventually caught, the blood in the murder scene consisted of ketchup squirts on saran wrap, which we placed very carefully on the victim's shirt and over the carpet, because under no circumstances was our executive producer (Kerry's mom) okay with unsupervised condiments and energetic nine-year-olds. We abided.

Kerry's uncle edited the VHS tape and added suspenseful music, which blew my mind. I had no idea sound could make someone… feel stuff. Watching our movie, I felt stuff. *We made something and someone put music in it and if you work really hard and are careful with ketchup you can do anything!* While we failed to garner an Oscar nod, I can still feel the tingles of wonder and awe 35 years later. I can still feel the slippery, saran wrap weighted with ketchup. I can still hear that ridiculous accent emanate from my prepubescent vocal chords. I can still see the joy on our faces, trying to make a story come to life.

Maybe energy, karma, the universe and my gut knew someday I would make a documentary long before I ever did. When we take time to examine our past, sometimes we can see the clues of our future. *I am careful with ketchup! I can do anything! I can make movies!*

Real documentaries proved much more difficult than *Murder in the Mansion*. Telling a story was one thing, but creating a film is another. Other than buying the lil' purple Bloggie, I had no idea where to find a real cameraperson or how to go about fundraising. Still in research mode on filmmaking in March of 2012, I put a few inquiring posts out on social media. The next day, a Facebook message appeared from my former neighbor, Dimitri Petropolis, asking whether I'd ever considered crowdfunding.

"Kathryn, I can't imagine that you would not mobilize an army of support. Kickstarter and Indiegogo have raised thousands for such projects," Dimitri said. "KB, you're definitely worthy. What do you think?"

Kick*who*? Indie*HuhHuh*? Crowd*what*ing? I'd never heard those terms. Google enlightened me on this new endeavor called crowdfunding, where people publicly seek financial support for a variety of projects—from film making to book writing to paying hospital bills. It was riveting. Dimitri suggested I could use crowdfunding to help me secure funding for a documentary. But what riveted me most were Dimitri's words *'you're definitely worthy.'* After feeling like shark chum for the past few months, I clung to this tiny word *worthy* like a life-preserver. I scheduled a meeting with Dimitri and his partner, Hildy Gottlieb, who ran a local nonprofit, Creating the Future.

"How exactly," I asked. "*Does* one create the future and stuff?"

Hildy and Dimitri explained their foundation helps people map out ideas on how to make something happen. Anything. Opening a business. Starting a project. Forming a mission.[26]

---

[26] Interactive Reader Guide: Creating the Future. Thank you Dimitri and Hildy.

"Whoa. So, if I want to make a documentary but don't know where to start... you could help me sort through such logistics?"

"Yes."

"And what would this cost?"

Hildy and Dimitri smiled. "It's free. We're helping you think. Thinking and helping are free." Proof there are angels dressed as humans walking around this world.

––––––––––––

At a modest office in midtown Tucson filled with whiteboards and markers, I showed Hildy and Dimitri still photos and videos from the little purple Bloggie I took with me on my Olympic points races in El Salvador, Venezuela and Europe. For a week, we researched, brainstormed and whiteboarded until a colorful map of possibilities unfolded in a glorious sprawl of bubbles, branches, solutions and documentary doability on the great big wall of their tiny office.

Then, Hildy pulled out her own camcorder and put me in front of it, explaining people/investors needed to see something, even if just a quick flash of photos and a voiceover. Apparently, saying "*I wanna make a film and I've never done that before but don't worry! It'll be great, trust me! Gimme yer money!*" doesn't exactly scream investment. Selling a verbal vision isn't easy. Physically *seeing* a vision is necessary. At least so they can assess my level of honestly/weirdness for themselves.

After a few more sessions of collaborating, deliberating, fine tuning and creating, we had a nine-minute video called "Kathryn's Quest" mapping out the mission statement of the documentary. "I plan to give a voice to the progress, development and drive of women's professional cycling," I spoke to the camera. "Women are starting to speak up, and the message is clear: We're stronger, faster, and better than ever—and we deserve equality. Now."

"I don't know about this whole 'Kathryn's Quest' title, though," I told Hildy and Dimitri. "This film isn't about me, it's about the whole sport."

"Yes, and you can change the title later, but right now—on this first go-round of crowdfunding—people know who *you* are," Hildy said. She had a point. I wasn't famous, wealthy or influencer-status, but I had some followers. "When you have enough film footage of others, *then* create a trailer for the documentary and give it the name you really want." Oh. Ok. Got it. Makes sense. Hildy and Dimitri are very, very good at creating the future.

"What's your timeline and budget?" they asked. After calculating travel costs, hiring a cameraperson, research assistants, photo/video rights, licenses, narration fees, video/film equipment, every possible miscellaneous expense over 12 to 18 months for completing the project, I estimated $60,000. If we ate at Waffle House, utilized homestays and kept everything very, very simple this project seemed doable. Especially having spent plenty of years on salaries below the poverty line. But $60K also seemed an unlikely goal for a first-time fundraising project comprised of a photo collage and promises of a non-famous, first-time filmmaker. So we cut it in half and set the crowdfunding platform for $30,000.

"Listen, even if you get a fraction of $30K," Dimitri said, "That'll probably be enough to create an official trailer for the film. That's the most important part. Then you can do a second round of crowdsourcing for the bulk of the film." We decided to wait until April to launch the crowdfunding campaign, after the Colavita-espnW team announcement in March. "When it comes to exposure and fundraising, timing is everything," said Hildy and Dimitri.

"When it comes to people helping people, you two are everything." I decreed.

On March 20, *The New York Times* announced the partnership of Colavita-espnW Pro Cycling.[27] EspnW would now be on the Colavita label in 15,000 stores, front-and-center on the jersey/shorts and the centerpiece of a team budget estimated at $500,000. I beamed. If my non-famous, non-wealthy self could make a business partnership like this happen, maybe there really was hope for the film. And to finally connect with ASO. Maybe we really could get women to the Tour de France. What brought even more joy was the last sentence of the Times' article:

"There will be eight members of the cycling team, Mr. Profaci said, which is to begin its 2012 season of competitions next month."

Eight members of the cycling team. I read it again and again, thrilled to know I was one of those eight members. Damn. *The New York Times.* It was official. Colavita Pro Cycling would not fold but thrive in 2012. My heart raced. *I am going to be a pro cyclist. For real, this time.* I publicly shared the news on social media. That weird, journalist, writer chick who first mounted a road bike five years ago as a Category 4 beginner would race professionally for Colavita-espnW Pro Cycling

---

[27] Interactive Reader Guide: NYT article on Colavita & ESPN

at the age of 37. I was the Rudy of bike racing.[28] *Never give up, Never give up! Yeeeehaaaaw!* I screeched, shared and blurted gleefully to anyone who would listen.

Behind the scenes, I took up Profaci's request to help build the team. The majority of women in pro cycling were already signed for 2012, but there were plenty of talented athletes who fell through the cracks of folded teams like I did with the Dutch/Unovelo squad. Over the next few months, we signed seven strong, talented, wonderful women: Mary Zider and Jamie Dinkins Bookwalter were our U.S. racers. Our Canadian racers were Moriah Macgregor, Leah Guloien, Joanie Caron, Laura Brown, Jasmin Glaesser Deuring... the latter two would go on to represent Canada in the 2012 Olympics. Rounding out the roster and representing St. Kitts and Nevis, I was thrilled to discover I wouldn't be the only Caribbean affiliate on our team.

Wynona Summerfield, a retired pro cyclist representing Jamaica, took the role of team director. I was ecstatic. Wynona was my idol. Not just because she was an incredibly talented former racer for Colavita, but because she was a half-German, half-Jamaican dual citizen pro triathlete competing for Jamaica in the 2000 Olympics. After she switched to road cycling, she won the Central American and Caribbean Championships, but failed to qualify for the 2004 and 2008 Olympics... likely for the same reason of the skewed points system. Wynona didn't know it, but she was a huge inspiration to me. Together we showed the cycling world there *are* talented female athletes in the Caribbean, and the UCI better pay attention. I couldn't wait to meet her in person.

Better still, Wynona was set to co-direct our team with the legendary Tina Pic, a six-time U.S. criterium and road race national champion. Anyone who raced bikes in the USA during the 90s and 2000s knew, admired and laughed with Tina Pic. Her leadership, humor and kindness was as stellar as her physical talent. Not only would Tina co-direct but also step in to race with us on occasion, too.

I didn't know this at the start of the season, but there is an intense level of sisterhood in pro cycling. There is no deeper bond than baring our physical and emotional guts to one another in the midst of pushing our humanness to its limits. We're all a little bit crazy, a little bit broken, a little bit independent and a little bit

---

[28] The indefatigable Rudy Ruettiger who, at 5'6 and 27 years old, walked onto the Notre Dame college football team in 1975.

stuck with each other. Equally the same as we are different. Half this, half that, all family. I loved this team before I ever met them.

With the announcement of Colavita-espnW Pro Cycling fresh in the media, I gathered my courage launched the documentary's Indiegogo campaign on social media. Using Facebook and Twitter, I shared the link daily and watch as donations began to slowly trickle in. *Whoa. This is amazing. Cover your ears, Tanya! People DO want to see a film on women's pro cycling.* On my next espnW column in the tiny byline sentence, I included a link to the Indiegogo campaign. *Want to see a film on women's cycling? Donate here.*

The espnW copy editor deleted the link before publication. "Raising money for a documentary we're not producing... that's a conflict of interest," she decided. Right, of course it was. ESPN neither wanted to produce nor assist a film on women's cycling.

Slowly, the numbers inched upward. When we hit $5,000, I started looking for a cameraman. At least with that amount, I could possibly hire him/her to get to the upcoming Exergy Tour in Boise, Idaho where we could gain access to interviewing some of the best international racers.

I had no idea, of course, where to find a cameraman/cinematographer. But I was gaining confidence in the outreach of social media. With the Indiegogo campaign on the rise, I gathered up my courage and put a request out in April 2012:

"Ok Facebook, Twitter... I am looking for a professional cameraperson to help me make the documentary on women's cycling. Who do we know?"

A few days later, Melissa Bailey, a Facebook friend whom I had not met in person but was a reader of my ESPN days, sent me a message. Her husband, Kevin Tokstadt, was a cinematographer. They lived in Hood River, Oregon. After years working at Nike, Kevin branched out on his own. Having just finished up a videography project, he was looking for the next opportunity.

"I can't answer for Kevin, but I think he'd be up for this documentary. Can I connect you?" she asked.

"Yes, please!" I answered. "But tell him the film isn't really 'Kathryn's Quest.' The official name of the film will be *Half The Road: The Passion, Power and Pitfalls of Women's Pro Cycling,*" I said, explaining half the road was a play on the adage that women hold up half the sky. Yes, and half the road in cycling, too. Kevin signed onto the role of cinematographer and editor and became my partner-in-filmmaking.

Behold, the power of social media. Behold, the power of asking for what we want. Behold, the power of getting what we want, feeling the equal rush of exhilaration/fear, and jumping in head first because our gut tells us this is what we're supposed to be doing.

13

No One Climbs Hills Smiling

On the floor of the Houston airport, slumber was fitful at best. Crumbs, odors, stains, and the remains of Cheetos embedded into the carpet beside my head. In the middle of the night on May 11, I reached into my backpack and opened the birthday card my father tucked in there before my red-eye flight to Venezuela. *I'm so proud of how you've chosen to live your life*, my dad wrote. I am equal parts touched and amused. I am in love with the journey of Olympic dream chasing and documentary film making, but sometimes the physical exhaustion of it all brought emotional introspection. Between the dozing, shifting, dreaming and Cheeto-dodging, I wondered about life paths and choices. Did I take/make the right path? *How much do we choose versus how much is hardwired*? Who knows. That was a big question to tackle on too little sleep. Sandwiched between 11pm and 5am connecting flights, it made no sense to dip into the documentary funds and pay for a hotel room or a proper dinner. The airport floor and Cheetos were just fine. Such are the logistics of a dream in progress. I loved and hated my immediate surroundings with equal passion.

I spent my 37th birthday en route to Venezuela and El Salvador, in pursuit of 2012 Olympic qualification points. The Colavita-ESPNW Pro Cycling team wasn't scheduled to race for a few more weeks, but a composite team made room and invited me to join them. For the fourth time in five years, I spent my birthday in Central or South America. Uruguay, Colombia, Mexico, Venezuela twice. All in attempt for Olympic points. The odds were usually stacked against small-nation-athletes earning qualification points, but I was motivated to thwart the skewed system. At the very least, I could expose the injustices.

With my little, purple, plastic Bloggie camcorder and its tiny little tripod, I filmed the athletes of women's pro cycling. I knew only three things about filmmaking: Keep the light behind me, keep the volume high and always keep the camera rolling. The best stuff happens when we don't expect it. In the dorms of Venezuela and the dining halls and start lines of El Salvador, I asked my competitors if they would chat with me about their experiences in pro cycling. *I'm making a documentary!* I told them, which probably looked anything less than official when I pulled a four-inch, grape-colored camera from my pocket.

As I gained their trust, my competitors slowly opened up. Athletes from across the world all sat down and talked to me. Openly. Honestly. Because I was one of them, now. In the dorms of El Salvador Sport Center, Pia Sundstedt of Finland told me how the UCI rescinded her points, and she hired a lawyer to fight for her right to the Olympics. In a quiet corner of the athlete's cafeteria, Flavia Oliveira from Brazil, with her broken collarbone in a brace from a crash the day before, talked about the gender pay gap at the Tour of Flanders. Veronica Leal Balderas from Mexico spoke of low salaries and fewer race opportunities for women, and how the politics of cycling were very corrupt in her country. In the Venezuelan hotel's storage room, the national team from Panama talked to me as they packed up their bikes. The race directors were sending them home mid-stage race, deeming them not good enough to be with the rest of the athletes when some Panamanians finished toward the bottom of the results. Strange, seeing how all results of all races will have winners at the top and finishers at the bottom. To be sent home mid-event was far more discriminatory than the dreaded broomwagon.

With every interview, my passion for the documentary grew deeper. Cycling was a supporting role. Inequity was the lead.

I asked each interviewee, Do you think the pro women should be allowed to race the Tour de France? If you had the opportunity, would you race? The yeses came forth on all accounts, from all cyclists, from all countries.[29]

"It's working!" I Skyped breathlessly with my husband. "We're getting amazing footage down here." From that moment on, I understood this wasn't my documentary. It was ours. Mine, George's, Kevin's, Hildy's, Dimitri's, Colavita's, every single cyclist we interviewed, even my Cerberus of self-doubt... together we

---

[29] The only Nos came from track cyclist sprinters who often joked, "A three-week road race? No thanks, I'll stick to the three-minute sprint events." We always shared a good laugh over that. 99.9% of track cyclists respected the right for their endurance colleagues to have equal opportunity to the Tour de France.

were making this happen. This wasn't my film anymore. This was ours. From that moment on, there was a permanent pronoun shift in making *Half the Road*. *I* became *we*. I wasn't making a film. We were.

In Venezuela and El Salvador, I garnered three top-twenty UCI finishes. A strong showing, but not strong enough. Classification points only went to the top eight places, and I left South America without qualifying for the London Olympics. There was one more event left before the qualification cutoff date: The Exergy Tour in Boise, Idaho. But before heading there, was something even better was on the horizon: Colavita-ESPNW Team Camp.

Serendipitously and conveniently scheduled in Tucson, our team camp was based at a Radisson two miles from my home. Tingling with excitement, I couldn't stop smiling. There was an instant connect and positive vibe among us. Getting to know one another, we told stories of our cycling lives. Jamie told us of living in Girona with her husband, Brent Bookwalter, a world tour pro cyclist. Joanie Caron, Leah Guloien and Moriah Macgregor discussed the upcoming Canadian national championships, Mary Zider talked about getting time off work from her day job in Boston to make it to camp. Trying to race professionally on low salaries and having to carry a second or third career to make ends meet was not easy, and we all carried two jobs. We shook our heads, lamenting how the men of pro cycling had base salaries and women didn't.

Wynona dispersed team clothing—summer kits, winter gear, casual wear, shoes, helmets, glasses, backpacks, luggage—as I sat there like a kid on Christmas morning. The outside temperature was 95F but I threw on my Colavita-ESPNW Pro Cycling hoodie sweatshirt, and basked in warm fuzzies. *I'm never taking this off*, my inner five-year-old rejoiced. *Neither am I!* my 37-year-old-with-two-functioning-ovaries-and-a-pro-cycling-contract agreed.

"Here," Wynona says, handing me a giant duffel bag emblazoned with *JAMAICA*. "We're short one Colavita-ESPNW duffel bag. But you can have my old national team bag. You're an island girl, now." *Omg my idol just handed me her own personal stuff. To keep*. I gladly accepted and told Wynona I was honored to uphold the Caribbean sisterhood.

The next day, we took team photos amidst the stunning desert backdrop of Redington Pass. Individual headshots, action shots, team shots. Posters, postcards, websites. *So this is what it's like to feel pro. Amazing.* At the end of the shoot our photographer, Jonathan Devich, came over to me.

"Kathryn, we're going to have to re-do your hill climb action shots."

"Why? Something wrong?"

"You're too smiley," he laughed, with kindness. "No one climbs hills smiling."

"Then you're going to need a faster shutter speed," I said.

Jonathan and I became instant friends. His photography would end up as the cover of our documentary, as well as terrific stills throughout the film.

Each day at team camp started with breakfast at my house, just down the road from the team hotel. The Colavita-ESPNW mechanic tuned up our Jamis Xeniths in the garage while we bonded with one another over oatmeal and coffee. *I still can't get over the fact I have a team bike with my name emblazoned on it. A metaphorical diamond encrusted golden Ferrari sitting in my garage.* George chatted with my teammates and assisted the mechanic working on bikes, while the cats purred in appreciation of the extra attention of ten women.

On the wall in our living room hung *The New York Times Vows* article from our wedding, and some teammates paused to read. Death, love, past, present, cancer, cats… all of it. I was proud of the article's honesty, but also got nervous when guests read it. Vulnerability is a fascinating thing, leaving us equal parts freed and judged. Even two years after our wedding, I still harbored a faint but present ache of sensitivity; a mark imbued by some of George's friends who were not happy he remarried and occasionally channeled their passive aggression toward me. These were not hanging on our living room wall: The negative comments on social media. The guy who would publicly post all the race results where I lost. Anonymous emails calling me names. The program from our wedding reception with my face scribbled out.

I did my best to grow a thick skin. I framed and hung *The New York Times* piece as a bulwark against unkindness, for in this house—*our* house—love triumphed.

Moriah pulled me aside in the kitchen. "The story of your marriage is beautiful," she said. "This is a testament to love and strength." Moriah became my closest friend on the team.

14

MASTERING ALMOST AND U-TURNS

After team camp, we headed to Silver City, New Mexico to race Tour of the Gila; one of the most grueling bicycle races in the United States. Altitude, terrain, volatile weather and tough competition was the perfect combination for professional bike racing. It also brought joy and full-circleness. Five years prior, Gila was my first amateur stage race as a Category 2 cyclist during my ESPN Olympic assignment in 2007. I'd only been on a road bike for four months and finished nearly last. Now I stood on the start line as a pro. That day, I finished the time trial as the second fastest member of Colavita-ESPNW, just behind Jasmin Glaesser, who would soon qualify for the 2012 Olympics.

When I first shared the news I was signed by Colavita-ESPNW, doubters and trolls commented my presence was tokenism. That I wasn't rostered because I was good, but because I worked for ESPN. I was old. Undeserving. No good. But that time trial proved otherwise. *Wrong, motherfuckers. I deserve to be here.*

On the second day of racing, an athlete went down in a crash. Right in front of me. For any cyclist directly behind the fallen, there is no time to think. Only react. Sometimes there is not even enough time for that, and we fall like dominoes. But on this day, instincts prevailed. Before my mind could process the crash, my brain calculated an exit. *There, to the right!* The back wheel of the athlete's bike lay tilted in such a manner that it became an exit ramp.

Instinct took over. I accelerated, held tight and used her tilted back wheel to catapult myself up and over the rest of her, somehow landing upright, back within the flow of the peloton. The riders around me were as awestruck as I. *Sweet bunny hop,* someone said. That was no bunny hop. That was a unicorn waltz. Something never to be seen nor replicated again. Life lesson learned. In the midst of fear and chaos, find the ramp. The gut usually knows where it is.

As we left Silver City, Wynona handed me a paper napkin. She and Tina Pic penned a brief note on it, thanking me for being a good teammate. The note was probably nothing to them, but it meant everything to me. To receive kind words from the two women I looked up to for so many years as athletes, now serving as my very own team directors, telling me I was worthwhile… my heart was full. Better than any stage win. Better than any unicorn waltz. Better than a sleeping Cerberus. After a five-year cycling journey with countless bumps along the way, this little paper note gave me the one thing I was missing: The feeling that I belonged. I framed the napkin and kept it on my desk for years.

———————

In the last week of May, we headed to the Exergy Tour—a five-day UCI stage race in beautiful Boise, Idaho. My newly minted cinematographer partner, Kevin, brought his gear and an assistant with him. Kevin and I obtained terrific interview footage of 2012's "who's who" of international Olympians and superstars at Exergy Tour; Connie Carpenter-Phinney, Kristy Scrymgeour, Evelyn Stevens, Alison Powers, Amber Pierce, Olivia Dillon, Addy Albershardt, Alisha Welsh, Emily Kachorek, Maria-Luisa Calle, Ally Stacher and Rochelle Gilmore… The latter of whom would play an enormous role further down the road, teaching me a monumental lesson in the journey of activism: When a woman puts on make-up and wants to talk to you, always, always say yes.

On the final day of Exergy, Kevin and I finished a three-hour block of filming interviews at a team hotel about an hour away from my team hotel. I was exhausted, dragging. Trying to race and film was proving a challenging physical obstacle. We had an interview scheduled with Commonwealth Games champion, Rochelle Gilmore of Australia, who also founded and managed one of the strongest teams on the circuit. When we arrived at her hotel, she didn't show up. We called, knocked, waited. Still, no answer. Finally, we broke down the interview cameras, dismantled the lighting, packed up the set, piled into the car and drove off. I was bummed. We didn't have the budget to fly across the world and interview Australian champions, so missing Rochelle in Idaho was such a shame. Just as we approached our hotel nearly an hour later, my phone rang. It was Rochelle.

"I'm so sorry, I was stuck in a director's meeting!" she blurted. Can you come back?"

I began telling Rochelle I was zonked, and like her, had to race the next day too.

"Sorry Rochelle, but—"

"Please. I believe in what you're doing. This film matters," she said, adding with a laugh, "I've put on makeup and everything. Please come back." That did it.

"Kevin, turn the car around," I sighed. The sisterhood of pro sports prevailed: No woman left behind. Not when they've showered, blow-dried and put on make-up in the midst of five-day stage race fatigue. "Ok, Rochelle. We're on our way."

This would become the most pivotal U-turn of my life. Just didn't know it for another two years. All I knew then was Rochelle believed this film mattered. That women standing up and speaking the truth mattered. That including others mattered. Turning around mattered. May we all pull a U-ie on the interstate for truth.

———————

On the final day of racing, I did not win the UCI points needed to garner a berth for St. Kitts and Nevis to London 2012. Disappointed, yes. Terribly. But eventually I understood the greatest gift is not always reaching the goal, but the new paths that open up during the quest. Maybe I was never supposed to qualify for the Olympics. Maybe I was supposed to change the broken system so others could. During this crazy journey toward equal opportunity, the mission became clearer: I wasn't supposed to win. I was supposed to be the domestique so Progress would.

I wasn't the only one for whom Exergy Tour was a turning point. My teammate and close friend, Moriah Macgregor, announced her retirement. Satisfied with her pro racing career, she wanted to start a family. I asked Moriah if there was one stand-out memory from her near-decade in pro cycling, one victory or moment above all others. Moriah thought for a while, then answered with abounding eloquence.

"The greatest thing about this sport isn't the win. It's the process of Not-winning. Of finding personal improvement and paths *toward* winning," Moriah said. "I don't remember half the races. But I do remember all the times I did something where I exceeded my own perceived abilities. Where I went above and beyond, you know? That's why I kept coming back. I remember a race where I came in fifth. So close to the win, but not the win. I stayed in the sport because of all the 'almosts' that gave me hope. It was the 'Almost' that kept me going."

Moriah's insights struck a deep chord of authenticity. During my first Olympic quest, I rarely won a thing. Mostly losses. People kept reading the column because I kept trying. They were drawn to the humanness of Almost. After the Exergy Tour, many readers of the old ESPN column wrote in asking, "Did you make it to the 2012 Games? Are you an Olympian?" Now I had the answer.

"No. But I'm a proud Almostian."

Before leaving the Exergy Tour, a Tucson friend snapped a photo in our living room. May 29, 2012. My husband was live-streaming my race, crouched in front of our TV, searching for me in the peloton. So attentive and focused, not even aware our friend was in the background taking a picture. I was overwhelmed with love. May every athlete with a dream have a spouse this supportive.

Not just overwhelmed with love, but grounded. Rooted. Thriving. Settled. Free. Two and a half years since we wed, the peace and joy I felt with George grew daily. We both knew my opportunity to race professionally was a limited window of time. We both knew this documentary film would be a two-year endeavor. I felt honored, focused and steady to be with someone who not only understood such opportunities but encouraged me to grasp them. George was the epitome of love, support and equality. A good man doesn't tell his wife to follow her dreams. He insists on it.

Sometimes, though, insecurities pawed my thoughts. Not a full mauling, but a prodding poke of doubt. Since parting ways with ESPN, my Cerberus sometimes growled that I was worthless because my income was so low. That maybe my husband didn't like carrying the financial load. *No*, I countered with a quiver in my voice, *My husband sees the value of this project, he believes in the mission. Just because I make less doesn't mean I am less. Shut up, you big dumb, stupid, demon bully.*

15

DRIVING THE BUS OF PROGRESS

At the end of May 2012, I sat glued to the internet, watching donations trickle in as our Indiegogo deadline neared. We were only about a third of the way to $30,000 and I started to worry. What if we didn't raise enough capital to shoot the footage we needed? I reached out to my incredibly talented screenwriter pal, Will Conroy, asking his advice on what to do if we didn't reach our financial target.

"It's okay to run out of money," Will assured. "Stop when you have to. Start when you can. It might take longer. Just make the movie you want to make." His logic quelled my neuroses. He was right. Do what we can with what we have. We'd make something happen, somehow.

We netted $11,330 from our first attempt at crowdsourcing. 77 donors throughout USA, Canada, England, Belgium and the Netherlands. Way short of our goal, but at least it was enough to start. To make the trailer for the film. My inner optimist didn't even look at the fact we failed to make 66 percent of our goal. *Look,* she cheered, fixating on the 33 percent win. *People believe in us! Wheeee!* The majority of contributions were made by friends and acquaintances but what struck me deeply were the donations from total strangers. *Maybe this film really does matter. Maybe my ideas matter. Maybe I'm not so worthless after all.*

Testing the waters of crowdsourcing was fascinating. My sensitivity was alive and well during that six-week run of public fundraising. Tweeting, posting and sharing our donation link over and over again came with more than a few swipes at my confidence. Comments from strangers trickled in every now and then, insinuating I was looking for personal handouts. That I wasn't a real filmmaker. That women's cycling races weren't interesting. Or—one that really irked me— making a film wasn't a real job, but rather a frivolous recreational endeavor. *Must be nice,* they wrote, *riding your bicycle and making movies while the rest of us work.*

Ah, the Must-Be-Nicers. Their comments got under my skin for two reasons: They were completely wrong. Also, completely right. The wrongness was in their assumption that filmmaking was solely about entertainment, not platforms for education and effecting change. On the literal side, their Must-Be-Nice mentality was spot on. It *is* absolutely nice to race bikes, to be creative and to work a job that pays shit but gives us joy. Many people equate work with misery. Which is why passive-aggressive Must-Be-Nicers usually take aim at anyone who attempts to combine work and joy. While I adhered to a strict policy of not engaging with nasty trolls, eventually I figured out how to answer the Must-Be-Nicers. Direct honesty is the kryptonite of passive-aggressiveness.

"Must be nice to race your bike and make movies."

Yes, it is nice to use professional bike racing and filmmaking to expose injustices and fight for equal opportunity. What did you do at work today?

"Must be nice to have such a flexible lifestyle to do whatever you want!"

Must be nice to have a salary, health benefits, a 401k, continuous food in your fridge, and a sense of feeling necessary, understood, and worthwhile all the time!

Whether or not these exchanges changed anyone's mind didn't really matter. It made me feel better, though, to occasionally call out the ignorance of Must-Be-Nicers. As disheartening as public ignorance can be, it is equally vital to activism. Ignorance reminds activists we're on the right track. As long as ignorance exists, so does the need to eradicate it. Activism is usually a journey into uncharted territory. Change brings newness, and too often people are afraid of unfamiliarity. Rather than join the movement of progress, many prefer to stand on Comfortable Ground. The Doubters, the Nay-Sayers, the Must-Be-Nicers, the Trolls.... they all share one trait in common: Ignorance. Which is why the most essential element of activism isn't fighting, but enlightening. Education is where the battle for change is won.

Also, we must recreate the image of activism. Too often, activism is portrayed as one leader, one lone warrior fighting for a cause. What if, instead, we envisioned activists as bus drivers. Just regular Joes/Joelles, sitting down at the wheel of a large caravan, picking up people along the way, explaining the route of their plan, taking passengers to the site of exploration, handing them a map, then heading back out to collect others. Repeat, repeat.

I felt much more like a bus driver than a warrior. I was a non-famous woman who once worked for ESPN and was now a bike racer in her late-thirties earning $5,800 a year living in Tucson with her husband and five cats. Shit, if I could drive this bus of progress down the road toward equity, picking up passengers along the way, collecting $11,330 in proverbial gas fare, then *anyone* could effect change. We're all bus drivers of progress. We're all passengers of change. With the right map, together we can go anywhere.

––––––––––

Another factor that helped quiet my demons of worthlessness; I signed with a new literary agent in May 2012. Andrew Blauner followed my ESPN career and we kept in touch. Six months after my previous agent severed ties deemed unmarketable, Andrew believed otherwise. I briefed Andrew about the documentary in progress, and that I was in the midst of an essay collection compiled from my ESPNW[30] columns, including the essays they refused to publish. I also told him my private dream.

"Maybe someday," I confided, "I will write about racing at the Tour de France."

"Maybe you will!" Andrew said. "I look forward to that."

––––––––––

In early June, I sat down to outline *Half the Road*. Who to include, what to cover, how to craft a compelling narrative. Kevin got to work on creating the film trailer, so this time we could launch a second Indiegogo campaign with footage that would show the world a glimpse of *Half the Road*. Before sending Kevin all the footage shot with my Bloggie camera, I watched the videos. When Moriah took ice satchels from the team car in El Salvador, shoving them into the neckline of her jersey, I could feel the cool chill on my own spine. Watching Pia's frustration with the UCI, I felt my own blood pressure rise. Flavia's broken collarbone made my own bones ache. The flyer taped to a wall of an athletes' dining hall advertising "Doping Negative!" supplements made me laugh and cringe. The resounding *yes*! of every woman answering the question, *Do you think there should be a race for pro women at the Tour de France?* stirred my soul.

The most beautiful thing in these clips wasn't the drama or the struggle, but the joy that came through in the persistence, voices and faces of these athletes. Even the dilapidated housing, the paltry prize winnings, the unsafe conditions… the film clips showed such a visible, profound love for their sport, no matter how stacked the odds of unfairness and inequity. From the footage we shot in Idaho, Venezuela, El

––––––––––

[30] Since the company changed it from espnW to ESPNW around this time, so too shall I.

Salvador and the upcoming trip to World Championships in Limburg, Netherlands I knew we had enough stellar material to compile an incredible trailer.

The best films and books are never about the setting or the character. They're about substance and journeys. *Seabiscuit* wasn't about a horse. It was about perseverance. *Unbroken* wasn't about an Olympic prisoner of war. It was about a human who didn't give up. Even Rocky Balboa—one of the most iconic-yet-fiction sports stars of all time—resonated not because he was a boxer, but because he went on a quest to get into a ring with the best fighter of all time. A scrappy underdog with a will of determination. No one even remembers Rocky lost the match. We only remember he won his quest. We remember he stepped into the arena.

We didn't have a bestselling book or a Hollywood budget for *Half the Road*, but that didn't matter. We were stepping into the arena. With substance, journeys and heart.

One day in mid-June, my 75-year-old father living in the suburbs of New York asked to set up a Skype chat. A sinking feeling sprung in my gut. Skype? Instead of just calling? Something was wrong.

That "something" turned out to be my father's diagnosis of congestive heart failure and the immediate need to repair the mitral valve in his heart, along with a Maze procedure; the equivalent of "freezer-burning" the heart to create strengthening scar-tissue. Neither of those sounded appealing. Over Skype, my dad educated me on function of mitral valves, weakened hearts, and how his leaky valve is causing a regurgitation of blood. I do my best to recall seventh grade science images of valves, aortas, red and blue arrows and the direction of blood flow amidst the fascinating, jumbled neatness of life's intricate little pumphouse.

"So, your heart is puking?"

"Yes, I have a puking heart. Surgery will close its mouth," Dad said. My eyes welled, filled and spilled. My father is my best friend. This was way too scary. "Don't worry," he soothed. "Heart surgery is very, very common these days."

"Super. Then let someone else's dad have it," I bickered. After pouting like a toddler for a few minutes, I grew up just enough to ask the date of surgery, promising I'd be there.

Timing was on my side. My father's heart surgery was scheduled for Montefiore Hospital in the Bronx the day after the Philadelphia Classic, just a two-hour drive from my next race with Colavita-ESPNW. One of the most historic and respected races in America, the UCI Philly Classic attracted the best pro teams and world-class competitors via invite only. I was thrilled to be going. For an east coast native, it felt like coming home.

At our pre-race meeting, Wynona delivered the game plan on tactics. For this particular event, we would need a sacrificial lamb.

"The race will be broadcast live on a TV network serving all Northeast states," Wynona explained. "This is Colavita's main geographic market and we must give them visibility. I need one of you domestiques to go on an immediate solo breakaway. Right from the gun. Then the commentators will discuss Colavita and ESPNW on TV. I need you to get a huge lead on the peloton and keep it. Go so hard that you blow up on Manayunk Hill. If you crack so bad you get dropped from the race, I'll consider that a victory."

The scene unfolded in my mind and I loved every painful minute. I knew breaking away from the peloton and storming ahead at the front of the race wouldn't raise flags in the minds of the experienced racers. They would know the break was too early, and the athlete would likely die on Manayunk's steep, slaughtering climb known as "The Wall." But the TV crews would follow the drama, desperate to see whether our sacrificial lamb was just plain foolhardy or just that arrogant. Whoever signed up for the role would burn bright and fast until she burned out like a dying star.

"So. Who will be our Sacrificial Lamb?" Wynona asked. My hand shot up with gusto.

"Baaa!" I bleated. A win-win situation; ride hard, blow up, get broomwagoned, drive home… just in time to take my dad to the hospital, all while doing my job. The most perfectly imperfect plan ever.

As the race rolled down beautiful Kelly Drive, past the boathouses I knew well as a collegiate rower, past the famous steps of Rocky Balboa's climb, I immediately launched an attack on the right side of the peloton. The teams took notice, yet few responded… the attack was too soon, they surmised, letting me go. For 20 minutes, I stayed away, with TV cameras and commentators discussing the products of Colavita and the influence of ESPNW. Pushing with every molecule of power and intensity, fueled by physical and emotional mitral valves, I rode that day not with legs but heart until there was nothing left to give.

On the Manayunk Wall, the peloton caught me; chomping, swallowing and defecating my presence out the back of the bunch. Spent. Done. Dropped. That was the end of my day. On the next lap, I rolled into the feed zone. Wynona marched toward me, smiling, nodding and hand raised for powerful high five. "Well done!" she slapped, commenting on the bountiful TV coverage attained. I beamed joy. This domestique, sacrificial lamb thing was my jam. God, I loved blowing myself to bits so my team could thrive. *I was part of something.*

At Montefiore Hospital in the Bronx, my father's operation was successful but not without complications. He remained in the ICU for ten days. I stayed by his side as we talked through the What Ifs, went over requests for Do Not Resuscitate, wrote lists of people to call, jotted notes for obituaries. All the painful thorns of adulthood and reality. Luckily, I would not need those notes anytime soon. What became immediately clear though, was my father's need for a lifestyle change. The cold winters of New York were too oppressive for his weakened heart. He would spend the rest of 2012 in the Bronx, but plans began for relocation to Tucson.

"I'd like to find an apartment and retire near you and George," Dad said, neither of us having any idea how much this would impact my life in the coming years.

After caring for my father for a couple weeks in New York, I flew to Nature Valley Grand Prix in Minneapolis, where I proceed to have my worst race with Colavita-ESPNW. As much as I attempted to suppress the exhaustion of caregiving, it all bubbled forth on race day. Speed drained from my limbs. I got dropped on the first stage within minutes. Not as a planned sacrificial lamb. Embarrassing, not to mention worrisome. *What if Wynona and Tina think I'm a totally useless shit? What if they never race me again? What if everything falls apart and life is an empty shell of nothingness?* Emotion and fatigue are terrible bedfellows. Over in the team tent, I slunk into a corner, trying my best to hide from the spectators and cycling fans. My teary heap of hot mess was not what fans were looking for. Still, two women approached the Colavita van, holding a book.

"We're so inspired by your journey," said one kindhearted soul named Meg.

"*This* journey?" I said, pointing toward the race course, as the peloton careened around the criterium corners without me.

"This one," she smiled, and extended a copy of *As Good As Gold*. Then pointed to the race. "*And* that one. You made it to the pro ranks. You're here. You did it. Everyone has a bad race sometimes. It's okay."

Despite tears streaming down my face and the spittled, snotty detritus of exertion clinging to my cheeks, we engaged in lovely conversation and their kindness left a mark on me. Even on the days we're at our lowest, people still believe in us. Even if we can't see it. They're out there. They're watching. They care. On the tough days, the bad races and trying times our most authentic self remains. That's who people connect with most. Not the victors, but the souls who try with all their might. The Almostians. At my worst race, I was reminded of the power of kindness and human connection.

16

LIST OF NAMES

s the 2012 UCI Road World Championships approached in Limburg, Netherlands, we used the remainder of our crowdsourcing budget to get Kevin overseas to film all the great pro cycling stars we missed in Idaho. I reached out to Olympic medalists Marianne Vos in the Netherlands and Emma Pooley in Great Britain, and countless others hoping they might agree to sit for an interview. With social media paying more attention to our documentary in progress, our followers were growing.

The more I tweeted or posted about the documentary, the more support came in. But so too did the trolls, doubters and ignoramuses of social media. I knew most of the trolls were simply looking for a rise, so I did my best to ignore the vitriol. What bewildered me, though, was the *amount* of people who took issue with women being equal to men. Had we not progressed from the dark ages? (I was yet unaware of the Loophole of Progress, but that education would come later).

Instead of responding to trolls,[31] I started keeping a list of all the names I was called and all the colorful adjectives hurled my way. The first word was "Impossible." As in *you're impossible*. That one fascinated me. My very existence clearly irked someone so much that I was simply impossible to tolerate. *Talentless*. Ouch. *Edgy*. True. *Loose cannon*. Beg to differ. I am not a loose cannon. My targets just move around a lot.

To keep balance, I also wrote down the positive words. *Untrammeled* was my favorite.[32] A beautiful, eloquent word of the past whose modern synonym is

---

[31] Golden Rule of Activism: Never respond to trolls. Hungry for attention, that's what they want. Starve 'em.
[32] The Susan B. Anthony quote: "Let me tell you what I think of bicycling... it has done more to emancipate women than anything else in the world. It gives women a feeling of freedom and self-reliance. I stand and rejoice every time I see a woman ride by on a wheel...the picture of free, **untrammeled** womanhood."

Unfuckwithable. To not be walked upon. To not be messed with. Incapable of being held down. To rise above. Untrammeled became my spirit word...

List of Names Called on Social Media as an Activist for Women's Equality[33]

Impossible	Slow	Ball of Energy	Plucky
Idiot	Old	Optimistic	Optimist
Self-serving	Bitch	Driven	Quirky
Talentless	Cunt	Passionate	Trailblazer
Worthless	Mad	Do-er	Not Normal
Embarrassing	Rare	Victorious	Visionary
Mediocre	Epic	Pushy	Pioneer
Painful	Rebel	Persistent	Strong
Talky	Weird	Loose Cannon	Bold
Incompetent	Wise	Prolific	Fearless
Rabblerouser	Edgy	Pulchritudinous	Tsunami Starter
Good Egg	Boss	Pain in the ass	Troublemaker
Annoying	Aggressive	Assertive	Ambitious
Unfocused	Unrealistic	Unusual	Ugly
Unflattering	Undefinable	Unstoppable	Untrammeled

Luckily, I was able to let many of these oddities and insults go by, finding comfort in my tangible friends and supportive husband. They had my back, hushing the growls of my sensitive Cerberus. My columns on ESPN apparently led the public to regard me as strong, confident and capable. Perhaps I am. Sometimes. But so true is this: pendulums swing both directions. My Strength and Sensitivity were equally weighted. I was a Deep Feeler of Things, with secret caves of vulnerability. Shocked me, sometimes, the depth of these caverns. I was becoming very aware of the Paradox of Happy People, my birth tribe. Happy People were a mark for the Unhappy. The weak, the cruel, the mean, the lost, the jealous, the vicious... anyone unable to grasp their own happiness inversely treats Happy People like shit. I was fast learning this lesson. No way I would've been able to survive this weird activism journey without my tribe of support. For those who want to support people standing up for change, I highly encourage the following methods: *Hug an activist. Hug the*

---

[33] This list represents 2012-2017. Updating it every few chapters would drive us both nuts.

Happy. Hug someone speaking out for what they believe. Hug the strong person who doesn't look like they need a hug. They're the one who probably needs it the most.

Around this time, it became apparent not *all* women of the pro peloton were voicing their support on social media. While most of them talked to me at races, saying very positive things about the documentary in progress, very few spoke about the need for equal opportunity publicly. Perhaps they didn't want their very own List of Names. Maybe they feared backlash. Maybe they were contracted not to speak out. *Huh,* I remember thinking. *Maybe their team directors weren't as supportive as Wynona and Tina.*

———————

As World Championships approached, filming plans fell into place. We secured interview dates with cycling greats Emma Pooley, Marianne Vos, Amber Neben, and Ina Teutenberg. But we also needed representation from the sport's governing body. I once more reached out to Pat McQuaid. Made sense to include the President of the UCI. A perfect opportunity for him to speak freely about his thoughts on women's pro cycling. As much as I didn't support his indiscretions, all successful documentaries show both sides of the story. McQuaid's secretary responded they'd set something up.

With two bicycles, a backpack and a notebook full of questions, off to Europe we went for Worlds. Kevin and his wife, Melissa, stayed near the race course in Limburg. I found a homestay with the lovely Deswijzen family, just across the Dutch border in neighboring Germany. A kindhearted elderly couple, George and Resi were fascinated that women race bikes professionally and lovingly insisted I eat more at every meal. They were also fascinated that I raced for St. Kitts and Nevis, and proudly flew the SKN flag outside their home.

"Is it hard racing bicycles in the Amazon?" Resi asked. I giggled, informing her St. Kitts and Nevis is in the Caribbean, not the Amazon.

"It's hard for women to race bikes anywhere," I smiled.

"What does your husband think of all this racing?" she asked.

"Oh, he's wonderful," I said. "George rides, too. He gets it."

"But you are going to have babies soon, yes?"

I paused. It wasn't the first time I'd been asked this question. Each time, I wondered: *Why do people expect motherhood is a given for all women?* I hold hope that fighting for equity in sport makes a difference for all children of the next generation, even if I don't have my own. With that in mind, I gave Resi an answer that rings true.

"I already do. Three billion daughters."

Assembling my road and time trial bikes in the Deswijzen's garage, I unwrapped the meticulously padded frames and set to work reattaching the forks, chainrings, derailleurs, handlebars and pedals. The Deswijzen's friend, Huub Harings, came over to watch. Huub, now in his 80s, was a five-time Dutch National Champion in cyclocross and a four-time Tour de France rider during the 1960s.

"Doesn't your team mechanic do that for you?" Huub asked, waving at all the parts and tools strewn about the garage.

"I *am* the team mechanic," I laughed, informing him that most of cycling's smaller nations aren't able to afford sending staff to events. Riders learn how to be their own staff. This was my fourth World Championships without a mechanic, assistant or someone in the feed zone. Huub picked up the tiny derailleur set screws, inspecting their ant-sized minuteness in his palm.

"You must have done this hundreds of times, Huub," I surmised.

"No, never," he says. "We always had a mechanic. Men's teams always have mechanics." Huub, in his two-decade career of bike racing, had never disassembled or reassembled a bicycle. Holding his palm out, lightly stroking the miniscule screws as if they were baby birds, Huub asked where they went and peered closely as I installed them into the derailleur hanger. I couldn't help but smile. In a tiny German neighborhood, a female cyclist of St. Kitts and Nevis showed a Dutch champion forty years my senior how to build a bicycle. My love for this sport and this journey grew in so many wonderful ways.

Embarking on a recon ride of the time trial course, Kevin drove behind to gather some B-roll footage.[34] At the top of Cauberg Hill, a favorite climb of Dutch cycling fans, we passed one of the sport's greatest icons: Didi the Devil.[35] An aging German man with a long white beard costumed in a devil suit and carrying a pitchfork. For decades, Dieter Senft has pranced, run and jumped alongside pro cyclists at the steepest part of every course, cackling encouragement and stabbing his fork skyward. *Allez, allez! Up, up!* Never interfering with the athlete's safety, Didi's

---

[34] B-roll is supplemental footage that is intercut with the main story. The stuff often used during documentary interviews, so viewers aren't staring at a talking head the entire time.
[35] Interactive Reader Guide: Didi the Devil

silliness and weirdness became a staple of pride for cycling fans worldwide. Didi was part hero, part mascot, all uniqueness. I screeched to a halt on my bike.

"DIDI! Hello!" I panted, out of breath from the climb. "May we film you?"

"Daaaaaaaa!"

Kevin grabbed the camera. (So too did a photographer for the Associated Press standing nearby.) We asked Didi his thoughts on women's cycling, and despite the language barrier, he told us he agreed it is crazy there are no women at the Tour de France these days. He remembered when there used to be, in the mid-80s. Didi asked if I would like to try his bicycle, waving at a fabulously bizarre custom-made sculpture; a monstrous two-wheeled rig comprised of titanium pipes and plastic waterbottles. *Absolutely*! I sat on the bike with him, smiling proudly. *Click, click,* chirped the AP photographer's camera. The shot went worldwide the next day. May we all be so lucky to meet benevolent devils.

What didn't go worldwide were my time trial results the next day. Feeling overconfident, I took the turn too hot at the base of Cauberg Hill and careened straight into the padded fence. Without falling, I simply thwumped myself broadside into the pads and remained upright... and at a dead stop. At the base of a climb. Not good.

European spectators are hardcore fans of cycling, and they knew just what to do. Three men came running over, hopped the barrier and placed their hands on my butt, pushing me forward so I could gain momentum for the climb. While ass-grabbing is highly discouraged in most capacities, this particular situation it was highly encouraged. My fence smackin' error produced one of my least impressive but most memorable time trials ever. Moriah's words came back to me; *I stayed in the sport because of all the 'almosts' that gave me hope... all the memories.* World Championships—and I was fortunate enough to compete in eight during my cycling career—never once failed me on memories.[36]

Four days separated the time trial race from the road race at Worlds, and in the interim I donned my filmmaker hat. We arranged to meet Emma Pooley at the main hotel where wealthier cycling federations like Great Britain were staying. Emma, one of the world's most talented racers, was the proud winner of the 2008 Olympic silver medal and 2010 World Championship gold. Before our meeting, Emma emailed me. "*Kathryn, I must prioritize my rest, and will only be able to grant you*

---

[36] Interactive Reader Guide: 8 World Championship memories that have nothing to do with racing.

twenty minutes for the interview, I hope you understand." Yes. Fully understood. I promised Emma I'd keep it short.

As Kevin set up the camera on a quiet balcony, Emma walked over. I greeted her with a hug, which I immediately learned is not the most comfortable salutation when meeting Brits for the first time. They're not a huggy culture. Feeling like an idiot, I silently hoped I hadn't offended her. Made a mental note: *Be professional, dummy. Stop trying to hug all your interviewees. Geez. People already think you're weird enough.*

Emma sat down, threading the microphone through her National British Cycling Team jacket. Her physical presence was remarkable. Emma is petite, only 5'2. Small but strong. When she enters a room, no stranger would guess the power and ferocity of her talent. So too is her passion and personality, which unfolded gloriously in her answers and opinions on camera.

From prize money inadequacy to base wage absence to Pat McQuaid rulings, Emma regaled us with stories about team corruption, Tour de France desires and prize-winning teapots.[37] Just minutes into the interview, Kevin and I exchanged a knowing glance that Emma was giving us the most golden footage we could hope for. Her unabashed honesty, candor and truth sent shivers down my spine. Emma would be the star of the film, no doubt. As we discussed the gender pay gap, I alerted Emma to the twenty-minute time limit approaching fast.

"May I keep talking?" she asked. "I have more to say."

"By all means, yes. Please keep talking," I smiled. Emma stayed for an hour, not knowing she was opening a door that would change history. Neither of us knew that yet. All I knew was the chill that ran down my spine when she looked at me and asked, "Why are there still no women at the Tour de France? I want to race the Tour de France."

I hadn't even gotten to that question yet. But I knew in that moment Emma was more than an interviewee. She was an ally. So far, every pro woman I interviewed spoke openly about wanting to race the Tour de France. But now we had star power—an Olympic medalist and World Champion—standing up and asking why. ASO and UCI didn't give a hooey about what I thought. But Emma? They very well might listen to her. And other stars. I wondered if Marianne Vos would feel the same way.

---

[37] Because prize money at women's pro races was so low, Emma celebrated her wins by buying teapots, which is about the only thing she could afford. The photo of her teapot shelf became one of our favorite B-roll shots in *Half the Road.*

After Emma's 20-turned-into-75 minute exhilarating interview, Kevin and I drove to meet Marianne Vos. I did not hug her. Well, not then. I already did in 2008 when we both raced Vuelta El Salvador. Today I kept my fangirlism in check as we reminisced about the sweltering days and volcano climbs of San Salvador.

We quickly got Marianne into a chair and off her feet. The road race was less than 48 hours away, and no cyclist wants to waste precious energy standing. Marianne told us her story about learning to ride a bike at age four and standing on her first start line at six. Last month at the London Olympics, she won gold in the road race. 7.6 million fans tuned into BBC's coverage to watch women's cycling as Marianne won her *second* Olympic gold medal. (The first was in track cycling at the 2008 Beijing Games). Marianne amassed over twenty national and World Championship titles during her career.[38] She was the GOAT of women's bike racing. Greatest of all time.

Marianne's ego, however, was the exact opposite of her title count. Humble, kind and supportive of others. I recalled her actions at Vuelta El Salvador, where despite being the leader, Marianne doubled as domestique, drifting back to the team car, stuffing her jersey with water bottles for her teammates. Pure class. With the cameras rolling, we got down to the nitty gritty. I asked her if she wanted to see a Tour de France for women. Not only did she want to *see* one, she wanted to race one. *Win* one.

"Before my career is over, I want to race the Tour de France," she asserted. Marianne was 26. Damn. I didn't even have a road bike at 26, yet she'd already been racing for 20 years. Like the interview with Emma, my spine tingled. My gut butterflied. With every mention of the Tour de France, something inside me knew we were one step closer. Thanking Marianne for her time, I wished her luck in the road race.

"You will be there too, right?" she asked. "For St. Kitts and Nevis? In the Caribbean? Good luck."

"Yes!" my heart soared. She actually knew who I raced for! And that I didn't live in the Amazon! There were still women in the pro peloton who questioned my presence and value, sometimes feeding my Cerberus kibbles of worthlessness. Small moments like this, receiving kindness and recognition from cycling's greatest

---

[38] Interactive Reader Guides: The indomitable Emma Pooley and legendary Marianne Vos.

champion, burrowed into my soul and hushed the Cerberus. I didn't feel the desire to tell Marianne about the latter. But I did thank her profusely.

Unsurprisingly, the UCI failed its promise to grant me an interview with president Pat McQuaid. He was probably hanging out with the King of Holland. But, his secretary arranged an interview with a different employee of cycling's governing body.

"Tomorrow, you will meet with the President of UCI Road Commission; Mr. Brian Cookson," she said. Thanking the secretary, I hopped online to research Cookson. Having served as president of the British Cycling Federation for over 25 years, I held hope he was far more progressive that McQuaid. After all, he was on hand for the rise of Britain's powerhouse Olympic medalists in cycling—Emma Pooley, Victoria Pendleton, Nicole Cooke—and surely paid attention to Britain's triathlon and marathon phenoms, Chrissie Wellington and Paula Radcliffe.

"This is great," I said to Kevin, with utmost confidence. "Brian will be just the interviewee we need; a man who truly sees the power and potential of women. He'll be vital to our quest for inclusion at the Tour de France!"

17

PARADOX OF TRADITION

The next day, I pulled on my compression socks, desperately-in-need-of-laundry sweatpants and giant, frumpy Colavita-ESPNW sweatshirt, tucking my unkempt, dirty hair into my SKN Cycling Federation hat. Tomorrow was race day, today was dress comfortable day. With a water bottle and some energy bars, Kevin, Melissa and I headed over to the UCI Press Tent to await our meeting with Brian Cookson. We were led to a private room where we could shut the door and close out the whirring, clicking computers and telephones of the media tent.

The room, sparsely equipped, held only a folding table and three chairs. Kevin set up the camera as we waited for Cookson to arrive. Fifteen minutes passed. Then thirty. At forty-five minutes, I crawled under the desk. The ultimate rest position. I laid down on the dirty, temporary floor, unfolded my legs, shut my eyes, and drifted in and out of napping. An hour later, Brian arrived. Crawling out from beneath the table and not wanting to appear unprofessional, I salvaged an attempt at why I was down there.

"Dropped my pen!" I offered, praying there was no evidence of dried drool on my face.

Our interview began. Cookson was tall, pushing sixty and his deep voice, direct eye contact and snazzy blue blazer connoted the image of a well-educated man who knows what he's talking about. *Perfect,* I thought to myself. *I'm so glad McQuaid couldn't be here. Cookson'll be so much better. This guy knows his shit.* Within five minutes, I realized what an idiot I was to assume anything.

While Cookson was kind, polite and very professional, his outdatedness and ignorance came tumbling through his words. His opinion was sadly based on the incorrect foundation that women's racing was not at very high levels. He gave platitudes of wanting to see women's cycling grow, but spoke of no initiatives to make that happen. His reasoning implied if women wanted to grow the sport, they'll have to do it themselves. Not a very progressive outlook. Then, things got worse. I asked Cookson if he thought women should be allowed to race the Tour de France. He paused, then said, no. Women aren't physically capable of the Tour de France, he reasoned. They're slower. Weaker. If women raced Le Tour there would be massive "devastation."

My professional self and personal self battled it out for mental composure. The former wanted Cookson to keep talking, spewing forth documentary gold, baby. The latter wanted to stick a handkerchief in his mouth, bind it with duct tape and let loose a diatribe of verbal insults and perhaps a small beating. Putting on my big girl pants, I chose the former. Catching a glimpse of Melissa as she helped Kevin with the filming, I watched her eyes grow wide as saucers as Cookson kept talking about how slow women are.

Moving on, we spoke of the UCI sanctioning races in war-torn nations. Cookson absolved the UCI of any wrongdoing when it came to holding Olympic qualification races in countries like Syria. I asked why UCI sanctioned three pro women's races in the Golan Heights of Syria in 2011, when: a) Syria did not allow certain ethnicities/nations to enter their country b) had a history of crimes against women and c) there was a fucking *war* in progress. I crossed my fingers hoping Cookson would agree the UCI was in desperate need of overhauling race calendars to ensure safety and fair accessibility. Instead he deflected.

"Well, that's a visa issue," Cookson responded, as to why not all women were allowed to compete in Syria. *Um, no. That's a human rights issue. Keep talking, Cookson. Keep talking.* The truth? UCI will sanction races anywhere they want because of the money they earn for the rights to UCI accreditation.[39]

The more he spoke, the more I believed in our need for *Half the Road*. Cookson's shudder-worthy comments on slower, weaker women was one thing, but *where* they came from was an equally important concept to explore. After we parted ways from the interview, the Cookson experience stayed with me, latching onto my brain and begging me to understand where exactly, such opinions came from. Enter the Paradox of Tradition.

During Cookson's interview, he spoke the truth. Not my truth. *His* truth. Sitting there with him, it was very easy to see Cookson truly believed what he was saying;

---

[39] As of 2020, the cost for UCI accreditation at World Championships: $8.8M starting bid.

that women are slower, that a Tour de France wasn't possible, that holding a race in Syria was a good idea. Our truth is what we're taught. No one usually bats an eye about tradition until people start asking, *why?*

Once that tiny question escapes someone's lips, we can begin exploring tradition's powerful potential for elasticity and growth.

As my best friend Ralph Waldo Emerson once wrote, "If I see a trait, my children will see it after me. Man cannot be happy and strong until he lives in the present, above time." Right on, Ralph. Without the flexibility to live 'above time' and be open to change, tradition will repeat unchanged. The bravest thing a soul can do is ask "*What if?*" and walk proudly toward the unknown answer.

Maybe Cookson lost his way, bound by the ropes of traditionalism. During our interview, it dawned on me that women are not the only victims of tradition. So too are men. They too will be left behind when the world catches up and moves forward without them. *Maybe our film could hold up a mirror up so the Cooksons of the world can see and hear their truths alongside the truths of others. Maybe we can all move forward together.* My inner optimist really liked that one.

Cookson wasn't the enemy; he was the norm. And when we want to create change, we must never hate the Cooksons. We must teach them. And let them teach us. Perhaps I could find someone to interview who would snap the elastic band of tradition and refute Cookson's truths in an honest, hate-free way.

As we packed up our cameras in the UCI Press Tent at World Championships, minds still reeling from Cookson's interview, I knew three truths: Marianne Vos wanted a Tour de France. Emma Pooley wanted a Tour de France. So did all the other women we interviewed for the film. All my heroes, all my idols, all the women I aspired to be like on the bike... amongst these stars, I saw the constellation of Change. The way forward was to align our points of light. It was time to push for a Tour de France together.

Not me; we. The Emmas, Mariannes, even the Cooksons... they're the stars. I was no superstar. Space dust, at best. But every constellation of change needs an organized story and a true north. That I could do. With every interview for *Half the Road*, the stars shone brighter and my role became clearer: Organize the right team, create the plan and initiate change *together*. To every Normal Person out there, know this: We don't need wealth, fame, Olympic glory or star power to create change. We can be the space dust that drives the constellation bus.

As the winter of 2012 approached, my first professional race season concluded and Kevin and I jumped into full-time documentary mode. We needed to extend our reach far beyond the cycling world. We needed to interview exercise physiologists, doctors, politicians, CEOs. We needed history, humor, relief, ideas, solutions and non-cyclists to make this film work.

I sent emails to amazingly talented people and squealed with giddy glee when answers of enthusiasm began rolling in, *Yes, I'd love to be in the film!* We secured U.S. Surgeon General Richard Carmona. Kathrine Switzer, my running shero. Doug Loveday, an exercise physiologist specializing in women's endurance joined us. James Carkulis, CEO of Exergy and sponsor of the Exergy Tour. Chrissie Wellington, eager to share how she broke down the barriers of physiological possibilities in Ironman triathlon. Nicky Wangsgard, Robin Farina, Alison Tetrick and a plethora of awesome pro cyclists. Even Kristin Armstrong was on the schedule for her dual roles of motherhood and Olympian. As my inbox provided jolts of joy with each interview confirmation, so too did a new endeavor: bike tourism.

A small cycling tour company, Bike Costa Rica, asked if I might be interested in leading a bike tour with them in Central America. "We've followed your work with ESPN and your pro cycling career," owner Henry Perez said. "With your visibility, we can pull in more clients. More clients, more income. Everyone wins." I joined forces immediately. Being paid to ride my bike in Costa Rica for a week? Yes please. The extra income of two thousand dollars would help immensely. Financially and emotionally. *Maybe someday I'd even earn five figures!*

The $200 twice-a-month articles for ESPN wasn't much of an income. Kevin and I had about $3,000 left in the film budget, but we still had three locations to shoot. I hadn't (yet) had to sink any of my own funds into the film, but I feared that might change soon. My Cerberus wasn't barking loudly, but a low, throaty growl rumbled from within, issuing a warning that my lack of salary rendered me worthless.

I had no pocket change for small pleasures like going out for coffee or dinner, but I didn't care about that. The passion for the film sustained me. Most days I was strong enough to silence the beast. *Hush Cerbie! This film is worth it. This film is necessary. Sit!* If I had to sink my own paltry income into this film, I'd do whatever it took to make it happen. Being paid to lead a bike tour in Costa Rica would go a long way. The trip was set for February 2013.

Costa Rica wasn't the only bike tour on my schedule. Part of my pro cycling contract with Colavita-ESPNW was to assist Colavita with their cycling tour for recreational cyclists that rode, ate and wine-d their way through beautiful Italy. *Ok, twist my arm. Fine, I'll do it, Mr. Profaci.* While Colavita covered my flight and lodging, I wasn't paid to lead the tour. Ironically, I spent my $1,000 salary from Colavita-ESPNW Pro Cycling on a plane ticket for my husband. He deserved this trip. With the support George showed me during my first year as a pro athlete and fledgling filmmaker, I wanted to give something in return.

Through the Dolomites and villas along the Amalfi Coast, we reveled in a week away from racing, filmmaking, barking Cerberai, pharmaceutical sales and daily grind. George and I bonded over what truly matters in life; embracing the moment, seeing the big picture and spending time together. Whether the film succeeded, whether ASO would ever return my emails, whether I would ever be hired to write again… none of that mattered. I had love, support and true partnership. That was more than enough.

Returning from Italy, I touched base with John Profaci. 2013 was fast approaching, and at this point in the year, teams were usually deciding on kit orders and gear logos for the upcoming season.

"We're not going to partner with ESPNW again," John said. "They didn't uphold their end of the marketing budget." They barely did any advertising at all. Disappointed but not surprised, I felt a pang of sadness ESPNW didn't see the marketing potential. I also felt a pang of fear, wondering if this meant the end of my pro cycling contract, too.

"No, no. We're partnering with *CookingLight* magazine for 2013 and I'd like you to stay with us on the team," John said, mentioning Wynona would continue as head director. A wave of relief washed over me. It wasn't just about the personal glory racing professionally for another year at the age of 38, but how it affected my role as an activist. Maybe ASO and UCI would finally listen up. Especially now that I had the likes of Emma Pooley, Marianne Vos and other talented powerhouses on board.

In December, I called Wynona to discuss our 2013 team schedule, so I could prioritize racing first, filming second. After getting to know her this past season, I liked Wynona that much more. As an Olympian from the Caribbean, she was a hero of possibility to me. To race for her again in 2013 was an honor. A dream come true. Or so I thought.

When Wynona answered, something was off. The Wynona I knew from our 2012 season wasn't on the phone that day. This Wynona was different. Her tone was harsh, exasperated. Borderline mean.

"I will sign you to the team, Kathryn, but now that we're not with ESPNW, I'm doing this out of the kindness of my heart." Wynona began, explaining Tina Pic would be racing, not co-directing. This year, Wynona was the boss. "Won't be like last year, Kathryn. Don't expect to race much. Oh, and you will not be paid," she continued. *Whoa. Wait. What*? Caught off guard, I stammered ums and okays into the phone, giving Wynona benefit of the doubt. *Maybe she's just having an off-day. We all have off-days.* My gut knew something was wrong, but my pain-in-the-ass inner optimist wouldn't yield. I was too naïve to understand that a co-director-turned-solo-director power shift emerged.

I called a fellow teammate to check how her call with Wynona went.

"Great!" she said, confirming Wynona offered her a salary and a preliminary race schedule. A sinking feeling set in. Having no other pro team options and very much in need of keeping my title of 'pro cyclist' for the sake of the film and activism, I signed the Colavita-CookingLight contract Wynona sent. The wage section read "$0." My heart sank and my Cerberus barked. Loud. This time, my worthlessness wasn't figurative. It was literal.

In the last weeks of 2012, Kevin and I flew to St. George, Utah to film Nicky Wangsgard, a recently retired pro cyclist with an important backstory we wanted to include in *Half the Road*. Like all pro cyclists, Nicky worked her way up the ranks and paid her dues of struggle, working part time jobs while pursuing her PhD and racing professionally. But unlike other pro cyclists, Nicky had to hide two things: her pro racing career and her sexuality. Nicky is gay. With a partner of eight years. While most modern, progressive Americans no longer care about someone's sexual identity, Nicky was a college professor in rural, conservative Utah.[40]

The university suggested Nicky keep quiet about her bike racing job—*we don't condone such hobbies of female professors racing bicycles*—and keep her sexuality and relationship status hidden. Two women "living in sin" in St. George was an

---

[40] The Supreme Court decision legalizing gay marriage was still a year away from being passed in 2013.

obstacle for professors seeking tenure. And since women's pro cycling had no base salary allocation, Nicky needed her teaching income to support her pro cycling career. She and her partner, Jenna Behm, kept quiet. Nicky entrusted us with her story, despite the fact she had not yet received tenure.[41]

"Whether I get tenure or not, it's time to tell it, anyway," Nicky said. "To hide oneself—be in cycling or professorship—it's not okay. And to hide because we're worried about whether or not we'll get paid? Definitely not ok."

Nicky was calm and soft-spoken and we often had to turn up the microphone when recording. But when she mounted a bike, Nicky was anything but temperate. Her power, speed and intensity made her one of the best sprinters in the U.S. and she had over 100 wins in her career. We followed Nicky through her mornings teaching on campus and her afternoons training on the roads. I sat shotgun as Jenna drove their Prius and Kevin hung out the back of the trunk, filming Nicky as she motorpaced.[42] Between the Utah mountains, the couple's conversations, and adorable footage of their little dogs, filming Nicky and Jenna was a turning point. This film wasn't about bicycles, inequity and everything that's broken. It was about love, humanity and all that remains whole.

---

[41] Nicky received tenure in 2013. I was still "that SKN, ESPN writer weirdo" yet she trusted me with such incredibly personal information that could have "outed" her before she was ready. What a gift to give and receive such trust. Thank you, Nicky.

[42] Motorpacing/motopacing is when a cyclist drafts behind a car or motorcycle. This intense workout forces the athlete to adapt to high speeds, high watts and high cadence. Keeping up with a vehicle at 40mph is no small feat to for human muscles. Interactive Reader Guide: Video of motorpacing at 4:23.

18

Dog Days and Broken Arms

A lso in need of fixing in women's pro cycling: rider protection and health insurance. Most athletes were on their own for health care coverage.[43] Most pro contracts offered no guarantees of job security should injury occur. In cycling, injury occurs frequently. Taking a spill in professional cycling is not a matter of if, but when. Which I had to learn the hard way.

Three weeks after signing my contract with Colavita-CookingLight and just days after returning from our filming trip to Utah, Kevin came to Tucson to shoot some B-roll of cyclists training. One of the best group rides in the country is Tucson's infamous Shootout.

For ten years, this 60-mile Saturday morning slugfest of pain, progress and awesomeness was part of my weekly training—along with the shorter Tuesday Shootout—and I credit these two group rides with giving me the ability to become a professional cyclist. Saturday was the main event, a race-simulation training ride where over a hundred (sometimes even two hundred!) of the best cyclists of the Southwest and across the nation showed up. All the cycling strategies and lingo ensued: Calculated breaks, brave attacks, strong bridges… countless riders blown up and discarded from the effort of exertion.

Took me years to get the hang of—and the strength for—this ride. A tremendous journey. From being dropped in the first few miles to breaking away, my brotherhood of the Shootout always treated me not as a woman, but as a cyclist. An equal. As it should be. Showing up, week after week, year after year, I earned

---

[43] As of 2020, there were at least *two* UCI women's pro cycling teams sponsored by heath care companies where riders were *not* provided free health care.

their trust and respect as a decent athlete, a knowledgeable bike handler and someone who won't cause danger or drama.

At first, I wanted to train with these men to become a better athlete. But something much greater happened. I became a better person. At some point, The Shootout turned from training tool to societal tribe. These were my people. My community. The guy who taught me how to launch an attack was also my lawyer. The counter attack, my mechanic. The two guys up the road in a break? My dentist and realtor. The lead-out up Sprint Hill came from my doctor. These guys were my friends. There is a bond among all athletes that share the intimacy of physical pain and mental progress that comes with sports. A camaraderie shows itself in beautiful, humbling, wordless ways. I had no idea, at the time, how this tribe would hold me together in the coming years.

For filming, Kevin and I hired a friend, Holly, to drive (safely) alongside The Shootout as the peloton wove its way through the traffic-less roads of the Tohono O'odham Indian Reservation in the desert south of Tucson. Respecting the safety of the peloton, we filmed for about 15 minutes on the safest road, then I pulled over and watched the group recede into the sunrise. Kevin got back in the car, but I still needed some training miles, so we made a plan to meet for breakfast in a couple hours. After my workout I pedaled toward Tucson, soaking up the desert views, feeling the satisfaction of progress and the joy of cycli—*BAM*! The Rottweiler came out of nowhere.

Hiding in the desert vegetation, a massive stray dog bolted straight into my path. Roughly the size, shape and weight of a park bench, this pooch was one solid beast. My bike bounced off his gigantic sidewall of furry largeness and my body went flying over the handlebars. Upon hitting the ground, reflex took over and I curled into a ball, clamping my hands over my neck in attempt to defend an impending attack. Lying in the middle of the road, I wasn't sure what to fear more—the enormous dog or the approaching car. As the rumble of the engine grew near, I unwrapped my fingers from my neck and peeked up. The dog wagged its tail, slobbered at me and ran off into the desert. The driver swerved around me without stopping to assist.

Dazed and alone, I stood up and took inventory. The bike was fine. My legs were ok. My head and helmet spared. Blood ran down from my thumb, but it appeared a surface wound. *Hot damn*, I thought. *That's some lucky shit*. I mounted the bike, clipped in and pedaled. As I gripped the handlebars, pain seared through my left arm. Something was nauseatingly wrong. With my right hand, I fished my cell phone out of my jersey pocket. "Holly? Kevin? I, uh, need a little help."

Twenty minutes later, Kevin hopped out of the car with the camera rolling, asking what happened. *Oh, nothing, my arm is just a little jacked up.* While I didn't yet know my arm was broken, I did know what sometimes happens when professional riders get injured: They get released from the team. At 38 with a broken arm and a director who made it clear I was the low woman on the totem pole, I had to hide the broken arm. If a bone breaks in the desert and no one is around to hear it, does it make a sound?

Yes, it does. *Snap!* Perhaps I had a harder time hearing the bone break because a car was approaching and I had my hands clamped around my ears while lying in the fetal position in the middle of the road. But snap it did; my left radius, one inch below the elbow. Six weeks recovery. Doctor's orders: No riding outside until it heals, as complications with elbow arthritis may ensue. Panicked, I grabbed a calendar. *Six weeks?! If we have team camp in January, I'm fucked.*

With what might be the luckiest break of all, Wynona scheduled team camp for March. The Costa Rican tour guide job was in late February. My only itinerary for January was filmmaking. And finding a stationary bike and lying to Wynona about my arm. No social media posts. No photos. The doctor put me in a removable soft cast instead of hard plaster. My dear friend Jo Roberts lent me her spin bike, which we set up so I could pedal vertically and not lean on the handlebars. Next to the bike, a makeshift desk for film work. Unable to reach behind my head, George made my ponytails for the next month and a half. Here's to the doctors, friends and family who Humpty Dumpty our broken selves back together again. Not to mention, insurance. Luckily, as a spouse, I was covered under George's policy. My arm was an annoyance, but the outcome of the crash was a gift. Could've been so much worse. Could've been my head. I was lucky and I knew it. With a full ration of hope, a half-confident heart and a most definite broken arm, I gimped forward into 2013.

19

LET'S GET EXCESSIVE

What wasn't so lucky was the image of cycling itself in January 2013. The infamous Oprah interview where Lance Armstrong finally admitted to doping ricocheted through the news. Society floundered, trying to make sense of the disappointment, vindication, sadness, validation and general mess of how it feels to accept the truth of a fallen hero. In the quagmire of all things wrong with professional men's cycling, I saw a silver lining: The door was open for the professional women to shine. The women could move the whole sport forward past this disaster of doping. Now more than ever. As a rising tide lifts all boats, a clean peloton lifts all cyclists. I altered my Tour de France pitch to ASO and emailed them again. Now, in the midst of Armstrongeddon was the perfect time to flip the script and invest in women. To reinstate women at the Tour de France, reshape the sport's image and give the fans—and society—exactly what they want: Something to believe in.

Grillons, grillons. No response.

For rest of my pro cycling career, Lance's name came up regularly. Less so now, but incessantly after his fall from grace. It was impossible to be a pro cyclist in 2013 without people constantly inquiring how we felt about That Texan. For me, Lance Armstrong was two people. Lance A: The cheater and liar who did a bad, bad thing. Lance B: A ray of hope for cancer patients and survivors. There was a personal element, too. Lance met George's first wife while she was sick. And when she passed, Lance gave my husband kindness, hope and joy when they rode together in Austin.

No matter how much EPO coursed through Lance A's blood, I held no hatred for Lance B. Hate doesn't interest me. Far too much energy. Lance has to live with himself, and that is enough. In the murky waters of *"What do you think of Lance*

Armstrong?" my only solace was (and still is) to redirect the person by answering them with a question: *What do you think of women's professional cycling?* Usually the inquisitor answers, *Well, uh, I haven't seen… I don't know much about… is there even such a thing?* Redirecting shifts the paradigm. When we redirect with education, passion and kindness we can use the troubled past to shape a better future.

––––––––––

Using the good arm, I hunt-and-pecked my way through websites and articles on the history of women's pro cycling. We needed to include history in our film. Current stars and influencers were key, but it wouldn't mean as much without knowledge of the past. The internet also brought me Alice Roepke and Shelley Lucas. Roepke is the great-niece of Tillie Anderson, the Swedish immigrant who dominated the wooden velodrome in America's early track cycling boom. Roepke kept an archive of Tillie's entire history, and kindly let me use it for *Half the Road*.

Shelley Lucas, PhD, a professor of Kinesiology at Boise State University, had an archive of fantastic data on the history of sports, gender discrimination and endurance events. Lucas provided us information and photos of Jim Rabdau, the race director America's premiere stage race for women in the mid-1980s, The Ore-Ida Women's Challenge. Rabdau blasted UCI's ridiculous rule where women's race distances were cut in half and dumbed down. Instead of upholding UCI rules, Jim made his own: A 15-day race with 17 stages, 663 miles and 22,000ft elevation gains. The UCI sent Rabdau a memo claiming his race had excessive days, excessive distances, excessive climbing and excessive duration. Rabdau responded by printing t-shirts claiming, *"Let's Get Excessive!"* The race ran for nineteen years.

Rabdau, a former Green Beret, Vietnam veteran and member of E-Company 506 (portrayed in Steven Spielberg's *Band of Brothers*) was an unsung warrior for women in sport. A longtime fan of cycling, it made no sense there were so few women's races. He didn't just want to change the system, he wanted women to know they were just as deserving.

"If you can be around people who are excellent, then you'll know what excellence is. That's what I was trying to do with the Women's Challenge. To get girls to that level," Rabdau told VeloNews in 2008.[44] Rabdau passed away from

––––––––––

[44] Interactive Reader Guide: Rabdau reflects on the Women's Challenge

cancer in 2013, before we were able to interview him. Including his story in *Half the Road* was a given.

Researching for the documentary was teaching me more than I ever imagined. There were so many activists and trailblazers I never knew about. Things and people I was never taught. While I'm thrilled we live in an era that celebrates the Ruth Bader Ginsburgs, Gloria Steinems and Rosa Parks, there are far too many female pioneers out there who remain unknown. We still live in a culture where education fails us by teaching the same leaders (often men) over and over again, without diving deeper to uncover the unknowns. There were/are so many women (and men) who stood up for change and progress, falling into the enormous silent chasm between the borders of history and media. The very least we could do in making *Half the Road* was to give some of them a face and a voice.

———————

At the end of January 2013, a wonderful event called Cyclovia closed off five blocks of downtown Tucson to traffic, so people could ride their bikes all day without cars. In attendance was actor Patrick Dempsey, an avid cycling fan and supporter of women's racing. Hoping I might be able to find Patrick amidst the crowd, I grabbed my Bloggie and headed to Cyclovia. Maybe he'd be willing to say a few words on camera in support of equality. My broken arm had just passed the six-week mark of healing. Cyclovia was my first time riding outside since the Rottweiler tumble.

At the start of the event, I found Dr. McDreamy who was just as lovely in person as he was on Gray's Anatomy. Patrick kindly stood by as I fished my plastic, purple camera out of my jersey pocket and gave a rapid-fire, super-brief explanation of *Half the Road*.

Keep it short, I told myself. *Don't be a bumbling idiot. Go!*

"HiPatrickimmakingadocumentartyfilmonwomen'sprocyclingandIknowyoure abigsupporterwouldyoumindtellingmewhatyouthinkofwomen'scyclingandhowyou dliketoseeitgrow?"

"Oh, I'm a big fan of women's cycling," Patrick attested, articulating the sport was desperately in need of a proper media package to help it grow. *Agreed!* What struck me most was the fact he'd obviously thought about the matter way before some weird chick shoved a Bloggie in his face. We then rode together for a few blocks, chatting about Tucson and bicycles. I did my best not to fangirl/drool, and thanked him for his willingness to be part of our film.

As Patrick rode away, I was reminded of the power of asking. Asking is how we build armies of awareness and support. I doubt Patrick had any inclination how much he helped our film move forward, or how much he bolstered my confidence in asking, but his 15 seconds of camera time was a very important part of our underlying mission. When men stand up for women, we all move forward faster.

The interview with Patrick also reminded me of the importance of being prepared. Since purchasing the Little Purple Sony Bloggie, I never left home without it. Unexpected footage popped up everywhere. Like when I met six-year-old Lauren Wade riding her bike outside. I asked her what her favorite thing is about cycling. Without hesitation she looked me straight in the eye, and said, "Winning." My heart burst into glitter and rainbows. That plastic camera was the best $99 ever spent. I rode home from Cyclovia high on gettin' good work done. Whistling happily and smiling like a kid on Christmas, I hopped online to upload the video files to Kevin. There was email from Wynona. My mood switched abruptly.

As January faded, time sped up. With our team camp approaching in March, I asked John Profaci if Kevin could come out and film Colavita's athletes for a day. Maybe two. Shooting some training rides would serve as terrific B-roll. We already interviewed John, so getting Colavita's brand on the big screen made sense. *As well as some pretty stellar advertising. Duh.* Since Kevin's expenses were covered by our film budget, it wouldn't cost Colavita a thing. Nor would it interfere with the camp's itinerary.

"Yes of course," Profaci agreed. "No problem." I emailed Wynona, letting her know Profaci gave the OK for filming a couple days at camp. Wynona, however, was not OK at all. She was downright pissed.

"I don't know the details of your documentary, or in what light the team may be portrayed," Wynona said. "But the attractive veneer of a film and publicity is masking the fact that you are doing what *you* want to do at camp, Kathryn. This is…unacceptable behavior from a rider."

Veneer of a film… Doing what I want… unacceptable behavior… my Cerberus chomped away on the bones of Misunderstanding. I was crushed. This woman—my role model—misinterpreted the film not as a documentary of activism, but a narcissistic video where I was the star. That it was all self-promotion. That I valued fame above team. Wynona's words stung, but also showed me a perspective I had not considered: What if others saw me this way? What if everyone thought I was making a film all about me, me, me? Some selfish yahoo with a reality-star agenda. After all, we did title the original Indiegogo campaign as "Kathryn's Quest." *Oh shit*. Shit. Shit. Shit. The idea of *Half the Road* being perceived as a self-indulgent mission nauseated, horrified and educated me. For the past year, we'd interviewed incredible athletes, profiled fascinating leaders, compiled amazing historic data… but Kevin and I were the only ones who visibly *saw* our footage. Even the interviewees didn't have access to the footage yet.

Such is the conundrum of vision; it is ours alone until we generate proof. The big picture of *Half the Road* was so crystal clear… to me. Without tangible evidence, not everyone trusts the process of creation. While more and more fellow pro cyclists began trusting me, Wynona was a painful reminder that not everyone did.

Deep inside my dark caves of sensitivity, my heart ached terribly. I called Kevin as he worked on the footage.

"How long is the trailer?" I asked.

"About four minutes," he said.

"Please, please make sure my face isn't seen for more than 10 seconds, ok?" No way would I let this film be labeled a vanity project.

"You're hardly in the trailer. We have 30 hours of footage you're not in," Kevin tallied. "No one's going to think this film's about you."

"You'd be surprised," I muttered.

We set a deadline to wrap all filming in March, after team camp, and spend the next six months whittling those 30 hours down to ninety minutes. Our final cut was set for September 30, 2013 motivated by the Sundance Film Festival entry deadline. Whether or not we were accepted didn't matter. We set our World Premiere launch for *Half the Road* in exactly one year: January of 2014 in Tucson, Arizona.

20

ROLL CAMERA, ROLL COSTA RICA

Before I left for Central America, Kevin and I went back to Boise, Idaho for our penultimate filming block. On tap for interview: Two-time Olympic gold medalist Kristin Armstrong, U.S. National Team members Alison Tetrick and Kristin McGrath, and James Carkulis, CEO of Exergy, an environmental engineering company that pumped $1.5M into the pro women's Exergy Tour. By this point, I was very conscious of the fact we needed good, strong, role-model men in the film. As many as possible. We didn't want to fall victim to the stereotype that *Half the Road* was a "women's film." This was a film about equal opportunity. It was important to strike the perfect balance and feature men who supported, commended and invested in women.

In a swank, stunning office in downtown Boise at 7am, Carkulis came in dressed to the nines in CEO business attire, impeccably groomed. He gave a terrific interview on why he invested in both women's and men's cycling. He even called out the UCI for pandering to the media, promoting false virtues instead of fixing blatant inequity. Halfway through the interview, Kevin paused to change batteries on his camera. Carkulis' demeanor loosened up a bit, as many people do when the camera isn't rolling. Off the record, he launched into a speech about how great women are, how his company has a female president, how he has three daughters, how he can't conceive of unequal pay, how women—

"James," I interrupted. "Can you please say it *while* the camera is rolling?"

Luckily, he did. Kevin often set up two cameras, so when one needed a battery or SIM card change, the other camera kept rolling. Some of our strongest footage came from the instances where our interviewee thought they were off the record. From Emma Pooley to Brian Cookson to James Carkulis, it was a great awakening for me to observe the different selves we humans choose to share with one another when we are on (or off) the record.

After Carkulis, we interviewed Alison Tetrick, who worked as Carkulis' assistant to help fund her pro cycling career. She also brought to light her harrowing ordeal in a crash that left her with a broken pelvis and traumatic brain injury in 2011. The pelvis healed faster than her head, and Tetrick wept openly on camera as she questioned whether this bike racing thing was all worth it.

The footage moved me. I couldn't figure out whether her post-crash comeback was beautiful or stupid. Death in professional cycling was rare, but it still happened. Kevin and I recently finished editing a segment of the film paying homage to the professional women of cycling who we lost along the way; many of whom succumbed to life-ending brain injuries while racing or training. When Tetrick spoke about her near miss,[45] I thought to myself, *Man, my broken arm was a gift. So lucky I didn't hit my head. Can't imagine what that must be like.*

On a snowy February morning in beautiful Boise home, Kristin Armstrong delivered an interview just as she delivered time trials; with power, grace and passion. Her two Olympic gold medals from Beijing and London nearly paled in comparison to her story of persistence. After a fall during the Exergy Tour time trial in 2012, Kristin shattered her collarbone just two and a half months before the London Games. Everyone—especially the media—wrote her off. She was done, they said. USA will surely send someone else in her place.

Hell hath no fury like a champion written off. With an insatiable will that fed off the energy of impossibility, Kristin fought her way back and was selected to Team USA for London. Then she promptly won the gold. At age 39. With her three-year-old son, Lucas, in tow on the medal podium.[46]

I thanked Kristin for her time and also her trust. When I first started racing, Kristin was on every podium while I struggled just to hang on to the peloton. When I was granted dual-citizenship with St. Kitts and Nevis, Kristin was kind. When ESPN followed me around, she held no ill-will toward the media attention I received. Now, six years later, to be invited into her home and speak with her on camera was extremely meaningful.

---

[45] We didn't end up using the footage of Tetrick crying. Part of me feared the critics, vultures and trolls would pick apart a woman who wept on camera. Years later, I wish we'd kept it in. Screw the critics, trolls and vultures. Emotion and vulnerability is strength, not weakness.

[46] I still get chills listening to this part of Kristin's story in *Half the Road*. May we all be so brave as to look media in the eye and tell them exactly what they're going to write.

Leaving Idaho, Kevin and I received confirmation that Kathrine Switzer officially agreed to be in our film. However, she was spending the winter in New Zealand. There was no way we could afford a trip to New Zealand, so we outsourced a local videographer. The footage was fabulous. With $300 left in our film budget account, we had just enough left to outsource one more interview: Chrissie Wellington, four-time Ironman World Champion and one among the constellation of my personal heroes.[47] But not in her home base in England. I'd be meeting her in Costa Rica.

––––––––

A year had passed since I wrote about Chrissie for ESPNW after she obliterated multiple Ironman course records for both men and women, sometimes missing the men's podium by mere minutes. She truly changed the sport. When Chrissie returned my call for our interview, I was driving. Not wanting to miss the opportunity, I pulled over and scribbled notes on old napkins from the glove compartment of my Prius. Neither of us knew this call would morph into a lifelong friendship and a history-making endeavor. *Note to self: always carry napkins.*

Since then, Chrissie and I kept in close touch. The British phenom was transitioning from her incredible run as a four-time Ironman World Champion into retirement from the sport. Chrissie was a badass, both physically and mentally, and I held her in the highest regard.

She was also a human being with the same fears and insecurities we all possess. We bonded and emailed regularly, letting down our guards and exposing our vulnerabilities. Body image, inner demons, success, failure, pressure. She told me about a media photo she hated, thinking the angles made her look disproportionate and heavy. I told her about the cover of *As Good As Gold*, where they had to Frankenstein my head and body together from two different shots. In an eight-hour photo shoot, I was incapable of producing one 'perfect' photo. We laughed at the concept of perfection and found solace in one another's authenticity. We also shared a strong dislike for the state of inequity in professional sports.

I told Chrissie about the documentary we were making. Finally, my inner lightbulb flicked on... *Hey! Dummy! Ask her, ask her!*

"Chrissie," I asked, wide-eyed and fingers crossed. "Will you be in *Half the Road*?"

––––––––

[47] Interactive Reader Guide: Chrissie Wellington, Professional Badass.

"Yes, definitely!" she agreed. When Chrissie learned I was leading a bike tour in Costa Rica, she asked if she could join me and we could shoot the interview there. Absofreakinglutely.

When we announced Chrissie's presence, the Costa Rica tour sold out within 48 hours. In mid-February, with my arm freshly healed, I flew to the land of '*Pura Vida*' for a week-long job of cycle touring. Twenty wonderful folks, most of whom were triathletes or road cyclists from the U.S., Canada, Mexico and Germany comprised our group. Some of us formed lifelong friendships as we rolled through the Costa Rican countryside basking in the warm, sunny weather of a Central American winter. I took great pleasure observing the inspiration Chrissie served daily to the campers, most of whom were middle age. One day, a woman pulled me aside, wondering if it felt difficult for me to be in Chrissie's shadow, being not famous and all. I smiled. No, no. No shadows here. Just space dust. And I loved it. Watching Chrissie empower and inspire others was awesome.

During the rides, she would often hop off her bike at random, taking pictures, exclaiming, "Don't forget to look up from your handlebars, everyone!" I saw firsthand her desire to embrace life to the fullest. And with it, something I recognized in myself, too. A smidgen of that wacky Type A neuroses that comes with high-achiever mentality. On February 18, in middle of the trip, we celebrated Chrissie's 36th birthday. It began with a rocky start, as she awakened pissed off at herself for sleeping until nearly noon on our one rest day off the bike.

"I always do something new and exciting on my birthday, and now I've squandered it!" she lamented with dejection. "I never sleep late!"

"But you *did* do something new, Chrissie," I countered. "You slept till 11:30am. That is an exciting first! Especially for a triathlete. Congratulations!" This is what friends do: provide perspective, hope for the best and see what sticks. Something stuck. Chrissie and I bonded. For the rest of the week, we dove deep into the big conversations of life. We talked about journeys and paths, what we're doing now and where we want go next. We discussed the conundrum of being equally motivated and utterly directionless, how jarring it is to be so sure of ourselves one minute and so sensitive the next. We spoke of children, and whether or not they'll be woven into the patterns of our futures. We laughed at our control-oriented personalities, robust with private issues and public compassion, wondering whether we're trying to save the world or save ourselves. Maybe both, we agreed. It's a tough excursion to bushwhack through the thicket of our own thoughts, let alone find a proverbial hiking partner willing to thrash away at the stubborn overgrowth of who we are.

Despite the newness of our friendship, Chrissie and I shared a bond strengthened by openness, vulnerability and the willingness to wield gentle machetes along the trail of introspection.

On the last night of our Costa Rica bike camp, I gave a quick talk about *Half the Road* and showed a rough cut of our film trailer. These 18 campers were the first to see any footage at all, and my nerves were abuzz. *Will they like it? Will they get it? Will it matter? Will it... anything?* Or would my worst fear prevail: no emotion or reaction whatsoever toward everything I just spent the last year and a half of my life working on. Oof.

As the trailer concluded, something magical happened. They clapped! With an intensity higher than politeness. *When can we see the whole film? Where? When? What theater?*

"Next year! 2014!" I grinned ear to ear. "We're, uh, still making it!"

I was smiling so hard my face hurt. *Holy shit, they liked the trailer! Maybe we really have something here!* The woman who asked me about being in Chrissie's shadow walked up to me again and took my hand.

"I just want you to know," she said, "You're doing something that matters. You may have not won four Ironman world championships, but this is just as important. Don't forget that."

Her words burrowed deep in my heart. I thanked her, though she probably never knew how much it meant to hear the words *you matter*. My Cerberus did, as he whined and slumped off into his doghouse and stayed put for a long, long time.

Beneath a palm tree in rural Costa Rica, Chrissie gave a terrific interview for *Half the Road*, using her journey to highlight what women are physically capable of achieving in sport. By 2013, Chrissie held the four fastest times ever recorded by a woman in Ironman triathlon, with a record-breaking *nine* sub-9 hour finishes, often missing the men's podium by only minutes. A whole new endurance era was afoot.[48] She gave our film a fantastic boost of awesomeness. What neither of us knew at the

---

[48] I was a pre-Wellington era pro triathlete. In 2006, pro women racing Ironman in 10-hour finishing times could still place in the top 20. Today, a 10-hour finish wouldn't even earn women a pro license. All pro women—and many top amateurs—are in the 8-hour and 9-hour range. Chrissie truly set the bar at a new level and women rose to meet it.

time was how this new friendship and film footage would lead to something bigger, a historic-game-changer, just a few months down the line.

When the tour group dispersed at the end of the week, I remained in San Jose to guest ride for a local elite squad called Team Rayita, at the inaugural UCI Vuelta Costa Rica. Henry, the owner of the bike tour company Chrissie and I just finished, offered me a spot to crash at his house, alongside another young woman from the team, Julissa. Henry, like most cycling tour guides, was a far cry from wealthy. His home was a kitchen, bathroom and bedroom. In the bedroom, two mattresses lay on the floor. Typical of Central America, there was no air conditioning. Julissa and I, both well-accustomed to plight of accommodations and professional women's cycling, were just happy there was a toilet and a refrigerator. As we headed out to the start line each morning with our bikes racked atop Henry's car, one of us would direct Henry's rearview-mirrorless truck while the other held back the giant mango tree branches so our bicycles didn't get stuck. I was not yet aware how fleeting memories and moments of mangos and mobility were the ones I would treasure most about pro cycling.

21

TEAM CAMP AND WATER BUFFALO HORNS

A fter the races in Costa Rica and El Salvador, I flew to California for our Colavita-CookingLight team camp. In two beautiful homes in the rolling hills of Borrego Springs, our team of ten women and three staff members settled in for a week of training, bonding and promotional photo shoots. From the 2012 roster, Wynona re-signed Jamie Bookwalter, Leah Guloien, Mary Zider and myself. Added to the 2013 roster were Heather Logan-Sprenger, Laura Brown, Lindsay Bayer Goldman, Jackie Kurth, Jen Purcell and Tina Pic, transitioning from co-director to full time racer. I shared a room with Jamie. A perfect match. Both of us preferred early nights, dark rooms, fans on and cell phones off.

On the first day, Wynona handed out team clothing. I ran my hands over beautiful new kits, smiling at the CookingLight logo that now replaced the space where ESPNW had been. After the disbursement of team kits came the allocation of team casual clothing, the logoed shirts, jackets and pants we were contracted to wear at venues and events when not on the bike. As Wynona passed around the clothing, I noticed every athlete received three sets of clothes. I received one, and brought the oversight to her attention.

"We're out," Wynona said, flatly, without eye contact. "Will mail you some."

Right. Ok. No big deal. Just a shirt. Let it go. My gut did not. After clothing, we moved onto divvying up the technical gear. Tires, tubes, flat packs and such are passed to each athlete. Except me.

"We're short," Wynona said. "Will mail you some." Finally, we approached the garage and the beautiful new, carbon fiber, matte black Jamis Xenith bikes stood in formation against the wall, each one emblazoned with the name of its rider on the top tube. The moment of receiving the team bike is the holy grail moment all pro cyclists look forward to. We eagerly milled about, admiring the fine carbon steeds as we sought the one bearing our name emblazoned on the top tube. I was still searching when Wynona called me over.

"Kathryn, I need you to ride last year's bike," she said. "We just don't have one your size this year." Confused, my brain took inventory. *Wait. That doesn't make sense. Last year's bike was yellow. This year's bike is black. All the components are different. Shimano, not SRAM. I won't look the same as everyone else.* My gut screamed bullshit, but my vocal chords remained still. To appear anything less than a team player or question Wynona amongst others would put the nail in my roster coffin.

"Ok," I smiled. "Whatever you need!" I covered my disappointment by wandering around the garage, oohing and aahing as my teammates tinkered with the saddle heights and handlebar positions on their sleek new machines. In the corner, I noticed a lone bike unattended. Size 54cm. My size. In personalized italic script, the top tube bore the name *Wynona Summerfield*. Hold up. A director doesn't need a bike.

"Hey Wynona, can I use this one?"

"No. That's the spare bike. Every team needs a spare bike," she said, exasperated. "But you can hold it during the photo shoot." My denial had nowhere left to hide. Something was definitely off. My Cerberus woke and my soul stirred with the vibration of its low, throaty growl.

Say nothing, my instinct guided. *Not if you want to race this year. Keep your mouth shut, let your legs do the talking. You are super fit after Vuelta El Salvador. Ride hard and prove yourself.* The notion of "proving oneself" in terms of optimal performance was one thing, as every rider on every team must do. But this was different. Now I understood I had to prove my worth just so Wynona would consider me an equal member of the team. The clothing and bicycle were the first two clues of Wynona's discontent with my presence, but the worst was yet to come.

For the first two days of camp, I almost forgot Kevin was there. Inconspicuously shooting B-roll footage for the documentary, Kevin rode in the team car accompanying us on training rides. He was quiet, unobtrusive and upheld the wallflower philosophy of what all videographers strive to be: invisible. Done, dusted. Footage obtained. Kevin went home after 48 hours. That's when things got worse.

———————

The mental disappointment and the physical exertion of team camp were concepts of discomfort I understood. Sports are hard. Every athlete hurts. What came next was a different type of pain. Something that blurred the boundaries of tangible and emotional hurt. For well over a decade, I had received massage therapy to aid in recovery and optimal performance. For all elite and professional athletes, massage is as normal as food and water. Never once was I disappointed, touched inappropriately or put in a bad situation. Until team camp.

Wynona hired Bobbi, a woman, to oversee massage duties for the team. When it was my turn for the table I rattled off my short list of niggling issues and tight muscles, which all therapists want to know ahead of time. Without telling Bobbi I broke my arm two months ago (for fear she would tell Wynona), I simply said I had an "old" injury along my left radius and to please tread gently there.

"I'll start with your back," she said, coolly. While neither rude nor mean, there was a curt tinge to her tone. Seemed odd, as I'd observed her interacting so pleasantly with all the other athletes. *Let it go*, my gut warned. *You're imagining shit.* I climbed on the massage table, face down.

Bobbi began, her pressure immediately strong. *Ok!* I thought to myself, *fantastic!* Nothing better than a massage therapist with a firm grip digging deep into stubborn muscles of the lats, traps and rhomboids; our skeletal Bermuda triangle where human stress loves to settle. Everything felt gr—

And then it didn't. Bobbi began pushing so hard my chest constricted from her weight and I had difficulty breathing. Suffering along for a few minutes, I finally asked her to go a bit lighter. This was a first for me, as I was accustomed to asking for more pressure. Not this time.

"I know what I'm doing," Bobbi barked. "This *is* light." She resumed pressure, then stopped. Fumbling in her bag of equipment, I breathed deeply, taking in as much air as possible as if to internally pad myself against her touch. Bobbi returned to the table. Pain shot through me as she raked something over my left scapula.

"*What the...?*" I jolted, instinctively rising from the table.

"Stay," she commanded, pushing my back down and scraping something sharp along my right scapula. As my blood met the air, the stinging sensation of broken skin arose across my back. Bobbi explained my muscles were being "healed." In her hand, a long, five-inch sleek, solid object that looked something like an animal bone.

"Water buffalo horn," she clarified. The horrendous pressure with which she raked this horrible horn down my spine felt as if the water buffalo was still attached.

I knew nothing of water buffalo horn scraping, but I was quite certain massage therapy is not supposed to make someone bleed.

"Bobbi, I don't—" I protested.

"Are you not tough enough for this?" she asked sharply, with a hint of taunting. "Hold still."

Against my better judgment, I did. Filled with panic/dread that if I showed "weakness," Bobbi would carry the message back to Wynona and give her one more reason to keep me from racing. I stayed still, bit my lip and held back tears. When Bobbi finished skinning my back, she skipped over my legs and picked up my newly-healed arm. And the horrific horn of death. In what may have been divine intervention, my teammate Mary walked in at that very moment for her scheduled massage. Bobbi let go of my arm and told me to leave.

Dismounting the table, I stumbled to the kitchen of our team house, grabbed two bags of frozen vegetables from the freezer and walked into the living room where my teammate, Jen, laid on the couch reading a book. I flopped onto my belly, lying prostrate on the carpet, and asked Jen if she would place the frozen bags on my back. She obliged and lifted my shirt.

"Holy shit," Jen whispered, gently unsticking my back from the bloody patches on my shirt.

"I know, right?" I winced. "How bad is yours?"

"What do you mean?" she asked.

"Your water buffalo horn exorcism. Did you bleed, too?"

Jen had no idea what I was talking about. Horns? Blood? Extreme pressure? She told me Bobbi did a light-pressure flush of her quadriceps and calves, then they joked around and chatted for a while. My gut couldn't let this one go. Tears welled up again in my eyes, but not from physical pain. *No, no, no,* I told myself. *I can't be the only one.* I put on a fake smile and staggered around the house, asking my other teammates how their massages went. *Great!* they all chirped, commenting how much their legs really needed that light flush. By the time I got to Tina Pic, I came undone. Tears spilled down, she asked what's wrong. Handing her my iPhone, I asked Tina to take a photo of my back. As a veteran pro cyclist ten years older than me with six national championship titles, Tina's been in this sport forever. I asked her if bleeding was normal for a pro cycling massage.

"No," she says. "It's not normal for *any* massage."

"Don't tell Wynona, ok?"

"Ok," she said, giving me a gentle hug.

Finding a quiet space in the team house, I had a good cry that night. Years would pass before I was ready to accept the impact of that situation. While I'll never be able prove a direct connection between Wynona's distaste for me and that Bobbi inflicted hurt on purpose, the writing was on the wall. None of my other teammates had bruised, bloody bodies. But the physical wounds somehow ached less than the emotional pain. For the rest of camp, I put on a mask. While being happy around my teammates was not an act, feeling good about Wynona, Bobbi and my status on the team definitely was. Pain is a complicated journey.

"That's nuts," my husband said on the phone that evening. "You need to tell someone about this. Why aren't you telling someone?!" I knew he was right. Not only was it nuts, but I was smack in the middle of my own double-standard. Here I was, an activist making a film about the injustices in women's pro cycling, yet I was too scared I'd lose my own spot on the team if I spoke out. Lobbying for pro women to be included at the Tour de France, yet simultaneously being excluded by my own manager. Every sign pointed me toward fleeing this team and voicing the issues, but instead, I became co-dependent. I *needed* this team. Leaving Colavita would give me less access to the professional races. To no longer hold a contract as a pro cyclist I feared would be a step backward. Making a film and pushing for Tour de France equity would carry less weight if I were no longer a pro. I knew the reality: Change has to come from within a broken system. I was in the system. Yet here I was, my own skin literally breaking.

So instead of leaving the team, I absorbed the unkind, mean, painful things both physically and mentally and lied to myself it was all for the best in the long run. In the short run, there were more lessons and more pain on the way.

"Next!"

Wynona's voice echoed through the hallway of our team house. All ten members of Colavita-CookingLight Pro Cycling were gathered about the living room, chatting quietly, reading or surfing the internet. We were also schnockered. Exhausted. Rightfully so. That morning, we were evaluated on our climbing skills in the steep, punchy pitches of the San Ysidro Mountains of Borrego Springs. Knowing I had to prove myself to Wynona, I finished in the top three amongst my teammates. Racing the hills of El Salvador the week beforehand was a blessing of fitness. From endurance rides to sprint lead-outs to hill climbs, I had done my job at team camp and I did it well.

That night, Wynona met with each of us privately to discuss our individual race assignments for the first three months of the 2013 race calendar. Some terrific events on the U.S. professional circuit were coming up in California and New Mexico—Redlands, San Dimas, Tour of the Gila. I was excited. Loved these stage races. Not to mention, most were within driving distance of Tucson, so my southwestern proximity was an asset to the team's airfare budget. Despite the horrible massage, withholding team gear and bicycle and the less-than-subtle personal angst radiating toward me from Wynona, I proved myself as a rider during camp. At least I could bring that tiny nubbin of confidence to our meeting.

"Next!" Wynona called again. It was my turn. I slid the wood-paneled roller door open, shuffled across the shag carpet, and took a seat on the overstuffed white sofa. Everything in this retirement-community rental home dated back to the mid-70s. Including myself. Next to Wynona sat Don, a tall man in his mid-fifties assisting her with logistics at camp; driving the truck, organizing group outings, etc. Struck me a tiny bit strange for him to sit in on a one-on-one team meeting, but whatever.

"Nice climb today," Wynona said, acknowledging our morning training session.

"Thanks," I answered, with a twinge of surprise and relief. *Whoa! A compliment! Meeting's off to a good start. Ok, speak confidently. You got this.* "Looking forward to the season, Wynona. Feeling strong for Redlands next month." Redlands Bicycle Classic, three weeks away, was our first official team race of 2013. Having raced it twice before during my climb toward the pro ranks, I had an edge of experience. Not to mention, I was fit. Ready. Hungry.

"Ok, Kathryn, so Don is here because I don't want it to seem like I'm picking on you," Wynona began. *Interesting way to start a meeting,* my gut gurgled. "Anyway. You're not racing Redlands."

Disappointment coursed through me, but there were still three more upcoming races, so I let it slide. Nodding in affirmation, I waited for Wynona to continue as my mind wandered to whether she'd choose San Dimas or Gila. *Ooh, maybe both*! What came next was a reality that hadn't even entered my brain.

"I'm debating whether or not to let you race at all this year," Wynona said. A pit in my stomach opened, excavating whatever was left of my confidence. The rest of the conversation ebbed and flowed between reality, disappointment and the strange, difficult place we must navigate when an authoritative person begins a verbal assault on one's dreams.

It then became clear why Don was in the room. He was a witness. Should I have questioned Wynona's decision, he could testify to Profaci that I was a troublemaker. A rabble-rouser. Someone who Questions Authority. His presence was her protection. I focused my attention back to the race situation. ...*Whether to let me race at all?* Wynona wasn't finished, though.

"If a teammate becomes sick or injured at the last minute, I *might* use you instead of a guest rider," she offered, "but you'll have to prove yourself." Good lord. The *Prove Yourself* conundrum. No manager needs to tell a Type A professional athlete to prove themselves. That's all we do, every day. From training to racing to self-care, we constantly compete with ourselves every damn day to make sure we're the very best version of who we are as an athlete. *Prove yourself.* Ha! All professional cyclists do this naturally. What's not natural and not okay—and sometimes very damaging—is when a team director makes an athlete feel they must prove themselves just to *stay* on the team. When those in a power position interfere with athlete's sense of self-worth *after* they've made the team... *that* is psychologically detrimental. Trust and encouragement are far better tools than faithlessness and belittling. Of course, none of that was apparent to me in the moment. Only worthlessness, disappointment, confusion and shame.

My heart sank. Wynona wrote me off nearly every race on the US pro cycling calendar. I was totally unaware her actions were illegal by UCI standards. All UCI pro teams must race each rider at least once a month. The wealthiest and best pro teams had rosters of 12 to 14 athletes. Since six athletes race per event, a 14-member team basically has two squads and two alternates, so they can do more races worldwide. Cycling's intense, demanding, injury-prone nature is well suited to the rotation of athletes. Not to mention, racing the same six people every single week would guarantee physical and mental burnout.

As a U.S. based domestic pro team, Colavita-CookingLight's roster of ten athletes was pretty solid: One squad, four alternates. Everyone would be shuffled around to various races, subbing in and out. If each athlete weren't raced at least once a month, that was a breach of contract. Unfortunately, I was three years away from learning this rule. In 2013, all I knew was how much it hurt to be benched. So I did what any co-dependent would do; internalize the pain, put on a smile and diffuse the situation.

"Whatever is best for the team," I said and left the room. The house was full of chatter, as my teammates cheerily chirped about which races they were assigned and who was going where. I offered nothing to the conversation but a lie, telling them

Wynona was still figuring out my schedule. Like the massage, this kind of pain took a long time to fully process.

The only way I knew to deal with the disappointment of Not Racing was to go into that weird little workshop deep inside my psyche where the detritus of bad experiences lingered, and fish through the bins of coping tools. Instead of letting Wynona get the best of me, I built the possibility that I could change her mind. *She wrote me off, but I'll write myself back!* Game plan: Operation Squeaky Wheel. Every week, I would email Wynona. Send her my training files. Let her know I was ready to race. To counteract the hurt of women not supporting women, I did the opposite, and voraciously tweeted, shared and posted positive accomplishments of other women. From journalism censorship to water buffalo horns to managerial dislike, shining a light on other women kept me from wandering in the dark caves of hurt.

22

NORMAL KATHRYN

A month after camp, Wynona called. *My weekly emails and persistence are paying off*! I thought to myself. Like usual, I was wrong. Well, wrong-ish. Redlands Bicycle Classic was fast approaching, and I held hope this phone call meant my addition to the roster. Quite the opposite. The conversation began with a berating.

"Kathryn, stop tweeting about other riders on other teams. You're only to promote Colavita-CookingLight cyclists, not all the other women in the sport," Wynona decreed. Her tone was angry, aggressive. She was incensed.

"I am wrestling with a deep decision," she snarled. "I'm debating about whether or not to let you race Sea Otter. We are short one rider. If I let you race, you need to make me a promise."

"Anything!" I breathed. Sea Otter was right after Redlands. *OhmygoshmaybeIgettorace*.

"I need you to promise me you will be 'Normal Kathryn,'" Wynona continued, her tone sharp and cold. "That you'll do whatever I ask of you. That you'll not interact with any of our sponsors. That you won't talk about that movie, or your self-serving ESPN journalism and all of that self-promotional stuff you do." Whoa. Anger, meanness and a tinge of dinosaur outdatedness. This wasn't sisterblocking, this was something else. She was on the hunt to tear me down, despite being a member of her tribe. A She-rannosaurus Wrex. Wynona kept going, her voice growing agitated with every sentence, each syllable gaining momentum with unkindness. She wasn't done yet.

"And stop telling people you're an Olymp—" she said.

"But I've never—" I interrupted.

"—and don't tell *anyone* about St. Kitts and Nevis," she counter-interrupted. "People hate that you race for them. There is a lot of controversy about you getting citizenship and racing for a country that isn't yours. That, and this movie you're making about yourself. You are nothing in this sport, Kathryn. You are a no one."

Time stopped then. Or perhaps it was my heart. Either way, the pause was long enough for the words to etch themselves into permanence. To be called a *no one* by the woman whom I once idolized was a devastating blow. Words are a fascinating weapon, how they can escape from people's brains and mouths completely unaware of the outcome they may inflict. Wynona's words plunged daggers into my confidence and trust. *You are a no one. You are nothing in this sport.*

"Normal Kathryn is looking forward to Sea Otter Classic," I quipped, using humor to deflect pain. I have long used humor as a salve for the pain of misunderstanding. I kept the tears back until we hung up.

Sea Otter was a disaster. Despite my peak fitness, doubt burrowed into my head and wrapped its powerful talons around my confidence, pulling it someplace dark and just out of reach. Instead of riding boldly and taking calculated risks, I positioned myself poorly and rode passively. Consumed by the fear of drifting toward the back of the peloton, that's exactly what happened. When racing, the best thing we can do is not think at all. Turn off our brain. Let instincts and training reign. But I couldn't flip the switch. There was too much clutter of non-confidence in the way. *No one. Self-serving. Be normal. No one likes you. You'll never race again this year.* Instead of turning my brain off, it roared to life with Doubt. I rode like shit. My teammates saw it, too. After the first two stages of Sea Otter, their lack of eye contact at meals and meetings gave it away. My gut knew what was coming. It was April, barely the start of the season. Wynona would not race me again. For the first time since I climbed onto a bicycle seven years ago, I felt like quitting.

There's a saying in sport that when we feel like giving up, we must remember why we started. I tried remembering the good stuff. How I was ESPN's Olympic guinea pig experiment. Then I fell in love with cycling. How I loved the crazy physical pain, the gains in progress, the safety and the danger, the broken arms, the stupid dogs, the guys on the Shootout, the women I raced, the cliffs in El Salvador, the flats of Shanghai, my beloved Tucson, the backside of Gates Pass, the views from Saguaro Park, the descent of Mt. Lemmon, the rolling river path of The Loop, shortcuts through neighborhood streets, and most of all, the inner-whisper of

Wheeee, again, again! I loved the ultimate gift of riding a bicycle; the way cycling anchors us to the present yet moves us forward all at once. The *Wheeee* was gone now, and I didn't know how to get it back.

"Screw that," my husband said. "Screw Wynona. You're going to sign up for races that don't require a six-person squad and you're gonna go by yourself. You're still a pro cyclist. Don't give up. Show 'em what you're made of." Such is the power of love and couplehood, to hold one another up when life throws its punches at our partners. George and I grabbed a calendar and planned out events for the rest of the year, targeting races Colavita was not attending so Wynona couldn't technically stop me from participating. The two biggest ones were World Champs and Caribbean Champs in the fall. There, I could represent SKN.

My confidence didn't bounce back completely, but at least lifted its head off the floor. Off the bike, Kevin and I dove into the long, tedious editing process of filmmaking. Keeping to our timeline, we were set to release our second Indiegogo fundraising campaign—complete with official film trailer—in May 2013. We're in full swing, editing 30 hours of footage using a software program called Final Cut, allowing us to work together online despite being a thousand miles away. Still, we needed to put in some face-to-face work time. I headed to Hood River, Oregon to stay with Kevin and Melissa. Setting up my bike on a stationary trainer in his office, I pedaled away next to Kevin as we clipped, cut, chopped and created our film.

23

INCHING TOWARD THE COMMA

On a white board in Kevin's office, *Half the Road* grew from an idea conceived into a fetus of Post-It notes and magic markers. Every time we added or moved a topic, I swear I could feel its heartbeat. I deeply loved this perceptual pregnancy of progress. As we categorized our footage into themes and timelines, cascading down in colorful columns, I noted the enormity of what lay before us. No film had yet been made on women's cycling. To explain the present, we needed the history. The rules of racing. The current professionals. UCI issues. Salary inequity. Gender discrimination. Age discrimination. Small/poor nation inequity. Women's physiological capabilities. Tour de France. Sponsorship. Injuries. Crashing. Doping. Memorials. Media coverage. Rise of the next generation.

Red Post-Its for themes. Yellow Post-Its for people. Blue Post-Its for the special features. Kevin and I worked 8-10 hours daily for two weeks straight, hiring out a few last-minute videography services to get footage of junior teens racing Tour of Rimouski in Canada and the kids of Little Bellas, Olympian Lea Davison's mountain bike camp for girls. With every edit came the reality of emotion... I wanted this film to run the gamut of the psyche. We needed the audience to experience everything we feel as women of pro cycling: joy, anger, frustration, sadness, pain, humor and hope. The latter, especially.

The toughest section by far was constructing the memorial clip. In the past twenty years, pro cycling lost 10 beautiful souls of the sport to incidents of training, racing, accidents and cancer. We needed the world to see their faces, to remember not their deaths but their lives. They were our sisters. *Are* our sisters, always. No cyclist ever wants to talk about the reality of death. Every time we mount a bike, we know something tragic could happen. Instead, we prefer to focus on the act of living.

We sign a silent contract with ourselves, acknowledging reality but accepting the risk. *Still, cycling's so dangerous!* Many people comment. *Aren't you afraid?* Yes, of course. I'm afraid of lots of things. But not cycling. There is one thing that scares me way more. A sedentary life.

While in Hood River, I received an email from Inga Thompson[49], who raced for the United States in the 1984 Olympics; the inaugural Games where women were finally allowed to compete in road cycling.

"Kathryn," Inga wrote. "I hear you are making a film on women's cycling. I raced in the Tour de France Feminin in 1984 –1989. May we speak?" *Oh hell yes!* One of our many Post-It notes was tracking down riders who raced the Tour de France in the 80s. But we'd run out of money from our initial film budget to conduct any interviews.

"I live in Oregon! I'll come to you," Inga said, and made the six-hour drive from her home in Halfway to Hood River. Confident, kind, tall, fit and lean from years of farm work and bike racing, Inga's brilliant blue eyes danced with vigor as she told us her story of racing through the Alps of France and the Olympic streets of Los Angeles. In 1986 and 1989, Inga finished third in the Tour de France Feminin, including a stage win in the time trial and capturing the coveted climbers' jersey.[50] Energetic, well-spoken and unafraid to use her voice, Inga was not only fabulous in person, but played a vital role in our film.

We embedded Inga into the film by splicing her story into Brian Cookson's opinions. For every point Cookson made about why women can't race the Tour de France, Inga made the exact counterpoint of how they can—and *did*! She provided a beautiful blend of smackdown and balance. *Women can't race three weeks.* Oh yes they can. Inga did. *Women's cycling doesn't draw spectators.* Yes, it does. Inga brought photos of thousands of fans lining the Alps, cheering on the women's peloton. *Women are slower.* Hardly. Inga explained the average speed of the women's peloton was only 6/10[th]s of a mile slower than the men in 1986, when Maria Canins and Greg LeMond won.[51] The difference between a rider traveling at 22 or 23 miles per hour isn't even visible to fans.

---

[49] Interactive Reader Guide: Inga Thompson and Cyclingnews article
[50] In cycling stage races, there are typically four jerseys awarded to the best finisher in these categories: leader, sprinter, climber and best young rider.
[51] Winning Magazine's stats on Tour de France 1986: Maria Canins, 991Km in 27:13:37 (36.385 kph/22mph) Greg LeMond, 110h 35' 19" (37.020kph/23.003 mph).

"The fans *loved* the women's race," Inga recalled. "They traveled miles and climbed up those mountains to watch bike racing. People were so excited to see two pelotons come by, not just one."

Also interesting was the fact Inga Thompson and Brian Cookson were members of the same generation, just 13 years apart. To be told "it can't be done" by a man sitting next to a woman roughly the same age who *already did it* was pretty fantastic. By the end of our interview, I was aglow with hope. Inga was a goldmine of terrific information and awesomeness; a great reminder of how many women in this sport paved the way for our gender to thrive. On a personal level, I was desperately in need of a new role model. Inga silently helped replace the toxicity of Wynona. She was kind, encouraging and believed in our film. Although there was nothing tangible to see yet, Inga never assumed the film was some self-serving showcase about me. She understood it was about *us*. This two-time Olympian, two-time Tour de France podium finisher and ten-time national champion badass got in a car and drove six hours to talk to me. Maybe I wasn't a no one after all.

In addition to the stellar interview footage of Inga, we needed something fun to break up the drudgery of patriarchal woes. We needed humor in *Half the Road*.

"How about a skit?" I mused to Kevin. "I mean, it would be so easy to change the ridiculous rules holding women back. What if we created an infomercial for a literal tool to make change happen? Like... an Equality Pen!"

"Go for it. Humor is important. And if the skits fail, you don't seem to mind looking like an idiot," Kevin reasoned.

"True!" I agreed. Between my deflated ego with Team Colavita and my growing List of Names called on social media, I was hardly bothered if we had to add Terrible Actress. I was becoming quite talented at vulnerability. We filmed a couple skits in low-budget creative glory, and to this day, they make me smile and cringe with equal fervor.

Also cringe-worthy was the price tag of Olympic footage. Obtaining proper permission, rights and credits were vital. Images, videos and quotes are not always free and may the courts have mercy on those who think otherwise. Kevin and I both understood the consequences of lifting intellectual property. No way. We did not want to get sued. We triple-checked everything. Some photos were free. Others ran $5. Some, like the picture of Kathrine Switzer getting accosted at the Boston Marathon in 1967, ran $500. Which was nothing compared to video rights.

I reached out to the United States Olympic Committee for a price quote. We wanted about one minute of footage showing Marianne Vos and Kristin Armstrong winning gold in the road race and time trial at the 2012 London Olympics. We *needed* this footage. It made no sense to feature these two champions and *not* show them achieving exactly what they were talking about. Seeing how the Olympics were broadcast in the U.S. on NBC Television, I assumed the price tag would be a little steeper than a $500 still photograph. *I bet this footage'll cost a thousand dollars!* I thought to myself. *Maybe even, like, $1500.* My naivety had a field day with that one.

For less than one minute—*we only needed forty-nine seconds!*—of Olympic footage, the price tag was $12,000. A shudder of reality coursed through me. Combined with all the other expenses, we would now need $65,000 to complete *Half the Road.*[52] Oof. Doubt crept in. How were we ever going to raise that much—especially when we topped out at $11,000 on our first crowdsource campaign? Still, I sang reality away with my weird genetics of optimistic denial and stubborn persistence. *Happy thoughts, happy thoughts. If you build it, they will come. This film matters. I matter. Untrammeled. Keep going. La la la la la.*

Kevin and I finished the final cut of the film's trailer. He did an amazing job whittling down our 30 hours of footage and creating a fantastic four-minute reel highlighting the core of *Half the Road.* Shining stars of our sport backed up with fantastic, action-packed B-roll of bike racing. Better still, only five seconds of me! Just a few quick words on women's rights. (Saved "Equality Pen" for the big screen).

Now came the moment of truth: Launching our second Indiegogo campaign to raise the necessary funds to make this film happen. Kevin and I each agreed to keeping our labor wages below the poverty line: $16,000. The rest of the budget was needed for photo and video licensing, paying our outsourced camera crew, distribution and all the travel, meals and unexpected costs that might pop up. Our target goal was $65,000. *Six times* the amount we brought in on our first round of $11,000. This number was terrifying. My current salary was $0 for Colavita-CookingLight. Coasting on savings and battling demons of self-worth, $65,000 looked a lot more like $6.5M.

My nerves were in full swing. If we couldn't hit this number, the film wouldn't happen. With our new *Half the Road* video trailer headlining our Indiegogo page

---

[52] Aside from trademark material, what else goes in an indie film budget? Plane tickets, car rentals, hotels, meals, voiceover work, editing work, crowdsourcing percentages, assistant stipends, etc.

and incentive perks like tee shirts, posters, inclusion in the film's credit reel, titles of Executive Producer, trips to Tucson for high-rollin' donors... we pulled out all the stops. Whatever it took to attract donors and investors. I was one step away from pledging a kidney.

On May 16, 2013, with sweaty palms, racing hearts and palpable vulnerability we launched the *Half the Road* campaign into the world wide web of wish, will and wonder. Fourteen months of turning a metaphorical vision into a physical one, we now had something visible to watch. It wasn't just a film trailer, it was a tangible step on the ladder of change. A wrung toward equal opportunity. Hitting *publish* on Indiegogo released the same electrical current within as when I hit *send* on the email to ASO four years ago. This time, there would be no crickets.

Since Indiegogo ran campaigns for seven weeks to secure the funds, Kevin and I divided the tasks: He would prioritize film editing while I oversaw the fundraising. Parking myself in front of my laptop, I dove into social media, sharing *Half the Road* on Twitter and Facebook, sending links and emails to everyone I knew. And everyone I didn't. *Reach, reach, reach. Ask, ask, ask. Give, give, give,* I chanted to myself. *Let no stone go unturned. Let no Maybe go unreached.* Less than twenty minutes after launching, a thousand dollars rolled in.

Over the next few days, I became transfixed by the fundraising bar on the upper right corner of the Indiegogo screen; a thin, green stripe that elongated itself with each donation under the target goal *$65,000* written in bold. Every time a contribution came in, the green bar wormed forward a millimeter, burrowing a tunnel of slow, methodical hope. On social media, I did everything possible to get word out about *Half the Road*. How strange it was to feel equal parts proud and angered in making a film about equal opportunity. Our prospective audience felt it, too. Three weeks later, we had $20,000. By the end of June, $40,000. The green line incheth!

Donations arrived from 16 countries, but what struck me profoundly was that 50% of our donors were men. Cycling's male-dominated fanbase wanted to see this movie just as much as women did. *Half the Road* wasn't a "chick flick." Sometimes *Half the Road* felt more like an action film than a documentary. As the donations rolled in, Kevin and I breathed a collective sigh of relief. Our message—our vision—was making its way around the world and people were taking notice. With a few weeks left to go on Indiegogo, I set to work on searching for the perfect narrator.

I was adamant we find a male narrator for *Half the Road*. While we had many men featured in our film, the cast was predominately women. To strike the right balance of parity—metaphorically, physically and auditory—having a male narrator helped break the potential stereotype of *Half the Road* being labeled a "chick flick" or marketed only to women. But we needed the *right* narrator, not just some random dude with a male voice. It made sense to seek out someone directly connected to the cycling world in some capacity. I made a list of all the celebrities/male actors in the U.S. who rode bikes.

Patrick Dempsey, Jake Gyllenhaal, Mark-Paul Gosselaar, Ethan Suplee... all terrific possibilities. But rising to the top of our list was the one-and-only king of unmatchable charisma, beloved jester of originality, human incarceration of creative awesomeness; Robin Williams. Robin was an ardent cyclist and fan of the sport. In 2002 and 2006, I raced the Escape from Alcatraz Triathlon in San Francisco, and the bike course went right past Robin's house. It was common for him to cheer from his lawn, sometimes cartwheeling his energy and appreciation as the pros and amateurs rolled past.

"Do you really think you can reach him?" Kevin asked.

"I don't know. But I'm gonna to try," I said.

I knew we'd have to contact talent agents of celebrities. John Scillieri, my husband's brother, lived in LA and often worked as an extra. John tracked down all the agents on our list, and I sent an email to Robin's agent at WME. Giving a brief synopsis of the film, I sent her the trailer and the narration script, asking if we could hire Mr. Williams for a two-hour voice recording. We'd pay, of course. I wanted our request to come across nothing short of professional. A few days later, Robin Williams' agent responded to our email, saying she would check in with him. The following week, she wrote:

> "Kathryn, Robin is currently filing a television series and he won't be able to commit to your project. But he wants me to extend his best wishes for your documentary."

The fact Robin even acknowledged our film, and possibly watched the trailer, made my heart sing. I loved this man. As a child, I was touched by his brilliance before I even knew what brilliance was. I just knew Mork was special. In the early 80s, *Mork & Mindy* was my favorite show. When I was seven, I greeted my childhood friends not with hello, but *nanoo nanoo*. More than once, I searched our attic and coat closets, hoping if I *nanooed* really hard perhaps he might appear there, too. As I grew older, the clarity of Robin Williams's brilliance and his openness about his demons struck me the way it did most people; he was just as human as he was alien, and we loved him for it. He struggled, but instead of keeping it secret, he let us in to take a look around at the detritus in his mind. I sure wasn't brave enough to show anyone my Cerberus. But Robin was. He loved bikes, too. Maybe someday we could meet and I could just thank him for being himself. In the meantime, I thanked his agent and extended my best wishes.

Since we couldn't get Robin to narrate, asking Patrick Dempsey made the most sense. He was already in the film and he'd been so gracious to me at Cyclovia Tucson. Through his agent, we reached out. She requested a rough cut of the film in progress, in addition to the trailer, which we sent immediately. A week later, we got a response. Patrick was busy filming another season of *Grey's Anatomy* and turned down the request.

"Patrick reviewed and feels the film should be a woman's voice," his agent wrote, turning down the request. Sticking to my guns, I explained a male narrator was best. "When men speak out on behalf of women's equality, both genders move forward faster," I wrote, thanking them both for their time and promising to send Patrick a finished version of the film.

While the agents of the other actors on our list kindly returned my inquiries, nothing panned out. This turned out to be a blessing in disguise, as all roads led to Bob Roll. "Bobke" was a former professional cyclist in the 70s and 80s who provided U.S. color commentary for NBC during the Tour de France, was a much-loved personality of the sport. Cycling fans enjoyed his inside knowledge, relatable character and terrific blend of sharp articulation punctuated with jovial goofballism. Bob provided exactly what was needed in broadcast sports television: he wasn't a talking head, he was a talking human. Bob was also a staunch supporter of women's racing. A contemporary of Connie Carpenter and Inga Thompson, Bob was no antiquated stranger to the world of women's physical capabilities. He was rooting for the progress of women's cycling as much as we were.

I reached out to Bob and asked if he would do us the honor of narrating *Half the Road*. He answered my email exactly two minutes later. Which meant he hadn't even had the time to watch the trailer. I sat there for a few minutes, not wanting to open the email. *Surely, another rejection,* I thought.

"Yes, I'm in! Let me know the details," Bob said. Never, never, never doubt the power of asking. Never sit around wondering what an email might say. Rejection is not contagious. Our job as an activist is to open every email with as much strength and passion as it takes to send them. I fell in platonic love with Bob immediately. We booked the wonderful Bobke at a recording studio in San Francisco later that summer.

––––––––––––

As Kevin and I neared the end of our film's final cut, we began the search for music. Rights for music was the same as it was photos and videos; ya can't just drop in your favorite song without paying for it. Recording artists receive royalties for their work, rightfully so, and since our intention was to get *Half the Road* into as many film festivals, theaters, DVD releases, television networks and international downloads… we needed the proper rights or we'd get sued. At the same time, we were not in a financial position to acquire rights for mainstream music. It wasn't uncommon for a hit song to carry a price tag of $30,000.[53]

On social media, I asked the universe if anyone had connections to singer/songwriters who might be willing to donate a song to *Half the Road*, and take a chance that our exposure could help their visibility. Sure enough, a recreational cyclist Stacey Legg, a Facebook friend whom I had never met in person, connected me with her brother. Dege Legg—"Brother Dege"—was an incredibly talented, unique, hard-drivin' rock/soul southern singer-songwriter in New Orleans who just got picked up by Quentin Tarantino for the soundtrack of *Django Unchained*. Dege generously sent us links to his albums and told us we could use whatever we like (except the *Django* song. That one was under Tarantino's rights). Thankful and thrilled, we used five soulful songs from Brother Dege, with "The Girl Who Wept Stones" opening our film. We were also given "All Summer Glory" from Casey Neill and the Norway Rats. Canadian popstar Marla Guloien, as generous as Brother Dege, allowed us to use her beautiful work.

I was getting a firsthand education in how important music is to any film. Sound makes us come alive. I knew this as a figure skater in my youth. When the songs

––––––––––––

[53] In 2003, the preface of my memoir *All the Sundays Yet to Come* began with a quote from Bruce Springsteen's *The Promised Land*. Because published books are a for-profit venture, I had to pay $100 for the quote. I was 27 years old, struggling to make my way to the ranks of pro triathlon and holding down three jobs as a middle school substitute teacher, figure skating coach and freelance writer. I'll never forget sitting on the floor of my one-bedroom, furniture-less rental, writing a check to Bruce Springsteen, hero of the working class. Still makes me smile. No matter how many millions he might have, paying a writer/artist for their work is the right thing to do.

came on, my body moved. Now, as a first-time filmmaker, when the picture came on with sound, my mind moved. In the memorial section of *Half the Road*, Marla's voice and message of "Gone Too Soon" soothed us as we watched the lives of our fallen sisterhood move across the screen in an homage to the women we deeply loved and missed. Even to this day, many years later, a lump in my throat arises when I watch this scene and hear Marla's song. It's a beautiful ache that will never go away.

We were still in search of one final recording to run during the closing credits when, driving through the streets of Tucson, I heard a beautiful song on the radio by a local artist, Cathy Rivers. "Come on, Come on, Girl" was perfect; an underlying message of encouragement for girls and women to keep striving. To forget being labeled, just be who you are. Come on, Girl. You got this. Desperately wanting a Tucson singer/songwriter in our film as a personal nod to the city I loved, I reached out to Cathy. She agreed to let us use her work. In the final minutes of our film, Cathy subtly reminded our audience there is always hope. That no woman should ever see herself as something she isn't, but all that she is.

Dege, Casey, Cathy, Marla.[54] Four artists who gave us their voices and their talent. Four people who answered the call of Asking. Four artists who believed a low-budget indie film on equality was something worthwhile.   Perhaps they didn't have the international acclaim of Pink, Beyonce, Taylor Swift or Bruce Springsteen, but to me they remain the greatest of all time. Our film was no longer something to just watch. Now it was something we could feel.

––––––––––

We were still $20,000 away from our crowdsourcing target when I began reaching out to the cycling industry for large-scale donations. There was a new clothing company on the rise; Rapha. Originally based in London, the high-end cycling clothes manufacturer now had a U.S. presence.

The price tags of their jerseys and shorts bordered on ridiculous. No female professional cyclist I knew was able to afford their $500 Lycra ensembles, but Rapha targeted the upper echelon of the retail market and they were doing very well. Perhaps they'd be interested in title sponsorship of *Half the Road*? Rapha asked for an advance screening of the film. We had them sign an NDA (non-disclosure

––––––––––

[54] Interactive Reader Guide: Songs in our film by Dege, Casey, Cathy & Marla.

agreement) and sent it off. A week later, their marketing department was extremely interested in sponsoring *Half the Road...* but on one condition.

"We'd like to be involved," Rapha said. "But we need you to make some edits."

"Sure," I responded, figuring they wanted to be listed in the credits.

"We need you to cut out all the footage of the Specialized brand, and edit in women wearing Rapha. And also, cut the section with Brian Cookson," Rapha said. "You're a little too hard on the UCI." Couldn't believe my ears. Cut out Specialized? No, they were the bike sponsor for countless women's teams. Specialized was in the background all over the film. *Too hard* on the UCI?!

"I don't understand," I countered. "Cookson speaks for himself. The history section of the UCI is fact-based. We're not being 'too hard' on anyone. We're presenting the truth." I told Rapha this was a perfect opportunity to show consumers that Rapha stands for change and supports equal opportunity for women. "You would be *more* than a sponsor... you'd be a game-changer, Rapha. A leader."

"Kathryn, this film's too edgy. Edgy isn't marketable. You'd have to make changes."

Politely thanking Rapha for their time, I declined deleting anything from our film. I then dove deeper to understand why Rapha specifically wanted us to edit Cookson and UCI. Rapha sponsored Team Sky, Great Britain's star-powered professional men's team. Brian Cookson's son—Oli Cookson—was an assistant director of Team Sky. Shaking my head and muttering to myself, I internally thanked Rapha for opening my eyes to reality of marketing: Truth and Edgy are not a combo deal for most companies. If truth and equality comes second to marketability and sales, that's a sponsorship we can do without. *Harumph*! I sulked, momentarily. I'd rather our budget come up $20,000 short than edit truth out of our film. This wasn't our final interaction with Rapha. They didn't fancy *Half the Road,* but sure did like some other stuff I made for women's equality... maybe too much. But we were still months away from Rapha pilfering our jersey design.

––––––––––

Unable to race with my Colavita-CookingLight team, I accompanied my husband to the Fire Road 100 mountain bike race in Cedar City, Utah. On a lark, I signed up for the 60km event. I didn't have any mountain bike experience but the Fire Road 100 was, well, more of a wide dirt road than a skills-are-necessary, singletrack trail. Strangely enough, I won. Stranger still, I won *overall.* I took the podium with two men flanking my left and right, none of us professional mountain bikers. For a tiny moment, I felt as though I'd won the world championships. Later that afternoon, as I soaked my tired legs in the motel swimming pool, I tried not to focus on my anticipation and anxiety for the other big event happening that day. We were hours away from our Indiegogo campaign closing, and just a few thousand dollars away from hitting our target. There was an exciting deal on the table. In the final few weeks, we were able to secure two large-scale donors who pledged to donate $10,000 each... *if* we hit $45,000 in individual donations. We were at $42,000 with three hours to go.

In the final throes of ticking time, I tweeted, posted and shared one last push for *Half the Road*. Sitting there in a parking lot motel pool in rural Utah, donations trickled in from 16 different countries. When we hit $44,300, something beautiful happened: full-circledness.

In 2006, while on my ESPN assignment, I had been invited to the USA track cycling development camp to see if I had any talent in the sport. Alas, I did not. Others at the camp did, and Kat Carroll was one. A powerful athlete with a kind and gentle soul, Kat was one of the first women I met in cycling. Because of her demeanor, I saw the world of bicycle racing as a sport filled with good people, strong women, motivated athletes... just the kind of tribe I wanted to be around. Mere hours before Indiegogo closed, Kat donated $1,500 to *Half the Road*, pushing us *over* our goal. We tipped the scales at $45,808. *101 percent of our goal!* Because of this, Jeff Lund and Kellogg International matched funds and we secured $65,808.

I reached out to Kat immediately, thanking her from the depths of my soul. This was a huge donation. For most female pro cyclists $1,500 is the equivalent to 20% of their salary. "It was the right thing to do," Kat said. "We need this film."

At the close of our crowdsourcing, *Half the Road* racked up 579 supporters from 16 different countries, with a combined grand total of $77,138 over both campaigns. I stared at the screen for quite some time. A year and a half ago, I'd never even heard of crowdsourcing. Because of it, now we were now able to create change. To make a difference. To fight for gender equity. To matter. In that private moment of Indiegogo glory, my shattered confidence grew a small spout of strength.

With fundraising complete, I breathed a deep sigh of relief. Not just for securing the budget, but for the respite of hanging up the extremely time-consuming role of fundraiser. Phew! I thought. That shit is exhausting. Now I can focus on the film's completion. Little did I know a new branch of activism was stemming from the tree of *Half the Road*.

24

BUILDING THE SISTERHOOD

A fter watching the trailer for *Half the Road*, Emma Pooley—Olympic silver medalist, World Champion and general badass—sent me an email.

"I want to start a campaign for a women's Tour de France to run alongside the men," she wrote. "Where do you think would be the best place for such a campaign? It has to be noticed by Prudhomme and McQuaid. What would be brilliant is if the groundswell of opinion were so huge they could not ignore it. I want to embarrass them into capitulation!"

My eyes grew large and my heart raced. Emma had no idea I submitted multiple business proposals, decks, PowerPoints and pestered ASO and ESPN for *years* about getting women into the Tour de France. She had no idea I was planning to reach out to her and to Marianne Vos to work together.

With thumbs a' flyin' across my phone screen, I answered back immediately, detailing the three major points we needed to launch such a plan. First, we'd need a detailed mission statement and proper website. After all, this isn't really about a bike race in France, but about equal opportunity and women's oppression. Second, we needed to rally the masses, probably through social media, but maybe there were other tools; I'd look into that and get back to her. Third, and most important, we needed to get in front of ASO in person. Social media and email might get things rolling, but if we wanted to see change, we would need to get in front of our oppressors.

Giving my thumbs and heart a quick rest, I paused, rereading my words. Throughout the email, I used "we" instead of "I." *Oh my gosh, I've only met Emma once, she's a superstar hero in women's cycling, and here I am jabbering on without even asking if she wants anything do to with me!*

"Emma, I'm sorry... please keep in mind, this doesn't have to be a "we" but I think I can help bring some cards to the table if we're partners in crime. You're the star, I'm the crew. I'm so excited you want to take initiative and create change at the Tour de France. And I'm so happy you like Half the Road's trailer. A lot of my non-cycling friends comment that their favorite part is when 'that British lady calls out that UCI guy and tells him to do his job.' The world adores you, Emma. You have the gift of impact, and I applaud your courage to use it. Not many people take chances with opinion and activism, but when they do, change happens--for the better. Ok, that's a really, really basic outline of how we can start. (My thumbs are falling off!) If you'll have me as a partner, I'm in."
Let's do this!
Kathryn

As I waited for Emma to reply, I dove into the vast interwebs researching the best way we could possibly make an impact and enlist the public to help us fight for the Tour de France. Maybe a petition or something? I googled *petition*. Lo and behold, there was Change.org.

Founded in 2007, Change.org quietly rolled into the world as a way for people to lobby for change by online petitioning. By 2012, the company had offices on four continents, 100 employees, ten million members and received 500 new petitions daily. Anyone could join and set up a cyber-petition to share with the world. For free! The goal of Change.org, according to founder and CEO Ben Rattray, was to "change the balance of power between individuals and large organizations." Through online petitioning, regular people can expose injustices and fight for change. Using the metaphor of David and Goliath, Change.org was the modern slingshot.

Surfing through the successful petitions of 2012, the most efficacious ones had thousands of signatures. A few even had *one hundred* thousand signatures! Environmental platforms, legal reform, social injustice... from eco-conscious fourth-graders petitioning Universal Studios to local communities pulling together to stop the deportation of senior citizens, the success stories were inspiring. They also seemed quite a feat to pull off. Not everyone likes creating user profiles to sign something on the internet. But who knows? Maybe if a petition really resonated, people would be willing to do so. What an incredible platform. I couldn't wait to tell Emma.

That is, if she wanted to work with me at all. While I felt the undercurrent of support from my fellow riders affiliated with *Half the Road*, many were still reluctant to speak their minds publicly. Emma wasn't afraid to speak her mind on camera a few months ago, but she was still under contract with Lotto Belisol Pro Cycling. Would she really want to risk losing her contract by connecting with a rabble-rouser? When her next email arrived, I braced for an expected response of *No thanks, Kathryn. Best if I steer clear of Edgy.* Instead, I got:

"We need to get this Tour de France project started now so it succeeds in time for us both to still be young enough to take part ;-)". Emma was *in.*

Brainstorming on petition tactics, we knew people would need information on *why* there was no Tour de France for women. The more data we could present to potential petition signers, the better. We needed to show it wasn't just ASO holding back women, but there were other culprits in cycling's gender discrimination, too. Two of them were Tour of California and Tour of Utah. Weeklong events for men, with one-day tokenism events for women. Both run by the same race promoters, Medalist Sports. While at work on the first draft of our Tour de France petition, I got a call from *Half the Road* interviewee Nicky Wangsgard, our favorite pro-cyclist-college-professor in Utah.

"Kathryn, the Tour of Utah wants me to help promote their UCI men's race. They want me to go to elementary schools and get kids interested in bike racing. But these kids are going to ask when I'm racing, and I'll have to tell them women aren't allowed," Nicky said. "No way. I'm not doing that."

"Yeah, don't," I agreed. "Let's expose Tour of Utah, instead."[55] I called the race's management company, Medalist Sports, and asked why there wasn't a women's field at Tour of Utah.

"Our clients basically watch races like the Tour de France then call us and say, 'I want that,' manager Chris Aronhalt said. "It's just what the sponsors see. Or in this case, what they don't see."

I asked Aronhalt why he doesn't inform his prospective clients there *is* a professional women's field and adding it *is* marketable. Especially when consumerism stats in 2013 showed 74.9 percent of all household budgets are controlled by women. "Adding a women's field could attract more sponsors and provide a larger return of investment," I countered.

---

[55] Interactive Reader Guide: Inequity at Tour of Utah

"Women's racing *could* be an asset, a true opportunity for investors to get in at the ground level. I think it's nuts not to include a women's demographic," he said. Then added, "But it's not our decision."

Beg to differ. A decision to leave out vital information *is* indeed a decision. Medalist Sports failed to see how race promoters could actually double their return of investment by selling sponsorship and media rights to women's races in addition to the men's. Were they blind to such investment opportunities? Were they just plain lazy? Then, I looked closer. Medalist Sports also put on Tour of California, which was owned by ASO. Who, as we already knew, had zero interest in equality. Go figure. Medalist Sports was merely a complacent rung in the ladder of traditionalism. Hmmm. Maybe USA Cycling could help. As our national governing body of cycling, surely they could do something proactive.

I asked USA Cycling director of communications, Bill Kellick, if they would mandate equal opportunity in U.S. races. If USAC took a stance that all top-tier pro races include a men's and women's field, they could vault the archaic sport out of the Dark Ages.

"To mandate equality as a condition to placing privately owned, operated and funded events on the USAC calendar is fiscally irresponsible and unrealistic," Kellick believed. Apparently dinosaurs are not extinct. Inequity in pro cycling always appeared to be someone else's fault or deemed unsolvable. The chicken-and-egg conundrum morphed to a five-point star. We explored the concept of chicken-and-egg cycles in *Half the Road* and renamed it The Pentagram of Blame.

Here's what it looked like:

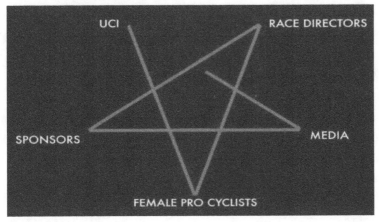

In the upper left-hand corner sits the governing body of cycling, the UCI. Since the very top of the sport doesn't value women equally, they get the ball rolling by not offering women the same distances, base salaries, age medians, etc. and decreeing, *Women are simply not capable of racing the same events as the men*, thus shifting the blame of inequity directly to the women. Female Pro Cyclists react: *Let us into the events so we can prove the UCI wrong!*, launching the trajectory over to the race directors. But directors like Medalist Sports, who can't see women as a viable way to double their ROI, then lament, *We just don't have the sponsorship dollars to add a women's field*, hurling the blame over to prospective sponsors. Most of whom are not aware there is a women's pro cycling field, claiming, *Wait, women race bikes too?! How come we don't see them in the media?* lobbing the blame over to multimedia. Media then rightfully slams the ball back to the UCI. *How can we show the women if they are not allowed to race the same events as the men, you big dummies!?* Exactly. To break the cycle of inequity, change must come from the top down.

Unfortunately, history had already shown us what the top thought of women's cycling. Because ASO discontinued the Tour de France Feminin, and *barred* the women from using the name "Tour de France" after 1989, UCI took up the torch, clinging to the erroneous belief "the money isn't there" for women's racing. Not true. When UCI *values* women equally, the money will come. The Top has the power to create value.

How could we make UCI see potential in women's cycling? Exposure, exposure, exposure. Also, benevolent shaming. Rather than use insults and anger, change happens faster and more effectively when we highlight inequity and injustice in a manner that makes the perpetrator feel ashamed... but also informed. Here's an example.

Bad shaming: "You totally suck, UCI." Benevolent shaming: "There are 370 UCI races for men, and 77 for women. This is unacceptable, unprogressive and sexist. Shame on you, UCI. What is your solution?"

When done correctly, benevolent shaming opens windows instead of slamming doors. Just might even change some antiquated UCI rules in the process, though we were still a few months away from knowing that yet.

———

June 2013 became a blur of drafts. Emma and I mapped out the basics of launching our petition for the inclusion of professional women's teams at the Tour de France. Timing was paramount. We would launch the petition during the second week of the men's Tour de France… when all eyes of sports fans and media are focused on the Tour. Statistics pointed to a lull in televised viewership during the second week of racing, after the excitement of the first week faded and before the epic mountain stages began. The media would be hungry for something new. A perfect time to pull the activism rip cord.

We were in total agreement on one key aspect of the petition: Calling for a 21-day Tour de France. Just like the men. No partial days. No tokenism. The only way this petition—and our mission—would work was to shoot for equal opportunity. Equality is like pregnancy. Can't be a little bit equal. It's either equal or it isn't.[56]

"Should we petition UCI as well?" Emma asked.

"Best to focus on one right now," I offered. The panacea effect of trying to fix too many broken parts with one bandage is a noble gesture, but won't get the job done right. As corrupt, sexist and outdated as UCI was, especially with President "Jim Burns" McQuaid at the helm, that was a whole other petition of change.

Right. Yes. The petition must target ASO directly. But behind the scenes, we still had to keep the pressure on UCI, as their outdated rules kept women's races at a 10-day maximum. (No max for men's races). Pressure matters. Constant pressure is the only way to staunch the bleeding of corruption. We also saw a window of opportunity… ASO and UCI didn't like one another. There was a long-standing Hatfield-and-McCoy-style rivalry between the two, dating back generations between the Amaury family and UCI. From pro tour calendars to media rights, the companies competed with one another rather than work together. The power struggle feud ran deep.

"If ASO agreed to put on a race, but the UCI blocked it with some stupid day-limit or age-median rule, the publicity for the UCI would be so disastrous they would have to back down," Emma said. "Women would race it no matter what." We also agreed we'd leave the topic of equal prize money out of the petition. First we had to secure a race, *then* we could tackle the issue of prize money.

"Besides, I don't really care about prize money or how shitty our conditions are," Emma said. "In some ways, our side of the sport is tougher, and being poorly

---

[56] Emma makes an excellent point in *Half the Road* that shorter races are far more exciting to watch, and a 3-hour women's stage is much more interesting than a 6-hour men's stage. She makes a wonderful suggestion for equity; Instead of elongating the women's races, let's shorten the men's races. Agreed! However, the argument for race distances was second to the big picture. First, we had to get into the race.

paid right now gives us a better image. It's like the way gritty, real cycling used to be… not like these overpaid, spoiled princesses of the men's peloton!"

My heart was full with platonic love and laughter. *Zing! Tell us how you really feel, Emma.* We were surrounded by a peloton of women who were too afraid to speak out because they feared being dropped from a team, but Emma was brave enough to do it. I was doing it. Didn't have the champion titles she did, but maybe others would come forward once they saw the likes of Emma speaking her mind. Hmmmm. Maybe we could add a few more pro athletes to our petition initiative.

"Emma, I'd like to reach out to Marianne Vos and bring her in. What do you think?" I asked. As the current Olympic gold medalist and reigning world champion, Marianne's voice and support might tip the balance in our favor. After interviewing her for *Half the Road*, she spoke on camera about wanting to race Tour de France, too.

"Absolutely," Emma said. "I was going to suggest the same thing."

———————————

Humbly reaching out to Marianne, I explained the Tour de France petition Emma and I planned to launch in the next few days, and would she possibly consider joining forces and coming on board. Her team was racing Giro d'Italia that week, and I figured chances were slim Marianne was even checking email while in race mode. She responded the next day with a heartfelt email of support. "Of course! I really think it's time for a women's Tour de France and I hope we can put some pressure on ASO," Marianne wrote. "It's great that you keep fighting for equality." Receiving a hell yes and supportive words from someone I greatly admired was (is) a true gift. Especially while struggling with my self-confidence… Wynona hadn't raced me since Sea Otter. Marianne's kind words and alliance helped diffuse the pain of being cast aside by Colavita.

Ok. Marianne was in. Emma was in. Two superstars with a combined total of six Olympic and World Championship medals, and one weird "no one" racing for St. Kitts and Nevis currently benched by her pro team. We were a three-person team. Then came a wonderful surprise to complete our quartet.

Later that day, I received an email with a photo. Chrissie Wellington, on a mountainside road in the Alps, getting ready to watch the men's Tour roll by. *What are you up to?* Chrissie asked.

"I'm working on a petition with Emma and Marianne. We're going to pressure ASO to let the pro women ra—"

"Can I be involved?" Chrissie asked, immediately. My eyes fell out of my head.

"Chrissie, you can be involved in anything I do, ever!" I typed frantically. I told her the whole plan; demand for parity at Le Tour, lobby for an in-person meeting with ASO, and work with them to create the race. The right way.

"I am 100 percent behind this – YES! Count me well and truly IN, girl!!!!" Chrissie responded with enough exclamation points to match her world championship titles. "Let's DO THIS!!!!" Four exclamation points and four strong-willed women was the perfect number.

Finalizing our petition, we knew it must be well-written, firm, concise and professional. If we did it right, the resounding sentiment of *Hey ASO, you're being a sexist dumbass* would silently scream between the lines. We also knew timing was critical. This wasn't some vague plea for change someday in the future. It was 2013 and we wanted change now. In time for the 2014 Tour de France, on its 101st birthday. New century, new rules: Allow the women to race.

Emma sharpened her points on the need for equal opportunity, I threw in some historic facts and Chrissie brought in the reference of marathon, reminding ASO how the 1960s believed women couldn't physically run such a distance and now 50 years later, how absurdly erroneous that idea was.

"Hopefully, 30 years from now we will see 2014 as the year that opened people's eyes to true equality in the sport of cycling," Chrissie rationalized. "Also, perhaps it is worth adding that Tour de France isn't just about elite athletes. It's about opportunities for women—people's wives, girlfriends, sisters and daughters—to take part in sport and in cycling. It is about encouraging grassroots action from the top down, and demonstrating that barriers are often human constructs that can be broken." Right on, Chrissie.

"We need to title this petition very clearly," Emma insisted. "We need people to question why there is no Women's Tour de France."

"Let's call it 'WTF is there no WTdF?'" I joked. No one agreed, but for a brief moment, we laughed. The salve of giddiness is a most necessary ingredient for activists. Sometimes the tiniest laugh can lift the colossal weight of oppression. Even if only for a moment. *Why the fuck is there no women's Tour de France?* would be well-articulated between the lines, but we officially titled our Change.org petition: *Amaury Sports Organization (ASO): Allow female professional cycling teams to race the Tour de France.*

Keeping the petition simple, clear and concise, we started in on the second step of our mission for change. A petition wasn't enough. We needed a manifesto and a website. A place where all supporters, naysayers and media could find their questions answered in detail. *Why does a Tour de France for women matter? What's the best way? Can it be done?* Pointing them to a website filled with answers was the only way to go. We also needed a name for our pressure group of activism and our website. Emma, bilingual in French, had a brilliant idea.

"How about *Le Tour Entier?*" Emma suggested. "It's French for 'The Whole Tour' and if we're targeting ASO, it makes sense to put it in their language." We all agreed Le Tour Entier was solid, and had a much more professional ring than *ASO are Dinosaurs*. From that moment on, Emma, Marianne, Chrissie and I became Le Tour Entier.

25

SPACEDUST SENDOFF

O n July 10 we finalized our Change.org petition to ASO.[57] It read:

For 100 years, the Tour de France has been the pinnacle endurance sports event of the world, watched by and inspiring millions of people. And for 100 years, it has been an exclusively male race (there was a separate Tour Feminin in the 1980s, but it lacked parity, media coverage, and sponsorship). After a century, it is about time women are allowed to race the Tour de France, too. While many women's sports face battles of inequity, road cycling remains one of the worst offenders: fewer race opportunities, no televised coverage, shorter distances, and therefore salary and prize money inequity. We seek not to race against the men, but to have our own professional field running in conjunction with the men's event, at the same time, over the same distances, on the same days, with modifications in start/finish times so neither the men's nor women's race interferes with the other.

The women's road race at the London Olympics was a showcase for how impressive, exciting, and entertaining women's cycling can be. The Tour of Flanders and Flèche Wallonne hold similar top ranked men's and women's races on the same day, with great success. Having a women's pro field at the Tour de France will also create an equal opportunity to debunk the myths of physical "limitations" placed upon female athletes. In the late 1960s people assumed that women couldn't run the marathon. 50 years on we can look back and see how erroneous this was. Hopefully 50 years from now, we will see 2014 as the year that opened people's eyes to true equality in the sport of cycling.

If you'd like to see more women's road racing on television and from the roadside, please sign this petition to call for road cycling to take a major step in the right direction. Help us break down the barriers that unjustly keep female athletes from the same opportunities as men.

Please sign this petition to show you agree that:

---

[57] Interactive Reader Guide: Our official ASO petition online

-- Women should have the opportunity to compete at the same cycling events as men.
-- Women should be on the starting line of the 101st Tour de France in 2014.

Thank you for your support,
Emma Pooley, GBR Olympian & World Champion Cyclist
Kathryn Bertine, SKN National Champion Cyclist & Filmmaker
Marianne Vos, NED World & Olympic Champion Cyclist
Chrissie Wellington, GBR World Ironman Triathlon Champion

Done. Dusted. Ready to launch. Uploading the petition to my Change.org account on July 11, 2013, that palpable twinge returned as I hovered over the *Send* key. Four years passed since the first email I sent ASO asking for women's inclusion. Four years of silence. Four years on a solo mission. Now, four years smarter. What started as one goal from one person was now four women strong and far more powerful. I understood the vital role of space dust, superstars, bus driving and organizational glue. I loved my sticky, sticky role.

Just before clicking *send,* I noticed a tiny box in the upper right corner of the Change.org screen. There was a tab asking if I wanted the recipient of our petition—Mr. Christian Prudhomme, Race Director of Tour de France—to receive an email every time someone signs the petition. *Oooooooh*!

Stifling a giggle, I fell in love with the visual image of Prudhomme sitting at his big fancy desk in Paris; email inbox ping, ping, pinging away as signatures rolled in. I envisioned him hunched in exasperation, muttering Francophile curses, gesticulating passionately toward his laptop aflood with the deluge of activism and the chimes of progress... *Hell yes*, I checked the box. Mr. Prudhomme was officially set to receive an email notification of every person who wanted to see women race the Tour de France. *Wouldn't that be awesome if we get a hundred signatures? Or maybe even one thousand?* I thought to myself, sharing the news with Le Tour Entier.

"I don't know," Chrissie warned. "That might *really* annoy him."

"I sure hope so," I smiled. Progress is a bitch. I brought my finger down on *send* and launched our petition into the weird, wild, unpredictable world of cyberspace. Then I made myself a snack and went out for a ride. Utterly clueless of the journey about to unfold.

Now more than ever, cycling offered me balance. Workouts were for training, but riding was for steadiness. The sweet equilibrium of physical exertion and rhythmic repetition soothed the frenetic pace of Everything. My plate was filled with Everything in July 2013; final film edits with Kevin, allocating funds to hire remote cameramen, shooting footage of things we forgot, purchasing rights to photos, researching festivals, distributors, promoters, publicity… the work was as daunting as it was exhilarating. Now here I was, throwing another log onto the activism fire with the petition to ASO. We were about to go head to head with the establishment of the Tour de France. I was equal parts alive and terrified. Two things brought me inner peace: my bicycle and my husband.

George was my rock, my confidant, my balance point. The partner with whom I could talk to about it all. During the mornings, I rode. During the afternoons, I thrashed about the keyboards, channeling all my energy into emails, edits, interviews and social media so maybe someday women would rise and prevail. Every evening, I cooked dinner for my husband—and I loved every minute of it, especially the comedic irony of striving for equity during the day and cooking dinner for my man every night. I was certainly not a talented chef, but being in the kitchen was enjoyable. Cooking and pedaling shared a similar vibe of rhythm and peace. Sitting together, discussing our day, confiding in one another our hopes and dreams. My husband gave me the equilibrium I needed to persevere. Every activist needs someone who will let them share, vent, confide, crumble, rise, laugh, weep and be their authentic self. George steadied me. The mast to my sails of balance. I truly needed him. Especially when the winds were about to pick up.

Two hours after launching the petition, I returned from my ride and logged into Change.org hoping perhaps a few dozen signatures might've accumulated. My eyes, heart and breath leapt out of my body in one collective surge when I looked at the screen. Five *thousand* people had signed the petition. *In the first two hours!* Within 24 hours, 10,000 signatures. Two days later; 20,000. That's when the first phone call came in from BBC requesting an interview. Europe was paying attention.

"The Dutch media is going crazy!" Marianne wrote, from the Netherlands. "This is the right time for change, that's clear." France, Great Britain, North America, Australia, more and more news affiliates—CNN, NBC, LA Times, BBC—were picking up the petition and running with it. I was dumbfounded, ecstatic, wild and wide-eyed. *It's happening.*

Also happening: An influx of trolls, doubters and haters. Overnight, my List of Names grew exponentially. *Assertive, Aggressive, Bitch, Unrealistic, Stupid.* While

I had the ability to let go the negative words, that didn't mean they disappeared. There is definitely something weirdly universal about being human when, if we're called 100 names—99 of which are positive—we still cling to that one derogatory, hurtful comment. I now understand that's just Vulnerability tapping us on the shoulder, reminding us we're human and it's okay to feel a little hurt. Acknowledging the sting is as important as moving forward. Whenever possible, I tried to find humor in every insult. There wasn't always humor. But sometimes there was. I was once called *hero, fearless* and *cunt* all in the same day. (Still happens today). I call this being Meat Loafed.[58] "*Don't be sad / Two outta three ain't bad…*"

"Remember," I advised Chrissie, Marianne and Emma, "When the Doubters, Ignoramuses and Naysayers come at you, be prepared. Don't respond to the haters. But if you must, use humor. Avoid sarcasm. And whenever possible, use the word "we" instead of "I" as it speaks for the whole movement of women's cycling. And if the media asks what's next, tell them we are planning to organize a meeting with ASO this fall/winter to further discuss the motion. (If I have any film budget left over, I'll use it to make sure the four of us are there.) Ladies, thanks for lending your star power to this movement. This is how change happens."

Sure enough, the petition spread like wildfire. After only a week and a half, we had over 50,000 signatures. We were averaging 5,000 signatures a day. Launching the petition during the Tour de France, when all eyes were on cycling, was the right decision. Not to mention, in 2013 Change.org petitions took a little bit more effort to sign. Wasn't as one-click-easy as it is now. People were still signing on and supporting us; an equal split of men and women around the globe.

It was also time to freak out. The petition gained so much traction Change.org got involved directly. Pulin Modi, an extremely kind and patient senior advisor at Change.org, reached out by phone.

"Kathryn, we'd like to translate the petition into multiple languages," Pulin said, "And we'd like to have the contact info for Chrissie, Emma and Marianne. Europe is going nuts for this petition, and we want to be able to put the press in touch with them. Ok?"

Yes, yes, ok indeed! Pulin connected me with three assistants in three different countries. While I was all for growth of the petition, a strange feeling bubbled to the surface. I couldn't quite put my finger on it immediately. Plumbing the depths of

---

[58] This is probably only funny to Gen Xers and/or those who had older siblings who educated us on the wonderfully ridiculous yet iconic songs and lyrics of the one and only Meat Loaf. Other generations may educate themselves here. Interactive Reader Guide: Meat Loaf.

my psyche, I fished around for whatever discord was clogging my thoughts. Found it! The fear of being left behind. Left out. Dismissed. Irrelevant.

Two days into the petition, the majority of news sites cited, "A group of cyclists including World Champions Emma Pooley, Marianne Vos and Ironman Champion Chrissie Wellington..." where I wasn't even mentioned. My ego was very, very okay with Chrissie and Emma and Marianne getting loads of attention and speaking on behalf of our petition. That gave me great joy. I loved being the space dust bus driver to my superstar friends. But I desperately wanted people to see that we non-famous, non-world champ, non-Olympian folks can effect change, too. That all our voices must be used and heard. That *being* greatness and *creating* greatness are two different things, and we're all capable of the latter. That we "no ones" matter just as much. If my name were added but no one knew who I was, that would actually be a good thing.

Between Wynona writing me off, the scars of ESPN dismissing *Half the Road* and my mind wandering over the cliffs of being left behind by my own activism group was quite a trilogy of Vulnerability. My Cerberus had a field day with the news articles that left my name out. *Maybe I really was a no one*, I sulked. *Shut the fuck up*, I countered. Alas, my adult maturity, my inner child and my weird Cerberus were all very much alive and well.

Luckily, there was way too much happening to pay too much attention to Cerberus Sensitivitus that July. Focus, focus, focus. Forget that mumbo jumbo vulnerability stuff... we've got 65,000 signatures (and counting!) on the petition and now ASO is finally starting to take notice. The press was doing a stellar job, using our petition as leverage to seek a response from race director Christian Prudhomme. On July 16, 2013, reporters approached Prudhomme in Vaison-la-Romaine, as he lingered near his car at the start of the 16th stage of the Tour de France. Swatting the air dismissively with the back of his hand, he brushed off the question:

"We are saying nothing for the moment," Prudhomme told the Associated Press, then walked away.[59]

With a cat in my lap and a cup of tea in hand, I beamed with pride reading this article from my home office in Tucson. Half a world away in France, the race director who ignored my emails over the last four years was now listening... and receiving a few thousand extra emails every day. Just as Chrissie predicted,

---

[59] Interactive Reader Guide: "Tour de France director has nothing to say about women's petition"

Prudhomme *was* annoyed! I was overjoyed. We stirred the pot, and it was simmering gloriously. Soon, we would act on following up with ASO to request a meeting date. But not yet. The petition was gaining full steam, so we watched and waited, relishing in the articles, interviews, tweets and posts from those who spoke out in support.

––––––––––

"You're becoming a national hero," John Profaci of Colavita said, with kindness and pride. My heart soared and ached. Profaci had no idea of Wynona's utter dislike of me. Nor that she raced me just once in the past seven months. For months, I pondered whether and/or when to tell him. *Immediately*, my heart said. *August*, my brain overruled. With the petition and media attention swirling throughout July, the most-often-used photo the press used featured me wearing the Colavita brand. If I rocked the Colavita boat, I feared getting fired and losing my voice as a pro cyclist. Profaci appeared to have my back, but if he didn't, that would be the end of my pro cycling career. I decided to wait until after the petition hubbub died down. In the meantime, I kept a notebook of all Wynona's emails, comments and antics.

I also kept quiet about the deep ache in my chest when reporters asked which race I was heading to next. *Not sure, I'll keep you posted!* I chirped from beneath my smiling mask of self-preservation. That summer, I was unable to notice (or at least acknowledge) the deepening pain of worthlessness. Better to focus on the progressive stuff happening now. Things were developing every day. Or in some cases, regressing. Oh, Cookson.

Less than five days after the petition went live, Brian Cookson announced his candidacy for UCI president. He was looking to displace Pat McQuaid in September. *Ooooof*, I thought to myself. With *Half the Road* still in production, no one had yet seen the interview footage where Cookson deems women less capable than men. When Cyclingnews.com asked for Cookson's reaction to our petition, he answered in kind.

"I have to say I think that's unrealistic," Cookson said. "I would like to see a women's Tour de France but I think it needs to be over modified distances, modified number of days and so on."

"You know," Emma said, "this doesn't surprise me at all. Cookson was on the 1997 committee when ASO banned the use of the name "Le Tour de France" to be used by the women." Unbelievable. *Of course he was.* During the summer of 2013, my eyeballs were constantly fighting over whether to pop out of my skull entirely or just continually roll upward. Cookson reached out to Emma directly. Clearly unnerved by the public response to the petition and receiving criticism for not supporting it, Cookson was nervous. The UCI election two months away. He raised the following concerns with Emma regarding the Tour de France. Unrealistic, impractical, lack of hotel rooms, quality of the women's field is too slow, the Easter Bunny is real, oh look there's a leprechaun … blah, blah, blah. Words, words, words. Traditionalism at its finest. What we're taught to believe is a fascinating science. *Buckle up, Cookson*, I muttered under my breath.

In all fairness, Cookson wasn't the only one out there with views on women's physical inferiority. There were still far too many Dinosaur Boyz who shared Brian Cookson's belief that women's racing was too slow. The depth and talent didn't compare to the men. As a racer, I knew this wasn't true. Perhaps data could help. Were there any graphs or data that proved women's cycling is just as powerful as the men's side of the sport, in their own right? I floated this question to the universe and the internet galaxy kindly sent me Thorsten Radde.

A German statistician, Thorsten analyzed data from speed, finishing times, peloton depth and performance of endurance events like triathlon, marathon and cycling. He does with data what Stephen Hawking did with physics, breaking it down for mere mortals to understand. When I asked him if we could prove the women's pro peloton was on par with the capabilities of the men's pro peloton, he agreed to analyze the results of seven major races where the men and women competed separately but over similar courses: Tour of Flanders, Tour of California Time Trial, Tour of the Gila, Tour de France, Giro d'Italia, Philadelphia Classic, World Championships.

The results were in.[60] The difference in speed averaged out to approximately 3 miles per hour. No human eyeball can see a discernable change in the speed of a bicycle going 30mph verses 33mph (any Dino Boyz who say they can are lying). The same is true in running. The fastest female pace is 5:06 minute mile. The fastest male pace is 4:38.[61] This 28 second difference results in 13 minutes over 26 miles. But 13 minutes over the course of two hours is not visibly noticeable to sports fans. Slower? Yes. Slow? No. The women's race is no less exciting than the men's. Thorsten's data was important. Now we had something tangible we could share with

---

[60] Interactive Reader Guide: Thorsten Radde's Stats & Charts on Depth of Field in Women's Cycling
[61] Brigid Kosgei and Eliud Kipchoge of Kenya, respectively.

the doubters and dinosaurs. The women's field has the same *depth* and *talent* as the men's field. Investing equally in women will lift the entire sport to a better socioeconomic level. For men *and* women.

26

THE WORLD RESPONDS (EXCEPT ASO)

On July 27, 2013 with the petition at 70,000 signatures strong, Christian Prudhomme surfaced again in the media, telling the UK Telegraph that he cannot possibly see how a women's Tour de France could be held in parallel conjunction with the men's race.

"Having women's races is very important for sure," Prudhomme said. "But the Tour is huge and you cannot have it bigger and bigger and bigger down the road. It is impossible." Ah, the irony… that women are important, but there's no room for them at the biggest event in the world. Which is outside. On open roads. Mostly in the countryside. He then went on to lament our petition, hinting at the fact we've blown up his inbox. *Ping, ping, ping!* "It would have been much easier to talk to us directly," Prudhomme continued, "instead of a petition and [finding out by] opening your mailbox one morning and you don't know what has happened." I couldn't stop smiling. *I did reach out directly, buddy. For four flippin' years. Maybe if you responded in 2009, you'd have a much tidier inbox today.*

As the first few weeks of the petition rolled by, the four of us—Emma, Chrissie, Marianne and I—were riding the wave of momentum and possibility. We emailed back and forth continuously, sending links to articles and interviews and comments from social media. The comments rolling in on Change.org were incredible. The world was responding. Men and women equally.

"If this sport is to grow and gain a wider audience there must be more inclusion!" —Jimmy Davis, Jr. USA

"As a participant at the 2013 Junior Road World Championships, I know firsthand how unbalanced the race distances and media coverage are for women. This is especially true for junior women. How will we ever get promising young women into cycling if the junior fields are laughable, no U23 category exists, and the professional prospects are negligible?" —Kelly Catlin, USA.[62]

"I'm so tired of women having to fight for their rights over and over and over." —Emma Pearson, UK.

"It's about time this shovenism stopped." —Anonymous, France.
(I immediately fall in love with the typo. Shove-nism is exactly how it feels.)

"Never truly registered, until seeing this petition, that the Tour de France was exclusively male. This is a ridiculous state of affairs, and should be brought to an end." —Dignum

"Freedom from gender stereotypes brings freedom for men as well." —Johnathan M., Germany

"What an amazing idea Le Tour Entier is. A women's Tour De France would be a true sporting spectacle. Before 1984 there was no women's marathon in the Olympic Games. Look at how things have changed and women's marathoning has moved on. Chrissie Wellington breaking in long distance triathlon and Paula Radcliffe in marathon and many other women in many different disciplines across the globe have repeatedly shown that women *are* endurance. I look forward to seeing my endurance cycling colleagues from around the world take on biggest cycling stage race in the world. This will help to further break down the gender barrier that exists in sport at all levels, it will promote great female role models for generations to come, and inspire a local, national and international women and girls to be active, achieve more and succeed more. Good luck, Le Tour Entier."
—Liz Yelling, Great Britain, Olympic Marathon

"Kathryn, the company you keep is like a real-life Justice League. Between the athletic talents, social fortitude and brilliant tactics of collaboration... Superwomen. And, to add to the analogy, you all just happen to wear spandex anyway." —April Whitworth, USA

"We shouldn't even need this petition." —Jeff G., USA

Right on, Jeff. Agreed. For all the supporters, so too came the Doubters, firing off their weak missiles of Can'ts, Won'ts, Too's and No's. *Women and men can't race on the same course, it wouldn't work! Too hard. Too far. Too long. No sponsors. No audience. No support. No hotel rooms. No no no.* With the petition closing in on 80,000 yeses, we fired back with knowledge, grace and humor. While

---

[62] Kelly was 17 years old when she signed our petition. Her words were as wise as her talent ran deep. I will speak of her again in this journey.

my reactionary impulse wanted to hurl insults, we knew arguing with ignorance and trolls was a waste of time. Education was better.

We reminded Naysayers that the very first Tour de France started in 1913 as a publicity stunt to save a dying newspaper called *l'Equipe.* Back then, no one even believed *men* could ride hundreds of miles. Impossible, the Doubters claimed. A hundred years later, here we were again—same argument, different gender. We laughed that we were simply upholding the tradition of doubt.

We laughed even more about this hilarious excuse: "There just aren't enough hotel rooms for a women's Tour de France." Still makes me giggle. Not a day passed by in Tour de France TV coverage where famed commentators Phil Liggett and Paul Sherwen didn't comment on the giant, empty castles throughout the French countryside. *Look at that splendid castle from 1756! What a magnificent estate.* Empty castles, empty fields. Everywhere. While the professional men at the World Tour level were used to 5-star hotels and catered meals, every female pro cyclist on the planet would happily make do with an empty castle, sleeping bag and camp stove for the chance to race the Tour de France. Besides, the women who raced in the mid 1980s made it happen. This no-room-at-the-inn baloney was just an empty excuse of a visionless Prudhomme.

Still, no response from ASO in regard to our request to set up a meeting. We issued a statement through Change.org in regard to ASO's "we are saying nothing for the moment" stance:

> "We are not worried about the critics, we won't be silenced by the push back. We are not surprised by Prudhomme's dismissal of our petition. It merely exemplifies our need to push forward and seek change. We look forward to meeting with ASO and to work toward a Tour de France based upon a model of equality. We will not stop until sexism and discrimination in cycling are solved."[63] -Le Tour Entier.

Weathering the impending storm, we gained strength from our petition signers. We knew everyone in the sisterhood of pro cycling had our back. Or so we thought.

---

[63] As the petition gained steam, debates stirred among the masses. Many asked, "Why don't the women just start their own Tour de France?" and "Why don't the women cede from the UCI?" Great questions. With long answers. Interactive Reader Guide: Why Ceding from ASO and UCI isn't the Answer.

At the end of July, CNN and The Daily Mail ran terrific pieces on the progress of the petition, with ample quotes from Emma Pooley on why equal inclusion matters. They also spoke to Laura Trott, Great Britain's two-time Olympic gold medalist in track cycling. Trott began by saying she believed women should race the Tour de France. But then added this:

> "Having [the women's race] run over the same distance as the men won't work," Trott said. "Only 20 girls will finish and I don't believe it will be as exciting. There aren't enough riders with top ability... The petition should change its plans. It hasn't been thought through very well," Trott decided.

Emma and I were dumbfounded. So too were Chrissie and Marianne. While I was no stranger to the Tanyas and Wynonas of Sisterblocking and She-rannosaurus Wrexes, Trott was our first experience with doubt and pushback coming from *within* our very own tribe of women's pro cycling. Worse, she was an Olympic champion. A role model. For her to articulate that women had neither the ability nor the excitement of the men's race factor felt like a gut punch. (Steeped in ignorance, too. She was a track cyclist, not a roadie. [64]) Yet another teaching moment in the life of activism: No matter how much we want to believe everyone is on board when it comes to equal opportunity, not everyone is. Opinions differ, traditionalism reigns and ignorance plays a major factor.

"It upsets me and makes me angry," Emma vented. "Even if there are female pro riders out there who don't think they'd survive a Tour de France, they should want to *aspire* to it! There are lots of young girls, and parents of young cyclists, signing the petition because they still have aspiration. Some of these current stars with egos… maybe they're scared that a big women's race like Tour de France might trump them."

Trott later commented on Twitter that she would not want to ever race a Tour de France for women. *Oh yeah? Well, I have zero interest in sprinting circles indoors but I'm not gonna burn down your velodrome, sister.*

I couldn't help but wonder if Trott would make those comments at age 40. My own personal awareness of, well, everything was vastly underdeveloped in my early twenties. Masters degree, yes. PhD in real world life experience, no. Zero. Zip.

---

[64] For scope of reference, a track cyclist saying they don't want to race a Tour de France is akin to Usain Bolt saying he doesn't want to run a marathon. Fair enough. But for one athlete to shoot down the event of another athlete? Unacceptable.

Zilch. Not a lick of Life Knowledge at 22. Not yet. Maybe Trott would change her tune in the future, but it sure wasn't gonna happen in 2013.

In addition to Trott, Olympic Gold Medalist and British Champion Nicole Cooke turned down Chrissie's request for a statement of support on our petition. Cooke, who twice won the Tour Feminin—a 14-day stage race which was the closest thing women had to the Tour de France without being able to use the name "Tour de France"—was quite annoyed with Le Tour Entier. Cooke felt our lobbying for the inclusion of women at the Tour de France undermined her accomplishments at Tour Feminin.

"I am pleased to have won it twice," she wrote to Chrissie. "I have attached a picture of myself riding alone in Yellow[65] at the summit of the Ventoux. Chrissie, I don't know who is advising you or your team but you need to do a bit more research." Chrissie quickly wrote back immediately, clarifying the situation. In no way did we mean to imply Cooke hadn't won the incredible Tour Feminin. We were simply seeking women's inclusion in the actual Tour de France.

We were saddened she felt her achievements were tarnished by our quest for equality. While it stung to not have Cooke's endorsement, it also taught me how vital opposition is to activism. Without opposition, there nothing to test the limits of our borders or mark our boundaries of progress. Opposition is a necessary tool to help us think through all potential flaws and pushback. I was also learning that sometimes opposition doesn't need to be solved. Just acknowledged and embraced. At the very least, tolerated.

Rather than dwell on the champions who chose not to support or sign our petition, we celebrated those who did. Like Gracie Elvin, the Australian national champion and Olympian, who said outright, "I don't personally want to race the Tour de France, but I'm signing this petition."[66] Elvin hit the nail on the head, delivering the inverse of Trott: Just because you don't want to do a race doesn't mean you block the path for others who want to race. We received tons of letters, articles of support and endorsement. Olympic gold medalists, international cycling federations, politicians and actors were writing letters to ASO on our behalf. But the letter that gave us greatest joy was from a twelve-year-old in England, who posted a fabulous missive online:

---

[65] In cycling, yellow is the color of the leader's jersey. Nicole wore yellow a lot. Interactive Reader Guide: Nicole Cooke
[66] Interactive Reader Guide: Gracie Elvin - Bigger than the Tour de France

"So I'm just a twelve year old girl. But my opinion still matters and I deserve to be heard. I'm a fan of cycling. Simon Gerrans, Cadel Evans, Tour de France and the Giro d'Italia. I've heard about all that stuff and I'm a big fan. But today my dad has taught me something very shocking. So apparently women aren't allowed to race the Tour de France?

Apparently, women aren't as good and strong as men. But people are forgetting one thing. People are trying to get kids into cycling, right? But they forget: 50% of kids are girls. And if girls can't see female cyclists on TV as much as the men, or hear cool news about them like we do with the men, well, I'm just going to say, 'Screw cycling! I don't want to become a cyclist when I'm older if I'm not going to be treated like an equal!' What kind of person wants to be treated like they're inferior? Like they don't matter as much as other people?

As a kid, I've had a taste of that feeling, and I do **not** want it when I'm older. Cycling used to be about fun. About being free. Feeling the wind go past you as you know nothing can worry you. You're **free.** Not anymore. How can you feel free when you're being mistreated? How can you feel free when you're **not** free? No one can be free when they aren't being given equal rights. I thought our world had moved on from that sexist-against-women era.

Women **need** equal rights. And they **can** get it. If you let them try. I will continue to support women's cycling, no matter what, especially my favourites, such as Bridie O'Donnell and Rochelle Gilmore, along with her whole team full of girls, the Wiggle Honda Team. I hope you can help to raise awareness of this issue and help support it with me."
    —Guest blog post by Kayla Beaconsfield, Age 12

Wonderful Kayla gave all of us at Le Tour Entier a renewed faith that our fight was necessary. *Welcome to the Space Dust Bus, Kayla.* I smiled to myself. *Someday you'll be driving this thing.* We also noticed a growing trend of men signing our petition and tweeting/posting photos of their daughters on bikes, daughters being active, daughters doing awesome stuff. So many men saw the Big Picture of progress, and it warmed our hearts to know we had such fantastic, progressive, anti-patriarchal men on our side.

Sometimes, support came from the most unexpected places. From Azerbaijan, we had an unlikely ally in Theo Maucher, president of the Azerbaijan Cycling Federation. Not only did Maucher sign our petition, but he wrote Prudhomme a direct letter:

Dear Christian,
Today I write you to support the petition of Emma Pooley, Marianne Vos, Kathryn Bertine and Chrissie Wellington. I remember some meetings at Gerolsteiner times in 2006 or 2007 and I got to know the power of the ASO....

Please make a clear sign towards equality of women's cycling. You have the power to change cycling. If you see a Marianne Vos riding, fighting and suffering, there's no difference to a Chris Froome or a Peter Sagan or any other of our male heroes. In athletics, swimming and tennis women are treated equal. Why not in cycling? Marianne Vos, Emma Pooley and all the others deserve it.
Kind regards, Theo

Maucher's email enlightened me on the vast trajectory of passion, change and the internet; the reach of our influence is far greater than we know. How incredible it was that a middle-aged Azerbaijan male and a twelve-year-old girl from England were doing everything in their ability to leverage our fight for change. Pausing to absorb the power of reach, it damn near made me cry.

We also noticed another trend; Silence. Many women in pro cycling reached out to me privately to express their support for the petition, but were too afraid to share or sign it. I asked Emma why.

"There are some pro teams that have clauses in their contracts where riders have to ask for permission to give interviews or share their own views on social media," Emma said. "It's ridiculous. But it means the difference between having a pro contract or getting fired, many women won't speak out on topics of controversy." I heard rumors of this. Now Emma confirmed.

"Wait, talking about *equality* is considered *controversial*?"

"Apparently. Image is everything when it comes to sponsors," Emma explained. "Team management just wants the riders to smile and say positive things about cycling."

For years, plenty of teams avoided me because I spoke my mind, but I didn't realize there were actual *rules* in team contracts limiting one's freedom of speech. It's one thing to carry ourselves with a professional demeanor. It's another thing to silence opinion. This blew my mind. To sign a contract where you can't be yourself? Our sport was a mess on multiple levels.

Also in the quagmire of Silence on the petition: The UCI, IOC and USA Cycling—and most national cycling federations—said nothing. In late July, *USA Today* finally got USA Cycling to issue a statement:

"A stand-alone women's Tour de France would be a great platform to showcase the top talent in women's cycling. But we also appreciate there will be major logistical, financial and broadcasting challenges and ramifications in having a women's race parallel the men's event," said USA Cycling.

But, but, but. Alas, the pronoun of ambivalence! *USA Today* called me after, and I fired back with this: "We're going to do everything we need to do to make sure we end this tradition of sexism in sports," I said. "We will do whatever is necessary so that our voices are heard."

We decided to wait till the very end of the men's Tour de France before reaching out to the Kings of Silence; Prudhomme and ASO. Perhaps they would say something by then. In the meantime, Chrissie, Marianne, Emma and I were spending so much energy on media requests, website construction and social media interaction that we truly needed help.

"I know someone perfect," Chrissie said, and introduced us to publicist Tracy Pinder,[67] who became our indispensable press secretary of Le Tour Entier.

Tracy became one of the most vital members of our pressure group. While I puttered around muttering "Duh!" and shaking my head with disbelief that we still have to prove women are worthy of investment, Tracy diligently dove into market research, using her astute skills to handle all the vital minutia; hashtags, media campaigns, websites overhauls and data points. Even better, she brought an extremely important perspective to the group: She was *not* a cyclist.

Thanks to Tracy's general normalcy and broader perspective, she brought fresh eyes to every discussion about inequity within pro cycling. Tracy was able to see the things the rest of us could not. One of her greatest points was on prize money. Women in cycling were making a mere fraction of the men's prize purse, like the Tour of Flanders, where men earned 75,000 Euro and the women's winner earned 1500 Euro. We—the women of pro cycling—simply couldn't envision a livable wage and equal prize money. We were victims of our own oppression. Tracy taught us to reach beyond our comfort zone. If we want to raise the entire sport for men *and* women, it made much more sense to shoot much higher. And Tracy knew it.

"A women's race at the Tour de France—no matter if it's one day or three-weeks—needs to offer women prize money in the six-figures, minimum!" Tracy countered, citing women who win one-day events in tennis, skiing, marathon, triathlon… they make at *least* six-figures. "Not only does ASO have the budget to do so, but they'd gain even more viewership with such a prize purse on the line. Shit, they could—and should—offer $1M for the winner of the women's race. Now that would send a message which would result in more sponsorship and revenue for the *entire* Tour de France," Tracy said, and continued passionately.

---

[67] Interactive Reader Guide: Tracy Pinder

"We will never get this monkey of inequality off our back if we keep highlighting shit we already know—race exclusion, shorter distances, poor prize money—That will put sponsors off immediately. So stop highlighting the negatives. When you pay peanuts, you get monkeys. We need millions invested in this sport. A few hundred Euro? That's bullshit. Piss off."

I liked Tracy very, very much. My beloved sister of *Duh!* Kind, compassionate, upbeat and tough. She was smart, she was right and although she never knew it, every time she opened her mouth my demons of self-worth retreated into their caves. Tracy was the much-needed voice of reason reminding me this whole crazy journey really was important. Hearing it from a non-cyclist mattered that much more. May every group of activists have a Tracy.

"We need to bring a few more people into the fold, behind the scenes," Emma suggested. "I'd like to reach out to Marion Clignet.[68] She's a retired French professional cyclist, and she has direct connections with Prudhomme. They're friends. Perhaps she can help us get a private meeting. And Kristy Scrymgeour[69] too, who runs Specialized-Lululemon, the highest-ranking women's pro team in the world."

"Also, I'd like to bring in Steve Beckett,"[70] Chrissie offered. Steve was in marketing and very close with British Cycling and Team Sky. "But we'll still keep Tracy as our main consultant on press and marketing." I loved the addition of Tracy, but the idea of adding more people to our Le Tour Entier campaign equally excited and terrified me. We were already four Type A women... would adding more strong personalities create conflict? Disagreement? Power struggles? On top of that, I could practically smell my own fear of losing control of our mission to strangers. Attempting to calm myself with reason and putting on my big girl pants, I was willing to open the door on one condition: We all had to agree on our stance of an equal, three-week Tour de France for women. If one of our new members suddenly said to the press, "Well, a full Tour de France for women is unrealistic, you know?" it would shoot our petition—and our movement—in the foot.

I was a little nervous about this Steve guy. Clearly, there were so many amazing men out there who were in favor of our mission, but the hundred-year patriarchy of cycling loomed in my mind. What if Steve were one of... *them*? I asked Chrissie if Steve could send us some general information about himself. He obliged.

---

[68] Interactive Reader Guide: Marion Clignet
[69] Interactive Reader Guide: Kristy Scrymgeour
[70] Interactive Reader Guide: Steve Beckett

A lifelong cycling fan (but not an elite racer), Steve's professional background was in media planning, measuring the return of marketing investments which brought him to Team Sky—the biggest team in men's pro cycling—where he was an operating board member. Steve also helped run Sky's partnership with British Cycling. In 2012, he went out on his own to create Bike Brands, which specialized in commercial development of cycling.

"I'd like to play a positive role in the restructuring of cycling," Steve wrote. "My overriding sense of purpose is helping cycling to manage change in a positive way. A better sport for consumers, better governance, a better commercial model."

A smart, knowledgeable guy for sure. Still, I carried that weird insecurity about possibly being left behind. That adding more voices might drown out mine. It was not yet on my radar that trust and vulnerability are the biggest parts of activism. That was a lesson waiting for me in 2014. But in the throes of the petition and creation of Le Tour Entier all I knew was activism felt like being the parent of a concept. Like you'd do anything to keep your mission safe and alive. So my initial reaction to adding people to Le Tour Entier wasn't *Yeah, great idea!* but rather *Don't you hurt my baby!*

As uncomfortable as it felt adding new people to our group, I knew it was the right thing to do. Change is uncomfortable. That's how you know it's working. So I swallowed my pride, swaddled my vulnerable, lil' activism baby and put her in my pocket. I hushed my rumbly gut and lowered my guard. Steve seemed progressive, intellectual and productive. *If we ever get a meeting with ASO, maybe Steve's maleness will pacify them*, I rationalized. *Ok. Steve can join.* We brought him— along with Kristy, Tracy and Marion—into the fold of Le Tour Entier. All of whom would bring valuable life lessons and educate me on activism's unspoken infrastructure of good, great and painful.

––––––––––

My first interaction with Marion Clignet was terrible, as email is a poor conduit for conveying emotion and personality. Her bountiful energy and penchant for ALL CAPS initially came across aggressive, and I interpreted her intensity as controlling. Luckily, I was completely, utterly wrong. Marion was as equally passionate as I. She turned out to be an amazing ally and huge asset to our team, and a much-needed reminder that sometimes a person's passion and drive can be wrongly mistaken online. May we all heed the golden rule of Internet: Never judge anyone by their email. Wait until you *talk* to them. After a few Skype meetings, it was clear to see Marion was awesome. As a dual citizen of France and the United States, Marion began her cycling career in the late eighties, racing for the USA. When she developed epilepsy at age 22, USA Cycling shunned and doubted her, despite finishing second at the 1990 U.S. National Championships. Hurt and dejected, Marion promptly extended both middle fingers to USA Cycling and switched allegiances to France, where she won six world championship titles and raced in two Olympic Games. *Allez, Marion!*

"Because my parents are French, we used to come to France for summer vacations and watch Le Tour when I was young," Marion told us. "The more I watched grueling mountain stages, the more I wanted to do it. One day in the mid-80s, I saw there was a women's Tour leaving before the men! I pestered my parents to take me to the start and when we got there I noticed a US team getting ready to race. An American, Marianne Martin, had already won the first edition of Le Tour the year prior. I noticed a woman preparing for her ride so I went over and started talking to her. Her name was Nancy Walker. She was called at the very last minute to ride, as she was in France and they needed a rider! We talked for a while, then I tracked down the US team manager and asked how I could race Le Tour like these women."[71]

During her cycling career, Marion watched the decline of women's pro cycling as the UCI and ASO cast women aside in the 1990s and 2000s. Marion had terrific insights on ASO that we did not. She also shared great information on how French society works, and how we could best leverage/align ourselves with ASO to gain their favor. As for the best part of connecting with Marion: She was personal friends with Prudhomme. Long before he took the reins as Tour de France race director, he started his career as a journalist.

"I was Christian's first subject in sports journalism," Marion said. "I was the new kid on the block on the French team. Christian followed me at Stuttgart Worlds in 1991... several years later he was head journalist at France's top sport channel. We go way back. I can get us an appointment with Christian." Behold the power of opening the door and connecting with others.

---

[71] While Tour de France Feminin was shut down before Marion could partake, she placed second overall at the 1993 Gran Boucle.

"Marion," I said, "If ASO doesn't to respond to Emma's emails by the end of the week, we'd love your help connecting with Prudhomme. Do you *really* think you can set up a meeting for us?"

"Absolutely," Marion said.

27

DINOSAURS LOVE SILENCE

At a coffee shop in Hood River, down the street from where Kevin and I were editing *Half the Road* in the summer of 2013, I approached ten strangers to ask a question. Holding a clipboard and smiling politely enough to convey I was probably not a serial killer, all ten people kindly engaged.

"Have you ever heard of the Tour de France?" I asked. All ten out of ten replied yes, they knew it was a bike race. "Did you know they don't allow women?"

I watched nine out of ten[72] crinkle their brows in confusion and respond with the likes of:

"But it's 2013… I assumed women had access to, well, everything."

Assumption is the silent assassin of progress. When we assume everything is equal, we fail to see—or question—what *isn't* equal. Traditionalism *loves* this loophole. What can't be seen can't be questioned. Traditionalism is a crafty little weevil. It lingers, thrives and grows stronger in the shadows of passive assumption. Half the reason there were no women at the Tour de France is because ASO said so in 1989. The other half is because we let them. Because we, the modern public, naively assumed women *were* racing.

ASO loved that silence. No one was asking, pushing or making waves. The great George Bernard Shaw once beautifully wrote, *There are those who look at things and ask why? I dream of things that never were, and ask why not.* We must peel back the layers of what we think is equal and ask, *is it really?* We must constantly turn over stones of Assumption and see what wriggles out from beneath.

---

[72] The tenth just wanted to talk about Lance. There's always one.

By late July 2013, with the Tour de France about to end, our petition had been live for nearly three weeks. We had 98,000[73] signatures, a media frenzy and we had *still* not heard a peep from Prudhomme. Neither had Change.org staff, lobbying ASO on our behalf. Pulin Modi, our point person at Change, suggested enlisting our petition signers and supporters to take over the social media #TDF hashtag during the last few days of the men's race. Not a day went by where our supporters didn't ask *How can we help*? Every solid plan of activism must be ready to give an answer. It was time to enlist the troops. We sent emails to our 98,000 soldiers.

> "You are helping us show Christian Prudhomme, director of the Tour de France, that the world wants to see a women's race run in conjunction with the men. Let's keep up the positive pressure and convince Prudhomme and ASO that women's cycling is worth watching. Together we can create change. Help us this weekend by sending a tweet to the organisers of the Tour de France asking them to agree to meet with us, so we can work together to build and equal opportunity Tour de France in 2014 for men and for women.
>
> A meeting of all interested parties will enable an honest and fair discussion to take place, so that a solution can be found benefitting everyone involved in the Tour and in cycling around the world. The initiators of the petition welcome the opportunity to continue to be involved in this important process. Use our hashtags #TdF and #Women4TdF" –Le Tour Entier: The Whole Tour, inclusive of all.

Chrissie, Emma, Marianne and I agreed the best possible chance to have a meeting with ASO meant targeting a specific date. Since the latter three of us were scheduled to race World Championships in Florence at the end of September 2013, we could feasibly get to ASO's Paris headquarters directly afterward. Planes, trains, automobiles… whatever it took. We'd ride our bikes from Florence if we had to.

Emma, who is fluent in French, would be our point person for emailing Prudhomme and ASO. Marion Clignet, in addition, simultaneously emailed Prudhomme as a personal friend, asking for a meeting. As a group, we were bonding. "Together we will drive change, babes. We are making it happen!" Chrissie wrote. "Shoot for the stars!!!!!!" There will never be enough exclamation points that could match my gratitude for these women.

---

[73] Full transparency: In 2013, we had over 98,000 signatures. Today, Change.org shows a number in the low 97,000 range. This fluctuation happens when people delete accounts, pass away, etc. Not lying about the numbers. Just keepin' it real, yo.

With the Tour de France completed, we decided to give Prudhomme a fair chance to respond to our—and the media's—attempts to connect. If nothing transpired by the end of the summer, we were ready to launch our next email.

As we waited for Prudhomme's response, August rolled in. Amidst the strength and power I felt on the activism front, my heart remained broken from not racing with Colavita. Wynona had written me off completely. Not a word since labeling me a "no one" in April. I saw it clearer now; her decision to bench me wasn't just because she disliked me. It was directly connected to the fact I stood up for what I believed. In modern terms, I'd been Kaepernicked.[74]

My demons of worthlessness were relentless. In an attempt to silence them, I decided to write John Profaci. Tell him the whole story. Stand up for myself. At this point, there were no more team races and nothing left to lose. *What's he gonna do, bench me? Already done.* Rather than run from my demons, I took a deep breath and ran toward them. Full speed, wielding a sledgehammer of truth.

In a five-page letter, I wrote everything. How Wynona started out great as our general manager 2012. How everything was cool when I was with ESPNW. Then things changed in 2013. How I wouldn't race. That I wouldn't get paid. That she said John didn't want me on the team, and that she forbade me to contact him again. How I broke my arm but couldn't tell her. How I paid my way to team camp. How I was not given a team bike. But a spare bike was labeled with her name. How I had 12 strong performances racing individually, including three podium finishes, but she took down all the photos I sent to Colavita's social media manager. I told John about the massage. The "Normal Kathryn." How she prohibited me to interact with sponsors. How I was reprimanded for posting/supporting other women doing awesome things in the sport. How I was told to be quiet about all this inequality nonsense. That I was deemed a "nothing." A "no one."

Ultimately, I told Profaci I wanted nothing more than to race for Colavita in 2014, but there was no way I could endure another year of Wynona's treatment. *John, I'm well aware this letter will come with consequences. Perhaps you will perceive me as a tattletale, drama queen or just plain honest. At this point, I have*

---

[74] In 2016, NFL 49ers quarterback Colin Kaepernick chose to kneel during the national anthem in protest of police brutality, racial injustice and oppression. His team dropped him. As of February 2021, he remains unsigned. Off the field, he remains a powerful activist. Interactive Reader Guide: Colin Kaepernick

nothing to lose. Despite everything with Wynona, I was so damn proud to represent Colavita. I always will be, no matter what. With utmost respect, Kathryn

John responded quickly and with kindness.

> "Hi Kathryn... Just finished reading. Heartbreaking really and unfair on so many levels. If there was such a thing called bullying in pro cycling... this would be it. I'm so sorry. She never told me about anything all season long and I've been pissed off for weeks even before your note. I'm looking for a new director and glad Wynona will be off the road. Once I find that person, I will have you meet her/him to review your 2014 opportunity and the team roster. Typically, I don't truly involve myself in the team roster picks which is the director's responsibility. Thanks again for your honesty and courage writing all that for me. – John"

Within a month, Wynona was fired. John began interviewing other directors. *Hold tight. I'll be in touch soon!* Sweet relief. I didn't care if he hired a Sasquatch or the Pope or the Easter Bunny to run the 2014 team. Anyone with a pulse would be better.

Bullying. The word reached out and slapped me in the face and woke me right up. Bullying was a term I always associated with childhood, conjuring up images of playground taunting and adolescent angst. It didn't occur to me that adults bully other adults. But they do. And she did. And it took me way too long to realize it. John's kind words—*courage, honesty*—were a breath of fresh air. And vindication. My inner child stood triumphantly in the playground of my thoughts and looked around, steadfast, smiling, fists raised, scanning the sandbox for bullies and whispering under her breath, *"Next?"*

In mid-August, my husband and I traveled to Colorado where George took part in the Leadville 100; a 104-mile endurance slugfest of trails, dirt and lung-searing 10,000-ft altitude. When he asked if I would be his crew, I was overwhelmed with pride. Absolutely! It would be an honor to drag coolers through the woods and wait for hours to watch him roll by for 10 seconds. *Love is patient, love is kind.*

I truly was thrilled for my husband. After so many years where George's priorities lay in the caretaking of his spouse's cancer battle, setting a goal for himself was big step forward in his journey of healing. Not to mention, he passionately supported my racing. Now I could finally support his race. We were two years into marriage and I glowed with pride to be with this man.

As his race day assistant, I set up shop at the feed station, handing him bottles, snacks and hugs. At 74 miles, George stopped for fuel. Excitement and nerves were in full swing. As he scarfed a wilted slice of cold pizza from our cooler, we embraced. Smiling and sobbing simultaneously, tears streamed down his cheeks. I knew these tears. Endurance events often bring out a raw, beautiful blend of exhaustion, exertion and emotion. But I also saw something else in his face. Couldn't put my finger on it at that very moment, but my memory gripped hold of the way he released his tears. Beneath the exertion, beneath the fatigue, a different source or sadness or pain ran deeper. As he pedaled away, I thought, "*Oh good! He needs to let that stuff out.*"

That "stuff," I believed, was grief. As a couple, we were very good at communication. I made it clear he could always share his depths of human emotion with me. Especially memories of his first wife. Sometimes he did, and I welcomed the authenticity of his vulnerability. Drew me closer to him. In the tears that flowed at Leadville, there was definite sweet release. But something weighted, too.

Getting down to the wire in our *Half the Road* final edits, it was time to hit the recording booth for narration. We booked a studio in Oakland, California near Bob Roll's home, and I joined over Skype to listen and direct. While I proofread the narration script five hundred times, I was insanely nervous. Our budget was gone. There would be no possibility for a do-over if this recording had any errors. My grammar nerd and typo neuroses were on fire. *What if Bob says Lea DaviDson instead of Lea Davison*? *The world will end! THE WORLD WILL END.* Bobke tolerated my high-strungness and did incredible job with the voiceover. The world did not end. In fact, he made it better.

In the middle of the script while reading about Chrissie Wellington's gender barrier-breaking achievements at Ironman World Championships, Bob's voice trailed off mid-sentence and he interjected,

"Wait, wait, wait… cut! Instead of saying 'Chrissie's achievement,' can I please say "Chrissie's *outstanding* achievement?'

"Yes Bob," my heart beamed. "You can absolutely say that."

By the end of August, ASO had not responded Le Tour Entier's petition. It was time to step it up a notch. On September 7, 2013 we (through Emma) sent an email to the three head honchos at ASO—Christian Prudhomme, Yann Le Moenner, Jean-Etienne Amaury—as well as separate email to UCI's Brian Cookson and PatMcQuaid, stating our case and asking for a meeting. I suggested we also copy Oprah, Mother Theresa, Bill Gates, Jeff Bezos, Dalai Lama and Jesus in the BCC. This idea was rejected in the literal sense, but embraced metaphorically.

> Dear Mr. Prudhomme, Mr. Le Moenner and Mr. Amaury,
>
> Further to our petition, we wanted to inform you about the launch of our campaign on Thursday. This campaign, known as Le Tour Entier, continues the call for a women's race at the Tour de France, and also includes a manifesto setting out our recommendations for exploring the opportunities to grow women's cycling to its fullest potential. We wanted to give you an advance look at the manifesto for your convenience. This is obviously to be kept confidential until our launch date on Thursday Sept. 12.
> We truly believe this is a win-win situation for all involved, but progress will require dialogue and discussion. We welcome the opportunity to meet with you to discuss the issues outlined in the manifesto. May we suggest a meeting within the margins of the Road World Championships, as it provides the perfect opportunity for all of us to meet between Sept 25 and Oct 1?
> Please let us know if these dates will work for you, or if you have other suggestions.
>
> With kind regards,
> Emma Pooley, Chrissie Wellington, Marianne Vos & Kathryn Bertine

The letter's professionalism was perfect, but stronger still was the message written between the lines: *Hey ASO boys, we're not going away. Ever. Let's meet. Soon. So we don't have to launch another petition for common sense, yo.* In addition to the email on September 7, we also sent a press release to all 249 countries, all media and all petition signers, launching our campaign for Le Tour Entier. This wasn't just a petition anymore, it was a movement, manifesto and website.

While awaiting response, I played the visualization game.[75] Envisioning our meeting with ASO, I pictured a basic office conference room, standard tables, nondescript chairs... the furniture wasn't interesting, but the occupation of it was. All of us were there. Every member of Le Tour Entier, every bigwig of ASO sitting down and conducting business together. Whether or not there is any karmic energy, vortex or wormholes where visualizing a result actually helps create it, who knows.

---

[75] When I was 12, my father gave me a copy of Shakti Gawain's *Creative Visualization*. For decades, I've been wrapping my goals in pink bubbles and floating them into the universe. Maybe this was the year one would float back.

All I know is believing in something *feels* good and shushes the whiny cries of Doubt. In a world brimming with Nos, visualizing Yeses is important.

We also decided to step up Le Tour Entier's global visibility game. I created a cycling kit for our mission. Something the public could buy to wear in support of equal opportunity at the Tour de France. I designed a simple black jersey with a white equal sign on the front, back, sleeves. Bib shorts to match. Basic and symbolic of our mission; equality is a black-and-white issue. We're either equal or we aren't.

Castelli Cycling, one of our sport's high-end clothiers, reached out and offered to make and market our kit. Within a month, they sold thousands. Within six months, Rapha—the company that declined investing in *Half the Road* because we were "too hard" on UCI and Cookson—saw our success with the equality kit and pilfered the design. To escape copyright infringement, Rapha changed the color and elongated the stripes, calling it their "Two Bar" style Brevet jersey.[76] Utterly annoyed at Rapha's copycat tactic, I had to let that battle go. There were more important irons in the fire.

Kevin and I were spending nearly six to eight hours a day making sure all edits and details were in place. Striving to hit the deadline for 2014 film festivals, we needed to get crackin' and wrap *Half the Road* by October 1. Not a day went by where I didn't second-guess myself and uber-scrutinize. Did we have everything we needed? Too much? Too little? Did we leave anything out? Should we leave anything out? History, check. Facts, check. Humor, check. Spellcheck, check. Check, check, check again. Wait, humor. Are the funny parts even funny? Fingers crossed. Am I going to look like an idiot? Probably. (Already used to it).

Without a doubt, the hardest part of the film was creating the memorial section. Paying tribute to our women of the pro peloton who passed away. These were our sisters. There were too many riders who were killed in accidents while training. Races, too. In 2000, Nicole Reinhart, a nine-time U.S. champion, was on her way to winning the Saturn Race Series. A four-series event—the first three of which she won—that would've banked her $250,000 upon winning the fourth. On the final day of racing, in the last corner of the course, Nicole was in the lead when she lost control of her bike and collided with a tree. The fatal accident claimed her life at

---

[76] Rapha calling their equality jersey knock off "The Brevet" cracked me up. A Brevet is a former type of military commission for outstanding service, where an officer was promoted to a higher rank... but without corresponding pay. This pretty much sums up the state of women's pay equity in pro cycling. Also, brevetting was declared obsolete in 1922. Rapha bringing it back made me cringe-giggle.

just 24. We wanted to make sure the world remembered these women.[77] We chose photos of them racing, smiling, happy. Celebrating life to the fullest. Each and every one of them helped the sport rise, and as with all women who take part in male-dominated traditions, so too did society rise.

Done. There was nothing more to add to *Half the Road*. With confidence, we wrapped up all sound and color technical edits and rendered the film into its final, finished format. On a warm September afternoon, after a hard training session for Worlds, George and I sat on our couch and uploaded a private preview link of *Half the Road* to our big screen TV. Under the very same roof where I whispered, *I'm going to make a documentary!* two years ago, now here it was. Dimming the lights, we watched. Even the cats joined in, rather pleased to snuggle couchbound humans in the middle of the day. For the next hour and forty-five minutes, I stole glances at my husband's face. He was the first person to see the finished project. His opinion meant the world to me. My nerves ran amok. "So proud of you," George said, with calming kindness. I exhaled relief. The cats were nonplussed, but affectionate nonetheless.

I confided in George I was struggling a bit with the fatigue. The filmmaking, training, racing, activism-ing. They were adding up. The road was long, but the finish line was in sight.

"We're almost there, baby," I told him. "Once the film is released, we'll ride the wave of film festivals and media for a couple months. But all movies have a life span. I'm looking forward to the return of normalcy." He agreed, comforting me with understanding and support.

---

[77] *Half the Road* pays tribute to Nicole Reinhart (USA), Amy Gillette (AUS), Michaela Fanini (ITA), Zinaida Stahurskaya (BEL), Carla Swart (RSA), Carly Hibbard (AUS), Amy Dombroski (USA). Since then, we've lost Erica Greif (USA), Annefleur Kalvenhaar (NED), Ellen Watters (CAN) to crashes or cars. We also lost Jackie Crowell (USA) and Sharon Laws (GBR) to cancer. Rest peacefully, sisters. You're still with us.

28

CRICKETS BE DAMNED

On Sept 13, 2013—six days after we launched our Le Tour Entier manifesto and media campaign, two months after we launched the petition—we finally heard from ASO. Prudhomme agreed to set up a meeting in Paris at ASO headquarters on Monday, September 30. With my jaw hanging open, victory and disbelief vied for control of my thoughts. Again, a pause of stillness. Four years passed since the spring day in 2009 when I sent my first email to ASO, asking for a meeting. 1,500 days later, a response. I sat there for a while reveling in the strangeness of this four-year journey of waiting.

The pause gave way to a flurry of excitement and Le Tour Entier launched into prep mode. We had a meeting, yes. But that was no guarantee women would race the Tour de France. Now it was our job to convince ASO why it was in their best interest. A barrage of drafts and emails went into effect on how we'd carry out the meeting. We outlined the stats, monetization and financial gains of adding a women's race. Strategic and commercial rationale, impact on grassroots participation, increased revenue from cycling related purchases, increased viewers/spectators, improved reputation of cycling. We nailed down all the major aspects and also took a close look at how we could use leveraging UCI to our advantage…a tricky aspect.

We had to make ASO our ally, not enemy. With the ongoing outdatedness of UCI's roadblocks for women—age rules, shorter courses, zero media—we wanted ASO to understand they could be the true gamechangers. How they could take the reins of equal opportunity and show UCI how it's done. We knew we had to present ourselves with utmost professionality. A giant bitchfest of all that's wrong with the Tour de France wouldn't get us anywhere. In addition, we readied ourselves with rebuttals on how to answer all the Nos and the Can'ts that ASO might hurl our way.

- *We can't have a three week Tour de France. The UCI has rules on maximum length of a women's race.* We will lobby the UCI to change this and point out the ridiculousness of the rule. If the UCI blocks a women's Tour de France, they will look the bad guys. ASO can be the hero.

- There aren't enough women who can finish the race. The stages are too long! Incorrect. The top 15 UCI teams have riders strong enough to finish.

- *There simply aren't enough lodging accommodations for a women's race.* There were enough hotels in the 1980s. We will use empty castles if we have to. Caravans and tents, too.

- *Tour de France clashes with the pro women's calendar, most specifically the Giro d'Italia.* The UCI doesn't release the annual calendar until Fall/Winter, so there's still plenty of time to address this issue of scheduling races so there is no overlap.

- *We just don't think this is worthwhile.* Oh yeah? Come at me, bros. (Ok, that last one didn't make it into our outline. But each of us felt it.)

We created a PowerPoint of all facts, marketing, data and strengths about what is right, prosperous and successful. We cued the trailer of *Half the Road* to add visual impact, too. We dug deep into investigating who within ASO might be at our meeting. Prudhomme may be the kingpin race director, but the power of the peripheral people is just as important. Maybe an Amaury family member? Perhaps. ASO's CEO? Likely. *Rule of activism: Always know—or at least anticipate—who's coming to the table.* The more details, the more confidence.

Marie-Odile Amaury, widow of ASO's founder, Phillipe Amaury, owned the bulk of the shares in ASO. She effectively held the reins as chairperson while her son, Jean-Etienne Amaury, held the role of president. In addition to cycling events, ASO runs 90 sports events in 25 countries, totaling 240 days of annual competition in sailing, golf, tennis, marathon and motor sports. In addition, they own media, marketing, merchandise and travel enterprises.

Yann Le Moenner, CEO, no stranger to the world of endurance sports, was an age-group triathlete. Christian Prudhomme, race director of the Tour de France, began his career as a trained sports journalist. Working for French television stations like La Cinq and L'Equipe TV, he became editor-in-chief and served as commentator for Tour de France in 2000. After serving as assistant director of the Tour de France, in 2007, Prudhomme replaced head director Jean-Marie Leblanc who served since 1985. Prudhomme's distaste for the terrible doping situation ravaging the men's sport through the 90s became apparent, as he cracked down on testing protocols at Le Tour.

Something about Prudhomme's experience in journalism and anti-doping activism lifted my spirits. Perhaps he would see the light. Perhaps he would understand why equal opportunity matters. No matter who showed up at the meeting, we would be ready.

"Prudhomme is very curious about us," Marion said. "I think he will want to know exactly how we envision a women's tour will work, who is going to make it happen and where the budget will come from. We must be prepared from all angles." Indeed, we must. But I snickered. The answers were already right there. *This is not rocket science. A Tour de France for women will work. It did in the 80s. We will work with you to create a sustainable modern version. Together.* But sure enough, we'd have to "prove" why it is worthwhile to invest in women.

As personal friend of Prudhomme, Marion also mentioned an important part about what makes Christian tick. "He is most concerned about the state of men's cycling... if one more doping scandal comes to life, Christian believes it's over for cycling and Tour de France investors will completely pull out," Marion said. "Which is why this is a terrific time to use women's cycling as a platform for change, and how Prudhomme could use this as a marketing strategy to invest in the women's side." Indeed. The time was right. The black cloud of professional cycling has a silver lining: Women.

"Emma should be our point person in the meeting," Chrissie suggested. "She's fluent in French. She's the current Olympic silver medalist and a time trial world champion and ASO is already impressed with her. Kathryn, the French aren't always thrilled with Americans, and since you're the one who launched the petition, they already think you're a troublemaker."

"Agreed," I laughed. "Emma's perfect. Besides, we were all going to be there."

"On that note," Chrissie responded. "I don't think we should all go to the meeting."

"Wait, sister... no, you've *gotta* be there," I urged, thinking Chrissie was excusing herself from going to Paris. "You're a vital part of this team. You *have* to be there!" What happened next nearly crushed me.

"I would strongly urge *against* having a whole team of women attend the meeting," Chrissie expressed. "I think this would send the wrong impression, and be incredibly overwhelming. We also risk diluting our message, or seeming to appear like a female revolutionary guard. In short, a team of 7 women will be off-putting, and get ASO's backs up immediately... I would suggest that only 2 of us (from Le Tour Entier) attend, as well as Marion... I feel strongly that Emma should attend given her ability to speak fluent French." My gut tightened into knots. She wasn't done.

"I would also suggest that we invite a male to attend, and one that is commercially astute and understands the business side of the industry—whilst also having a grasp of the tradition, history, the institutional framework and politics (and also the campaign and its mission). I would suggest that Steve Beckett would be one such person," Chrissie orated.

Wait. WHAT!? Something was wrong. Something was off. Something hurt. Bad. My gut doubled over and the Cerberus started howling its guttural song of worthlessness. I read between the lines. My hero, my friend, my confidant... Chrissie didn't want me there. My sensitivity welled up and the tears came down. The very meeting I—*we!*—worked so hard for was now something where I was unwanted. Unnecessary. Unworthy. Three days ago, the high of securing a meeting with ASO infiltrated my soul, but now the low of Chrissie's email came crashing down upon me. There is no greater pain than being misunderstood and cast aside from your own goals. I slept little that night. Activism is equal parts daydream and nightmare. In the morning my vulnerable rawness turned from sadness turned to anger.

Hold up. "A team of seven women will be off-putting?!"

Never in the course of history has the concept of seven men in one room for a business meeting been considered "off-putting." How did we get to 2013 and still believe that seven women in the same room as men might be considered *off-putting*? The loopholes of tradition were still here, still gapingly wide open. Just because I had envisioned a mixed-gender meeting with ASO since my lil' pea brain came up with the idea in 2009 didn't mean everyone else lived in my weird lil' brain. (Lucky for them.)

Our demons are not to blame for everything. I too was an equal contributor to the ugly weight of my worthlessness. One of my (many) faults lay in holding these amazing women—Chrissie, Marianne & Emma—in such high regard that I viewed myself beneath them. *Ok, Self, that has to stop.* If I kept considering myself less important than these women, then I would be a hypocrite of my own belief that *anyone* can create change and progress. *Space dust bus driver, yes. They are the stars. But remember, Self. You built this damn bus and sat down at the wheel. Remember that.* My sensitivity reeled at Chrissie's inference that perhaps I should not go to our meeting, but my gut begged me to stand my ground. Mustering up my threadbare courage, I wrote back to Chrissie and the others of Le Tour Entier:

> "I am not *not* going to this meeting. If that were ever to be considered, it should have been discussed long before this point, long before the four of us asked for a meeting over email and signed four names to it, long before four of us petitioned for an opportunity to discuss this with ASO. If you're worried that I'm some loud American who the French won't like, grant me the understanding I can change this stereotype... We have all worked so very hard on this campaign. All of our names are on it, with equal weight. It isn't right to say only two can go, and insinuate I can't be one of them. If you don't want to go the ASO meeting because you feel we're too many, don't go. But don't take away from me the right that I've earned to be there. I'm going. -KB"

Over the next few days, heated emails continued to fly back and forth. Chrissie stood her ground, remaining steadfast on the cautionary side. Ultimately, it was Marion Clignet—whom I didn't get along with at the start—who saved the day, saw the value of inclusion and shushed my Cerberus. She believed the four original members of Le Tour Entier, joined by auxiliary members Steve Beckett, Kristy Scrymgeour, Tracy Pinder and herself was a good move and would be well-received by Prudhomme.

"Everyone can contribute, but the majority of speaking should come from a few key people," Marion said. "I just want you all to be prepared that France is not like other countries in all senses. THE FRENCH ARE AT LEAST 15 YEARS BEHIND OTHER COUNTRIES, in particular the U.S. in terms of women's rights, pay, etc. Just saying that we need to be ready for some 'tennis' during the meeting."

Marion's all caps made me smile. Once again, she delivered passion. This time, I loved it. Marion's inside knowledge on French life was so important, so necessary. All this from a woman I first thought too pushy, too opinionated. A woman whose ALL CAPS freaked me out till I took a good hard look in the mirror. *Hey weirdo, you're pretty damn opinionated, too.* Marion was such a wonderful lesson I was desperately in need of learning: Let others in to help. With that, I sent an email to the group with my travel arrangements booked for Paris on September 29. Confidence slowly wrapped its roots around the cornerstone of inclusion and whispered, *Always show up. Always go. Always be there. Never let anyone make you feel you don't belong. Especially YOU, dummy. Never let your own brain get in the way. YOU HEAR ME, WOMAN?*

In the end, it was agreed we would *all* attend the meeting. There was no more talk of off-putting women and loose cannons. In fact, the situation taught me one of the most valuable lessons I needed to learn: *In life, there will be times when our closest friends have different opinions. What happens next?* Answer: Argue, bicker, listen to others, stand your ground... but never throw away a friendship over disagreeing viewpoints when compromise can be achieved. Chrissie and I made it through the melee. My demons quieted down, finally retreating to their caves and barns. For a while, anyway.

Logistics of plotting my route to Paris took some creativity. My plans were already in place for Florence, Italy, for World Championships, where I would represent St. Kitts and Nevis in the road race on September 28. The race would end by 4pm. Not enough time or money to catch a flight, but if I really hustled, I could ship my bike home via DHL, stuff everything else into a backpack, and run to the train station on time. There was a twelve-hour overnight train from Florence and Paris. *This was doable!* I booked the cheapest possible train ticket; sharing a sleeping cabin with three strangers. After a life of women's pro cycling teams, I was just thankful to have my own bed.

Chrissie arranged to take the underground "Chunnel" from London. Emma would fly from Switzerland. Marianne's family would drive their camper van 14 hours from Florence to Paris. Marianne was racing World Championships, too.

In addition the four original members of Le Tour Entier, our auxiliary members—Marion, Kristy, Tracy and Steve—would also join us in Paris.

Drafting our five-year plan for women's inclusion at the Tour de France, Le Tour Entier members all willingly acknowledged a three-week event was not likely to happen in time for 2014—just nine months away. Getting the ball rolling with a shorter multiday event, however, was definitely possible. Three to five days was doable. And a terrific starting block. Then, growing Le Tour incrementally each year by three to five days would be exciting for fans and also help grow the infrastructure of women's professional cycling. The women's pro teams could then budget properly each year for the predicted growth of the Tour de France.

We wanted to be abundantly clear with ASO: Le Tour Entier wanted to work *with* ASO. Not just dump the project in ASO's lap and run away. ASO needed to understand the current public/media/commercial climate for women's cycling is different today than it was in the mid-80s. We needed to show the data. Pitch and tone are vital in all business meetings, and we all agreed we wanted ASO to look like the winner. How Prudhomme would be seen as a "savior" and "visionary" of women's cycling in creating equal opportunity... and how his efforts could elevate the entire sport, and that sponsors truly want to be part of such a forward-thinking operation.

We all agreed this business meeting must be seen as a "wooing process" of ASO. Rather than barging in and making demands. The best partnerships engage in a give-and-take approach. We wanted ASO to see the value of working together. And finally, the big DO. What is our desired outcome? Whether or not ASO agrees to a Tour de France on the day of our meeting, we needed to make sure we would leave our first meeting with a second meeting scheduled. We were not going away. Ever.

PowerPoints, bullet points, data, stats, strategies, procedures, objectives, feasibility, finances, psychology... we were ready for anything. While it's impossible to plan for the unexpected, it is possible to remain unwavering, unrelenting and untrammeled. To stay firm and hold our line. Everyone in Le Tour Entier was playing a crucial role in gathering everything possible to support our cause for women at the Tour de France.

Christian Prudhomme emailed Le Tour Entier to request we keep our September meeting top secret. Under no circumstances did he want the media to know ASO was meeting with Le Tour Entier to discuss the possibility of women at the Tour de France. *Oooh, secrets!* I couldn't help but snicker. ASO didn't want people to know they were talking about—*shhhh*!—equality. They didn't want to be seen with us. Behold, the secrecy of activism! Progress is a mistress of the night.

Despite the fact I wanted to sing from the rooftops about achieving this milestone meeting, I agreed to keep it under wraps. Journalists worldwide still checked in with us every day, wanting to know if/when a meeting might be held. All of us Le Tour Entierees agreed to a wonderfully vague but truthful response: "We are working on arranging meetings and communication opportunities with the ASO." Secrets, mistresses, meetings, whatever. The truth would come to light in time.

On September 26, 2013, I flew to Florence for what would be my most underprepared World Championships. Physically, I was doing quite well. My watts, intervals and data were stronger than ever. My mind, however, was having a field day with denial. Despite repeating the mantra all athletes recite as they head into their most important competition of the year—*Everything's great! You're fine! You're strong! Wheee!*—I was zonked. Schnockered. Sacked. Plumb tuckered out. Not just physically. Mentally. Emotionally, too. Filmmaking highs, Colavita lows, activism overload. All of it barreled full steam ahead like some surreal runaway train where I was the conductor, passenger and brakeman. Hunter S. Thompson famously said that our role in life is to "Buy the ticket. Take the ride." I was very much on that ride. Yet I had no idea if I was supposed to be driving or coasting or flailing or anything. I desperately wanted to whisper, *Hunter, am I doing this right?!* to which I envisioned him answering, *For fuck's sake, woman. Turn off your damn brain.* Oh, ok. Good idea.

I arrived at the Florence train station, dragging my cumbersome bicycle bag (without wheels) seven blocks to an Airbnb near the finish line of the road races. I was solo for this one, as George was saving his vacation days for my last race of the season in Curaçao. Hauling a bulky suitcase was hardly a complaint. I was well aware of the glorious awesomeness of how lucky I was to be in this stunning Italian city, racing world championships as a professional cyclist for St. Kitts and Nevis at the age of 38. Exhausted, yes, but life was awesome and I knew it. I had my health, my husband, food on the table and a roof over my head. Cornerstones that allowed me to build this house of activism, and I did so with pride and gratitude. If my race sucked because I was tired, so be it. I was here. I showed up. Kept my promise to represent St. Kitts and Nevis, reminding UCI there were small countries and poor federations in cycling who deserved to be recognized, acknowledged and counted equally.

The day before the women's race, I took my cycling kit to be officially okayed by the UCI henchmen. As I waited in line, Rochelle Gilmore walked by. I asked the kind man from Moldova Cycling Federation to hold my place in line and rushed over to give Rochelle a quick hug. Over a year passed since interviewing her for *Half the Road* in Boise, Idaho when Kevin and I turned the car around. Rochelle had since retired from racing and now managed Wiggle-Honda Pro Cycling. The team she created. Signing some of the best women in the sport, many were here racing world championships and Rochelle was there as TV commentator.

"Great to see you, Rochelle," I said, smiling. A familiar face in a faraway place gave me a much-needed boost of energy.

"You too, Kathryn," she said. "I'm psyched to see *Half the Road.*"

Thank you, thank you! As she hurried off, I walked back to my place in line. A man from Australia stood behind me and we chit-chatted.

"Did you hear there's a film coming out on women's pro cycling?" he asked. "I can't wait to see it." I beamed with joy. Strangers around the world knew about *Half the Road*, and it wasn't even out yet.

Making my way from UCI headquarters, I wandered through the festive tents of vendors. Gear, souvenirs, memorabilia… everything in the village was abuzz with the fanfare of cycling. And just about everything on display was targeted toward men. Missing out on potential sales for half the population. The "maleness" of world championships was overwhelming. *We need to remind people that women are here too*, I thought to myself. *If only we had a stage where we could stand up and*— Wait a minute. We *do* have a stage. Tomorrow. Next to the start line.

Before the start of UCI races, athletes of each national team are required to sign in under the watchful eyes of UCI officials and take stage for a team photograph. I too would have to sign in, even though I was the only member of the St. Kitts and Nevis Cycling Federation. I too would have to take the stage before a huge crowd of fans and media. Hmmm. A stage… Perhaps this was an opportunity to do something. To literally stand for something.

But how, exactly? We only had a few brief moments to stand and smile as the media took photos. No microphone, no speech. Just standing. Ok, then. If I were going to send a message it had to be quick and concise. A visual to remember. Something that would get the people talking, asking questions. There, in the tourist village of vendor tents, employees of Team Sky—pro cycling's most prominent men's team—were passing out free glossy posters of their leader, Chris Froome. On the front, a shot of cycling's golden boy riding toward victory at the Tour de France. On the back, nothing but blank white space. Perfect. Walking back to the apartment, I grabbed some thick, black kinesiology tape from a local pharmacy.

———————

The next morning, the kindhearted man from whom I'd rented the Airbnb kindly offered to drive me to the start line of the road race, which was almost 50 miles away from downtown Florence. There were so many moments like this during my cycling career where the help of strangers was the only thing that made it possible for me race. Logistics were often a huge obstacle. Just like it takes a village to raise a child, it took a village to race a Kathryn. I thanked Manuele for his assistance, unloaded my bike from the trunk of his car, reassembled it in the parking lot, shoved two waterbottles in the cages, stuffed energy gels in my pockets and rolled over to the sign-in stage. After scribbling my signature, the Italian announcer annunciated,

"Kaaatreeen Berrrrteeeeen, San Keeeeets e Nehvus."

"Neeeeeeevis!" I corrected with a smile, and marched forth to center stage with the clippity clop of my cycling cleats clicking their rhythmic cadence on the wooden floorboards. From my jersey pocket, I fished out the poster I made in the kitchen last night. On the blank, white, back of the Chris Froome poster, I had attached two black, foot-long strips of kinesio tape into an equal sign. On stage in front of the spectators, I held it over head, stood tall and waited. Neither the announcer nor the crowd was quite sure what do with this strange interruption, and in all truth, neither was I. All I knew was I had to do it. To stand for something. Until women's cycling is equal, if they give me a stage I will give them a show.

I stood there for about five seconds, the rough equivalent of one deep yoga breath. Just enough time to let the sign speak through the silence. Just enough time to feel like it mattered. A photographer wearing an official media vest wandered over to a snap a picture. *Namaste, buddy.* I lowered the sign. A few people in the audience clapped. The UCI officials did not.

Leaving the stage, I put my weird little kinesio equality poster in Manuele's car, and rolled off to the start of the race. While I had no intention of keeping the handmade poster, it didn't feel right to throw it away. En route to the start line, a fellow competitor saw the display on stage and asked what that was all about. From shorter races to lesser prize money, we engaged in conversation about the rampant inequities in cycling and how the first step in solving the problem is generating exposure. Especially to the UCI.

"Aren't you scared about the backlash?" she worried. "They could fine you."

"Oh please. UCI isn't going to penalize me for holding up a sign," I laughed, releasing just enough endorphins to perfectly balance out the start line nerves. "That's silly."

2013 UCI World Championships was fabulously brutal. About two-thirds of the entire field was broomwagoned (in both the men's and women's races), myself included. I made my way to the finish line in central Florence in just enough time to watch the winner approach. There in the distance approaching the chute, a flash of orange... yes, yes, YES! It's VOS!!! Marianne Vos, our Le Tour Entier superstar, crossed the line and claimed her third road world championship title. I commenced a series of internal fist bumps, flooded with joy, pride and hope. The woman who just won world championships—*again*—will sit down at the table of ASO tomorrow to lobby for equality. Picking my way through the crowds of fans, I finagled my way over to congratulate Marianne with a quick hug and a whisper, "See you tomorrow."

"See you tomorrow!" she smiled.

Pedaling back to my Airbnb, I packed up my bike, shipped it home, stuffed everything else in a backpack and headed out for the midnight train to Paris.

29

THE MEETING

Making my way to the economy cabin, I opened the door to my four-person room expecting to find three other passengers. There were six. A large Korean family occupied three of the four bunks, two of them sandwiched into each plank barely wide enough for one. I threw my backpack onto the remaining top bunk, hunkering down for the twelve-hour journey when a conductor knocked on the door and entered.

"Passports," he commanded, hand extended. I took mine out, and flipped to the photo page to assist the verification process. He snapped it shut, collected each one and made his way toward the door. Life experience bubbled forth with visceral impulse.

"Wait!" I yelped, dismounting the bunk and following him out of the room.

Fifteen years ago, before bicycles orbited into my universe, I was a professional figure skater.[78] In 1998, while on tour with a Mexican company in Argentina and Chile, my employers asked to see my passport. I trustingly gave it to them. Hollywood on Ice kept it behind lock and key for five months; an illegal scheme to keep employees from quitting. I was young and naïve, unaware that passports must always be kept by the person who owns it. Watching the Eurostar train conductor exit with my passport induced panic.

"Where are you taking my passport?" I questioned, nervously.

"To the office for safe keeping. It's procedure."

"No, I'll keep it with me," I said firmly, reaching for the little blue book.

The conductor attempted to persuade me, citing theft within bunks. I dissented and snatched my passport back. *Mine, mine, mine.* He had a point regarding

---

[78] Interactive Reader Guide: All the Sundays Yet to Come

safekeeping, though. Before entering the cabin, I shoved my passport into the back of my panties and climbed into bed. No way in hell was passport drama keeping me from meeting with ASO. I settled uncomfortably into my bunk, dozing off with fatigue, equal parts thankful and annoyed to be a back sleeper. Just before noon, the train pulled into Paris. I pulled the passport from my underwear, curved with a subtle bend that would last the rest of its existence.

———————

That morning, the cycling world was abuzz with election news: Brian Cookson defeated Pat McQuaid in a 24-to-18 vote to become president of the UCI. While the majority of the cycling world was thrilled to see a changing of the guards after eight years of a downslide into performance enhancing drugs and political corruption, I too was thrilled to see McQuaid ousted. (Now he had plenty of time to party with the King of Norway.) But my gut reeled with the reality of what was coming: Another white, middle-aged, European man of privilege who considered women to be less capable than men. I shook my head. No one yet knew the outdated mindset of Cookson, as *Half the Road* wouldn't be released for four more months.

At the very least, Cookson's election win gave us a solid talking point to bring up with ASO. Perhaps the exodus of McQuaid and the entrance of Cookson was something ASO and Le Tour Entier could share as a common ground.

As the members of Le Tour Entier began trickling into Paris, I received an email from Olympic gold medalist Connie Carpenter-Phinney, who also raced the women's Tour de France in 1984-1989. We kept in touch since her *Half the Road* interview. Confiding in her about the meeting, Connie offered some last-minute advice on dealing with the Good ol' Boys.

"Remember not to treat ASO as the enemy or antagonize them," Connie said, "but to offer the opportunity to work with them to create change. Don't attack The Tour, just work to make it happen. Don't back anyone in the corner. Be kind, but hold your ground."

Connie then told me about her days racing the Tour de France in the 80s and how ASO was stupid to cancel the event in 1989.

"IMAGINE how big our sport would be today IF women's cycling had continued on that trajectory? Even if women raced 100 kilometers less than the men each day, still the impact would be huge, making those French towns happy because they'd have more activity and excitement and income. If that were done, women's cycling would surely already own half the road. Press onward, Kathryn!"

With motivation, strength and warm, happy fangirl fuzzies, Connie's words were just what I needed to hear.

Making my way from Gare de Lyon train station to Issy-les-Moulineaux, the southwest quadrant of Paris, I checked into the Hotel Luxor and did my laundry in the sink while awaiting the others. My professional self was calm and collected, but my inner child was rampant with excitement. I've done my job and kept my mouth shut about the meeting on social media. Feeling giddy about the big day, I decided it was safe to post something very innocuous on social media. '*Interesting things are happening today. Stay tuned!*' I tweeted and Facebooked. Besides, with all the other stuff going on in my life, from *Half the Road* to racing world championships, there was no way ASO could infer my tweet was about them. Freedom of speech, yo.

Within 30 minutes, ASO emailed and asked me to remove the tweet. Ha! They were watching, closely. To censor the phrase 'interesting things are happening today' is like silencing a meteorologist for predicting there might be sun or clouds or rain later. After a good bout of giggles, I deleted the tweet. *Fine, ASO. But someday, there will be a women's race at the Tour de France, and I'm gonna write a book about this journey. Good luck deleting that. Oh, and one more thing. The more you tell me to be quiet, the more I will rain down upon you.*

Chrissie, Emma and Kristy arrived first, and we walked to a café just blocks from ASO headquarters, where I met Marion Clignet and Tracy Pinder for the first time. Both of them absolutely lovely. Steve Beckett walked in next. Somewhere in his late thirties/early forties, I thought, *Ok, good. Not a Dinosaur. He's one of us.* Finally, Marianne arrived, and we all broke into big smiles and cheers, congratulating her Worlds victory.

"Where's your family?" I asked.

"They're in our van in ASO's parking lot," she answered.

After a 14-hour drive in the Vos family camper, her entourage—mom, dad, brother and the family cat—were content to stay in the van and remain inconspicuous. How many world champions drive 14 hours overnight with their family (and cat) to fight for equality? Humbly acting like it's no big deal? Not many. Marianne Vos is downright special for many reasons. Glancing around the café at our group of incredible, high-achieving souls, it was not lost on me I was in the presence of greatness.

We grabbed a quick snack and ran over our notes before heading to the meeting. We reminded each other to be cool, calm, collected and kind… but also strong and forthright.

"Remember," I added. "No matter what, we must all stay united on our petition's request: There needs to be a women's Tour de France, equal to the men's. We're only nine months away from the next Tour. Whether we get one day or three weeks in 2014, we must not relent from the standpoint of full equity. If we ask for less, women will remain less." All the women nodded in agreement and my heart grew a layer of confidence knowing we're all on the same pa—

"Actually, I don't think the Tour de France needs to be three weeks for women," Steve said. The thickness of his words poured molasses into my time-space continuum, and I felt my head swivel toward him in slow-motion, like when films foreshadow impending doom. *Noooooooooooo*, my brain screamed silently as I brought my gaze to meet Steve's.

"What are you *talking* about, Steve?" I asked, flabbergasted and defensive. "That's our *entire* mission of Le Tour Entier. Three weeks has been our position since July. Since we brought you in. We have a hundred thousand people who stand with us. We're fighting for equal opportunity. We can't walk into this meeting and change course."

"Look, the women would be fine to do a 10-day race. Doesn't need to be three weeks," he said, matching my tone. *Ten days. Exactly what Brian Cookson said.* The hairs raised on the back of my head and Tracy sensed it. My defenses and nerves moved to the frontlines. We were about to walk into the meeting I've sought and envisioned for four years. The thought of our lone male member saying, *"Hey, we don't need three weeks, just ten days would be fine for women!"* nearly put me over the edge. Red flags went flying and my personal sanity teetered. It took all the courage I had to open the doors of Le Tour Entier to people I'd never met, but I did it, believing Steve was on the same page. *What if he isn't? What if he sinks this meeting?* My Cerberus started its low, throaty growl.

"Come on, time to go!" Tracy interjected. "We'll stick to the plan. Let's go, meeting time!"

For the few short blocks we walked toward ASO, I commanded the remaining remnants of my calmness to band together. *It's go time. Don't obsess about Steve's comment. Put on your Big Girl pants, woman. If the topic of ten days vs. three weeks arises in the meeting, take charge. But first, be patient and wait. Exciting stuff is about to go down. You're ready, you're prepared, you're here. Now, be confident and pretend you've got your shit together. Oh, and smile. Men love that shit. Right. Good plan.*

As we made our way to the building, I took in the surroundings, wanting to remember everything about the day. ASO's modern building stood at the intersection of historic battles, Avenues Stalingrad and Flanders, in the heart of Issy-les-Moulineaux. The Seine flowed a few blocks away. Roundabouts were everywhere. The deliberate yet unhurried pace of European pedestrians, the warm, early autumnal weather, the clear skies. The click of our shoes on Parisian cobbles as seven women (and Steve) walked into the lobby of ASO as one collective movement. The sound of our presence traveled through my ears and straight into my soul. Without a doubt, it was the right decision for all of us to be here.

The receptionist called Christian Prudhomme, who promptly greeted us in the lobby. True to his images in the media, he was tall, well-spoken and professional. Nothing short of cordial and businesslike. We chitchatted in the elevator en route to the meeting room. *Our journey to Paris was fine, the weather was wonderful, world championships was fantastic, we're about to bring the equality hammer down on ASO.* The last one was internal dialogue, but still.

———————

Six floors above the streets of Paris, in a small office conference room with walls bearing photographs of men racing bicycles, I took a seat between Chrissie and Emma, setting my digital voice recorder on the dark, oval table. Compact, portable, smaller than a cell phone. Not on, but ready. We kept our promise to ASO. No one knows we're here today. The five main men of Amaury Sports Organization shuffled in and took their seats. As race director, Prudhomme sat down at the head of the table. The CEO, Yann LeMonner, next to him. Across from me, Jean-Michel Monin, Sports Manager. Monin, a dapper, square-jawed, blondish-grey man in his mid-forties, is a 1996 Olympic gold medalist in track cycling team pursuit. Amongst our Le Tour Entier group, my role was secretary. I flicked the recorder switch on; a tiny, red light winked in compliance. I've always used as recorder for meetings and interviews. This is how writers take notes with accuracy, transparency, honesty and openness.

"May I see that?" Jean-Michel said, pointing toward the recorder, smiling, his eyes and expressions conveying a *hey, that's cool!* interest in gadgetry.

"Sure," I responded, smiling back. Best to start off this meeting by conveying a sense of trust, amicableness. I slid the device toward him with a plasticky woosh across the table. Picking up the recorder, he flicked off the red light and put the device in his pocket. His smile switched from *hey, that's cool* to *gotcha!*. We locked eyes. Unbelievable. ASO just pocketed my recorder.

"I'll give it back after the meeting," he grinned, winking at me, with a tilt of his giant, geometrically splendid chin.

"No problem," I smiled, bigger. *Game on, pal*. Reaching into my bag, I pulled out my laptop.

Chrissie, sitting next to me, observed what was going on and lowered her hand above my backpack, motioning to keep the laptop at bay. *Don't piss him off*, she communicated. *And don't risk losing your laptop*. Fine. I retired the laptop, deterred but not defeated. Keeping my eyes locked with Jean-Michel, I leaned into my bag and fumbled for my last two weapons of activism; pen and notebook. Placing them before me, I opened the cover and uncapped the pen. His smile faded. Mine did not. The meeting hadn't even started but the power struggle was well underway.

The pause of that moment was as palpable as the pause four years prior, before sending my first email to ASO. Something within me registered change was afoot. I knew not what the next four years would bring—victory, defeat, devastation, heartache, brain injuries—but in that secret boardroom meeting in Paris, my soul knew this: Equal opportunity is a necessary war and I was ready for battle.

The meeting began with Christian Prudhomme introducing his staff, Emma introducing our members of Le Tour Entier, and then what I will forever remember as The Great Finger Wag.

"You should not have initiated that petition," Prudhomme stated, speaking sternly and wagging his index finger at us. "That was highly unnecessary. You could have asked for a meeting." I suppressed a smile and restrained myself from blurting out *Dude, I've been asking for a meeting since 2009. And seriously, the finger scolding? Come on, br—* Luckily, Emma interrupted my mental monologue with a far more appropriate response.

"Mr. Prudhomme, the petition is what brought us together today. Society as a whole is inspired by the Tour de France, and the petition shows a direct interest in women's cycling. As you know, we believe including women equally at the Tour de France is not just the right thing to do, but the smart thing to do, which will be lucrative and positive for all…"

Emma glanced at her notes and kicked off the meeting. Something was different about Emma today. Here in the boardroom, Emma's voice was soft, her gaze downward, her nerves on full display. This was not the Emma Pooley I witnessed in front of our documentary cameras; outspoken, strong-willed, dynamic, ten feet tall not five-foot-two. *Uh oh*, I thought, and began channeling every possible iota of positive energy toward her. *Come on, sister. Come on. You got this. You are prepared, eloquent and awesome. Do NOT let these Suits break your vision. Come on, champ.*

Within a few minutes, her nerves steadied and confidence returned. After explaining the mission statement of why Le Tour Entier was there—to work with ASO to establish a women's race at the Tour de France and create a multi-stakeholder group to make it happen—Emma shared a bit of history of women's cycling, then segued into investment strategies, focusing on the commercial rationale for women's inclusion. With each example, her voice grew stronger. As she talked data points and marketing stats, I scanned the room. Some of ASO's men were taking notes. Consumer interest, revenue streams, commercial viability and gain, media coverage, the groundswell of public demand…evidence, proof, data, stats. Emma nailed each point, demonstrating we did our due diligence regarding the viability of a Tour de France for women. My mind drifted to the paradox of tradition and loopholes of modernity. Never in the history of time have white men needed a visual presentation on why they deserve to be somewhere. Here we were in 2013, sitting in a meeting 'proving' to men why women must be included. *Complete with a slide show, for fuck's sake.*

Emma gave the floor to Steve to present his PowerPoint deck on marketing research on why women are a sound investment. *If you say anything about just wanting a 10-day race, Steve, I will dislocate your kneecaps beneath the table,* I seethed. He did not. However, when Steve spoke, the men in the room definitely sat a bit straighter, listening more attentively.

During the meeting, Yann LeMonner stared at Chrissie Wellington. As an age-group Ironman triathlete with an upcoming trip to Kona for the World Championships, he was taken by her presence, and we all sensed it. While Yann did not cross over the Creepy Border, he was definitely engrossed by anything Chrissie said, hanging on her every word. When Chrissie spoke about the lack of men's professional teams affiliated with a women's professional team, Yann agreed, going so far to say that Team Sky's lack of a pro team for women is "pure discrimination."

When he asked about data for women-specific growth in the industry, we provided it and Yann agreed.

"When I look at the questions and the details of cycling today, the Tour is different now," Yann said. "The Tour de France has four main sponsors. Adding a non-competitive fifth sponsor could add the women's field." *We're off to a good start*, I breathed to myself.

We then tackled the wider framework of stakeholders, race rules, calendars, with an emphasis on collaboration. We needed to make ASO feel they were in charge. We laid it on thick, reminding ASO they could be the hero of pro cycling's tarnished reputation. That including women equally would make them heroes. Stroking their ego without losing ours, we made a strong case that Le Tour Entier could help ASO make such an event happen.

"What is it, exactly, you would like to see in terms of the race?" Yann asked. My head swiveled toward Steve. As I watched him open his mouth, I quickly opened mine first.

"We want full parity, just like the men. Three weeks." I stated. "However, we know there's only nine months till the next Le Tour, so we suggest three to five days for 2014. Then, each year, expanding 3-5 days incrementally until full parity is reached." I gave the floor back to Emma, who explained the incremental growth of expanding the race over the next five to seven years would not just be helpful in creating a sustainable budget, but also exciting for the fans. The crowd appeal of adding more stages each year would be a breath of fresh air—and attraction of viewership—for a sport now steeped in staleness and tradition.

"Well," LeMonner interjected. "The logistics are not so simple." Alas, the moment we most anticipated: ASO's stance on why a women's race *can't* be done. True to our predictions, Prudhomme started in on the List of Nos. Too complicated for men and women to race the same day. Too difficult for officials. Too expensive. Not enough hotel rooms. Too many this, not enough that...

"Actually, yes, it would work," I interrupted. This time I made eye contact with Christian, Yann and Jean-Michel, slowly looking each of them in the eye. "Gentlemen, the majority of the men's start times for Le Tour are 10am. The women would happily rise early and stand on the start line at 5am, if that's what it takes." For a moment, there was silence. Prudhomme and LeMonner looked at me with confused expressions.

"The... the women would do that?" LeMonner asked, bewildered. "They would race before 10am?"

"Yes," I respond, equally bewildered. "Most of us do already." I watched their eyes widen, as the concept of women riding early in the morning coursed through the room like a biblical revelation. These guys had no idea about the history—or current state—of women's racing. How, for decades, we played second fiddle to the men's pro peloton, racing much earlier in the day or on completely different dates.

"We would sleep in castles, tents and caravans. We would do whatever it takes to race the Tour de France." For the first time in the meeting, the men smiled. Some even laughed. I feigned taking notes and scribbled in my notebook, tilting the page toward Chrissie. "*They're responding to passion!*" Chrissie nodded, smiling.

Emma, now brimming with confidence, took the helm to discuss multi-media process, naming rights, UCI sanctioning, team selection process, number of participants, country/continent representation, ambassador protocol, commercial structure of sponsorship, and more prove-ity proof n' data.

"Well, that's good," Prudhomme said. "But Rome wasn't built in a day."

Oh geez. The Roman Paradox. When activists call for change, it is not uncommon for the opposition to deflect progress or delay action by using this somewhat flawed phrase. Yeah, Rome wasn't built in a day. But because of corrupt politics, Rome was ransacked and rebuilt seven times. Perhaps if Rome got their shit together sooner, it could have built a stronger foundation and skipped the devastation. The Tour de France isn't quite as ancient as Rome, but it has been around for over a century. So too has ASO. And UCI. For ASO to claim they can't offer a multiday women's race because it's just too much all at once? Horseshit. There *were* two Tour de Frances for women in the 1950s and 1980s. The blueprints were already there.

We concluded our presentation by showing ASO the four-minute trailer for *Half the Road*. I let the men know our film had its world premiere scheduled for the end of January.

"We can edit in an announcement for the 2014 Women's Tour de France," I offered, with a wink. We turned down the lights of the boardroom and started the film clip. I watched with great delight as ASO laughed at all the parts where UCI appeared less than favorable.

By the end of the meeting, the mood lightened. ASO realized we did not come here to skewer them, but to build something together. We concluded by asking ASO to consider our proposition for the race and that we looked forward to another meeting. They asked us to continue keeping today's meeting secret while they decided on the next steps. We agreed. We also agreed to ASO's request for a point person from Le Tour Entier to communicate via email. Chrissie accepted the role. Yann smiled a lot.

Across the table, Jean-Michel removed my digital recorder from his pocket and slid it back. I didn't thank him for returning something he took, but I did hold eye contact, gave a hint of a smile, narrowed my eyes and nodded once. *Not intimidated by you, buddy.* Sometimes the last word is a look.

"Thank you, ladies, we'll be in touch," Prudhomme said. "We appreciate your time in coming all the way to discuss this with us." As we made our way to the lobby, Prudhomme congratulated Marianne on winning Worlds the day before. I told him how Marianne made the journey overnight with her parents, brother and cat in the family van, and that they're in all hanging out in ASO's parking lot. Prudhomme stopped abruptly, mortified the Vos family was sitting in a van in their driveway for two hours. He quickly made a detour to greet them.

Before we left, I gave my trusty Bloggie camera to Tracy, who snapped a quick picture of us in the lobby of ASO. Our smiles, our postures portraying a shared vibe of confidence and composure. *We organized. We fought. We showed up. We were making stuff happen.*

"Please do not share that photo publicly," Prudhomme warned.

"I won't," I promised. Well, not for the next eight years.

Skyping home immediately after the meeting, I relayed the entire day to George. The flow, the vibes, the notes, the reactions, all of it. How something good was happening. "I'm not sure what, but something," I said, grinning through every syllable. What a ride, these past few months. Years. Hours. Without the teamwork of our marriage, his moral support of my racing, his encouragement as I stepped away from ESPN to make *Half the Road*, his emotional support as I struggled through the bullying of Wynona... none of this would've happened. "We're on the verge of something great, baby," I said. "2014 is gonna be big for us!"

That night, Chrissie, Emma, Marianne, Steve, Kristy, Tracy, Marion and I met for dinner before dispersing to our own countries and continents. We discussed the Maybes, the Could Bes, the What's Nexts at an outdoor café around the corner from Hotel Luxor. I don't remember much more about the conversation that night, just a sweet release of inner peace that we all achieved something together. We all sensed something positive was coming.

Before flying home, I spent the next day with Chrissie in Paris. Finally a chance to reconnect, bond and catch up on life outside of Le Tour Entier. Any differences we had in our activism melted away in friendship. Talking for hours, we walked through the streets of Paris, and took an obligatory selfie at the Eiffel Tower. While under strict gag order notice not to say anything on social media about ASO, something about the Eiffel Tower seemed both neutral and empowering. Like we should all stand tall for what we believe. *Eiffel Tower selfie power*! I tweeted, with Chrissie and me standing in front. No big deal. Just a couple of women sightseeing in Paris, trying to change a hundred years of history. We strolled to the Champs-Élysées and circled the famous arch, which always serves as the final stage of the men's Tour de France.

"Maybe we're one step closer to seeing women race around the Champs, too," I said, watching the traffic looping the famed cobblestones.

"Maybe," Chrissie smiled. "Maybe we are."

Seventeen hours after our meeting, ASO wrote us. On October 1, Yann emailed Chrissie to connect on next steps. Chrissie scheduled an in-person meeting with Yann at the Ironman World Championships the following week in Hawaii. She also sent him a high-end, fancy triathlon race suit and custom-made goggles complete with the French flag. Smart woman. *Allez, Chrissie!*

30

ADDING AMY

Returning from Paris, I began the task of submitting *Half the Road* to international film festivals and working to secure a location for our world premiere in January. Our film 18 months in the making was finally complete. Nothing left to add, nothing left to edit, no changes to be made. Until October 5, 2013, when we had to re-open the files and make a heartbreaking addition to the memorial section. We lost Amy Dombroski that day.

Amy, a beautiful soul in our pro cycling sisterhood who hailed from Colorado was killed during a training ride in Belgium, struck by a car as she motorpaced through a roundabout. She was only 26. I wept reading the news. We all did. This one hit too close to home. I knew Amy.

Six years ago on a rainy, summer afternoon in 2007, I wandered aimlessly along the shoulder of the rural road in Seven Springs, Pennsylvania serving as the staging area for the US National Championships time trial. I'd only been racing a bicycle for seven months. Green as could be, I qualified for Nationals by the skin of my teeth, reaching the Category 2 level just two months prior. I was very much in the early stages of my ESPN Olympic assignment to get to the Beijing Olympics.

As I wandered the wet roads, watching all the well-prepared women warming up under dry, tented protection, I sought shelter from the rain. As a newbie, the thought of bringing a tent or tarp was nowhere on my radar. There, up ahead, I saw a young woman spinning away on her stationary trainer under a makeshift tent. Next to her, there was space.

"Excuse me, may I set up here?" I asked, nervously.

"Yes, go ahead," Amy Dombroski said. She never knew the relief of her words, or how much in need I was of kindness and acceptance at that moment. Or that she would serve as a role model to me for years to come, despite the fact she was a decade my junior. I followed her career from that day on, watching Amy grow stronger year after year, cheering as she rode herself onto national teams, professional teams and world rankings in the cyclocross division. Later, when we raced together in the pro peloton, I often told my teammates, *"That's Amy! She's the one who let me in when a lot of people didn't."*

With tears in my eyes, a lump in my throat and the reality of cycling weighing heavily in my heart, I called Kevin and asked him to reopen the fully-rendered film files. We added Amy into the memorial section of *Half the Road*. The hardest edit I've ever made in any creative endeavor. Selecting a photo of her smiling, charismatic face, Amy expressed pure love, joy and even a hint of mischievousness as the lyrics of *Gone Too Soon* echoed the over the screen.[79]

I reached out to Amy's brother on Facebook, expressing condolences and letting him know we were doing our small part in preserving her immortality through *Half the Road*. Dan Dombroski responded with a photo of Amy's bookshelf. There were copies of *All the Sundays Yet to Come* and *As Good as Gold*. Wait... I was the one who admired *her* all these years, yet she had *my* books on *her* shelf? I cried for the rest of the day. Never underestimate the power of reach, of connection. May we all have the courage to ask for help. May we all let weird strangers share our tents on rainy days. Inspiration flows both ways, though we might not ever know it.

Days after Amy's passing, a small ray of hope and progress shone into the dark world of women's cycling: The UCI finally ended the archaic age median rule. Twenty-eight was no longer considered geriatric. Female racers of all ages were now able to chase their pro cycling dreams. While this ruling came under the new leadership of Brian Cookson, it was UCI's head of road cycling commission, Matthew Knight of Cycling Canada, who issued the proposal. But I also went ahead and thanked Amy for that one. Maybe on her way Up, she threw some karma thunderbolts toward UCI. Maybe, maybe not. Who knows. Doesn't matter. I still enjoy that mental picture.

---

[79] Amy went after her goals and her dreams, epitomizing the gift of athleticism and tenacity. Our sport is better for having Amy in it, and we carry her spirit--and those of all our fallen sisters--with us. Her legacy lives on in the Amy D Foundation, which helps rising women cyclocross racers follow their dreams. Interactive Reader Guide: Amy D Foundation

Half a world away from Paris, in a relaxed Hawaiian atmosphere for the VIP athletes of Ironman Kona, Yann and Chrissie sat by the pool discussing strategies for securing a women's race at the Tour de France. Yann told Chrissie he was extremely passionate about our meeting, and was pushing it through internally, getting more traction with others at ASO who were initially skeptical. He asked for Chrissie's opinion on creating a storyline for the race.

"I suggested the story could be the perfect mark for the 101st Le Tour birthday[80] and that ASO is representing a new century, and 'new beginnings,'" Chrissie said. "Yann loved it, and suggested emphasising the fact ASO would be doing something that people didn't think possible—defying expectations, carving new paths and paving the way—and that this would inspire the world... and help drive participation by men, women, girls and boys at all levels."

Continuing the conversation, they both agreed marketing the race properly was of utmost importance. That female riders and teams must be presented as strong, successful, accessible, open, friendly and within reach of the everyday person. The months leading up to the race must be equally loaded with attention so potential and existing sponsors saw more value and exposure. Yann agreed. This was much more than a race.

Chrissie went on. "Yann was 100 percent in agreement with my assertion that adding a women's event should not be 'window dressing' but a very competitive, combative race. He also said ASO does not want to hold an event unless we can guarantee the best teams/riders will be on the start line. We now have a mandate: Yann wants us to go to the team managers and ask them, hypothetically, if this race were to take place whether they would they attend. Then, once we are able to "go public" we will all discuss marketing and promotion, ambassadorship, charitable causes, expos, etc.

Oooh! A mandate! Action minus talk equals getting shit done. I was ecstatic.

In addition to Chrissie's chat with Yann, we received an email from Baptise Kern, ASO's marketing and business director. Kern, who was with us at the meeting, stated ASO began a "feasibility study" of staging a race on the final day of 2014 Le Tour de France on the iconic Champs-Élysées. My eyeballs nearly fell onto my keyboard. *Oh my god. This. Might. Happen.*

---

[80] Also interesting, as Tracy's research discovered, women in France finally gained the right to vote in in 1944. Holding a women's race at Le Tour in 2014 would mark the 70th anniversary of women's suffrage in France.

My inner child began to whine about the one-day part, but my semi-adulthood-self hushed her. Whatever gets our foot in the door of the patriarchy, whatever it takes to get women officially on the course of Tour de France, whether one minute or one day… it doesn't matter for the first year. All that matters is we're there. Three weeks will come someday. But not until our foot is in the door. *So quit your whining, kid, and remember this*: All change starts with one day.

Still, even one day was not a given, yet. There was much work to be done. Kern asked Le Tour Entier to take the reins of creating a sellable storyline for investors.

"What is the rationale behind women coming to ride on the Tour de France?" Kern asked. I stifled yet another chuckle that we're being asked—yet again—to prove why it matters women are included. To offer a 'rationale' for equality. I desperately wanted to suggest the rationale for having a one-day women's race was so the athletes could hurry back to the kitchen afterward.

"Not funny," Chrissie said, "We're not writing that."

"Kind of funny?"

"Kind of. But we're still not writing that."

As per usual, ASO requested their "feasibility study" be kept absolutely confidential. Yet a double standard presented itself. If they wanted us to start talking to team directors about a hypothetical women's Tour de France, there's no way the secrecy cat would stay in the bag. News would travel and the press would pounce.

"Chrissie, they can't give us a gag order and simultaneously ask us to do public research," I said.

"I know," she agreed, "but we have to do what we can to keep it quiet until we know the next steps."

Steps indeed. The continued secrecy was fascinating. What was the big deal? Why didn't ASO just tell the media we were working together to create a race? Within Le Tour Entier, we chuckled about this to ourselves. We were quite certain ASO wanted to take full credit for the race's inception. If ASO wanted to keep it a 'secret' and then suddenly announce "*Hey! We've got a great idea! We're going to put on a women's race!*" then so be it. We didn't become activists to take credit. We became activists to take charge. To create change. To do something right. *Ok, ASO. We'll be quiet. 98,000 people who signed the petition already know what we're up to, but whatever. Lol, guys.*

Our petitioners were asking, too. While gag-ordered by ASO, we decided to draft a public statement for our Le Tour Entier website—without naming ASO directly—to let the public know we were still working on the fight for women at the Tour de France:

> "After our initial campaign for a women's race at the Tour de France which gathered over 98,000 signatures and significant positive media exposure, we are now working with various stakeholders to explore the ways in which this vision can become a reality for 2014 and beyond. In addition to the Tour, we will work toward the implementations outlined in our Manifesto to ensure wider reform of women's cycling. We are encouraged by the in-depth discussions we have already had, and look forward to working with a range of organizations and individuals to help drive much-needed change." -*Le Tour Entier*

Our deadline for turning in our research to ASO was November 10. We immediately got to work creating the storyline, stats and "rationale" for the women's race, as well as reaching out to the top professional teams to gauge their interest in racing at the Tour de France. All of them said yes, of course they wanted to race. Including Colavita. I went straight to Profaci. *Yes, of course, we want Colvita to race and yes we would invest to help make a women's Tour de France happen.*

I was equal parts thrilled and sad. Thrilled Colavita wanted to be there. Maybe the new director would keep me on the roster and I could be there, too. Still, it was time to sit down and have a stern talk with my ego. The quest for women racing Le Tour was never about me. It was about moving our gender forward. *Right, I know, I know*, my ego understood. But goddamn, we wanted to be there. We being all of me; heart, brain, soul and ego. To stand on the start line of my dream, to stand with my compatriots of pro cycling. To feel the formerly forbidden cobbles of Le Tour de France beneath my feet. To chase away the demons of traditionalism, ageist governing bodies, outdated organizations, bullying directors. To show kids in the Caribbean that St. Kitts and Nevis was there in Paris. To let my soon-to-be 39-year-old pro athlete presence silently scream, *I belong here, too.*

Hold up, dreamer. I was getting ahead of myself. There was no official start line in Paris yet. We had work to do.

31

BROKEN THINGS

A
t least there was one definite start line in my future. Caribbean Championships were two weeks away and I had a bone to pick with my Cerberus. After an entire year of feeling crappy about Wynona's shunning and non-racing, I channeled every ounce of energy into training for the Caribbean Championships and representing St. Kitts and Nevis in the final race of my 2013 season.

While afternoons and evenings were devoted to ASO research, entering film festivals and spending quality downtime with my husband, mornings were devoted to training with grueling motorpace sessions and challenging intervals. With the last of my airline miles, George and I flew to Curaçao in mid-October. I was down to the scraps of my personal savings, so it made sense to attempt packing my road bike and my time trial bike into the same travel case. That way we wouldn't be dinged an extra $200 each direction by the airline mafia of baggage extortionists. Besides, I had done the double-bike packing before. Nothing bad happened. I was quite skilled with foam padding and bubble wrap. But apparently not skilled enough. This time, luck finally caught up with me and celebrated my idiocy by cracking the frame of my time trial bicycle. The bike I needed most.

"Shit," George said, inspecting the damage to the right chainstay. "You can't ride this." We both knew the rules. All bikes had to pass check-in protocol by UCI officials in order to be rendered "race legal." Broken bikes were not allowed to race. There were no shops in the vicinity, no chance to rent or borrow another bike in time.

"Shit, shit, shit." I confirmed. Took three flights, most of my money and what was left of my sanity to get to Curaçao … No way I *wasn't* going to stand on that start line. There had to be a way to fix this. Morality bubbled to the forefront of my thoughts. Not only is it illegal to ride a broken bike, but it's potentially quite stupid. If the chainstay didn't hold up during my time trial race, it could cause a crash. *But!* My inner-optimist provided, *This is a time trial. You might crash, but no one else would be hurt!*

I took a closer look at the splintered carbon along the chainstay, jutting inward toward the disc wheel. Of all the triangulations on a bicycle, the chainstay is geometrically important. But… not as important as the big triangle of the downtube, top tube and cross tube. Which were all unscathed. The two smaller chainstay triangles were the backup singers to the big triangle. One of the two chainstays was just fine. Then I noticed the crack also ran along the gray paint of the bike brand's logo. *Hmmm.* An idea came to mind. I looked at my husband. Our jetlagged eyes met.

"Find me some duct tape?!" I ask-begged. George took my undamaged road bike and cruised the island, returning with a sacred, silver roll of hope. To this day I don't really know what duct tape is made of, but I'm quite sure the three main ingredients are denial, faith and glue. *Two outta three ain't bad…*

"What are yo—" George started.

"Don't ask, don't tell," I responded. Somewhere between the reality of carbon's fragility and the strength of my repudiation, my mind saw a path of possibility. Unrolling the sticky circle of duct tape, tearing off thirteen long, half-inch wide strips, I wound each piece over the cracked carbon in a corkscrew pattern, once, twice, three times, leaving just enough of paint from the bike logo peeking out each side. Shaking the frame, torqueing it with all my might, it held. George, uncertain and nervous, mounted the bike and shook it harder with his additional fifty pounds of bodyweight. The bike still held. He dismounted, convinced. Grabbing my hands, he looked me straight in the eyes.

"Ok, here's the plan," George said, now on board with Operation Duct-Taped Dreams, just like he was three years ago during Operation Let's Tape Trident Gum to the Handlebars and Outsmart the UCI Officials. "Tomorrow, if you pass inspection, you're gonna ride *the shit outta this bike*. Your brain is going to tell you to be gentle because it knows the bike is broken. You can't think that way. Ride twice as hard. The faster you go, the less time you'll be out there on a broken bike. So ride like hell and get back here fast." There is no motivation greater than love, logic and swearing. T-minus twelve hours till check-in.

A memory. 1981. Riding my little single-speed bicycle to kindergarten one day, the chain fell off. Somehow I figured out how to put it back on. My fledgling mind had no idea what pride or confidence meant at age six, but both coursed through me with all their might and splendor. That day in school, our teacher asked us what we wanted to be when we grew up. With chaingreased hands, a gigantic grin and mind wide open, I knew exactly what I wanted to be when I grew up. *I want to be a Fix-it woman*, I wrote in the neat, block letters on the wide-lined paper with tiny, blue dashes in the midline that looked like important little roadways for words merging into stories.

"So, you want to build things? Like construction?" my kindhearted teacher asked.

"No. I want to *fix* broken things," I said. "I want to make things work."

What was supposed to be a handwriting assignment turned out to be a premonition. Bicycle chains, cracked frames, equal opportunity for women... thirty years later, I still just wanted to fix broken stuff and make it better.

The next morning in Curaçao, I rolled to the time trial start line, perspiring equally from the Caribbean sun and crackling nerves to which no duct tape could adhere. This was the moment of truth. Well, truth-ish.

"What is this?" the UCI official asked, measuring my bike then wagging his finger at the chainstay's silver duct tape, crouching down to inspect closer.

"I had to cover-up the logo," I told him, pointing out the tiny bits of logo sticker peeking out from beneath the tape. "Conflicting sponsorships, you know?" This was as true as it was false.

He nodded, and called to the woman behind me. "Next!"

With an exhale of unbelievable relief and probably a small bit of urine, I took my seat in the time trial corral and gathered my nerves into the complicated internal basket of fear, excitement, apprehension, conviction, adrenaline and a hearty dose of *f*ck yeah*! It was Go time.

Rolling off the start ramp, I felt a swelling surge of confidence. Apparently the duct tape wasn't just holding my bike together, but my heart as well. Colavita had benched me from every team race that year, but they couldn't take Caribbean Championships away from me. Into every pedal stroke of the time trial, I unleashed the pent-up pain, boxed-in sensitivity, growling Cerberus, the hurt, the frustration, the terrible, lingering sting of being called a "no one," the anger—good lord, so much *anger*!—all of it turned to beautiful energy, sweet release and physical agony (the good kind.) Somewhere over those 24-kilometers, my heart acknowledged the brokenness and my body responded like a proverbial fix-it woman, cauterizing my inner wounds with intense physical effort and lots of drooly saliva. Both of which are the metaphoric duct tape of every endurance athletes' dream.

Saluting the pain, releasing the demons, channeling the energy… it all came together that day, fixing/healing the cracked, broken stuff as I rode through the streets of Curaçao on a duct-taped bike that never wavered.

I won the time trial. By 25 seconds. Just over 26mph. [81] Joy was an understatement. As I stood on the podium donning the Caribbean Champion jersey, I felt joy indeed, but more so a deep sense of personal peace.

I emailed John Profaci immediately, letting him know my results and asking how the search for a new director was going. I was so looking forward to Colavita under new leadership in 2014.

"Congratulations!" John said. "Yes, I've hired a new director. What do you think of Jimmie Harney?"

My heart, breath and brain stopped. I re-read the sentence over and over again. If there was one person in the cycling world who disliked me more than Wynona, it was Jimmie.

Jimmie, an Olympic track cyclist, and his professional cyclist girlfriend, Ella, lived in Tucson. When I started gaining media coverage from ESPN, Jimmie didn't like it. Such media attention, he believed, should go toward Ella. He seemed offended I didn't write articles about Ella, or include her in the filming of *Half the Road*. We actually had two photos of her in the film, and indeed, Ella was a talented cyclist. Most women in pro cycling understood we couldn't interview everyone, and that it wasn't personal. [82] Still, in the few times Jimmie and I overlapped in person (or through his comments on social media), it was clear he was not a fan of my general existence.

"Jimmie knows I want you on the team," Profaci said. "I'll make sure he reaches out. It'll be fine." November passed quickly and a sinking feeling in my gut

---

[81] Had I raced in the pro/elite men's field, I would have placed 10th.

[82] There were 403 other women with a UCI race license in 2013 who did not appear in the film. They understood we couldn't get to everyone. Many of them even donated to *Half the Road*.

arose. Jimmie had neither reached out nor returned my emails. All the other professional teams had finalized their rosters. As mid-December rolled around I reached out to Profaci.

"Look, Kathryn, I'm sorry to tell you this, but Jimmie dropped you from the 2014 roster," Profaci said. When I ask what reasons he give, the response was semi-shocking. John continued. "Jimmie doesn't like that you didn't include his girlfriend in *Half the Road* and that you haven't given her any media attention."

"John, Ella *is* in *Half the Road*! There are two photos of her on the podium. I *did* include her," I explained. "The film will be released in January. You'll see!"

"I'm sorry, Kathryn. My hands are tied," Profaci said. "I hire managers and trust them to do the best job possible. When it comes to the roster, it's ultimately Jimmie's decision about whom to hire. I don't want to get involved. It's out of my hands." I was dropped from the team, released because a team manager wasn't able to keep his professional life and personal grudges separate… a resentment based on a film no one had even seen yet.

Part of my brain understood Profaci's "out of my hands" philosophy. Roles, rosters, managers. Business is business. Time to move on. Find another team. Makes sense. Sort of. But the other half of my brain struggled deeply with the "don't want to get involved" part. I understood it was easier for John to avoid confrontation and step aside. But in my world, getting involved and confronting problems is how we move forward. To remain impartial is a step backward. There are times in life when it *is* important to take sides, to use our voice, to stand up for someone or something.

Sometimes activism is no different than chemistry; the catalyst for change literally gets burned in the experiment. Speaking up about Wynona's actions, I became the catalyst for a new director. Then burned by the new one. Ooof. Chemistry is one cruel bitch. Neither Jimmie nor John wanted anything to do with me. Maybe I just wasn't worth standing up for. *Rabble rouser. Self-serving. No one…*

Stop, stop, stop, I told my brain. *Do not go down that rabbit-hole*. It was late December 2013. In a last-minute effort, I reached out to every pro team on the international circuit. They were all full. But I couldn't throw in the towel. Not yet. Not on these terms. I wasn't gonna let jaded directors get the best of me when I was only getting better, faster and stronger. Not with *Half the Road* slated to release and the Tour de France opening the door to women. Change must come from within oppression, and I needed to stay *in* pro cycling. I came up with a plan. *Ok, Self, you're going to start 2014 as an individual. Race under the banner of the St. Kitts and Nevis Cycling Federation. Ask for guest ride opportunities. Check in monthly with every pro team and ask, ask, ask if any vacancies have opened up. Persist. Put all your energies into* Half the Road *and the Tour de France and hold on tight. Let no one see you falter. Smile, fake it when you have to, and pretend this teamlessness thing is all part of the master plan. Who knows? Maybe it is. Don't crack now. You got this.*

While the final letdown of Colavita was soul crushing, two very uplifting bits of news came in and heaved my sanity/equilibrium back to balance. We secured The Loft—Tucson's local independent theater—for the world premiere of *Half the Road* on January 29, 2014. This beautiful theater was a landmark with a fabulous auditorium of 500 seats.

"We're going to sell every damn ticket!" I gleefully promised Jeff Yanc, the theater's kind soul and general manager. He smiled at my childlike excitement, but offered some reality.

"We hope you do sell out, Kathryn," Jeff said. "But that's never happened before. We've been around since 1972. There's never been an independent film by a first-time filmmaker that's sold out The Loft's 500 seats."

"Fantastic!" I told Jeff. "Those are my favorite odds."

Tickets were set go on sale January 1. In the meantime, we upped our game with *Half the Road* posters, t-shirts, a giant push on social media and entering just about every film festival on the planet.

My literary career took a turn for the better that month. Three years had passed since the release of *As Good As Gold*, the dissolution of ESPN Books and being cut loose by my first agent. A writer's life is synonymous with getting one's creative heart ripped out on a regular basis. Often with a rusty ice pick. Or dull butter knife. For years on end. But my new agent convinced Triumph Books to give me a chance, landing me a book deal for my ESPNW essay collection, *The Road Less Taken*; *Lessons from a life spent cycling*. The release date was set for September 2014. Most of the essays I'd already written, but working on new chapters began immediately. There were some personal essays I wanted to include. Topics from my private life. George was a huge part of my world, and I looked forward to including some stories about us in the book. My creative brain was in full swing, and I found great peace in the vortex of my writing life, activist life and athlete life merging toward tangible progress.

What also mattered that winter: Love and balance. As 2013 began winding down, George and I celebrated our third anniversary. He would often wear his *Half the Road* t-shirt around the house as I beamed with pride and gratitude. That fall, George also celebrated his third anniversary of Team Colleen, a charity he founded to help cancer survivors train for and ride El Tour de Tucson; a wonderful community cycling event with distances ranging from 25 to 104 miles. No small feat for anyone, let alone those struggling with (or survivors of) cancer. Such a terrific, empowering, heartfelt organization that George named after his first wife.

That year, my dear friend and former college rowing teammate, Jenna Doucette Auber, finished her final round of chemotherapy for breast cancer. We flew her to Tucson to ride with Team Colleen. Our college teammates came out support Jenna and we housed five of them in every corner of our home, which overflowed with love, joy and happiness for a week straight. Jenna provided the much-needed reminder of the Big Picture. All my personal struggles of the past few years—job loss, team issues, bullies, trolls—none of it mattered. I had a film coming out, a book in the works, a race at Tour de France possibly being created, a loving spouse, supportive family and the biggest gift of all; good health. Hot damn, life was good. No, it was *great*. My soul was full.

George's soul, however, was not. That winter, he often came home from work with something between despair and exhaustion etched into his face.

"I hate my job," he said, sinking into the couch, day after day. Pharmaceutical sales sucked the life from him.

"Ok, baby," I attempted to console. "This is fixable. Let's look for career paths that will bring you some inner peace." We also talked about how the next few months were likely to be a whirlwind of high-energy and vast unknowns. With film festival acceptances, world premieres, working with ASO and the possible media attention that might accompany it... this was bound to be a busy stretch. But I also knew it was just that; a stretch. Books, films, historic events... such achievements possess a very short lifespan of newness. The hubbub of *Half the Road* and possible Tour de France would all die down at the end of July.

"I'm so excited about these next few months, George, but I'm also a little scared," I confided in my husband. "Can't wait for the calm after the storm!" Despite the nuttiness of filmmaking and activism, my favorite part of the day was snuggling with George and our assortment of cats, renting movies and just plain being together. My need for togetherness and recharging was just as strong as my need for independence and action. My heart ached for his current situation of feeling stuck in an unfulfilling job. Years of freelancing, waitressing and adjunct-ing made me sympathize. All I could do was pull up job search websites on his iPad and encourage him to browse.

32

SECRET MISTRESS ACTIVISTS

As we awaited a follow-up meeting with ASO, they asked Le Tour Entier to create a headline message and offer supporting stories for the proposed women's race at Le Tour. They wanted race format research and team selection protocol. We spent hours drafting everything requested. We lobbied for 2014 to include a three-day women's Tour de France. A time trial and/or a team time trial and two road races near Paris—all of which synced perfectly with the final three days of the men's race—would give fans and media more bang for the buck. ASO was not budging from wanting a one-day format. *Ok, fine. Whatever gets women there for the first year.*

We explained a circuit race—a multi-lap course that would draw thousands of spectators—created the best option for exposure. The best place for an historic race would be the final day of the Tour de France, encircling the Arch d'Triomphe on the Champs-Élysées of Paris, filled with sprint bonuses and an exciting finish. That would get the fans—and media—riled up. Equal prize money a must, correlating with the same earnings of the men on that day.

Despite my Cerberus spending most of its time snoozing in the doghouse, there were a few occurrences where I still felt Steve wasn't embracing the Big Picture of our mission. As he began corresponding with Cookson to embrace change and progress within UCI, Steve's wording rang some alarm bells.

"Brian, rather than chew your ear off about the women's (LTE) campaign, which I don't think is appropriate," Steve wrote to Cookson, "It's important you don't have the wrong idea about Le Tour Entier - it isn't about three-week tours and equal pay." *Hold up,* I panicked. *That's exactly what Le Tour Entier is about*! I thanked Steve for making contact with Cookson, but asked him to run all emails to UCI and ASO past our group first.

"I respect your opinion, Steve," I wrote. "But for those of us who *do* believe it's possible to achieve a three-week Tour and have equal pay, let's make sure all future emails sent on behalf of LTE share a common platform."

"Kathryn, I appreciate this is a long-term ambition but we need to extinguish these thoughts of a three-week tour and equal pay as far as we and the UCI are concerned—for now," Steve countered. He firmly believed the best way to get in with UCI was to buddy up to the president. But if extinguishing thoughts of equal races and equal pay is what it took to get into the Good ol' Boys club, I didn't like it one bit. The hairs on the back of my neck stood up. My Cerberus stood at attention.

Steve also believed the women shouldn't actually race the tour de France, but rather do an Etape event—which is a non-competitive group ride with amateur cyclists. In other words, ride with the amateur fans rather than race. *What?! Hell nooo…* we were not going to ask ASO to add women to the Tour de France by pimping the female pros to ride with fans. Nope. Nope. Nope. The rest of us quickly struck that down. Steve also thought we should all start acknowledging the men's side of pro cycling more.

"Tweets congratulating men who win races would help build trust," Steve said, in regard to gaining pro cycling men as our allies. He was as right as he was wrong. We very much wanted our beloved brotherhood of pro cycling to stand up for us. Showing support is important. But gaining men's approval/trust by stroking their egos was so… 1950s. Men's pro cycling had millions of congratulatory fans, yet very few of the pro men even publicly *acknowledged* women's pro cycling even existed. We were more than happy to high-five our brotherhood's accomplishment. Most of us already did. But to tweet congratulations to prove we were worthy of their trust? Yeeech. No thanks.

"Look, Le Tour Entier isn't a women's lib organization," Steve surmised. "But the danger is we look like this on social media." My snark-o-meter went haywire. I had to sit on my hands from reaction-emailing and firing back *Oh no! We look like a group of people who believe women are equal! Quick, HIDE!* Despite the fact Steve was just a few years my senior, he had already drunk the proverbial Kool-Aid: women's liberation is dangerous. Here's what women's liberation actually means: Women want to be as free as men. Politically, socially, economically equal. That's it. Women's liberation is not dangerous. The danger is people who *think* women's lib is dangerous.

For generations, society sunk their ignorant hooks into words like liberation and feminism, sequestering them to the dungeons of Misunderstanding where words like socialism and retardation rot with misappropriation. These words were rebranded and hurled around as insults. I don't think Steve truly meant to expropriate the definition of 'women's lib" but I was worried. Tracy sensed my anxiety, and counseled me to relax about the Steve vibe.

"His heart is in the right place. We are a team and we will get through this sticky weird patch," Tracy soothed. "Have patience...and faith! We're all a little worn right now."

She was right. The eight of us on Le Tour Entier were working our butts off. We were all tired. None of us were getting paid, some of us worked two jobs and all of us were gag-ordered by ASO. I wasn't sold on Steve the Activist but I really liked Steve the Person. Besides, he was teaching me something; the importance of tolerating different views. I had to remember to cool my sensitivity jets sometimes, especially when it came to responding on email. We were a team and we were heading toward progress. That's what mattered most.

––––––––––

On December 13, 2013, Le Tour Entier's second meeting with ASO took place in Paris. I was all out of airline miles, so Chrissie, Emma, Marion and Steve represented us. After all the hours Le Tour Entier spent together over emails and Skype, the weird apprehension/anxiety I felt about being 'left behind' dissipated to a dull pulse. I was thrilled half our team would be at the meeting, and that the idea of too many "off-putting" women was never resurrected. Still under ASO's gag-order, it took every restraint I had to keep from tweeting "Nothing interesting is happening today!" Adulting is *hard*.

My pulse raced with excitement reading Chrissie's bullet point email of how the meeting transpired. The most important one: ASO secured a one-day race for July 27, 2014, on the traditional loop of the Champs-Élysées, where the men's race would conclude hours after the women's race. Same finish line, separate staging area at the Place de Concorde. The women's race would begin at 1pm and would last just over two hours, totaling 80km—twelve laps around the 6.5km loop of the Champs-Élysées. In addition to the typical podium for the top three finishers, ASO agreed to take on a historic role: The prize purse for the women's race would be equal to the prize purse for the men's stage that day: 35,000 Euro. I nearly fell out of my chair.

HOLY SHIT THIS IS HAPPENING! THIS IS HAPPENING! I bellowed at my laptop in Marion-esque all caps joy. Yes, the race was one day. Yes, the race was too short. Yes, none of that mattered. Not this year. All that mattered was that in eight months, women would finally race at the Tour de France. Officially part of the event. On the same day as the men.

Took a good fifteen minutes before my heart rate settled enough to focus on the rest of the email about the ASO-Le Tour Entier meeting. ASO wanted our help and research on everything. On the issue of team participation, we agreed team selection would be governed by UCI rules for World Cup events; invitations would go to the top 15 to 20 trade teams and three national teams, with 6 riders per team. Teams would be informed/invited at least 60 days before the race. ASO requested our input on team selection, should they have to make decisions on the five teams between rank #15 and #20, though ASO would have the final word.

The biggest win in visibility: ASO secured Eurosport and France TV to broadcast the race. With the event still eight months away, this was a key factor and a fantastic springboard for us to continue negotiating with other broadcasters for international coverage. For the first time in Tour de France's 104-year history, the women would be covered equally in the media.

When it came to the topic of race name, ASO offered "The Ladies' Ride" but Le Tour Entier shut that down quick, as images of petticoats and bloomers clogged our vision. We needed Tour de France in the name; reclaiming the naming rights that were retracted in 1989. *Course Feminin Tour de France* was our original frontrunner, but with Emma, Tracy and Marion's better grasp on the language, we shortened it to **La Course by Tour de France**. Like a mullet of gender equity activism: Feminine in the front, badass in the back. "The future is female" combined with reimagined traditionalism. I truly loved the name. While my sarcastic side kind of wanted the race to be called Tour de Functioning Ovaries, my inner-grown up was very satisfied with La Course by Tour de France. ASO agreed, and La Course by Tour de France was official.

Next up, media/PR strategy. Publicity was a must. We reiterated the necessity of building a compelling and interesting story focusing on the terrific athletes/characters and driving public awareness and engagement. The earlier the better. We suggested all forms of social engagement; gala dinners, billboards, organizing grassroots rides. While ASO needed to launch these projects, we agreed to help strategize and organize.

"ASO noted that *we* made this race happen," Chrissie stated, "That Le Tour Entier pushed them to react and create the event. They would like us to continue to be on their internal Advisory Board. They suggested that in future (after the first race) they would utilize us in a more formal capacity and that we would be remunerated for this." *Well, that's promising!* I thought. *ASO is actually going to pay us for doing their job.* Even better, Chrissie told us: "ASO stated their intention is that 2014 is just the start, and the multiday stage race will evolve over the coming years." My heart soared.

Finally, ASO discussed The Big Announcement. A press release about La Course by Tour de France would take place on January 30. Until then, the gag-order remained in place. Personally, I was thrilled the announcement for La Course would be made on January 30, 2014. Our *Half the Road* world premiere on January 29. Kevin and I added an "Update" reel to the closing credits, victoriously sharing La Course by Tour de France would take place on July 27, 2014. I quickly did the math. Seven-hour time difference between Arizona and France... Our film would end at 9:30pm MST on January 29, which was 4:30am CET January 30. Just in time for the gag-order lift.

Less than a month before *Half the Road*'s premiere, an unforeseen budget oversight sank its fangs into my wallet. Checking the status of our Olympic footage rights for the 49 seconds of Kristin Armstrong and Marianne Vos winning the Olympics, I wanted to confirm our $12,000 fee was received and we were in the clear for upcoming premiere and future film festivals. We were not.

USOC informed me film festival rights would run another $4,465. What?! That doesn't make any sense! I already bought the theater rights. Film festivals are held in theaters.

"You purchased rights for mainstream theaters. Not independent theaters and film festivals," USOC said. *Price-gouging at its finest*, I grumbled. My first-time filmmaker naivety didn't see that one coming. The total was now $16,465 for less than one minute of our film.[83] While we budgeted properly for the $12,000 in the beginning, the rest of the budget was loooong gone. Spent the last of it months ago. That left me with two choices: A) I could try to recreate Kristin and Marianne's Olympic glory in Claymation or B) suck it up, avoid getting sued for copyright infringement and put $4,465 on my personal credit card.

I reluctantly chose B. Probably only a few years until USOC starts charging us for thinking the word *Olympics*. Till then I had to believe every penny was worth

---

[83] The new cost of *Half the Road* ($83K), divided by its length (106 minutes/11,236 seconds) means each minute cost $774. Each second cost $7.50. Omg, math is cool.

the journey. From *Half the Road* to petitions, losses and victories to new beginnings, these were the five lessons I learned in 2013: Never give up. Sometimes give way. Always keep the camera rolling. Interesting things are happening *every* day. And, in the words of Reddit guru Alex Ohanian, "Magic happens when you give a damn. Give lots of damns." Damn straight. Bring it on, 2014.

33

WORLD PREMIERE

There are moments in life—few and far between—where we are wide awake, extremely present and fully conscious that *this specific moment* is a turning point. A benchmark. An unveiling of truth. An awakening. A reckoning that *this* is exactly what we were meant to do with our lives. That moment presented itself to me on January 29, 2014, when *Half the Road* premiered to a sold-out crowd of 500 people at The Loft Theatre in Tucson, Arizona.

The day before, every single ticket was sold. Before the film began, Jeff Yanc went on stage to introduce the film, and in doing so, proudly admitted his defeat. "We've never sold out a screening of an independent film before," he said, "and I didn't think Kathryn could do it. But she did. Here we are, sold out!" I was giddy with delight. While I'm usually comfortable speaking to a crowd, that night I trembled when Jeff handed me the mic. Speaking from the heart, I thanked everyone for making this film happen through their donations and moral support.

"This is *our* film," I said. "Not mine. Someday, I'll tell you the whole story of what it took to make this film. There were heroes and villains, victories and defeats, and everything else it takes for change to happen. For now, I will just say this: When you commit to seeing the Bigger Picture, there are a lot of Small Picture people who try to knock you down. Stand firm, take the hits, and surround yourself with people who believe in you. Because in the end, the Big Picture is the only size the whole world can see. Thank you for believing in *Half the Road*. Now, hands up… who wants to see a film on women's cycling?"

The crowd roared, hands soared upward. I had to restrain myself from jumping off the stage and surfing the audience.

Sitting in the beautiful, art-deco theater, five rows from the back, I gripped the hands of my husband on my right and my dear friend and fellow pro cyclist, Amber

Pierce, on my left. I was an equal mix of adrenaline and peace; both thrilled and terrified this day was here. Nearly two years had passed since that switch-flipping moment where ESPN rejected the documentary proposal, and my brain/voice released the words, *I'm going to make this film anyway*. And here we were, about to watch it all unfold onscreen.

Despite the fact I watched *Half the Road* about two million times on computer screens during countless edits and revisions, no one else had laid eyes on it except for my husband. I was terrified. Hoping for the best reaction to the film, my Cerberus stood on point, ready to pounce and shred me to pieces and tears.

"I don't think I'll survive if they start booing," I confided in Amber earlier that day. "On the other hand, I'm going to burst into tears if someone actually claps. I'm a bit of a wreck. I might lose it."

"It would be beautiful if you lost it," Amber said, handing me a tube of waterproof mascara before the screening. "Here, now you're ready for anything." Cementing my confidence, eyelashes and life-long friendship, I kept that mascara for five years. Even after it was empty and *Revlon* faded to *evl n*, I still can't throw that plastic yellow tube away. Sparks too much joy, and apparently my soul clings to it like a metaphoric life preserver. *Look out, world! I have bold, sassy lashes! Nothing can destroy me! Ok, maybe soap, whatever. I. Am. Unstoppable. Wheeee.*

As the 106 minutes of *Half the Road* unfolded, I watched the audience. They weren't just staring at the screen, they were active participants. Brows raised in surprise, heads shaking in disgust, eyes narrowed, laughter rising, collective gasps at Cookson's election win, giggles at our spoof infomercial for the Equality Pen, groans of UCI disappointment, a variety of adjectives hurled forth, and my deepest wish as a filmmaker was granted: people were *feeling*. Something, anything! They were experiencing anger, disappointment, confusion, happiness, laughter, sadness, and best of all, hope. So too did I. Hope coursed through me like a river in flood, especially when a young, millennial male in the middle of the audience started loudly booing at Brian Cookson's comments on women's physical "inferiority." The echoing hum of his *Booooo* was the same sweet tenor of a yoga class *Ooooohhhm* and I swear my soul opened. There in that theatre, between the literal darkness and figurative light, the intangible present wound its beautiful grip around my heart. Writing, filmmaking, activism, fighting for change… this is exactly what I was supposed to be doing with my life. *Namaste.*

Two days before the premiere of *Half the Road*, we received an email from ASO. They pushed back the announcement of La Course by Tour de France from January 30 to February 1. *Shit, shit, shit.* I was still under ASO's gag-order. Our four-second clip in the credits of *Half the Road* revealed the news of La Course by Tour de France. With 48 hours until ASO's press release, if I spilled the beans, ASO could turn nasty.

But to stop *Half the Road* before the credits finished wasn't okay either. What to do, what to do? I informed the theater technician about the issue. "Well, we can keep the film rolling, but turn off the sound and black out the screen with a piece of blank paper," he said. "Five minutes before the Tour de France scene, run up to the booth. Bring paper!"

So I did just that. Just before the film's conclusion, I ran up to the booth of The Loft with a large, blank sheet of paper, ready for "the blackout." The audience was somewhat in on the plan, too. Before the film started, I announced that very big, game-changing news for the cycling world was coming on February 1, but until then... we had to keep quiet. And I needed their help.

"When you see the screen go blank for four seconds, know that progress is on the way!" I said. *Oooooh*, the audience whispered. One hour and thirty-nine minutes into the film, I squeezed into the film booth and awkwardly dangled a blank sheet of paper in front of the projector, blacking out the news of La Course. Flashbacks to posters of kinesio tape equal signs darted through my thoughts. For four seconds, I was alive with a strange pulse of secret knowledge, yet simultaneously deflated by the reality of ridiculous things we do for progress and equality.

When *Half the Road* ended, the audience erupted with kindness. The applause felt amazing but two things made a bigger impact. First, the positive comments from non-cyclists. It was a huge win for our intended goal; making a film not about bike racing but equal opportunity hurdles. Second, receiving looks I refer to as 'benevolent disbelief.' For the last two years, many people in the audience knew I was making a film. Most of them assumed it would be some sort of home movie shot on a smart phone. Their comments in The Loft made me both smile and cringe. "Whoa, you made a *real* film." "There was a *real* plot!" "I didn't think you were making an actual, you know, *movie*."

While the comments from our viewers were intended as compliments, it also unveiled the undercurrent of women being underestimated. While I thanked each bearer of kindness, the benevolent disbelief was palpable. If anything, *Half the Road* helped break through one more layer of doubt when it comes to proving what women can do. Daniel's comment was the much-needed humorous icing on the cake.

A kindhearted middle-aged man came over and bestowed praise for *Half the Road*, expressing his enjoyment of the film and his disdain for the inequality I smiled and thanked him.

"I just have to ask one thing," Daniel said. "I'm a huge fan of Bob Roll. Did you like everything he said?" It took me a moment to process the question. That Daniel thought our narrator free-versed the entire film. As if we sat Bob down and said, *'Ok, Bobke. Say stuff.'* I broke into a big grin.

"Yes, Daniel, I like what Bob Roll said. I *wrote* what he said."

"Ohhhhh... you *wrote* that stuff?"

"Yes. Is this your first documentary experience?"

"No, I've seen lots. This is just the first one I've seen that's been written."

Alas. Sometimes it's best to let sleeping dogs lie. On the upside, apparently Daniel wasn't surprised a woman wrote a documentary. He was surprised *anyone* wrote documentaries. I took that as a victory for equality and I still smile about our conversation to this day.

When the lights went up in the theater, we held a Q and A session so the audience could interact with the seven pro cyclists in the film who flew in to be part of the screening. Lauren Hall, Janel Holcomb, Amber Pierce, Jade Wilcoxson, Nicky Wangsgard, Addy Albershardt, Alisha Welsh… the very women I looked up to so for so many years were now seated beside me as friends, teammates, competitors. They were also my grand jury, the only ones whose verdict I truly cared about. *Half the Road* was *their* story, and I desperately wanted to get it right. Nicky Wangsgard put me at ease.

"Our stories showed the world the true meaning of drive and determination," Nicky said. "I believe everyone in the audience walked out the door thinking '*Yes*, female cyclists can race the Tour de France and I want to be a part of the movement that makes this happen.'" I exhaled relief. When I finally had a moment to take it all in, tears started streaming down. The mascara did not. All was right in the world.

――――――

On January 31, the day before ASO's announcement for La Course by Tour de France, I tweeted, "Keep a close eye on women's cycling right now!" in an effort to set the stage of anticipation and get people talking. I received an immediate email from Chrissie. "I just got a call from Thibaud at ASO. Please delete the tweet. He isn't happy!" Yep, they were still policing Le Tour Entier's social media (and mine). Sheesh. ASO was happy to work with us behind the scenes, but they really did not want the public to know. The fact I didn't have optic nerve damage from eye-rolling was a medical miracle.

On February 1, 2014, ASO announced La Course while I loaded bikes into a minivan on the side of the road in Guatemala. Hired to lead another cycling tour with Bike Costa Rica I spent the week taking tourists to the Mayan ruins. The timing was perfect. I had five thousand dollars of credit card debt for film festival rights. Freelancing as a tour guide helped immensely. With the launch of *Half the Road*, the next six months were not conducive to holding a normal job. Slinging bikes in Central America was a multi-faceted gift.[84]

Every moment not pedaling or sightseeing, I fielded calls and emails from journalists, regarding the news of La Course by Tour de France. The cycling world and mainstream media was on fire with the victorious outcome of our petition. On my way home, my flight connected in Honduras. I have distinct memories of roaming around the Tegucigalpa airport in search of an internet signal, smiling with great joy. Activism that started in Tucson by some chick with St. Kitts and Nevis scored a victory in France thanks to the help of Brits, Dutch and 98,000 international warriors and here I was reading about it in Central America. Indeed, we can all create change anywhere and see its effect everywhere.

———————

Two weeks after *Half the Road*'s premiere, we received incredible news: our film secured a distribution contract with First Run Features. International rights, DVDs, future downloads and current crowdsourced screenings were now possible. Film festival acceptances began flooding in. Within the next 11 months, there would be 66 screenings in 26 different states and seven different countries; England, Canada, Australia, Scotland, Switzerland, St. Lucia and the United Arab Emirates. That was just the beginning. My eyes grew wide and my soul, wider.

"George," I said to my husband. "It's happening. People who are not related to me actually want to see movies about equity, sports and women kicking ass!" I sat

---

[84] The Mayan cycling tour also took us into Belize, where our campers brought cycling gear to donate to their youth cycling federation. I would be remiss not to mention cycling is Belize's #1 sport. The Belize Cycling Federation, founded in 1928, has the longest-running bike race in the Western Hemisphere; Belize Cross Country Classic a 142-mile event spanning 92 years as of 2020. From Guadeloupe's Yohann Gene to Trinidad & Tobago's Teniel Campbell, there's a lot more cycling history happening in Caribbean than people realize.

down with my husband and had another heart-to-heart. Things were gonna get busy. Real busy. It was February 2014 and La Course was in July. Screenings were popping up everywhere, and some contacted me for speaking engagements. My final manuscript for *The Road Less Taken* was due in early May. The next five months would be intense, but the calm was on the horizon.

Beneath my excitement, joy and relief, my sense of need was in full swing. We so often equate "need" as something that comes into play when things are going wrong or when there is a void to be filled. But in that moment when everything was going right—the film, the book, the petition, the Tour de France—I was most in need. Not of tangible things, but support and balance and normalcy. I was becoming two people; public Kathryn and private Kathryn. My public self was strong, outspoken and fighting for justice. My private self was tired, sensitive and in need of a hug, some take-out food, binge-watching *Dexter*, singing to the cats and being around someone who let me be my weird human self. My husband was that person. There is no greater gift in this life than being around people who let us be who we are.

"You got this," he said to me.

34

TRY, TRY, TRY

What I didn't "got" was a pro cycling team. It was February of 2014, and since being permanently released from Colavita in January, there was little hope for me to sign a contract with a UCI team. All of them were full. Also, island politics were not in my favor. Despite my win at Caribbean Championships which technically secured me a spot to the Commonwealth Games, the St. Kitts and Nevis Olympic Committee refused to acknowledge their own national cycling federation due to an internal power struggle between feuding parties. There were so many aspects of corruption in sports and usually athletes were the ones who paid the price. I desperately wanted to hire Dexter to take out the garbage.

Trying to keep positive about being teamless, I wore the Le Tour Entier cycling kit every day, drawing as much power as I could from the equal sign emblazoned on my chest and back. Surely that had to add watts to my workouts. I pretended as hard as I could that being teammless didn't hurt.

On the inside, what stung the most was the irony. We were finally going to have women's pro cycling stand on the start line of the Champs-Élysées… but the person who fought for it would not be one of them. My public self was ok with this. All I ever wanted was for pro women to have access to the Tour de France. Mission accomplished. But what kept me going through the tough parts of the journey was the personal vision I held since 2009: Maybe someday I could stand on the start line, too. To be part of the mission. To be a stakeholder in my dream. To revel in the What-Ifs. To keep the demons of NotEnoughness at bay. To show that we—the non-Olympians, non-famous, non-wealthy, regular "no ones" of the world—all have the power to make stuff happen. I also wanted to show other grown women what's possible. I was almost 39. You know who else wanted to stand on that start line? My inner child. The one with unhealed wounds.

In the spirit of teamwork, my inner child, adult activist and mental demons of Not-Enoughness banded together and formed our own private justice league. We began planting seeds in the Possibility crop, emailing all UCI teams in one final search of a contract for 2014. Now that word was out about La Course, teams worldwide were excited to qualify for the Tour de France. Selections of the top 15 to 20 teams would take place on April 29. Till then, teams concentrated on upping their world ranking. To land a pro contract in February would be hard enough. To land a contract on a team that makes selection for the race? Harder still. Landing a contract with a team, then having that team make selection for the top 20, then being chosen as one of the team's six athletes? Dear Sweet Jesus and Dexter, that was a long shot.

Still, I had to shoot. With professionalism and honesty, I asked every team in North America and Europe if there was any possibility of room on their roster. This time, instead of the usual crickets, responses came back with kindness. *"Hi Kathryn, sorry, we don't have room for you but thank you for making La Course happen."* I received no contract that winter. Nor spring.

What I did receive, however, was an opportunity to guest ride with Optum Pro Cycling, the highest ranked U.S. team in 2014. They were coming into Tucson for two tune-up races and needed a spare athlete. My two closest pro cycling sisters Lauren Hall and Amber Pierce raced for Optum. To ride with them was a dream… and maybe even a doorway. Zipping up the stylish, powerful orange and black jersey felt like a great Lycra hug of hopefulness. My confidence soared and I performed well as their domestique at Tucson Bicycle Classic, clinging to the hope that perhaps a window of opportunity might open by July. Hope and pro-activeness seemed to be my most effective mental weapons. *There was still time.*

―――――――

When ASO announced team selection for La Course would take place on April 29 my inbox was flooded with team directors asking if I could help pull strings and grease the wheels of ASO. One of those teams was Optum. The selection protocol was in place; 18 teams would race La Course. The top 15 teams in UCI world ranking, plus three national teams selected by ASO. Behind the scenes we knew ASO decided the three national teams would be France, Australia and Netherlands.

I quickly scanned the UCI world rank stats. Optum was fluctuating between 15th and 16th place. Ooof. Right on the cusp. No wonder they wanted help.

Only one pro team from the U.S. ranked above Optum—UnitedHealthCare Pro Cycling. They were safe. But Optum was too close to the cutoff. The very least I could do was find the right angle and put benevolent pressure on ASO. Other than UnitedHealthCare, the remaining top 15 teams were all European. I scanned the rosters of those teams. There was zero representation from Canada. Optum was a US-based team, but half their roster was Canadian. Optum's Leah Kirchmann was the national champion of Canada. She also happened to be in my living room, as she remained in Tucson to train after team camp, so George and I took her in. Ok, now I had something to work with. Simply wouldn't be right for a historic World Tour race to have no Canadian representation on the Champs-Élysées. I immediately wrote our contacts at ASO to ask for the inclusion of Optum in La Course. *"Team Optum p/b Kelly Benefit Strategies has both the reigning U.S. and Canadian national champions, multiple UCI podiums and is widely regarded as the strongest team in North America. They deserve to be at La Course by Tour de France..."*

In the spirit of Asking, I reached out to Chrissie, inquiring if she might go to bat for me on another idea. With no representation of pro riders from smaller nations, we could ask ASO to create a composite team for La Course. A team of riders from Caribbean, Asian, African and Middle Eastern countries... what a perfect opportunity to show the global growth of cycling and right the wrongs of UCI's exclusionary ranking system.

"Chrissie, I know we don't have ultimate say, but Yann & Thibaud definitely listen to you... can you help me? Can we try? I will do whatever it takes. Thanks babes, love you," I wrote.

"I can try," Chrissie said.

In March and April 2014, *Half the Road* gained serious momentum. From North Dakota to Virginia, film festivals were accepting us everywhere. Some even flew me out, like Richmond International Film Festival. RIFF was a big deal because Richmond, Virginia was chosen for 2015 UCI Road Cycling World Championships... a race that hadn't been held in the United States for thirty years! Originally, *Half the Road* was turned down by RIFF. But the big boss of RIFF, Heather Waters, stood her ground and emailed me.

"This rejection decision just doesn't sit well with me," Heather wrote. "Your film has an important message and it got 4 out of 5 votes needed. The fifth vote was a "no" because it was clearly not a big-budget film with any Hollywood stars. Frankly, that's not a good reason to turn this film away." Then she asked if I thought we could sell out a full theater. I told her we already did.

"Let us in RIFF and I'll prove it, Heather," I asked. She agreed. We took to social media and pre-sold enough ticket sales to score a screening on Saturday, the most coveted day of all film festivals. Then, the Richmond UCI World Championship committee came on board to sponsor our screening, despite our stance on UCI in *Half the Road*. Still, they stood behind us, supporting women's pro cycling. Rule of activism: rejection is not always final.

The night of our screening at RIFF, something even more incredible happened. Out of the sixty films selected, *Half the Road* won Audience Choice Award. The award where film-goers actually vote on their favorite film of the entire four-day festival. *Half the Road* was up against every genre of every subject matter. Documentary, fiction, narrative, animated, long, short, everything. Given the fact I knew only three people in the state of Virginia, winning this award was a monumental victory.

After the screening, a young couple came up to me and expressed, "We can't wait to share this film with our daughter!" I thanked them and asked if they also had a son.

"Yes, two!"

"Please share the film with your sons, as well," I urged, smiling, explaining we must raise the next generation to see women as their equals. Starting as early as possible. By sharing stories of strong women to boys, it'll help us get to gender equity much faster.

That night, I broke down in happy tears at the Richmond Holiday Inn Express. 90 percent of the tears were because of the Audience Choice Award. 10 percent were because of the gift basket filled with fancy truffles and fabulously snooty foods. *I have arrived.* Even breakfast was included. Ok, breakfast is always included for everyone at Holiday Inn, but still. These particular free cinnamon rolls felt like glorious, doughy Oscars.

All jokes aside, there was a bit more underlying my mini cry-fest. During the two years it took to make *Half the Road*, I was in relentless go-mode. Git 'er done, make it happen, go go go. Beneath that layer, something in my sensitive soul never truly got over being called a "no one" or being undervalued by women to whom I aspired. Until that night in Richmond, when a film originally eliminated was brought back by woman who saw its importance... and then went on to win the Audience Choice Award. Goddamn, that was some healing juju. It was as though Heather Waters buzzed her way into the nasty hive of Queen Bees who stung my soul and took the throne, decreeing, *In the hive of progress, women don't sting women.* Thank you, Heather.[85]

I cried a little that night because my go-go-go mode released its forceful grip a little. Sometimes we cry upon full, not empty. Because hurt is acknowledged rather than denied. This little film ESPN once dismissed was now truly connecting and reaching people. Strangers. Society. I was learning more and more each day. This journey of activism was much harder than I expected, but the sweet release of doing something that mattered gave rise above the pain.

———————————

Los Angeles, Napa, New York City, Tulsa, San Francisco, Newport Beach, London, Boulder... *Half the Road* was on fire in April 2014. The Loft even screened it again for an encore performance. New York City booked a weeklong stint, with *Half the Road* showing three times a day at Cinema Village. *Three times a day*! Screenings were pouring in around the world. Reviews were coming in. Most were downright positive. Every now and then, we'd get the comment about the 1-hour and 46-minute length. *The New York Times* critiqued *Half the Road* for being too long. This made me laugh. Too long? Yeah, well, so was waiting 101 years for women to be recognized by the Tour de France. So, let's try this math: A film about women's equality running 106 minutes averages 58 seconds per year of Tour de Francelessness divided by zero representation of women in 114 years of UCI presidency multiplied by our current society's attention span disorder = *Half the Road* is too damn short.

Also too short: time. I was in desperate need of someone to help me with the influx of *Half the Road* inquiries, bookings, appearance requests. Budgeting for an assistant had totally skipped my radar. There was no way I could afford one. Out of the blue, I received an email from a social media friend, Eric Berman, a recreational cyclist and realtor in suburban Boston who'd followed my career since the ESPN

———————————

[85] Interactive Reader Guide: Heather Waters & Richmond International Film Festival

days. Picking up on the vibe that I was overwhelmed with duties, he volunteered his assistance.

"Listen, if you ever need any help…"

I responded immediately and took on Eric as my assistant. What I didn't realize immediately was the gift of having a *mans*sistant. Slowly, the truth unfolded. When it came to the business side of screenings, bookings and appearance fees, people interacted/responded differently with Eric than they did with me. (Kind of like the way the ASO guys interacted when Steve spoke during our meeting). When I sent responses on screening prices and speaking availability, people would bargain. When Eric sent responses, people would simply accept or decline. Fascinating! The male/female business interactions and negotiation differences were real. Which prompted me to create a second email account.

While I passed most of our *Half the Road* emails to Real Eric, I became Fake Eric and answered quite a few myself. Using only his first name. Misrepresentation? Nope. Eric was in on the game, and if I needed a voice interaction to take place, he willingly obliged. He was a terrific manssistant.[86] Here's to all the real and fake men who help women thrive in this Not Equal But Getting There Weird Fucking World. Rule of activism: A woman's value is non-negotiable.

Now that La Course was a sure bet and *Half the Road* was in the spotlight, I was a tweet storm of energy, positivity and activism, hurling my thoughts into social media with confidence, spunk and joy:

"Progress is uncomfortable. That's how you know it's working."

"Find something you love in this world and stand up for it."

"How to have a fulfilling life: 1) Say you're going to do something. 2) Do it."

"I am not a loose cannon. My targets just move around a lot."

"Hush demons. Let's take a nap."

"It is amazing what you can achieve if you refuse to shut up."

"Anyone who puts down your dream lacks the courage to go after their own."

"Thank your demons. Growth & progress rarely stem from a life of kittens & rainbows."

"Thank your doubters. They're just as motivating as those who believe in you."

---

[86] I still use both Erics today. Thank you, Real Eric, for all the years of manssisting. Maybe this book will bring more emails your way. Our way. They'll never know. Fist bump.

The more La Course gained traction in the media, the more the trolls of sexism came out to play. This time, it bothered me less. Now we had a race. We won ASO. I stood taller, stronger, prouder. While the world responded positively to *Half the Road*, there were two people who were quite displeased. The first was Brian Cookson. He was often tagged in social media comments from viewers of *Half the Road* who disagreed with his antiquated thoughts that "women are slower" and less capable than men. Cookson did not like it one bit. He reached out to Emma Pooley, trying to track me down. He expressed to her that in his conversation with me at Worlds, "I had thought that we had a sensible and thoughtful discussion. It now seems this has been edited and I am presented in the film as being unsupportive of the developments of women's racing."

"Thought you might like to see this!" Emma said, forwarding me the email from Cookson. "Interesting that Brian claims his interview has been 'edited.' I suspect he has actually rather more accurately changed his views, due to the pressure of public opinion."

I reached out to Cookson, with an equal mix of honesty and empathy, to let him know he was not edited. If he'd like to see the original 20-minute clip of his interview in full, that could be arranged as well. I pointed out that people were responding to is his outdated philosophies, and he could use this opportunity in a very positive way to *change* his views of women's cycling. "Our side of the sport needs the men of UCI to champion us, and I think you can do it, Brian," I told him. "Let's use *Half the Road* to grow a new outlook, a new platform. Together."

Cookson still wasn't thrilled with me. Not everyone likes standing before the Reality Mirror of their own beliefs, but sometimes that's exactly what we need to do. Also nonplussed with their portrayal in *Half the Road* was Jonathan Vaughters, one of the most prestigious men's cycling team owners. Vaughters created Garmin-Cervelo, a men's and women's team in 2011, then cut the women's team after one year. Vaughters cited sponsorship withdrawal. Emma Pooley, who was on the team, argued a very well-articulated point. After shuttering the women, Vaughters signed former-doper Thomas Dekker to the men's team for near half-million dollars. Was funding women really an issue, or was the funding simply prioritized for men? Vaughters was not thrilled be called out by Emma.

"I should sue her," he grumbled to me on the phone.

"Don't," I diffused. "Emma said nothing libelous or slanderous. And it would only bring more attention to you in a negative way. Let it go. How about if we work on bringing back a women's team, JV?" Despite the grumbling, Vaughters and I got on quite well after that. In our modern society, not everyone has the guts to have an actual conversation about difficult topics. Rather than troll me on social media, Vaughters called. Speaking matters. Rule of activism: Use your voice whenever possible. (The literal one).

On the Le Tour Entier front, we were in the stages of helping ASO's marketing campaign promote La Course by Tour de France. Every week, we went back and forth over email. Talk about standing in front of the Reality Mirror... boy, was ASO stuck in the past. They showed us their first rendition of the race poster. It was a cartoon caricature of a thin, sexy woman on a bicycle dressed in pink and purple and wearing red lipstick. I'm not sure if fear or laughter was my first reaction but my first words were definitely *Nooooo!* and *Noooooooooooooooooooooooo!* Luckily my sisterhood of Le Tour Entier agreed wholeheartedly and we pressed hard for ASO to recreate the poster. Women sitting on a bicycle, no. Women racing, yes. Ponytails, ok. Lipstick and cartoon graphics, no way. None of this pink and purple gender assignment coloring. Please use greens and blues. Something, anything other than pink and purple. Eventually, ASO listened.[87] We were already doing the majority of ASO's job for them. What more could they want?

Everything. In addition to our still unpaid partnership, ASO also wanted access to the 98,000 people who signed our petition on Change.org. *Give* our valuable data to ASO? Absolutely effing not. I told them we'd post an update about La Course taking place, but no, they could not have our email listserv and bombard people with links to Tour de France merchandise... that didn't even include items for La Course.

Chrissie and Steve went to Paris for another meeting with ASO on behalf of Le Tour Entier, only to find ASO lacking serious direction just five months before La Course. Their marketing and media plan was abysmal, their investment stingy at best. They had no plan for a press launch, no desire to cover the costs for Ambassadors, nor budget established to compensate us for our time and effort. They did, however, encourage us to seek sponsors for ASO. They wanted Le Tour Entier to talk to possible investors and simply send them over to ASO. Without contracting us for commission. We shook our heads, once again cringe-laughing as how stupid they thought we were.

What we did do, for the sake of the race, was provide content instructing ASO on media coverage, ad content, social media announcements, spokespeople,

---

[87] Interactive Reader Guide: Final posters for La Course by Tour de France.

language, branding, story structure, historic key points, and all the ridiculously unseen minutia it takes behind the scenes to make shit happen. The list was never-ending. But we were committed do whatever it took so La Course by Tour de France would thrive. Except the extortion part of bringing them money without contracts. *Nous ne sommes pas si stupides, garçons.* We're not that stupid, boys.

––––––––

In late April, I traveled to Boulder for a speaking engagement at a sold-out screening of *Half the Road*, bringing with me a metaphorical basket of *How ya like them apples?* to Boulder International Film Festival, which turned us down the month before. Not only did *Half The Road* sell out once, but a second showing was added and that sold out, too. Rule of life: Make your own damn festival. The best part? I didn't have a ticket for either sold-out screening, so I sat in the lobby. Ten minutes from the end I wandered back into the theater, where Kristin Armstrong tells her story about coming back from a devastating, collarbone-breaking crash at the Exergy Tour and winning the Olympic gold medal less than three months later. Despite the millions of times I'd seen the film, Kristin's scene gave me shivers of hope every time. I leaned against the wall in the dark corridor of the theater, watching people's faces, smiling deeply within and trying my best not to drop popcorn on the floor. When one's biggest concern is dropped popcorn, life is very, very good. April was very, very good. At least the first half.

One of the best pieces of April news; ASO changed their invite format for La Course by Tour de France. Instead of 18 teams, there would be 20. The 17 top-ranked UCI teams, and three national teams. Optum Pro Cycling, previously on the cusp 16th place, was now set receive an invite. ASO agreed with my point, Canada needed representation. I was thrilled. No doubt Optum would put Leah Kirchmann on the roster for the race. A sliver of hope pulsed through me. *Maybe Optum would allow me to guest ride, too.* Deep inside, I couldn't help but feel a pang of karma about one specific team not invited. Colavita Pro Cycling didn't come close to qualifying in the top 17.

While speaking to filmgoers in Boulder, I noticed my reliance on the collective term "we" when talking to the audience and the media. Activism wasn't a solo journey. *We* spoke louder, clearer and more powerful than *me*. I loved the authentic symbolism of *we*-ness. Yet, as April rolled on, I sensed there was also something personal and vulnerable beneath the stalwart exterior of *we*. The word *we* also served as an emotional bulwark. With the film and La Course gaining traction, I was in the epicenter of activism. The constant state of being "on" was exhausting. Sometimes lonely. Using *we* helped. Every time I used the word, *we* channeled an invisible army of support. That I wasn't alone. That we were all fighting for equality. Together. *We* became my tiny, mighty noun of strength, bringing both ferocity and nurturing when I needed it most.

At the end of April, my demon of worthlessness came roaring to life while sitting in my friend Keavy's garage in Boulder. Cleaning the grime off my bike, which I brought with me to Colorado to train while at the screenings, I heard the ping of a new email. With our increased Le Tour Entier workload, our emails pinged often. This one was different. Steve was downright pissed that Cookson was being called out on social media for his interview in *Half the Road*. Steve was also ticked that I reposted/retweeted such opinions in solidarity. Clearly, Steve and Cookson were building a close relationship, and neither were happy that our timelines differed on most effective strategy for gender equity. (Mine: now! Theirs: someday!).

Usually, I am a huge fan of different opinions. The challenge of seeing someone else's view is a fantastic exercise in perspective. Also, a practice of tolerance and respect. There were times over the past year where someone in our group didn't see eye to eye with someone else, but we found solutions and moved forward. I often disagreed with stuff Steve said, but he made some damn great points from time to time. Except this time. Something was off.

Steve was concerned my background as a journalist and filmmaker was to make a name for myself. *Uh oh*, I thought. *Sounds just like Wynona.* He believed speaking my mind about Cookson/UCI would back me into a corner and label me counter-productive to the bigger picture of improving women's cycling. But rather than call or reach out to me personally, Steve chose email and CC'd everyone in Le Tour Entier.

"Kathryn, please do not shoot yourself in the foot," Steve warned, "Look to others for advice and opinion." I couldn't help but snicker, as *Half the Road* and Le Tour Entier *were* 100% comprised of advice and opinion. Steve had not yet seen *Half the Road* but went to bat for Cookson anyway, claiming, "Brian isn't in any way, shape or form a misogynist… He's a strong family man with a long-standing marriage and lovely family, including a daughter." To which I agreed; Cookson was a very kind, good human being. Also, a president with incredibly outdated views.

As I continued reading the email, it became very clear Steve got angry anytime I ruffled the feathers of the UCI patriarchy.

"Fostering an 'us' and 'them' type mentality won't work," Steve said. "And because your views often aren't consistent with Le Tour Entier, despite you being the founder, we should consider what the future may hold..."

Hold up, now. My blood ran cold. Steve wanted to exclude me from the very group I created. The group I brought him into. The mission dearest to my heart; equal opportunity for women. An arrow launched straight to the heart of my vulnerability trifecta: Left-out, misunderstood and worthless. In my friend's garage, with chain-grease on my hands, sweat in all crevices, hunger in my stomach and anger in my soul, I lost my shit.

Storming around Keavy's garage—which was luckily closed and she was not home—I knew better than to kick or punch other people's stuff. But my bicycle travel case was there, and its awkward, trapezoidal body was made of thick canvas cloth. With fists and feet and flailing limbs, I let loose a fury of physical angst I had no idea dwelled within me. This was a first. And it wasn't over quickly. Time became irrelevant. I just kept battering. When I was done with the bag, I took my rage to the air. My arms and legs thrashed and floundered in every direction, not necessarily waiting for the previous limb to finish. Also, I was crying. Also, mumbling. *Steve hasn't even seen the film. Fuck shit ass shit shit fucker. Criticizing me. Let him into our group. Mistake. Stupid, stupid. Dammit shit shit shit. Another middle-aged white man telling me what to do. Shitty damn shit fuck fuckin fuck. Misunderstanding is the devil of trust. Ahhhhhhflar. Rggggwu. Uuuuhhhh.* If there were such a thing as Zumba cage fighting therapy, I think that's what was happening.

Also happening; not just a reaction to hurt, but a reaction to fear. One of the greatest all-time quotes on fear belongs to original gonzo journalism guru Hunter S. Thompson, who instructed, "Never turn your back on fear. It should always be in front of you, like a thing that might have to be killed." Bravo, gonzo.

Throughout my activism journey, I made friends with fear. It was the only way to deal with the doubters, naysayers, trolls, bullies and enemies. But this fear was different. It wasn't coming from the public. It was coming from within a group I built and trusted. My mind wasn't equipped to wax philosophy in that particular moment of garage tantrum angst, but my body was indeed attempting to kill the invisible, intangible fear in front of me. Fight I did. When one of my spazzing limbs connected with a metal garage beam thingy, I collapsed into a pile on the floor, drained. Aching. Empty. Hollow. Nothing. Nothingness. Steve wielded the weapon I feared most and held it to my chest. Exclusion is the sharpest sword.

I made two phone calls from my post-Zumba-cage fighting fetal position. The first was to Tracy, who I hoped might sense my fear about being blackballed from Le Tour Entier. Being middle of the night in Europe, it went to voicemail. The second call was to my husband. After explaining the situation, George said,

"Why don't you just apologize?"

"Oh, I didn't break anything in Keavy's garage," I said, misunderstanding. "I'm a little bruised, but—" Took me a moment to realize my husband meant apologize to *Steve*.

"But I didn't do anyth—"

"Doesn't matter. Just say you're sorry."

Sorry? For standing up for myself? Bewildered and hurt, it took a moment to process that George's comment came from a place of love, yet rooted in avoiding conflict rather than dealing with it. In that sobering moment of suggesting apology, the Reality Mirror was held before me. I had two choices. I could apologize for upsetting Steve and Cookson, and turn in my card of authenticity. Or, I could stand my ground and continue to speak my mind, which meant battling demons of exclusion and nothingness. I went with the latter. Women have a long history of apologizing just to keep the peace. To yield in power struggles with antiquated men who feel uncomfortable amongst opinionated women. To apologize—to Steve or Cookson—for sharing my views of inequality in the film or social media was not an option.

While struggling with demons, it's incredibly hard to see the flip side of any situation. It's hard to pause mid-Zumba angst and philosophize, "Why is [the opposition] so threatened by public displays of opinion?"

While such answers lie in a far more credible psychology textbook, the kernel of truth was this: I disrupted Steve's comfort zone. He was wary that association with me would jeopardize *his* progress within UCI. But rather than removing himself from Le Tour Entier, he instead employed psychological projection: *I* should go.

Slowly, I collected myself and got up from the garage floor. While my Cerberus feasted for hours on the hambone of worthlessness, I learned a huge lesson from Garage Meltdown. Exclusion was the sharpest sword, but the shield of a team is always stronger. Tracy picked up the armor and stormed to the frontlines. Over phone calls and emails, she had my back.

"We're here *because* of Kathryn," Tracy defended, letting Steve know there would be no exclusion. That the strength of Le Tour Entier *was* our different viewpoints. That our varied perceptions made us question the norms and seek smart, balanced, creative solutions. "We have something quite special in Le Tour Entier and I am really excited to be part of it," Tracy continued. "What an amazing day it will be in July when we all stand together on the Champs-Élysées and celebrate the first race... I'm feeling very positive!" Immediately after our group call, Tracy sent me a personal note:

"Kathryn, I love the fact that every time I speak to you, you change my mind about something... you always have the best thing in mind for the sport and ask the right questions for the right reasons. Cycling is lucky to have you." I'm not sure Tracy truly knew how much her words healed. All hail the Tracys of Teamwork; Defenders of Inclusion, Soothers of Cerberai. Tracy was such a gift to our team. And my overall stability.Hold tight to the ones who lift you up.

That May, we were three months out from La Course by Tour de France. Dialing my training up a notch—*Operation: Just-in-Case-Optum-Calls*—I hit all the hard-core group rides in Tucson. On a Saturday morning Shootout, a 16-year-old boy on the El Grupo Youth Cycling rode up next to me.

"So cool to see women out here. Did you see that movie on women's cycling?" Christian said. "It's really annoying pro girls don't get paid the same as guys. Doesn't make any sense. The girls on our team work just as hard as we do. Anyway, you gotta see *Half the Road*." Then off he pedaled.

Be still my heart. Our future is bright.

35

NO MORE SIDELINES

In May 2014, ASO officially announced the route of La Course by Tour de France in downtown Paris, a circuit encircling the Champs-Élysées thirteen times. 20 teams were selected[88] and the prize purse set for 32,000 Euro; same amount as the men's prize purse that day. The French Police announced La Course would be lined by female officers. Marianne Vos, the winningest female cyclist in history, was chosen as the official ambassador.

"I have won numerous trophies, as you know," Marianne tweeted, humbly eschewing the fact she has two Olympic gold medals and countless world/national championships. "However, this day is even more special. It's a memorable day with the launch of La Course by TDF." That one hit me right in the Happy Feelz. Here was the incredible role model I looked up to for years in the sport, who once granted my fledgling rookie self a photo with her when we both raced Vuelta el Salvador in 2008. Six years later, she was my friend, my partner-in-activism and she was going to stand on the start line of a race we created together at the freakin' Tour de France.

Best news yet, the media was coming on board worldwide. Now that La Course was secured for July, Le Tour Entier was on the hunt to secure international broadcast coverage. While technically it was ASO's job to handle broadcast rights, we didn't fully trust them. One of the main reasons the women's Tour de France Feminin disappeared in 1989 was because ASO chose not to sell the broadcasting rights. Not wanting La Course to follow suit, Emma, Chrissie, Marianne and I took initiative by contacting all sports networks in our respective nations. I reached out

---

[88] Pro teams selected: Rabo – Liv, Ale Cipollini, Astana BePink, Boels Dolmans, Bizkaia Durango, Mexico Faren, Bigla, Hitec Products, Rusvelo, Lotto Belisol, Optum p/b Kelly Benefit, Orica – AIS, Wiggle Honda, UnitedHealthCare, Giant – Shimano, Specialized – Lululemon, Poitou-Charentes Futuroscope. National teams: France, Australia, Netherlands (Pays-Bas).

to Universal Sports, a subsidiary of NBC that cornered the cycling market with over 186 hours of annual footage. They were interested, and began looking into acquisition. Television and livestream broadcast rights were secured for Europe, Asia, Africa, Australia, The Americas, The Middle East… over 157 countries, 104 which would be live and 25 via direct channel access. Within weeks, Universal Sports signed to broadcast La Course in North America. They booked me for an on-camera interview at their Colorado Springs office, set for mid-June.

Sydney Morning Herald tallied the data and concluded La Course would be the most televised exposure a women's cycling race ever received outside the Olympic Games. The Business Standard projected a sponsorship windfall. Prudhomme, excited about the media coverage, tweeted, "Thanks to Le Tour, La Course will get an exceptional media exposure. Once we saw how confident, engaged & motivated the women were, we just had to do something." Which made me smile. *Thanks to us, women will get some recognition*!

Media in the U.S. was buzzing in the best possible way. All major newspapers and men's interest magazines were robust with articles about Tour de France finally having a women's race. Quite a victory when women's magazines like *Glamour, Shape* and *Marie Claire* outside the sports market were covering the story. ESPNW mentioned nothing, other than sharing a pre-written Associate Press article. The media appeared in full support of La Course—especially now that broadcast rights were secured—but there remained two people who were not. Once again, British track cycling Olympians Laura Trott and (her future husband) Jason Kenny weighed in on the creation of La Course. Both thought the one-day race was a great step forward, yet stopped short of advocating for full inclusion for women at the Tour de France.

> "I'm not so swayed on the whole Tour de France idea," Trott told the UK Daily Mail. "I just don't think it should run along the same course as the men's because we would never, ever complete 300 km. You'd get two riders rolling in after 10 hours. I just don't think it would be realistic. We ride a tour for five days and at the end of it we're completely knackered. For three weeks - no chance. I certainly wouldn't finish, put it that way."

> "There'd be deaths," Kenny predicted.[89]

---

[89] Interactive Reader Guide: Laura Trott and Jason Kenny on Tour de France for Women

Unsure whether to laugh or cry, I settled on cringe-wincing. There is no greater step backward for progress when two members of prominence—blinded by ignorance—speak to the masses. These talented sprint champions in their early twenties clearly had no idea that physiology catered to female endurance athletes in their thirties and forties. Rather than acknowledge the many women who *could* do and *wanted* to do the Tour de France, death apparently seemed an easier answer. Well, Kenny had one thing right. There will be deaths. When women are granted a full Tour de France, we will see the deaths of patriarchy, traditionalism and ignorance. I proudly volunteer to drive the hearse.

As long as it doesn't interfere with my bus driving schedule...

———————

Weeks after my near-exclusion from Le Tour Entier and unhinged garage tantrum, I was invited to race the time trial at AMGEN Tour of California. ATOC was the U.S. equivalent to the Tour de France. Like its famous French counterpart, ATOC was ridiculously behind the times. Hovering dangerously close to the cliff of sexism, ATOC developed a one-day criterium race in 2008, then added an invite-only time trial in 2011. Invitations for only ten to twenty women, selected by the race directors. While I still didn't have a professional team in 2014, I was the reigning Caribbean Champion in the time trial and I was given an invitation. A local California elite squad put me on their composite team for the criterium the day before.

At the enormous ATOC gala event filled with sponsors and patrons, all eight riders of each men's team were brought up on stage to parade before the audience. For the women's presentation, only one representative per team was allowed. An afterthought at best, making the women appear less equal and less important. In addition, all the women were brought out on stage together—like one long line of Rockettes from different teams. As we lined up for entrance, I was told by the race promoter, Adam Duvendek, that I could not take part.

"We already have a rep from your criterium team," he said, checking his clipboard.

"But I'm racing the time trial too. For St. Kitts and Nevis." I reminded him. "It's very important we show representation of smaller nations."

"No, you can't go up there. Too many women on the stage," he confirmed. *Ha! Heaven forbid twenty-one women stand together on one stage.* I wasn't sure if he feared the stage or the world would fall apart. Paying attention to the vibe, I felt there was something else going on. That perhaps ATOC didn't want me out there because of my reputation as a rabble-rouser. To step aside wasn't an option, but neither was being rude. With as much kindness, benevolence and smiley-ness, I looked at him and said, "Adam, please let me represent St. Kitts and Nevis. Otherwise, I will have to talk about women and small nations not being presented equally at Tour of California."

He stormed away. A few minutes later, he came back.

"You can walk," Adam said. "But don't ever put me in this position again. You've already thrown us under the bus."

Ah, so that's what it was… Medalist Sports, which ran Tour of California and also Tour of Utah, was not thrilled with the article I wrote for VeloNews on women not being allowed to race Tour of Utah. *There's the rub!* Clearly they did not like being exposed for inequality, and they certainly didn't like me for doing it. The Exposed tend to believe The Exposer has thrown them beneath the metaphorical bus. True activists never throw people beneath the bus of progress. We *drive* the damn bus. We offer The Exposed two choices: Get on board or get out of the way. Those who can't decide sometimes inadvertently throw themselves under. The latter achieves very little. Rule of activism: Drive the bus. Invite others aboard. If they don't accept, at least honk the horn so they get out of the way. *Beep, beep.*

I walked on the ATOC gala stage as the final athlete in the line-up, which must have suited the race promoters just fine. My on-the-end location made it very simple for Tour of California media to cut me out of the press photo, which they did. But alas, I was there and I stood.

That year, the time trial fell on May 11, my 39th birthday. I placed 16th, which suited me fine. These were twenty of the best time trialists in the world. 16th felt like a victory after being completely schnockered from the Le Tour Entier work, *Half the Road* promoting and full-time training for the remote possibility that maybe— just maybe—some team might pick me up mid-season.

While I knew the odds were stacked against me that any UCI World Tour Team would hire a 39-year-old rabble-rouser mid-season who got dropped from her last team... still I had to dream. I had to put my hope and energy somewhere. Even if Optum never signed me, I had to train as if they might. The best way to stave the pain of No-One-ness was training toward the possibility of a Yes.

———

While my Yeses for mid-season team possibilities were slim, the Yeses for *Half the Road* were pouring in. Word was really getting out! We weren't just booked for screenings but *sold out* in Chicago, Denver, Seattle and Baltimore. We then sold out Chattanooga, where U.S. Cycling National Championships were taking place.

In mid-May, an email appeared from two women in Dubai, asking if they could screen *Half the Road* and if I might be interested in coming to the Middle East to speak. Pascale de Jong and Louise Adamson were Dutch ex-pats living in Dubai and they filled me in on the flourishing cycling community and the need of more women's representation.

"Of course, yes, let's do it!" I responded, enthusiastically.

"Great! But be warned, the paperwork is ridiculous," Pascale explained, citing that shipping something to Dubai—even as simple as a DVD—incurred a magna carta of documentation. I filled out the documentations and we set a screening date for November.

Weeks after receiving the DVD, Pascale called. There was a problem. To screen in Dubai, they would need to edit the film. *Aww, come on*, I thought. *Was 104 minutes too long for Dubai?*

"No, it's not the length," Pascale said. "It's a subject matter about—"

"NO. No no no. Forget it. You do not have permission to edit *Half the Road*. We're done," I huffed, cutting Pascale off and immediately launching into a tirade on censorship, creativity and personal annoyance. *This film is my baby. No, you can't cut off a limb.* I didn't even hear her out. I was completely sure what she wanted to cut. The Cookson part, just like Rapha wanted to cut. Since there was a UCI Tour of Dubai, surely some Dubai representative didn't want political strife with the UCI. Yeah, that had to be it.

"That's not it," Pascale interrupted back. I finally regained some grown-up composure and heard her out. Pascale wanted to cut the section of the film about Nicky Wangsgard, the gay pro cyclist who shared her story of having to stay in the closet in order to keep her job. One of the most important scenes in the film! On inclusion, tolerance and equal opportunity! Not to mention, Nicky was my *friend*. I breathed fire into the phone.

"Absofuckinglutely not," I reacted/bellowed. As I reached out to disconnect our Skype session, Pascale said,

"Kathryn, wait... please hear me out. I'm gay."

Um, *what*? Now I was intrigued. Why on earth would a gay woman want to cut out the gay rights section our film? That made zero sense. Still brimming with anger,

I was hooked. *Please explain.* Pascale elucidated. In Dubai, films using the word "gay" or "homosexual" could not publicly be screened. In the majority of the Middle East, homosexuality is still labeled a sin and/or an illness. There was, however, one way around screening the film.

"Look, it's very clear in the film that Nicky and Jenna are a couple," Pascale explained. "We don't want to cut the entire section. We just need to cut out two sentences where she verbally says the word "gay." Everyone in the audience will know they're gay, it's very well implied. But if the word "gay" is in the film, the government won't let us show it." Pascale and her partner Louise were both cyclists, and they loved this part of the film the most. They wanted the people of Dubai to see a film empowering women and bicycles, but to do so, they had to get creative to get around the law.

"I would prefer to change the law first, but that will take years and will probably never happen," Pascale said. "But we can screen your film now, lift the curtain of oppression and help empower women in this country. Please help us do that."

Well, I'll be damned. Pascale did the one thing that plucks the iron string in the heart of every activist: She brought perspective to the table and sat me down to feast, holding up a mirror to the conundrum of progress. Should we compromise our personal beliefs for a greater good?

"I'll call you back," I told Pascale, wrestling with the decision. This was my movie and the thought of editing out the word "gay" would not fly in my culture. But Dubai wasn't my culture. And Pascale raised a remarkable point: Maybe not everything needs to be spelled out or spoken, especially when it's visually implied. But what I wrestled with most was the discomfort that comes with personal growth. Pascale made me take a good hard look at myself. My roots were steeped in my beliefs, but maybe I could bend my tree branches a little bit. Bending is not what we Type As do best. Which is exactly why I knew I had to do it.

During the petition campaign, I told the world *Progress is uncomfortable, that's how you know it's working!* Giving in to my own discomfort would make me a hypocrite. As for the technical element, well shit… the film was already released. The DVD with First Run Features could not be altered. That would be a royal, logistical and potentially legal mess. I called Pascale back with a compromise.

"Ok, Pascale. If you sign a non-disclosure agreement, waiver of non-distribution and allow me to view the edit before signing off on the screening rights… I will send you a non-watermarked original DVD. You hire the editors to remove the word 'gay.' Just this once."

Pascale agreed. We booked the screening and my trip to Dubai for November, six months away. Neither Pascale nor I had any idea how much my life would change in the interim. Or how Dubai would keep me alive.

A week after pro teams were announced for La Course, I scanned the list with hope. ASO did not honor our request for a composite team of pro athletes from smaller nations. But Optum was on there. So was Specialized-Luluemon, owned by Kristy Scrymgeour of our Le Tour Entier associates. Perhaps one of these two teams I knew personally might have room. I was fully aware this was a big ask, but I had to obey the What-Ifs by trying, hoping, training and asking.

Optum responded by thanking me for the help, then promptly said no. There was no room at the inn. Kristy said she'd love to help, but didn't feel it was the right thing to do.

"My riders are all vying for a spot to La Course, and it wouldn't be very professional of me to take that away," Kristy said. "I know you'd love to be on the start line but in your position, perhaps being on the sideline is a good thing. It might give you more of a chance to engage with media and do other things to promote the race." I understood Kristy's take, but I'd been engaging from the sidelines for the past seven years. I earned my way to the pro ranks. No more sidelines. I wanted in. I wanted to race my very own dream that was now a reality. Watching wasn't enough. I wanted to *feel* La Course.

I wanted to feel the cobbles vibrate through my bones. To inhale the air of Paris, feel it ricochet through my lungs, and exhale all the doubt, fear, demons and courage it took to build this race and leave it there to hover over the Arc d'Triomphe. From the corner of my eyes, I wanted to see the big, beautiful, bold blur of spectators at full speed. I wanted to hear the whirring gears and communal breath of my pro cycling sisterhood as we shifted physically and metaphorically on roads that once banned us from being here. I wanted to smell, touch, taste, see and hear every damn thing that happens on a day that was supposed to be impossible. I wanted to feel it all. And maybe, if I stood on that start line, maybe someone would see they could make some impossible shit happen, too. My inner athlete wanted to race, but my inner human wanted to be there for the hundred thousand people who helped build La Course, the six hundred plus who donated to *Half the Road*, for the legacy of Christina-Taylor Green and for my three billion daughters. Who likely had no idea I existed but whatever. Family is family.

I wasn't ready to stop swinging for the fences. Batter up.

Optum. Specialized-Lululemon. UHC. Hitec. The teams where I had connections said no. There was only one more team left that I knew, but it was such a longshot. For two reasons. First, Wiggle-Honda was ranked seventh in the world. If the all teams ranked behind them didn't want me already, surely Wiggle-Honda wouldn't either. Second, I learned guest rides weren't really possible at UCI World Tour events. Riders must be part of a team's official roster. As in, a team would have to sign me for the entire season. *Jesus. My odds were already bad, but now they were getting worse.* Still, I had to try. On May 28, I reached out to Rochelle Gilmore. Two years passed since we turned the car around to go back and interview her for *Half the Road* in Boise, Idaho at the Exergy Tour. Maybe she would be receptive. I had to ask. Ask, ask, ask.

> Hi Rochelle,
> I'm so glad Wiggle-Honda got an invite to La Course! Much deserved. I know you and I have the same vision of success for women's cycling & you've been so supportive of the film... Thank you for that, Rochelle. On that note, I wanted to reach out and see if there is any possibility I could ride for you for La Course. I know it is a very "big ask" but it is my dream to race... I'm the reigning Caribbean Champion & national champion of St. Kitts and Nevis, but as per UCI rules, ASO won't let me race as an individual. It would be of no cost to Wiggle. I will get myself there. I want to be there more than anything. I will gut myself for the team. Whatever you need. Do you think we could make something happen?
> Thank you, Rochelle & please let me know your thoughts.
> Kathryn

As I sent the email off to Rochelle, I smiled at the memory from 2012 Exergy Tour, where Rochelle was late to our date for filming *Half the Road*. Kevin and I left after thirty minutes. Then came the call. *Please come back, please come back... I've put on make-up and done my hair!* Sitting in my office chair two years later, as my email to Rochelle whooshed off into cyberspace, *I thought, please come back, please come back... I'm not so great with hair and make-up, but I helped make a race and I'm strong enough to be there and maybe that's enough to lift me from the sidelines okay universe do your thing I'm out wheeee.*

That night, I had a quick 24-hour trip to Denver for a screening/speaking. On my flight home the on morning of May 29, 2014, I received Rochelle's response:

Hi Kathryn,
My initial thought is YES! Let me speak to my PR/Media advisors & sponsors & get back to you later today. We've been discussing an angle for our media campaign in the lead up to the event & see an opportunity to make you a big part of that. More later today. Thanks for wanting to join us!!
Best regards,
Rochelle

My heart jumped into my throat, my pulse soared and my breath stopped. Just the *possibility* of racing for Wiggle-Honda alone was exhilarating. The visualization of putting on a Wiggle-Honda kit and rolling toward the start line of La Course pushed its way to the front of my brain. Early that afternoon, another email from Rochelle made its way into my inbox, and I hovered over the enter button for an eternity. *Has she decided? Is this the verdict?* Took me five minutes to gain the courage to open the email. Neither a yes or no, Rochelle had some questions and got down to brass tacks.

Kathryn, Can you give me a realistic expectation of your possible performance during the race? We will be there to look after Giorgia Bronzini[90] and execute a strong lead-out.... Or, ensure she's in position and fresh to follow Vos's attacks. You would be assigned to stay next to – or in front of Giorgia at all times and if she needs you to close a gap, chase or move up you will need to do that 100% and hopefully stay in to do it one more time. If we have you on the start line we will need to be confident that you have the form to be active for Giorgia and without ambition to finish with a result (or in the front group) for yourself. I need to know if you can do this.
Thanks, Rochelle

Excellent, important questions. I assured Rochelle that, as both a rider and a representative of the team, I would not let her down. She was asking me to be Giorgia's domestique. *Servant.* That's what my role had been since day one of my pro cycling career. And I loved this role; the epitome of teamwork. Gutting myself to the point of being unable to finish is the unsung win of the best teams. I wholeheartedly accepted the role of being Giorgia's wingwoman and doing whatever she/the team needs. I assured her I was fit, capable, ready and willing. Before telling Rochelle I'd give both my kidneys, I reeled myself in a bit. Better save that for later. No need to freak her out just yet. *Nothing is definite. Be cool, be cool.*

---

[90] Interactive Reader Guide: Giorgia Brozini

May 29 was turning into the most incredible day, and it was only getting better. Another email, this time from Universal Sports announcing they signed Dotsie Bausch[91] as color commentator for La Course by Tour de France. Dotsie was (is!) one of my heroes, not just for her 2012 Olympic silver medal in track cycling, but for her own streak of activism in animal rights and eating disorder awareness. Dotsie supported our ASO petition from day one. To know her voice—along with commentators Craig Hummer and Todd Gogulski—would bring La Course to the U.S. broadcast filled me with great personal joy. I was riding the high of happiness that day.

Everything was happening: La Course was a sure thing, *Half the Road* was thriving, *The Road Less Taken* was at the printers, media interviews were scheduled, possible race opportunities were in discussion, my Cerberus was slumbering, and my heart was full of life, love and confidence. I wasn't famous, wealthy or by any means perfect, but in my personal definition of what it meant to be successful, happy and fulfilled, goddamn... *I had arrived.*

Touching back down in Tucson after the over-night trip to Denver, I tweeted a quote from my literary hero, Dr. Maya Angelou: "I have a certain way of being in this world, and I shall not, I shall not be moved."

Then everything moved.

---

[91] Interactive Reader Guide: Dotsie Bausch

36

UNRAVELING

I remember coming home from my bike ride in the late afternoon of May 29, 2014. Four-ish, maybe 5pm. I remember how good the ride felt, as exercise always does after travel. Denver was a good, brief screening trip. The audience at the film festival responded fantastically to *Half the Road*. *Sushi tonight?* George texted that morning. *Hell yes!* I responded. It was a Thursday. I couldn't wait to tell my husband about the prospect of Wiggle-Honda. Couldn't wait to tell him that we just sold out all our June screenings for *Half the Road* in Chicago, Philadelphia, Boston and Burlington. Couldn't wait to be home and revel in the fullness of it all with the one person who knew how much it took to make all this stuff happen and to rejoice that it was all truly happening.

I remember sauntering into the house, bounding up the stairs to see George, who was home from work early that day. Sitting on the couch in the TV room, his tie and collared shirt were disheveled, his complexion pale and haggard. Staring blankly at the TV, which was off.

"I'm done," he said.

Oh shit. It's happened. Pfizer let him go. Layoffs had been rampant the past few months, and I mentally prepared for this possibility. In fact, I was secretly looking forward to it. Since his job-related depression set in six months ago, this layoff was a blessing in disguise. I shifted into SWAT team support mode.

"What?! Ok, honey. You know what? This is great. That job made you miserable, now you can—" I started. Slowly, George swiveled his empty gaze toward me and spoke again.

"No," he said. "I'm done with us."

I remember lying in a fetal position with my head on the carpet, downstairs, sobbing. But we were upstairs, and I have zero recollection of how I got downstairs.

Must've followed him, pleading. Begging. Something. Anything. I remember three sentences he said. *I feel nothing. I failed you. You don't need...* a sentence he never finished. Until it occurred to me perhaps that was the entire sentence. That I was incapable of need. I remember stuttering a chorus of No, no, no, nos and what what what whats? My inner journalist hurling all the Ws; when, where, what, why? Especially *why*. My inner everything else was stupefied and silent and unable to comprehend what was unfolding. My gut knew before my mind. *He is leaving you.* I crumpled to the floor, one arm wrapped around my gut, the other around my heart, as if throwing myself into the void of this fresh, gaping wound would somehow staunch the bleeding. What happened next was a bizarre mixture of incredibly sharp memories perforated by empty holes of utter blankness.

I remember the eerie coldness. The robotics. Whatever snapped in George that day replaced his kindness and compassion with drones and droids. I don't remember him blinking. When I reached for him, there was no embrace returned, just a stance of angles with hinges. Wherever his physical color drained to that day swept away his humanness as well. I crumpled again to a pile on the floor, a mumbling a word salad of syllables, questions, sobs and half-sentences.

I laid on the living floor for quite some time, still in my cycling clothes. The black and orange Optum kit. Which always felt like a superhero cape. But not this day. There is no cape nor kryptonite for the weapon of abandonment. *Exclusion wields the sharpest sword.* I remember the garage door shutting, as his words floated through the room; *Staying with a friend. Do not contact me.* Twelve days later, I was served divorce papers. I never saw my husband again.

I don't remember how I got to my father's apartment, but I spent the next two nights there, unaware those two nights would soon become two years. Unaware of the downward spiral waiting. Unaware of just about everything, except the act of putting on a Mask.

———————

Blindsided, reeling, lost and confused, I fragmented into two people the day my husband left. Person One was an incredulous mess quickly coming undone at the seams. Person Two put on the Mask of Normalcy, and began a lying spree in an attempt of self-preservation. Two days after George's sudden departure, I was scheduled to guest ride at the Philadelphia Classic. I called the team and told them I was violently ill with a stomach bug. This was a half-truth. I was grief-barfing regularly.

I had to go to Chicago, though, in three days. A committee paid my way out there to speak at the film screening. *Good*, whispered the voice of Person Two. *You need to work on this act of pretending you're fine. You've got media requests up the wazoo and if you're the face of activism in women's pro cycling, no one can know you're a sniveling mess. If you show weakness, everything you've worked for in equal opportunity will crumble. Get your shit together, Person One.*

I fucking hated Person Two. But I needed her. My codependency with the Mask was just beginning. I barely remember the Chicago screening in on June 3, 2014, but I do remember being in a trance of fakeness. Spending most of the screening in the theater lobby or bathroom crying silently, I was able to pull it together just before the Q and A at the end of the film. Toward the end of *Half the Road*, I'd watch through the theater windows or side hallway, and when Kristin Armstrong stood on the Olympic podium, I'd make a quick dash to ladies room and wash my tears and reapply make up, practicing my excuse for residual nose-blowing. *Allergies*, I lied. Ah, pollen; the glorious cover-up of fear, grief and self-loathing.

I used the allergies lie for the next year. Especially on the group rides, where my eyes would leak constantly from behind my glasses. 'Allergies' and 'pollen' were much easier conversations than 'unstable' and 'broken.' On the Shootout, I was a venerable fountain of snot and lies.

"Hey KB! How ya doing?"

Person Two: Oh man, the Palo Verde bloom hit me hard this spring.

Person One, who never spoke: *I'm hurting, bad. Oh my god, I'm dying. Can you see it? Can anyone see it? Please help me. I don't know what to do. I don't know who I am. Everything is strange and nothing makes sense and I think something is wrong, really wrong, I am coming undone and I don't know what that means and the only thing that stops the hurt for a few moments is when my legs push down on the pedals just hard enough to block out everything else.*

So that's what I did. Clipped in and kept pedaling. Sometimes up to five or six hours a day. Eating and sleeping were waning fast, and my weight began to decline quickly. In the cycling community, a sinewy physique is often associated with fitness. *Lookin' lean, KB! Riding strong!* Note to the endurance sports community: When a rider loses weight rapidly, don't tell them they look fit. Ask them how their marriage is doing. Then buy them a cheeseburger. Sit down and talk. Bring extra napkins to double as tissues.

Two days after George's departure, I showed up on the The Shootout. I don't remember the ride; my inner athlete was on autopilot. All I knew was I needed to ride, because if Wiggle-Honda called with a yes, I had to be ready. I hadn't heard anything from Rochelle for a week. Or was it a year? A minute? Time was an illusion. Still, I clung to the far-fetched idea that she might sign me. I had to believe in something. Anything. Because I sure as hell didn't believe in myself. I was a zombie of shame, sadness and defeat. Filled with questions to which I had no answers.

Still in a blur of upheaval, autopilot and wearing the mask of Person Two, I sat down with three of my training partners at Caffe Luce after the Shootout. Zeus, Matt and Jay. We had pastries and coffee. I was so sure they could all see something was off, something was wrong… but alas, the exhaustion of physical effort from an intense training session and the zombification of personal struggle look *exactly* the same. Choosing to keep my pain inside, I nibbled at the scone from behind my mask. It would be weeks before I was able to tell anyone my husband left. *If someone is abandoned, but no one is around to hear, does absence make a sound?*

It does. On June twelfth, there was a loud knock on the door and I was presented a manila envelope containing divorce papers. In the two weeks since leaving, I still held hope George's abrupt abandonment was a mistake, a temporary breakdown, that he would come back and this whole thing was just a bad dream that would go away. But then came the knock, the papers and the reality: He was not coming back. Ever.

I quickly learned two unexpected lessons. The hard reality of Arizona's legal system and my own glaring ignorance. I would soon be homeless. We bought the home when we were engaged, not married, and only George's name was on the title. I had no legal claim to this being my marital home. Worse, despite being a spouse, I could be forcibly removed by the police. The myriad of loopholes in marital law were astounding. I naively believed that in divorce—which I was certain would never happen—both spouses have equal access to the house. At the very least, the house would be sold and we'd split the difference. Wrong. I was given 60 days to vacate the premises.

On the same day I was served divorce papers, another piece of unexpected mail arrived. Something that again would change my life forever. Attached to Rochelle Gilmore's email was a contract to join Wiggle-Honda Pro Cycling.

"We've decided. It's happening. We're signing you to the team," Rochelle said. "You will race La Course by Tour de France." The black hole of despair spit me out for just long enough to register what I was seeing: I was going to stand on the start line of my dreams.

To have the best possible news and worst possible situation collide on the same day was a complete and total mindfuck. (Despite a degree in literature, there remains no better synonym.) Five years since emailing ASO. Five years of struggle, rejection, keep-going-ing and building. Also, five years since meeting my husband. The underbelly of activism was floating to the surface. Sometimes when we fight for everything we want, we lose everything we have.

Reeling from the impact of departure, abandonment and unable to think clearly, I was utterly lost. How does one raise their arms to celebrate an epic victory while drowning in a shithole of reality? Person One, Person Two. Masks, masks, masks.

"I'm going to the Tour de France! *My husband just left me!* I am an unstoppable force of strength! *I am having heart palpitations, shortness of breath and telogen effluvium which is science's way saying my hair is falling out!* I am a winning combination of persistence and power! *I've had two locks cut off my gym locker this month because I'm so fucking sad that I can't even remember the combination.*" Person One and Person Two were duking it out for mind control and I was a walking amalgam of disconnectedness. All I could do to keep some sort of balance was focus on the tedium of logistics. Ride bike. Book screenings. Call lawyer. Pack things. Fall apart. Despair, anger. Repeat, repeat.

I remember sitting at my computer, printing out the Wiggle-Honda Pro Cycling contract, when Grizzles the cat jumped into my lap to assist me with typing. She loved lying on the keyboard, which was far from helpful but wonderfully adorable and loving. Then it hit me. He would take the pets. He would take Grizz. My Grizzybear. Technically his Grizzy, but after five years of bonding and closeness, she was mine, too. Not anymore. Sobbing ensued. In that moment, I wasn't able to acknowledge the depths of depression into which I was wading.

I mailed my contract back to Rochelle with a card; a vague attempt at letting her know much it meant to me to race La Course by Tour de France with Wiggle-Honda. I still hadn't mustered the courage to tell anyone my husband left. Rochelle couldn't possibly know she was saving me. Three days later, Wiggle-Honda sent out a press release, firmly and publicly cementing my inclusion to the team and racing La Course was actually happening.

Wiggle Honda signs Kathryn Bertine for La Course

Rider jointly led ASO petition for La Course; "Wouldn't be right for her not to race" says Rochelle Gilmore.

The British professional women's racing team, Wiggle Honda, has signed Kathryn Bertine for the La Course by Le Tour de France race, which takes place on the same day and over the same route through Paris as the men's Tour de France finale. Bertine, who is the current Caribbean Champion and three-time national champion of St. Kitts and Nevis, is a co-founder of Le Tour Entier, which petitioned the Tour de France organising body, ASO, to create a race that ran over the same duration and distances as the men's event. Over 97,000 people signed the petition and the ASO announced La Course on February 1.

"Kathryn was instrumental in creating the La Course race and it simply wouldn't be right for her not to race in this historic event," said Wiggle Honda's owner and manager, Rochelle Gilmore.
"La Course is one of 2014's most important races in shifting the sport to where it deserves to be and we're delighted to make her dream of racing it come true."

"I am over the moon to be given this opportunity by Rochelle," said Bertine. "The ASO hasn't given us the full three weeks we requested, but this is a vital stepping stone in changing both the public's perceptions of, and the outdated regulations governing, women's professional cycling."

Training became an odd mix of necessity and contradiction. By late June, I lost twelve pounds from anxiety training and mental darkness. There was no Cerberus lurking within the caves of my mind. I *was* the Cerberus. I was a walking beast of NotEnough and Doubt. Not all of the worthlessness was figurative. Some of it was literal. According to my divorce attorney, women without children were actually worth *less* than women with children.

"If you had kids, you would've had a right to the house," she said. "But since you don't, you have to go." My scales of justice did not like it one bit that a woman without children meant she was not equal to a woman with children. My three billion daughters didn't seem to count. 14 months would pass for the divorce to finalize and it would get worse every step of the way.[92]

---

[92] Rather than relive every horrific step of my divorce, I'd rather share some tips on how to avoid legal loopholes. Here's hoping my mistakes and ignorance will educate others. Interactive Reader Guide: 10 things to know before marriage.

37

UNIVERSAL SPORTS

In the dressing room of Universal Sports studios, a makeup artist swooshed a foam sponge of foundation across my face, dabbing gently and tenderly at the crescent moons of darkness beneath my eyes.

"There," he said, with quiet kindness. For the first time in a month, I actually appeared to have a pulse. A vast improvement. Three weeks shy of La Course by Tour de France, I flew to Colorado Springs to tape a TV interview. How we formed Le Tour Entier, how the petition came out, how we traveled to Paris in the middle of the night after Worlds, what the meeting was like with ASO. How this victory of La Course by Tour de France had nothing to do with bicycles and everything to do with progress. I was totally in my element. On fire with coherent responses. Stringing together lengthy, semi-articulate sentences about progress, sustainability, return of investment and equal opportunity as if building an invisible shield of protection around my broken soul. I was even smiling. *Just don't ask personal stuff, please don't ask me personal stuff...*

Toward the end of the interview, sports anchor Todd Gogulski toed the almost-personal line and asked what it took to make this happen. I wasn't ready to release the Cerberus and unravel onstage, so I fake-truthed it:

"Sometimes when we shoot for everything we want, we lose everything we have," I said from behind the mask, still smiling, deflecting.[93] Todd threw a quizzical glance, so I keep my foot on the vague pedal. "It's hard fighting for change. There were all sorts of changes this year." I then punted the response over to the neutral territory of cycling talk. Eventually we crossed the bridge of being

---

[93] Interactive Reader Guide: Universal Sports interview. Looking back and watching this interview years later, I'm blown away by my ability to mask inner demons.

teamless for 2014 and how Wiggle-Honda came to the rescue, and I would stand on the start line of La Course by Tour de France. I teared up a bit.

"Will you keep racing after La Course?" Todd asked. I told him I would let that particular answer unfold. That seemed a safer answer than blurting, "*Look Todd, I really can't figure out if I want to keep racing because I love racing, or if I need to keep racing because the sound of the gears drowns out the heavy metal trio of Doubt, Worthlessness and Instability blaring through my brain like a 24hr freakshow rave holy shit can't you hear it, CAN'T YOU HEAR IT, TODD?*"

Apparently he couldn't hear it. But I could. All the time. I thanked Universal Sports for the interview and flew home to Tucson, taking my freakshow carnival bicycle brain to the Arizona State Championships. A perfect tune up for La Course. In theory, anyway.

Channeling my pain into the bike made me lighter, fitter and faster than ever before, but I had not raced since George left. The main thing that differs between racing and training is the way our mind reacts under pressure. For anyone wearing masks and splitting into two people, racing is not a good place. Not easy to put on Game Face when Tears Face whines, *But, it's my turn!* Normally, I love the pressure of racing. Digging as physically deep as possible when everything is on the line… damn, I loved that rush. A rush that grows from a foundation of confidence, happiness and joy. None of which I had. *Maybe I can fake this!* I assured myself, and started with the Category 1 men.[94] Yay masks! *You got this.*

Five miles into the race, when the first fast surge began on the rural roads of Show Low, I crumbled like goat cheese. Physically I was fine. Mentally my brain gave up. The peloton rolled away. My heart didn't know what to do or which mask to wear or how to fake it, so it just plain stopped.

Three thoughts went through my mind: A) Get your shit together. B) Sskjhfdayreagyfjzaghdlerrrrf. C) You might need help. My brain was a circus, indeed. There in the Tilt-a-Whirl of Coming Undone, gravity, demons and I spun round and round and round. Nothing made sense. Grief couldn't decide whether to speed or slow the clocks, so it did both simultaneously. *Did my husband leave weeks ago or minutes ago?* It was all the same. In the Carnival of the Unhinged, time is a terrifying haunted house. In an attempt to steady myself, I needed to see if I was

---

[94] I typically raced with Category 1 and 2 men in Arizona when preparing for women's UCI races. The men's elite amateur field was harder and the races were longer. While I didn't stand on the podium, I could crack the top 10 sometimes. Excellent training!

even ready to let others know what was happening in my personal world. I called Phil Gaimon.[95]

Phil and I were on the same trajectory through cycling, from amateurs chasing the pro dream to landing our first contract to World Tour team status. We became fast friends. Training in Tucson during the winter, Phil and I rode together often and shared many laughs and stories. It was so nice—and very important—to have awesome male friends who weren't looking for more. I confided in Phil about the sudden upheaval, the divorce, the meltdowns and masks.

"Shit, that's insane," he consoled. I felt a tiny surge of relief letting someone in behind the mask. Now, three people knew. My two sisters of pro cycling, Amber Pierce and Lauren Hall, and now Phil. I was so afraid that telling others about my mental state might cause me to unhinge completely. The mask was getting heavy, but I still felt the need to wear it.

During the three weeks before La Course, I trained and job searched. Getting signed to Wiggle-Honda Pro Cycling came with the glory of being able to race at the Tour de France, but my contract did not come with a salary. *Half the Road* was thriving and went to iTunes on July 11, but royalties on documentary films were infinitesimal sums. There were no royalties from *As Good As Gold*, and my next book wouldn't be released until September. Financially, I had jack squat. *Author, filmmaker, professional athlete, ESPN senior editor and columnist, equal rights activist...* With a resume like that, my husband's divorce lawyer believed my fortunes were stored in an off-shore account (in St. Kitts and Nevis) and she threated to search for it. *Please do*, I responded. *I would be thrilled to give you half of my secret millions.*

The truth wasn't pretty: fighting for change left me broke. Figuratively, I won the lottery of social justice. My soul was filled with joy. Equality was happening. Financially, I wasn't worth anything. Or so it felt. Either way, the writing was on the wall: I would have to quit professional cycling this year. The reality of "normal jobs" was okay with me, but here's what was not ok: If I were in the same situation as a man, I wouldn't have to quit my job as a pro cyclist.

Had I been a man on a World Tour team that year, I would have the guaranteed annual base salary of 37,000 Euro. While going through divorce is equally awful for

---

[95] Interactive Reader Guide: Phil Gaimon

any gender in pro cycling, at least I would still have had a wage. In 2014, there were no base salaries for women at the World Tour level. This, of course, on top of UCI's patriarchal belief that if women wanted a proper base salary, they had to *prove* their worth. Which was some serious Pentagram of Blame crap.

For professional cyclists, leaving the pro ranks comes down to three situations: chosen retirement (by the athlete), unchosen retirement (due to injury, illness) or being fired for bad results/misconduct. Those are all gender equal. But for a woman to leave the highest level of professional sport because she can't afford to eat and pay rent?! Not ok. Not right. *Someone's gotta do something about that bullshit*, I stewed, as I perused the classifieds in Tucson. *What if there were an organization that lobbied the powers at UCI to secure an equal base salary for women at the World Tour level... and in the interim, there was an actual, physical place—a residence, a program—where female pro cyclists could live and train without rent and expenses? Damn, imagine that.*

Alas, no such place appeared in the classifieds. I was far too deep in my personal sadness and emotional instability to realize a new seed of activism was planted in that moment. First, I needed to find a job. That was one helluva a necessity right now.

I reached out to every contact in my journalism and cycling worlds. Writing, editor positions, sales positions, pushing the mail cart, anything. Rejection after rejection came barreling back, or offered a wage beneath the poverty line. *Look at your resume, of course you'll get hired*! friends cheered in support. My confidence was in the gutter. My emotions were a wreck. My worthlessness was on fire. I decided to abandon the job search until after La Course and do something much more productive for the next week. Like go sleep with someone.

———

I was learning, albeit slowly, about vulnerability. And the need for human connection. The weight of loneliness grew heavy. Two months passed since my husband left and I was struggling to acknowledge how all-consuming the loss was becoming. Sorrow came in waves. One minute, so riled by anger that I hurled seething soliloquies of *FuckYous* toward his memory. The next minute, I'd slump into a pile of vacant humanness on the floor, soundlessly rocking back and forth for far too long; a gold medal contender for the Fetal Position Olympics. Mornings were the worst. In the few precious moments between sleeping and waking, grief won the race to the start line of memory, destroying all chances for a clean slate of day. Dawn and pain rose together in the mornings.

I confided in a lifelong friend, Mary, an older woman who'd known me since childhood, that I was lonely to the point of aching. She replied, *Go into the woods, but watch for bears*. At first, I thought she meant go camping and be mindful of garbage. *That's not what I mean*. Oh. She meant that it's okay to find companionship and human touch, but be careful of the predators. The bears. The vultures. The ones sniffing around for vulnerability, insecurity and lowered guards. I understood, but also, didn't.

While I did my best to keep my personal life quiet on social media, word got around about the divorce. Men began reaching out. Most were acquaintances, but also a few strangers who followed my journey. I named them the WannaTalkers. Their emails and messages began something like this, *"Hey, I hear you're going through a hard time. You poor thing. Wanna talk?"* I started to wonder if my vulnerability had a scent. If people could smell me through the internet. Never before did it occur to me that vulnerable and vulture share the Latin prefix, *vul*, which means to tear apart and/or being torn apart. Fascinating![96] I wasn't ready for bears and vultures. *No, I don't want to talk, but thanks*. Then, one day, I did engage with a WannaTalker.

I visited a man I barely knew, believing I could handle separating my physical needs from my emotional quandary. But my demons came along for the weekend and volunteered as the metaphorical grill master, skewering Love, Sex, Want and Need all on the same damn kebab, charring it terribly. My vulnerability was clearly unable to differentiate between "Booty Call" and "Booty All I Want Is A Life Partner Are You That Partner Please Love Me Forever." That didn't go well. He didn't really wanna talk and he definitely didn't call again. I wrestled with my insecurities. *Was I too much? Not enough?* Years would pass before I understood those two questions are exactly the same. Self-measurement is a vicious demon. Never, ever let that one near the grill.

My dear friend Greg Philip, who served as president of St. Kitts and Nevis Cycling Federation, hurled a stone in my direction, though I doubt he knew the

---

[96] Also fascinating, Merriam-Webster Dictionary uses divorce as its definition example of 'vulnerable': "He was very *vulnerable* after his divorce." No doubt the online editor for Merriam-Webster has been through it, too.

weight it carried. Not everyone in my personal circles saw or knew what was going on with my marriage. Life doesn't exactly schedule warnings of *Be kind, Kathryn is hurting!* on everyone else's calendar. Greg didn't know my husband left, or that my mind was falling apart.

For the past seven years I'd represented St. Kitts and Nevis, the cycling federation was proud of the visibility it received. When I asked Greg if he would register me for 2014 World Championships (just the paperwork, not the expenses) I assumed he would respond with the positive affirmation he always did. Instead came a blunt *No*.

Greg was pissed. He received word from UCI that, at the 2013 World Championships, I "made a scene" onstage by holding up an equal sign. UCI actually imposed a fine of €50 on the St. Kitts and Nevis Cycling Federation. Greg was terribly upset I had not cleared my kinesio tape equality poster with him. While my stronger self would've laughed this off and engaged in a strong-willed conversation defending the act of holding up an equal sign, my very fragile self was crushed.

"You should not have done that, getting up on stage and making a scene in Florence, Kathryn," Greg said, through Winston over a Skype call. "I do not want you representing us at Worlds this year." If there was anything left of my heart, it shattered in a million pieces. Which shocked me as I didn't realize there was anything left to break. But there was. For a near decade, St. Kitts and Nevis was my life preserver of hope. My ability to keep racing and standing for change, no matter how many pro teams and cruel managers tried to stop me. I proudly flew the beautiful red, green, black and gold SKN flag at six world championships, three national championships and Caribbean Championships. Helped build a cycling federation for women and kids on Nevis. Winston and Greg were my constant reminder that nothing is impossible. Until now, when an equal sign created waves on stage.

To feel we must apologize for who we are is a devastating blow to the soul. I was not sorry for raising an equal sign above my head, but I was very sorry for any tension or misunderstanding it caused. To be misunderstood by strangers and society is difficult. To be misunderstood by friends and family is soul crushing. The worst part came next.

Weeping profoundly, impulse took over and I reached for the phone to call my husband. Then remembered I didn't have one. The tears came down hard that day. *Just focus on La Course*, I chanted.

Forgetfulness was the new ride in my circus. Stress does that to people, as if sadness, confusion and grief have a direct line to our daily functionality, rendering us stupid and slow while we struggle. I'd forget to do the little things. Like eat lunch. Pay bills. Put stamps on envelopes. Bring my wallet. Things upon which my Type A-ness always kept a firm grip. I confided in my 78-year-old father, asking him if I should be concerned about my rampant absentmindedness. He hugged me and told me not to worry, that my forgetfulness was situational where as his forgetfulness was due to aging.

"I can't even remember President Obama's first name," my dad offered, consoling.

"Barack!" I assisted, chiding, "You know who our vice president is, right?"

"Millard Fillmore!" Dad responded, with such quick, deadpan whimsy that I still laugh to this day. Fillmore was indeed vice president. In 1848. There is no greater gift in life than loved ones who hurl brilliant bolts of laughter to light up the darkness of our private stormy skies.

38

LA COURSE BY TOUR DE FRANCE

A week before leaving for La Course, my sensitivity ratcheted up a notch. The public response to La Course hit a deep-seated nerve. People were incredibly supportive, celebrating with me when Wiggle-Honda brought me on board for Paris. While the overwhelming public sentiment toward La Course was victorious, knives of disappointment plunged into my chest when people responded, "La Course is just for one day? That's not enough."

Of course it's not. "Just" rattled around in my head, stirring up worthlessness with all its snide implications, as if one day doesn't matter or is too small or less than or not enough. But everything that ever mattered in gaining equal opportunity for minorities began with just one day. One day, Susan B. Anthony was denied the chance to speak publicly because she was a woman. One day, Margaret Sanger heard President Theodore Roosevelt declare it would be "race suicide" if women were allowed birth control. One day, Rosa Parks sat down at the front of a bus. One day, K.V. Switzer entered the Boston Marathon. One day, Billie Jean King played Bobby Riggs. One day Geraldine Ferraro, Sarah Palin, Hillary Clinton and Kamala Harris put their names on ballots and ran. One. Day. Matters. *La Course isn't just for one day, it's justice for one day. And there will be more days because of this day.*

What the public couldn't see was all the work behind the scenes it took to move the dial one inch forward for women. No one knew how much work went into getting ASO's attention, never mind all the work that went in after. I was truly cracking. Public self, private self… being two people was too much. The weight of the masks were dragging me down. It was time to merge and build the bridge back to one self.

I felt the need to say something publicly about the "just for one day" comments. Authenticity beckoned, but it also laughed. My ego and I were well aware that no one would really give a rat's ass about my divorce or my personal losses or my mental state, but I needed to say it out loud. Perhaps admitting struggle was the kryptonite that could forever destroy these horrible masks. Wasn't sure, but had to try. Grabbed my iPhone, wrote a few words, grabbed a few props, made a five-minute video called *Just for One Day* and posted it on YouTube.[97]

In the brief clip, I talked about my origins in cycling, the shift into activism, *Half the Road*, the petition's victory, La Course and Wiggle-Honda...how all the high points look like a life of sunshine and rainbows from the outside. Then brought the viewers inside for a quick glimpse about what really happens when we stand up to fight for progress and inclusion. I set the clip to my favorite David Bowie song, 'Just for One Day.' The video was honest, goofy, explanatory, ridiculous, equal parts heartfelt-authentic and mildly cringe-worthy and lo and behold it worked. For me, at least.

The masks fell off. I was no longer some chick who fought for equal rights, I was a human who had plenty of baggage and was just like everyone else. A proud mess! No more masks. From July 23 onward, I was certain things would be easier now that I was one person instead of two.

On July 24, 2014, three days before La Course by Tour de France, I arrived in Europe with a small carry-on bag and the three pieces of mental luggage every woman should carry by the age of 39: A passport, an opinion, and the knowledge of how to drive a standard transmission. While the rest of the Wiggle-Honda athletes were flying directly into Paris, I flew to the team house near Ghent, Belgium, where I was outfitted with a team road bike. For three days, I had the entire house to myself. Set up much like a college dorm or youth hostel, there were three sets of bunk beds in each of the three bedrooms, a living room with a trophy rack, and a kitchen where tins of tuna, boxes of cereal and jars of almond butter were Sharpied with the names of its owners.

Professional athletes—myself included—don't mess around with food. Hell hath no fury like an endurance athlete coming home from a five-hour training day to find someone else has eaten all the personal groceries they just spent the last hour fantasizing about. Sports fans often wonder about the secret ingredient in creating the best team in professional cycling. Signing the most talented athletes? Creating

---

[97] Interactive Reader Guide: Just for One Day

the perfect leadout train? Trust falls at team camp? No. The best teams have Sharpies in their kitchen so people can initial their own food. The rest will fall into place.

In the sparse living room of the Wiggle-Honda house, an enormous cardboard box the size of a refrigerator sat on the floor. My name was Sharpied upon it. Rochelle mentioned there would be some team apparel waiting for me. For the past three weeks I imagined receiving one team kit, one helmet, a pair of socks and maybe even a new pair of shoes... though I was certain they'd just give me some Wiggle-Honda shoe covers so at least I'd match everyone else. I assumed most of the gear would be second-hand or leftovers in the wrong size. That's how it goes when signed to a team last-minute. Getting signed *was* the gift!

I opened the massive box. My internal floodgates let loose. Plunging my hands into the depths of black, orange and white packaging, there seemed to be no bottom. By the time I counted six jerseys and shorts, a full wardrobe of winter gear, summer gear, rain gear, two sets of shoes, two helmets, two backpacks, head-to-toe casual wear for life off the bike, Adidas sneakers and Osprey roller luggage... I was in tears. Smiley-bawling all over the place. Weeping with joy not at the incredible product itself but the long-lost feeling of Belonging. These clothes weren't cotton and lycra. They were armor and Kevlar. I wanted to put on every piece and run-waddle around the streets of Belgium screaming, *TAKE YOUR BEST SHOT, WORLD!!! I FUCKING BELONG HERE!!!*

Of all clothes to try on, I first picked up the gloves. They were size medium. Phew. Had they been too small, I'd need to remove my wedding ring. Wasn't ready to do that yet. I kept hoping, believing that if I kept it on, maybe he'd come back. Mediums, perfect. Black, too. No one could see the ring. No one would ask. I emailed Rochelle immediately, letting her know how thankful I was. That she had given me a branch to hold onto when the rest of my world was slipping away. That, thanks to her, dreams don't have to disappear even when everything else does.

With the historic impact of La Course by Tour de France making its way around the world, interview requests were rolling in. Juliet Macur of *The New York Times*, Jason Gay of *The Wall Street Journal*, *USA Today*, BBC, CNN, NPR... all of them kind, supportive, strong pieces showcasing the importance of women racing at the Tour de France.[98]

---

[98] Interactive Reader Guides on La Course by Tour de France: *The New York Times* and *The Wall Street Journal*

During the photo shoot for *The New York Times*, I stood in the middle of a quiet Belgian road outside the Wiggle-Honda house. They put the article on the front page of the sports section the next day. The day before the race, Colavita reached out to me for quote. While team manager Jimmie surely didn't give a rat's ass I was racing La Course, the Colavita company did. No matter the personal pain, perspective mattered more. Colavita gave me my first professional contract, and for that I was (and always will be) thankful. No problem giving a quote. "I am thrilled to take part in La Course by Tour de France with Wiggle-Honda. I got my start in pro cycling with Team Colavita, and remain grateful for the doors it opened in my racing career." Definitely sounded a lot more professional and far more karmalicious than *Kiss my ass, Wynona! Suck it, Jimmie! Hey Bobbi, remember when you tore up my back and made me bleed with your water buffalo horn? Looks who's wearing the horns now, bitches. Come at me. I dare you.* My ego had a private field day with the first draft.

The evening before driving to Paris, I met Els and Wilfried for dinner; the wonderful couple who housed me for two months when I raced for the Belgian team in 2011 when I was trying, hoping to turn professional. Three years later, here I was, about to race at the Tour de France and they would be there to watch. I thanked them from the bottom of my tattered heart. Rule of activism: Seek out the people who played a role in your journey years ago. Let them know they mattered then and matter still. Always lift the ones who lifted you.

The 'Just for one Day" video made the rounds for a few days, and my anxiety over putting myself out there on the vulnerability tightrope soothed and steadied as responses came in. Turns out other people could relate. Kimberly Coats, the trailblazing woman behind Team Africa Rising—the incredible mission to put African pro cyclists on the map—sent a lovely email.

"Kathryn, I just watched your video. Selfishly, it couldn't have come at a better time. Sometimes I feel like all I do is bang my head against a wall trying to make these young men's dreams come true. Their dreams are my dreams. To see an all-black African team at the start of the Tour de France one day... will be *my* day. But it's not "one" day. You've changed thousands of days for women cyclists. This is just the outward "one day." The real one day is a lifetime, a movement in the world of cycling. You gave up a lot... but you never gave up your dreams. Our stories are similar. I lost my house and my marriage as well, but in the end I found my family. Who would've thought they'd be a bunch of Rwandan, Eritrean and Ethiopian cyclists? If I had to do it all over again, I wouldn't change a thing. When you sacrifice your dreams you lose so much more... your soul. Wish I could be there to see you race.

Oh, and by the way... houses are overrated! Love to you from all of the women in Africa who you inspire to ride and race. You're my hero! — Kimberly"

A lump rose in my throat. I wasn't as alone as I thought. Stories poured in from people—mostly women—who struggled in their quests to stand up for something. Kimberly was *my* hero. The impact of women supporting other women went straight to my soul, forever bonding me with strangers, many of whom became friends in the coming years.

In the days leading up to the race, we also saw an upswing in the professional men speaking up and supporting the women. Sweden's Magnus Backstedt, former Tour de France stage winner tweeted, "Good to see so many people are gonna be on the Champs tomorrow for La Course & Le Tour. Gonna be awesome!" Germany's Marcel Kittel of Giant-Shimano endorsed Dutch racer Kirsten Wild when asked who would win the inaugural La Course, while Andre Greipel backed Belgian Jolien D'Hoore.[99] The impact was making waves and the world was finally seeing this wasn't just a bike race, was a global opportunity for equal representation.

After the three-hour drive from Ghent to Paris, we arrived at the Holiday Inn Express on the Canal de la Villette not far from Charles de Gaulle Airport. Couldn't help but chuckle that the fight for international equal opportunity landed me in an American hotel chain. Loved everything about it. In my assigned room, I met my teammate Charlotte Becker from Germany. Lotte sized me up, and although pleasant, it was apparent she was less than pleased to room with the new girl. My presence disrupted the flow of a team who spent the last six months together and I completely understood.

Doing my best to make Lotte feel comfortable, I attempted to establish a connection where she felt recognized, appreciated, supported and that I was a team player there to work for her and Bronzini tomorrow. Like most things, I probably overdid it. After a few minutes of chit chat, she smiled then left the room. I didn't see her the rest of the day. *Right, ok. Be cool, KB. Stop smiling and talking so much. That's creepy.*

On my bed, there was another package from Wiggle-Honda. Rochelle sent me six more kits, jackets and full team wardrobe. This time, the sleeves were

---

[99] Interactive Reader Guide: Video of Kittel/Greipel & Wild/D'Hoore

emblazoned with my St. Kitts and Nevis national championship stripes. As I traced my hands along the green, red, black and gold bands that encircled my sleeves, I was equally undone and glued together. I held tight to the latter.

I was also equally glad Lotte was not present to witness my teary squeals of joy about the new kits. I needed her to see me as a tough badass teammate, not a spazzy kindergartner who just opened a box of glitter and rainbows and can't stop jumping on the bed. Holiday Inn Express has stellar bedsprings, by the way.

After a few moments, the high of jersey joy swung the other way on the pendulum, as past, present and impulse collided once again. I desperately wanted to call George. To tell him all about the jerseys. All about the team van with the washer and dryer. How the Holiday Inn in Paris looks exactly the same yet completely different as all the other ones. Again, I reached for the phone before remembering there is no one to call. The wave of grief started its rise. *I miss saying his name. Writing his name. Sharing joy. Sharing everything. I miss everything.* I pushed the grief wave down with whispered chants of *no no no no no not here not today not now not now not now. Remember where you are. Remember why you're here.*

Luckily, an interview with the media thwarted a total meltdown. Phil Sheehan of Sky Sports/InCycle TV knocked on the door and I composed myself in the nick of time before answering, *Hi Phil, thanks so much for coming, I was just about to spiral into the abyss of darkness, self-hatred and loneliness because I totally do not have my shit together and the Tour de France is 20 hours away and part of me wants to die but yay women's equality. Tea?*

I pulled myself together just enough for the video interview.[100] Afterward, I rode the tide of inner sadness till it washed up on the shores of reality: Tomorrow I would stand on the start line of my dream. *Be present, be here. For fucks sake, breathe woman.* Changing into my Wiggle-Honda casual gear, I made my way to dinner and met the rest of my teammates for the first time.

In the Holiday Inn dining room, I was amongst the goddesses professional cycling greatness: Giorgia Bronzini, Italy, three-time world champion. Emilia Fahlin, Sweden, seven-time national champion. Charlotte Becker, Germany, five-time national champion. Emily Collins, national criterium champion of New Zealand. Beatrice Bartelloni, national junior champion of Italy. Three of them were Olympians.

---

[100] Interactive Reader Guide: Video with Sky Sports / InCycle

I could only imagine some of these women might not want me here. Some—maybe even all—might not share the same sentiments as Rochelle toward my inclusion. Since I still harbored insecurities of being misunderstood in the women's pro peloton and carried the scars of Wynona saying "everyone" hated me, it was not the easiest thing to sit down at this table, wondering if they too felt this way. While my grown-up side figured out it was probably Wynona who hated me, not necessarily everyone else in the world, my inner-child was scared.

Hoping to take the edge off any awkwardness at the dinner table with my new teammates, I verbalized how thankful I was to be there and I understood it was a strange circumstance. Some of them warmed, and we switched the conversation to La Course. The waiter arrived and a few teammates chuckled at my fish selection.

"What?" I asked. "Is French fish bad?"

"This isn't America. They don't filet fish here," Girogia explained. "You're going to be picking out bones for half an hour before you get a mouthful." Indeed, she was right. We laughed. Bonded. Well, bonded as much as one can twelve hours before a race. That night, Rochelle sent an email to the team.

> Dear Athletes,
> I just want to say how proud I am of all of you for being selected to stand on the start line on the Champs-Élysées tomorrow. I hope you absorb the significance of this event when you experience the sensations of racing in front of such a huge enthusiastic crowd.
> You should feel extremely honoured to be a part of women's cycling (and sport's) history so please take a moment tomorrow to acknowledge that you've all assisted in achieving this dream for women's cycling... We've demanded a stage to perform on and now we have it, so let's make the most of this and put on a real exciting show for the 60 networks and 157 countries who are showing this race live on TV... Have fun, race like there's no tomorrow. I will be the most proud team manager in the world watching you all stand on that start line. Good Luck! X. –Rochelle

The morning of July 27, 2014, we drove from the Holiday Inn to the Champs Élysées in the team van. While Giorgia, Emilia, Emily, Bea and Lotte zoned into their personal pre-race modes of concentration via headphones, reading, or staring out the window, I absorbed the details of my immediate surroundings, still mildly obsessed with the fact this world tour team had a washer-dryer unit in their van. *I could live here.* We were about to make history on the Champs-Élysées and my energy channeled into wondering if the washer takes high-efficiency detergent and if the dryer beeped loudly or not at all upon completion. Nerves are fascinating.

A half-mile down from the Arc d'Triomphe on the Champs Élysées, all team vans parked near the Place de la Concorde.[101] Wiggle-Honda slid between Orica-GreenEdge of Australia and Specialized-Lululemon of USA. Staff set out turbo trainers for warm up, cyclists exited the vans to look around, fans milled about while blue skies and brilliant sunshine arrived to set the perfect backdrop for our historic day.

Ninety minutes till race time. 90 years since Alfonsia Stradi rode the Giro d'Italia. 30 years since women were unrecognized participants at the Tour de France, given zero media attention. Soigneurs set up folding chairs for the athletes in semi-circles beneath their team van awnings and cycling fans slowly ambled past the team caravans looking for a glimpse or maybe an autograph from their favorite riders. Other than a feeble rope marking off the team van area, cycling is one of the few sports where fans can get quite close to the action. Some of the more introverted riders remained on the bus, preferring to hide in private. I wanted to feel everything, everything.

The summer sun illuminated the angles and bulges of every ancient cobblestone under my snazzy team-sneakered feet. The mild humidity and electric current of excitement was evident in every breath. I breathed deeply, huffing history. I gawked at the Arc d'Triomphe and acknowledged the reality of standing in the middle of one of the most famous streets in the world closed down for the women to shine today.

"Excuse me... Kathryn?" a man in his mid-sixties asked, from the other side of the red rope where he and his wife stood next to the Wiggle-Honda van. I nodded, smiled and made my way over. "We've been following the La Course journey," he continued. "We signed the petition last year and we drove five hours today to watch the women race. We won't be staying for the men. We've come just for this. We're no longer interested in the men's Tour de France until the women are equal." I shook his hand, quite sure I felt a surge of watts transfer into my body. I'm glad positive energy isn't on WADA's banned substance list, because that's the strongest stuff out there.

---

[101] It would be remiss not to mention the Place de la Concorde was where executions took place in the 1700s, and most of those guillotined were people who questioned authority. Such as Marie Antoinette, who pushed political policies for women to wear less make up and hoop skirts. I like to think she was there cheering for the women racing La Course by Tour de France that day.

"One more thing... my wife and I saw your 'Just for one Day' video on YouTube. We didn't know much went on behind the scenes. People don't talk much about the personal stuff. The men never do. Thank you for sharing... we feel much more connected to women's cycling now." It would take a few more years until I understood the power of reach and how our actions extend far beyond the targets we first create, but I'll never forget that couple's kindness that day.

More spectators, handshakes, autographs and congratulations. *I saw your film!* strangers said, shaking my hand and saying kind words about *Half the Road. I read your books!* asking when the next would be released. *"I followed your column on ESPN!"* they laughed, in good-natured fun. *"I'm a fan of Wiggle-Honda!"* asking if I would sign their team jersey.

Just before settling into pre-race warm up mode, one more spectator approached the Wiggle-Honda van. A young woman from Chicago traveled all the way to Paris just for La Course. *Can we take a selfie?* Of course! Snap, click. She asked if I was nervous for the race.

"No. I was nervous we'd never have one," I smiled. "This might be the calmest I've ever been." We shared a laugh. She headed into the crowds to watch La Course unfold before I caught her name, but the universe took note of that moment and held onto it for me.

Glancing into the crowds forming along the race course, my heart bloomed. The fans were an equal mix of men and women. All different ages. Most were white, but not all. (Diversity in cycling was/is still a demographic in desperate need of change.) But in that moment, a rainbow of hope. The entire course was *packed* with spectators.

Half hour before the race, our team rolled up to the sign-in stage. No need for a kinesio tape equality poster today. Our pre-race team meeting with Rochelle was brief, succinct. We already discussed the plan. Cover all attacks, break away if possible, but keep the focus on setting up a lead-out for our sprinter, Giorgia Bronzini. With the multiple-loop, cobblestone finish on a flat course with a slight uphill grade, she was our best chance for the podium. *Roger that, Rochelle.* Together we rolled to the start line.

I took my place in the peloton, on the far left, mid-pack. I always liked starting on the left, for no specific reason but the comfort of tradition. (The good kind.) Before settling into race-mode, I scanned the peloton. Lauren Hall was two rows up on my right, her neon orange Optum helmet a comforting beacon of familiarity. Olympic, national and world champions everywhere. Leah Kirchmann and Denise

Ramsden, two Canadian champs, representing. Emma Pooley was toward the front. So too was Marianne Vos. Chrissie Wellington stood with officials at the start line, being the ambassador of General Awesomeness she was, as were Tracy, Marion, Steve and Kristy. All of Le Tour Entier was there. We are one minute from the start when the weirdest, silliest yet incredibly empowering thought flashed through my brain for a fleeting second. The scene from *Cast Away* where Tom Hanks celebrates a most important victory, bouncing about the beach, yelling to the universe, *I have made fire!* In that moment, my joy was on fire. That's exactly what it felt like to stand on the start line of a dream created. *We. Have. Made. Fire.*

Something else burned too, though. While the masks were gone, there were still two personas within me battling it for mind control; the athlete and the human. The athlete was focused on the race; all she cared about was clipping in and starting strong. The race would be less than three hours, there would be no dicking around, no lollygagging. The pace would be blistering fast, game on from the get-go. My inner athlete was ready to roll. My inner human, however, was trying to soak up as much as possible… the sights, the sounds the smells, everything, everything, everything. Except my multi-headed demons trying to wiggle out through the cracks. *Not now, Cerberus. This is not your day.* The starting gun fired, the wheels rolled out, the demons scampered. We were off. History was happening.

———

July 27, 2014. I remember everything and nothing about our day in Paris. Able body, masked mind, fractured heart, broken soul, fully present; bits of my shattered self grasped at every detail and held tight. Ahead of us, crowds of spectators flooded the streets of Paris. 157 countries—literally half of the world—watching us live. Women were finally able to race the Tour de France with equal media coverage to the men's event that day. Finally granted official use of the name "Tour de France." Finally, after 104 years, treated equally. For one day. One day, one doorway. Today mattered.

Behind us, the Arc d' Triomphe rose into the bluest skies. I remember the stunning magnitude of its rectangular rise as we approached each lap. Around me, a sea of women, ebbing and flowing into the peloton's amoebic shape of movement. *Take it in*, my heart begged my body and mind. They did. I remember tiniest edges, epic surges, the slick, wayward cobbles and physical vibration of every stone, every movement, every moment. Such is the strangeness of memory, assigning equal weight to the most significant and random details, forcing the splendid Arc d'

Triomphe, portapotties of Place de la Concorde and snippets of conversations with strangers to live together in the quagmire marsh of memory. How grateful I am now for this strange bog.

The next hour was a beautiful blur of badass racing; surges, attacks, counter attacks, re-grouping. The peloton was feisty, animated and relentless. So too were the cobbles. On the fourth lap, flying down the descent from the Arc d' Triomphe toward Place de la Concorde, the sharp edge of a protruding cobblestone dug with all its might into my front wheel and pinched the tubular. *Fssssssssssst!* the tire exhaled. Pulling over immediately, I popped off the wheel and readied for a quick change from the team car. *No need to worry. Flats happen. I'll make it back fine.* The caravan sped by. Wiggle-Honda had drawn the last number for caravan car order. Panic set in. *Too far back.* By the time the wheel was changed, the only way to make it back to the peloton was drafting off the team car. UCI officials don't like that, but will occasionally turn a blind eye if the journey is quick.

The journey wasn't quick. During my flat, the peloton sped up with attacks. Dramatically. The race was full gas, and physics upheld its decree that mass is stronger than an individual particle. The team car paced me for one lap at nearly 35-miles an hour, but we were no closer to the peloton. The officials waved the car to move away from me. Attrition was in progress. Riders were coming off the back of bunch. I dropped away from the Honda. As I passed a member of the Australian National Team, I patted my right hip, indicating for her to join me. Perhaps we could work together to make it back to the mass. She sprung to action, and we traded roles of leading and drafting for a couple laps… until the inevitable became clear. Our race was over. We were not going to make it back to the peloton. The officials waved for us to exit the course. We still had about a mile till the exit area, and during that stretch my perspective shifted from sheer disappointment to deep gratitude. What started as an unlucky mechanical became the greatest flat tire of my life.

In the deceleration of our pace and acceptance of my fate, I saw La Course from an entirely new perspective. My heart rate slowed, my disappointment yielded to exhaustion and as I encircled the famous Arc d'Triomphe for the last time, I physically saw what we achieved. Fans lined the *entire* course. Four, five rows deep. There were men and women and children of all ages, and they were not just standing listlessly. They were completely enthralled. Cheering and waving, as though the young Australian and I were not dropped from the race but winning it! I was close enough to see their faces. These fans understood what was happening. They knew we weren't winning. Still they clapped and hollered as if we were. They were cheering for us because we were there. Because the race was happening at all. And, like the racers, the spectators were thrilled to be there. The men's race was hours away, yet these spectators came for us. For the women. They cared that we were women, and at the same time, they didn't care at all... which was exactly our point.

Circling the Arc for the final time, I gave a little wave. The crowd roared and waved back. Shivers sailed through my spine. I did it again, waving and rolling slowly along. New sections of fans would cheer and wave back. I waved, Paris waved. Ride, wave. Ride, wave. We ebbed and flowed like this for a mile. *Holy crap*, it dawned on me. *My dream and I are waving at each other*. Faces of the fans blended together, but I felt as if each hand and hug and fleeting touch were tethers to something more stable than I. No one knew I was wavering on a cliff within. At that moment, I'm not sure I knew how close to the edge I was, either.

Tears spilled as I pedaled from the Arc to the Place. But these particular tears, falling over the very cobbles that deflated my race, were pure joy. I waved and cried and rolled myself over a finish line that wouldn't count for me as a racer that day, but would forever remain a benchmark of my life's journey. What a gift it was to have that flat tire, to let the Champs-Élysées soak in. To realize we can all create something good in this crazy world, and maybe if we do it right, our dreams will wave to us as we go by.

———

I came to La Course to feel it all, and feel I did. While the perspective of awesomeness was in full swing, so too were the raw emotions that come from emptying the physical tank of athleticism. I was tired, joyous, depleted, happy and very, very sad. It was all coming out now, like it or not, mixed together. Tears were streaming down my face but I was wearing sunglasses and smiling. While I'd promised myself no more masks, I needed one today. The Just for One Day video was a good first step, but I didn't want anyone to see the brokenness in person. Not today.

After the flat, I made my way to the shower tents. There was a section of dismally unclean portapotties and a ramshackle tent with sprinklers set up for mass showers. I have a high tolerance for modesty, but with cracks in the tenting, these showers were far more Moulin Rouge than Louvre experiences. I took a quick rinse using my dirty jersey as a towel, then made my way to the finish line to watch the final sprint. The peloton dwindled to the final sprinters, and as they rounded last the corner, I saw the rainbow jersey signifying the reigning world champion at the forefront. Marianne Vos took the win and my heart soared! *Holy shit, Le Tour Entier just literally and figuratively won La Course by Tour de France!* There is nothing sweeter than driving the intangible fight for change home with a physical victory. *Marianne. Has. Made. Fire*!

Dutchwoman Kirsten Wild took second, and Leah Kirchmann—the Canadian national champion of Team Optum—grabbed the bronze in an exciting sprint finish. Joy overload. Marta Tagliaferro of Italy nabbed the sprinter classification points and Coryn Rivera of USA scored the Best Young Rider title. Better still, the stats: In the top ten finishers, there were eight countries and ten different teams represented. Proof that women's pro cycling was a global force to be reckoned with.

Making my way to the post-race VIP tent for athletes, I found Emma Pooley, her face beautifully caked in sweat, grime and effort. She poured her heart and soul into the Champs-Élysées, playing the role of super-domestique to get her Lotto-Belisol Belgian superstar teammate Jolien D'Hoore to the line in seventh place. Not only did Emma have an incredible performance at La Course, but she won the time trial at British national championships three weeks prior... after taking the previous year off to finish her PhD. Now she was back, stronger and more badass than ever. To have Emma and Marianne there as competitors with Chrissie, Marion, Steve and Kristy on the sidelines was an incredible feat.

I made my way to a table to with Emma, Rachel Neylan, Sharon Laws, teammates Emilia Fahlin and Giorgia Bronzini (who finished 11th). All of them Olympians, five countries represented, a roundtable of Awesome. A fleeting memory entered my brain, where Wynona once told me to stop idolizing the competition. *Kiss my ass, Wynona.* Celebrating women empowers everyone. Makes us all stronger. I snapped a photo. Sharon Laws, one of the Great Britain's best cyclists, is smiling, happy and full of life. None of us knew we would lose her to cancer four years later. Like most of life, we're accustomed to focusing on the main event. Depth lives in the beautiful periphery. Look around, look around. Selfies, shmelfies. Take photographs with others whenever possible. La Course was so much more than a race that day.

That night, ASO paid for a hotel room at Mercure Paris on Rue Lauriston for each member of Le Tour Entier. Chrissie, Emma, Steve, Tracy and I met for dinner. Emma presented me with a small box. "It's a divorce present," she offered, as I opened it to find a necklace of a heart with a dagger through the center. "Look," Emma demonstrated, "The knife is removable!" As if there were more reason to love this woman. Gotta love a British sense of humor. Rather than skirt around the issue of pain, my dear Emma went straight for the jugular. I so desperately needed that laugh.

We celebrated the race with gusto, making plans to check in with ASO about the data of La Course. A Euro-style late dinner, strolling the streets of Paris, reveling in the social media, I didn't sleep a wink that night. I made my way into the lobby at 2am. There at the check-in desk, was Brian Cookson. I saw him before he noticed me. He was with his wife. The middle of the night in a foreign country with a spouse present is probably not the best recipe for a discussion on gender equity. Nor was it one I wished to breach on such a momentous, historic day. I stayed in the eaves of the lobby knowing we'd meet again someday.

39

LEAVING HOME

Back home in Tucson, the move cracked what was left of me. Disassembling oneself from a couplehood is a battlefield rife with emotional landmines. Lifting heavy items was simple. But the small stuff broke my heart. Removing individual books from a combined bookcase and my coffee mugs from the kitchen cupboard, then staring at the gap-toothed shelves where my presence used to be… the emptiness was an unbearable ache. CDs, movies, photos, shared clothes and cycling gear. A lost, lone sock of his turning up in my packing boxes had the power to make me come undone.

"It's all too much!" I announced to the kitchen and the living room one day. "I'm not sure how much more I can take." The furniture and appliances said nothing. Gathering the courage to send my husband a text as I boxed the last of things, I wrote, *It's all too much*. There was no response. There never would be. The last I saw of him was the day he left three months ago. I would never see nor hear from him again. I was years away from understanding closure does not come from others, but within. That day in August, there was nothing closeable. Just a gaping void impossible to fit in any box.

Also unboxable, the garden. When we married, instead of tangible wedding gifts we asked for gift cards to Lowe's or Home Depot, so we could build a garden in the dirt lot of our backyard. We created a small haven of plants and vegetables in an otherwise descriptionless row house with too-close neighbors. Oleanders, bougainvillea, desert willows, mesquite, fig, pomegranate and orange trees, brick patio and a vegetable garden built by hand. I took great pride, peace and comfort in tending, watering, weeding and watching everything grow in the space we built together. Now I was the one being weeded out. *It's just a backyard*, logic interrupted. *But I built that, it's mine*, my heart interjected. *Not anymore*, reality clarified. Reality is such an asshole. Leaving was more than I could bear alone.

Three stalwart friends, Marilyn, Jo and Dean, helped carry my four items of furniture—dresser, bed, couch and table—into a storage unit. *Don't slip, don't slip, don't slip*, I begged each of my feet as we shuffled stuff down the stairs. The idea of breaking a bone while being evicted during divorce was not how I wanted to end my pro cycling career. There was not much else I owned, but the few remaining items were dispersed among friends. Oliver took my bookcase, Marilyn claimed the TV, Adrian kept my drum set. I had essentially William Wallaced my belongings to every corner of Pima County; as if divorce were warning the world, *Don't marry that one*.

At the storage unit, I broke down. All brain power was lost. I couldn't engage in the Tetris required to see how shapes fit together and what boxes go where. What tipped me over the edge was disassembling my Team Colavita Jamis road bike. I had a Wiggle-Honda bike to use that year, but I could not bear to part ways with the very first bike I earned as professional rider. Unless I found a job pronto, I knew I'd have to sell the Jamis soon to pay my lawyer fees. But the act of taking apart a bike and wedging it into storage felt unnatural. They're supposed to be ridden, not dormant. Staring at the upside-down angles and jumbles of my disassembled life, my grief and I questioned the complicated trilogy of need, want and storage. Part of me wanted to hold onto everything. Part of me wanted to drop a match and walk away.

My husband's departure in May was, by far, the worst day of my life. But the worst night was the last one I spent in my home that August, alone. During our marriage we kept our bedroom door shut at night, as the onslaught of five nocturnal cats was not conducive to beneficial sleeping habits. But that night, I slept on the couch and they all came to visit me in their weird cat way. Jal checked in on me, Taz stalked by, Polar and Panda curled up for a bit, while I waited for Grizzy—the one with whom I bonded most—to nuzzle into me. She did, and I wept without end. Between fits and spurts of sobbing and dozing throughout the night, I whispered to the cat. Telling her I didn't want to go. That I had to, but couldn't take her with me. That I would never see her again. *Grizz, I know you don't understand words, but I need you to know that I don't want to leave, I want to stay here, I would never abandon you, holy shit I'm talking to a cat, I know words don't make sense but can you feel anything I'm trying to say? That I love you and I miss you and I'll hold you close in my heart and thank you for loving me…* When she reached out and laid her paw at the base of my neck, I cracked into a new fissure of brokenness.

Saying goodbye to a pet at the end of its life is a sadness I knew and understood. But to say goodbye to a pet very much alive was a new level of pain I was not equipped to process. My soul flatlined that day. I took a picture of each cat. I took a picture of the garden. I turned on the Apple TV and took a picture of *Half the Road*, downloaded on iTunes. As if to prove I still existed somehow in this home. Grief makes us do weird things.

I don't remember leaving the house. I do remember pulling into my father's apartment complex and parking my Prius next to my dad's car. Unaware the divorce was still a year away from finalizing, I do remember feeling that—after home, pets, sanity and marriage—at least there was nothing more my husband could take away. Or so it felt at the time.

I was 39 years old, homeless, jobless—*ooh, don't forget worthless*! my Cerberus chirped—and moving in with my father. Surely that was not in my dad's plan when he retired to Arizona just eight months beforehand. His one bed/one bath apartment had a den just big enough for a mattress, small bureau and a lamp. His heart, however, was the size of a palace and there was no place else I would rather be an emotional basket-case than living on the floor of my dad's den. My father wasn't just my dad. He was my best friend. When I confided in him that I was losing my sense of emotional balance and struggling to figure out who I was now, my father sat quietly through my lengthy ramblings. One day, he uttered a sentence that captured the heart of my predicament of change and loss.

"The struggle is when we try to be who we were," Dad said, "instead of who we are now." Bullseye. I was hanging so tight to who I was then, as the now-ness was so scary and unknown. My father is a wise man. He's also funny. Shortly after moving in, I asked him where he wanted to go for lunch on his 79th birthday.

"Hooters on Broadway!"

"No, Dad. Try again."

"Hooters Downtown?"

Persistence. It's a Bertine thing.

Days after the inaugural La Course, Le Tour Entier received an email from Thibaud Coudriou of ASO. They were thrilled with La Course's success. Primary data was already in for the first two countries. France Television had an average of 2.4 million viewers, which comprised 24 percent of the market share. The usual audience of this time slot averaged one million viewers at just seven percent market share. In the Netherlands, viewership soared from four percent to 31 percent. While math was never my strong suit, the numbers made perfect sense: Investing in a women's race at the Tour de France was a gain. Not just ethically, but financially. In typical ASO fashion, however, Thibaud asked us not to share these figures in social media. They were "just for Le Tour Entier." Made no sense why ASO wanted to keep secret this important data proving women's market value. Then again, most of ASO didn't make much sense. I desperately wanted to tweet *Interesting statistics are happening!* then set my watch to see how fast they would ask me to delete it. I let it go.

The effect of La Course was still circulating in the media that summer, articles coming out in *Glamour, Marie Claire, Real Simple* and other women's magazines and news networks that had nothing to do with cycling. Which was exactly what we needed for visibility, equality and change. I was keenly aware of the importance of media coverage, but unable to truly embrace it or be proactive. Strange were the instances when people engaged with me about the positive impact of La Course, and my voice said *thank you*, but my brain silently offered a different dialogue.

"Congratulations Kathryn, you did this! You made history with La Course!"

Thank you! Did you know storage units are just $79 a month if you book online with the coupon code?

"Read the article in *Glamour* and saw you on CNN. You changed cycling!"

Aww, thanks. He took the tire pump with the slightly broken dial. It wasn't in the garage. That was my favorite pump.

"You helped open the door to parity at the Tour de France."

Well, we all did our part. I miss my cat. She wasn't technically mine, but she really was, you know? She chose me. My lap. Not his. For five years. Fuck. I miss you, Grizzy.

"You are a force to be reckoned with."

"Wellesley College made you an honorary Wellesley woman!"

"I heard you on NPR last week and BBC's podcast this week!"

Thank you so much. I might want to die. I'm not sure yet. I don't know why or when exactly, but I do know this. When someone gives up on you, it's so hard not to follow suit.

Adding to the peculiar distortion of past, present and reality came the release of my third book, *The Road Less Taken*. The honor and gift of landing a book deal and seeing one's work come to tangible fruition is no small feat. Being published is a big deal. A time to celebrate. Not to mention, publicize. But I didn't feel like doing either. The final draft of the essay collection went to print two weeks before my husband left. No changes were able to be made. The book featured chapters about my personal life and loving marriage. In the acknowledgements, gratitude for my husband always being there. *To George… All roads lead home to you.* Four months later, those roads no longer existed. Who would want to read an essay collection by a worthless woman whose husband left her? My mind was in no state to promote the book.

Everything I strived to accomplish was happening. But the person I wanted to share it with was long gone. *Aww, screw 'em!* my kindhearted support crew commanded. *His loss!*

"Yeah!" I chorused, hollowly. My attempt at anger all fell short.

"Congrats on the book," friends cooed. "You are successful! Accomplished!"

"Thank you." Success is a mindfuck. Accomplishment is empty. People still leave. I am growing very, very tired of it all.

Within a few weeks, my internal dialogue stopped talking. For the first time in my life, the two-headed Cerberus of NotMattering wasn't there. Not quieter, gone. Doghouse empty. I didn't feel like a nothing, a no one, worthless or broken. I simply didn't feel anything. Apathy replaced emotion.

At first, I thought maybe it was good to stop feeling because everything stopped hurting. I wasn't sad, distraught or troubled anymore. I was vacant. The physical ache in my chest for which I saw the doctor a few months ago, that was gone, too. I stopped caring. About anything. Which is a bizarre situation for someone whose whole existence as an activist was caring about *everything*. I also stopped writing. Words came through me like bric-a-brac ribbon, this way, that way, kinked and cornered, never straight to the point. Jumbled mush at best.

As a writer, I was accustomed to channeling pain, discomfort and confusion into sentences that could help me dissect the tough stuff. For years, I held the words of Hemingway close in my heart when I stumbled into life's difficult trenches:

"Write hard and clear about what hurts." But when things stopped hurting, there was neither words nor clarity.

Maybe a change of venue would spark something. Maybe this was just a rut, I attempted to reason. Job applications were out everywhere, but I heard nothing back, adding to the void of Empty. I flew to upstate New York. Maybe if I surrounded myself with family and nature, things would get better. But even in the woods, the happiest place my soul knew, I was still vacant. I felt nothing at all.

There were film events and races coming up for which I was booked to attend; a mountain bike ride in Idaho, Worlds, Caribbean Championships, and screening in Dubai. I didn't care about any of them anymore. I understood I was broken, and I could see all the proverbial pieces scattered on the floor. But I couldn't pick them up. Didn't want to. The weight of emptiness grew to immeasurable proportion. Apathy took a dangerous turn toward numbness. My mind began nurturing the idea of death because there was nothing else growing in the garden of who I used to be. Somewhere in that unreachable void, the exit plan took root.

40

Exits

Depression never announced itself in my headspace. I never once considered myself depressed. Just empty, alone and unable to feel. Besides, depression was something clinical. Wasn't it? Something people are born with, I assumed. That's how advertisements made it seem. Depression was something people felt all the time, their whole lives, and if they took the right medication it would chase away that little, dark, cartoon raincloud hovering overhead. No, I didn't have *that*. I didn't have psychotic, bipolar or manic-depression, nor postpartum or perimenopause depression. If none of those definitions of depression fit me, then I wasn't depressed. Googled *depression* too, just to make sure. Yup. Nothing fit. Even if there was a name for whatever was going on in my head, I didn't care. I just didn't want to be here anymore in this unfeeling life.

There was indeed a name for my depression, just not in 2014. Situational Depression made its way to the medical journals by 2017, defined as a condition stemming from extremely stressful life situations like divorce, job loss, death of close friends/family and major life changes.[102] Situational depression lasts between three to six months, peaking at the halfway point. While the duration of situational depression is shorter than clinical depression, it is often equally (or more) severe. Therapy and psychotherapy are effective treatments, but this doesn't do much good for people who don't realize they have depression. People who think they're empty, unfixable and just want to put a stop to vacancy in their soul. Like I did.

I began sussing out options. Bullets and nooses were a hard no, I would not put the person who found me in such a horrific position. Had to be something peaceful.

---

[102] Interactive Reader Guide: Situational Depression.

Like pills. But I hated pills. Swallowing one pill was hard enough, let alone multiple capsules. Since I didn't drink alcohol, washing pills down with a sedative wasn't looking like a good plan. Then it hit me. What if my death could help someone else? My dad was struggling financially that year. If I staged an accident and pulled it off correctly, he would be the beneficiary of my life insurance policy. A very small policy, but at least it was something. Besides, sometimes people really do fall while hiking.

With a note pad, I stood in the woods of upstate New York, scouting the quietest location. Something secluded yet not difficult for my body to be found soon by other hikers near the base of a cliff. I'd been at this for a week before finding the right mountain with the proper angles. A few days later, I wrote a note and a letter. The note was easy. Left those on the kitchen table all the time, telling dad I was out for a hike. *Went hiking. See you later! Xoxo*

The letter was harder. Took some planning. I'd have to mail it the morning of the hike. Just enough of a small delay so police or hikers would find the body first, *then* dad would get the letter. If I remained missing for too long, the letter would have the coordinates of my location. The *why* was simple: *Dear dad, I have found something I am not strong enough for; emptiness. Don't tell anyone about this letter. Here are all the details for my insurance claim. I love you and I will see you on the other side. I'm sorry, Dad. Please don't tell anyone.* Even in my final plans, I was telling old white men what to do.

Relief—or so I thought at the time—washed over me. It wasn't relief, but simply the act of feeling. Feeling something, anything. Which felt like carrying out this plan was the right thing to do. I set the date for August 11. I was terrible at math, but loved numbers. Patterns. Sequences. The idea of being born on the 11th and dying on the 11th brought some strange sense of circuity to my troubled brain. I would be exactly 39¼ years old, exiting this world in the very month when I was conceived. (Troubled brains think up some weird shit.) A year ago, on July 11, we launched the petition for La Course. I loved the 11th. Back when I could love. This was the right day to go. On August 11, I would scribble the *Out hiking!* note, then mail the letter from town, then go into the woods. Done. Decided.

On August 11, 2014, I put on my trail sneakers, grabbed my backpack and went into town. The internet was strongest at the local library. I tucked myself into a quiet, hidden corner and opened Facebook and Twitter. I posted one last time about the upcoming screenings of *Half the Road* in Alaska, Colorado, New York, New Mexico, Canada, England and Ireland, as if I were trying to reach every corner of the world one last time before I go. While starting to type a new post about what a great day it is for a hike, I glanced at the newsfeed. The headlines were everywhere. Robin Williams had taken his life.

Emotion rushed into my heart with such a powerful force it took many breathless moments to figure out pain and sadness were alive and well within me. Sitting at a small wooden table in the back of the library, I clicked out of Facebook and devoured every news site while chanting *no, no, no* in whispered tones. How could such a vessel of humor, joy, creativity and laughter carry the weight of such despair? No, no, no. Not Robin. Not Mork. Not Mrs. Doubtfire. Not Professor Keating. Not Dr. Maguire. Oh captain, my captain... come back, come back. I watched you cartwheel across your lawn at the Escape from Alcatraz. You wished us luck on *Half the Road*, remember? You couldn't be our narrator because you were busy making more characters of awesomeness. We were gonna ride bikes someday. No, no, no. Not that incredible mind capable of electrifying a moment in ways no one else could, incorporating past concepts and future thoughts into digestible bits of here and now. Nanoo, nanoo. No, no, no.

I searched for the whys. How did he break? What was he missing? I needed something tangible. A very specific reason. Every emotion flitted through my head as I clicked, scrolled, refreshed and exhausted every possible paragraph on the suicide news unfolding. When I couldn't find a reason, that's when I knew what happened. The Empties got him. Even that beautiful, incredible, iconic brain was not exempt from the weight of emptiness.[103]

I closed my laptop. Hours had passed since opening it. My body was overwhelmed with sadness, my mind was pinging with feelings. Robin Williams's death shifted everything. I did not go to the post office that day. I went outside and ripped the letter into tiny, untraceable shreds and deposited them in two separate bins in our Adirondack town, beneath the ice cream cups and chicken wing cradles of summer tourism. I then went for a very long walk on a different trail, without cliffs. Back at the cabin, my dad was on the porch. Sitting down next to him, through tears I finally sobbed, "I think I need help."

------

[103] Unknown until autopsy, Robin had Lewy Body Dementia (LBD), a very difficult branch of Parkinson's. These particular biological Empties were physically taking away the mind we all knew and loved. His wife Susan Schneider Williams wrote a beautiful, educational piece on LBD. .

Returning to Arizona, I began sessions with a therapist after seeking out someone who specialized in divorce, depression and suicide prevention… and offered a sliding scale for payment. She was a lovely middle-aged woman whose gentle, cognizant vibes emoted trust. We met weekly, but I knew therapy alone wasn't going to be enough to get me over the hurdles of emptiness, darkness and loneliness. I had to be an active participant in my own healing, and for me, research was one such method. If I were going to get through this storm of depression, then I had to show up with an umbrella of knowledge when The Emptiness rained down. After perusing countless websites on suicide prevention, what resonated with me most was the power of distraction.

The reason I aborted my plan on August 11 was because I was completely distracted by the impact of Robin Williams' death. My mind shifted gears and all of a sudden, the idea of ending my own life took its seat in the nosebleed section of my mental stadium. Distraction *is* a feeling. While distraction often carries the burden of a negative connotation, it can be a saving grace and a powerful, wonderful tool for rebuilding. My life as an activist brought me into this place of struggle, but perhaps it could also bring me out. I started drawing blueprints for planned distraction, both physical and mental.

First, the physical distraction. I resuscitated the races and events coming up which I had given up on during the exit plan. Now, they were points of positive distraction: Go there. Be present. Do stuff. Engage body and mind. One day matters. When the Empties come, hush them with planned distractions. Rebecca Rusch— multi-world champion of endurance mountain biking and eco challenges—invited me to her signature event, Rebecca's Private Idaho in Kethcham. Rebecca offered to fly me out. So I went, entering the 25-mile mountain bike gran fondo. Physical distraction, achieved! My mind, however, was still a mosh pit of unfocused-ness. I missed the turn off for the 25-mile event and found myself on the 80-mile course. I was clearly still missing a sense of normalcy, but the distraction was working. I did not think about dying that weekend.

During the long ride in the woods, I saw a cyclist ahead of me wearing our Equality Kit from Le Tour Entier. A middle-aged man, no less. When I rode up next to him in my Wiggle-Honda jersey, he recognized me and introduced himself. Greg had signed the petition. Donated to *Half the Road*, too. His kind distraction of encouraging words while wearing our equal sign gave me hope and peace. If a stranger could make me smile, maybe I was capable of feeling some joy again. This is all I remember of that weekend: Rebecca Rusch is awesome. Strangers give hope.

Sometimes wrong turns make us stronger. Distraction wasn't smooth, but it was working.

Returning from Idaho, Winston Crooke, the SKN team manager, called me. He and Greg Philip thought hard about the World Championships situation. None of us liked how things were left on our last call. St. Kitts and Nevis registered me to go to 2014 Road World Championships in Ponferrada, Spain. *You can go, but no more signs and stage antics, ok?* Compromise isn't always fun, but often necessary. *Ok guys, thank you. I'll save the equal sign and use it somewhere else someday.*

Ponferrada was not easy to get to. Four hours from Madrid, the journey was a jumble of planes, trains, taxis and homestays. Luckily, Wiggle-Honda had my road bike there already. With such late notice, I would not be there for the time trial, but the road race gave me something to focus on. That's what I needed most; distraction. The race itself turned out to be an unremarkable personal result, but there were three moments that made the whole trip worthwhile. During the race, a mid-peloton crash splintered the peloton. Those of us behind had to chase like demons to get back to the bunch. Most of us solo. Marianne Vos had gone down in the melee, and her stalwart Dutch teammates waited. Protecting Marianne from the wind, the Dutch domestiques passed me like a speeding train. Ellen van Dijk patted her hip, which is cycling language for "Get on board, we'll help tow you back to the peloton." While we didn't know each other personally, Ellen knew what Marianne and I had done with Le Tour Entier. That brief moment of inclusion made me feel part of something bigger. To feel part of anything when one is broken is a beautiful, healing thing.

After the race, a woman from the Israeli National Team told me she saw *Half the Road*, and the women cyclists of Israel were then able to use the film to help make changes in their own country. A rider from Romania told me her national team was empowered by the film, too. I was blown away. The film really was making its way around the world and effecting change. Talk about distraction! These nuggets of knowledge became tiny footholds and handles for me to keep hanging on. While I did not hold up any equal signs at World Championships in 2014, it finally felt like maybe I didn't have to.

Two days after Worlds, ASO confirmed La Course by Tour de France would take place again on the Champs-Élysées in 2015. That same week, Vuelta España announced their inaugural race for women and Tour of California added more race days to their event in 2015. The ripple effect was happening, and each undulation was a most necessary, beautiful, personal distraction.

––––––––––––

Back on good terms with Greg and Winston, In October I flew to Puerto Rico to represent St. Kitts and Nevis in the Caribbean Championships. A wonderful Puerto Rican, Isis Casalduc, whom I befriended on social media invited me to stay with her. She was a kind, compassionate triathlete and former Miss Universe competitor; gorgeous in all capacities. Isis followed my activism journey. I struck up the courage to confide in her about how things were pretty bad behind the scenes. That I wasn't exactly okay, but trying my best to get there. On the morning of the time trial, Isis left me this note:

> "I know maybe you don't think about it that much, especially when you are down... but girl, let me tell you something. When someone looks for the definition of LIVING in the dictionary, your face should come up. You're not tied down to anyone's standards but your own. You give the middle finger to the status quo. Many might have 'more,' but what most people describe as more is usually a life full of way LESS. Less freedom, less happiness, less satisfaction, less of leaving a mark in someone else's life, in a future generation, in the world. I celebrate you. Keep going. —Isis"

Isis' healing words helped tremendously. I was hurting hard that day, flooded with memories of my husband at Caribbean Championships one year ago. The duct-taped broken bike, the win, the togetherness. (The bike was properly fixed. My heart was certainly not.) Uncertain whether my mental fatigue and physical prowess would suffice enough to defend my time trial title, there was something interesting that distraction provided. I was slowly coming to terms that this year—from *Half the Road* to La Course to divorce to a near-miss with suicide—was, well, *pretty fucking heavy*. The weight was equal parts unbearable and perspective-shaping.

The travails of bike racing now paled in comparison to the hard stuff. Perhaps this was the only place where feeling empty could be a temporary asset. All the stuff I stressed about in training and racing like calculating watts, heart rate, power and intervals suddenly took a much-needed backseat to the bigger picture of bike racing. Nothing on the bike could possibly hurt as much as this year had. And if it did, then fantastic! Hurting was feeling and feeling meant the Empties were leaving. So I used it to my advantage. To stand on a start line and say *I just don't give a fuck* would either yield victory or disaster.

Luckily, it was the former. I won my second Caribbean Championship that day in Puerto Rico, fueled by the Empties, Isis's emboldening note and the simple distraction of wheels going 'round and round.

On the Le Tour Entier front, all of us were equally thrilled and annoyed when ASO confirmed La Course for 2015. Thrilled it was happening. Annoyed it hadn't grown. Our plan, to which ASO agreed, was to start with one day then add two to three stages each year.

"I think they are all missing the point here," Tracy said. "I think we should state publicly that another 'one day' is not progress… 2014 was a litmus test and it worked, so why is 2015 another litmus test? Somebody needs to say this is NOT progress. Going from opportunity to tokenism is not progression. THIS IS INSANE."

Fascinating too, was the news from Steve, who spoke to ASO's commercial department. Jean-Etienne Amaury, chairman of ASO, wanted La Course to become seven days.[104] Even Paris was on board for growth.

"Paris has given permission to use more of the city for the final stage of the men's race, so hopefully this will extrapolate to La Course," Steve said, adding, "We need to be very careful. We don't have a budget to just keep helping ASO." Indeed, Le Tour Entier worked our asses off for free helping ASO get La Course off the ground. No more freebies. Rumor had it ASO was opening a US office to run the Tour of California, so I made a mental note to reach out to ASO in a few months to discuss La Course. But right now, my head and heart needed to focus on their own course. Distraction, help and healing were a most intricate, internal stage race.

---

[104] Interactive Reader Guide: Jean-Etienne Amaury & Women's Tour de France

41

CAMELS IN DUBAI
AND OTHER PLACES WHERE I LOST MY SHIT

In November of 2014, I boarded a plane to Dubai for the much-anticipated screening of *Half the Road*. Pascale and I came to an agreement where permission was granted for her to cut the word "gay" from one scene, so the film could legally be screened in Dubai theaters. Pascale and her partner, Louise, raised funds to bring me to Dubai to ride bikes with the local cycling community, speak with the Saudi Minister of Sport about adding a women's pro cycling race and to give a talk at the screening.

"You could help us open some doors here," Pascale said. "We need you to come." The word *need* poured into my ears like liquid healing. While I was faring much better with therapy, I was still reeling from the side effects of abandonment. To be left without warning harbors terrible feelings of unneeded-ness. *Dubai needs me! Ok, let's go! Wheee, camels!*

Screening *Half the Road* in Middle Eastern society was a big deal. While Dubai is a very modern, popular city for expats of all race, creed, color and denomination, the country is governed by an ideology biased toward heterosexual men. Saudi women and the LGBTQ community do not share equal opportunities, freedoms, or rights. I happily flew half way around the world to experience this culture myself.

Pascale picked up my stinky, disheveled self in Dubai. I liked her immediately. A jovial, good-natured, get-it-done type of woman whose general temperament I very much appreciated. Taking me to Wolfi's Bicycle Shop, Pascal set me up with what would be my eighth rented or borrowed bike of the year. There at Wolfi's, a Sheik was buying a $10,000 Ferrari road bike equipped with a commuter saddle and regular pedals. Apparently, this type of purchase was common practice. Pascale dropped me off at the DoubleTree by Hilton, which I expected would be a typical, modest DoubleTree. Like usual, my preconceptions were wrong.

The lobby was decked out with swanky tea room pagodas, gilded cornices and Persian rugs; a QuintupleTree of high-class lodging. After my jet-lag induced nap, Pascale dropped me off for the most fascinating group ride I have ever experienced during my eight years of cycling. From camel race tracks to highways without light posts, this adventure was distraction at its finest. The Dubai Roadsters evening group ride was just like the Tucson Shootout but completely different. Went something like this…

Me: Hi, I'm new here. I like your country. So, how does this ride work?
Local Guy: First we start on the camel track.
Me: There are camels? On a track?
Local: Not today. After a lap on the camel track we get on the interstate.
-The interstate? Won't it be dark by then?
-Yes.
-Are there lights?
-Sometimes.
-Are there cars?
-That's how we get our light.
-Right. Then what?
-We ride two hours on the highway. Watch for runners.
-There are runners... on the highway?
-Sometimes. They are hard to see.
-Anything else?
-On the last lap there is a sprint for the city limits sign. It's in Arabic and English. Try to follow someone with a light.
-Light, Arabic, runners...ok, what else?
-You're going to need arm warmers.
-But it's 75F.
-Then knee warmers, too.
-Anything else?
-My heart rate is 100.
-That's... wonderful.
-Do you have a husband?
-Ooh, look... A camel! On a track!
-That's not a... Hey, where you going?

I fell in love with cycling and all its characters all over again that night. Long live camel tracks, dark highways and the luminescent glow of new life experiences. A gentle sense of joy found its way through my soul in Dubai.

The next night, our *Half the Road* screening took place at the Vox Cinema at Mirdif Mall. Liv-Giant raffled off a bicycle for women and female students from the local colleges came to see the film. The audience was a splendid mix of age, gender, sexual orientation and religious backgrounds, equally filled with men and women. I stifled a giggle as the audience booed Pat McQuaid and Brian Cookson's antiquated ideals and laughed at the humorous parts. I barely even noticed the edited section of Nicky and Jenna's story. Pascale was right. Cutting out one word did not alter the presence nor message of their journey. Afterward we held a Q & A, discussing the victories of La Course and changing minds at ASO. Women wearing burkas bought the last of my *Half the Road* tee shirts. Never in a million years did I think our film would screen in Dubai, and I was overcome with emotion and gratitude. Pascale and Louise opened my eyes and educated me on adaptation, flexibility and personal growth.

On my final day in the United Arab Emirates, Pascale drove us to the Dubai Sports Council (DSC) headquarters to meet with the Ministry of Sport. After their three-year run of a UCI men's race, it was time to lobby for a women's equivalent of Tour of Dubai. In this particular country, the money was there. The DSC augmented its 2014 sports budget to $120.3 Million. *Million!* That ranked the UAE the second-best international sport event destination in the world.[105] I asked Pascale how she finagled the meeting with DSC.

"I've been talking to them for years. They're aware of what we want," Pascale said, "But when it comes to a meeting with the government in Dubai, you don't wait to be invited. You just show up." I smiled and felt an immediate kinship with Pascale. Show up, indeed.

The chairman at DSC heard us out and asked a few questions about women's bike racing. They had followed our ASO petition and La Course and paid attention. We went over some numbers and data about why inclusion of a women's professional race would be beneficial to Dubai's economy and societal progress. The meeting was positive, but Pascale was quick to point out that progress takes time in the Middle East. We might not see a result for many, many years...if at all.

"But you have to start somewhere," Pascale reasoned, with wisdom and patience I admired. Exactly. Everything starts with one meeting, one day.

After a wonderful, healing, distracting experience in Dubai, I packed up my suitcase in the QuintupleTree of awesomeness, getting ready for the trip back to Arizona. My father called on Skype, which sent a shiver through my spine. Dad only called on Skype when something was urgent or wrong. Usually the two went hand in hand.

---

[105] Behind London. Our British friends had some damn good sports marketing across the pond.

"Honey, I don't want you to worry, but just wanted you to know that when get home, your car won't be here," my father attempted to explain calmly.

"Are you ok!?" I panicked, assuming he borrowed the car and an accident ensued. "You're not calling from a hospital, are you?"

He was not calling from a hospital. Nor had he driven the car. My father explained that George sent two men to repossess the Prius. Since my website listed when and where I was away at screenings, George waited until I was out of the country and sent two men to my father's apartment to retrieve the car. At first, my father refused, telling the men they cannot have the keys. That cars were to be handled by divorce lawyers.

"If you don't hand over the keys," said one of the henchmen, "we will have Kathryn arrested for grand theft larceny the moment she sets foot back in the United States." Since my name was never added to the title, my husband could legally claim it was stolen.

My father was concerned I could be arrested in Newark airport. Worse, he was physically unnerved, worried he was not strong enough to block these men from forcing themselves into the apartment. Dad, angered but afraid, gave them the keys.

Marriage. Love. Husband. Home. Income. Car. All of it, gone. And now, something else: personal safety. The idea of people showing up to harass my father was incredibly unsettling. Back in Tucson, my nervousness escalated to the point I jumped out of my skin every time our neighbor or the FedEx man knocked on the apartment door. Maybe my husbands' repo henchmen would show up again. *They had only taken one car key, not both.*

While I'd just gotten a handle on positive distracting tactics, this particular stressor was an outlier on the distraction borders. I sat at the kitchen table in my dad's apartment and took literal inventory of the situation, mapping the best escape route of a second-floor apartment, should someone kick down the door. I could probably make it out one of the windows or the balcony, and if I hung by my hands it would only be about a ten-foot drop, so barring broken ankles, I could probably make it to the car, then… *Fuck. There was no car.* Somewhere between plotting escape routes and unpredictable repo men, and remembering my car, home, husband and safety were no longer there, I exhaled deeply and waited for the flood of sadness and anxiety. Instead, the Empties crept in. *Shit, shit, shit.*

When the awful sensation of Not Caring arose, I knew it had the power to transport me to the dark places of exit plans. The loss of the car itself was awful, but the act of taking was worse. I was already empty, what more was left? Trying to keep positive, my therapist and I hammered home two truths I kept on repeat mode: When there is nothing left to lose, there is everything to gain. Rock bottom is solid ground. *Rebuild, rebuild, you got this!* I tried convincing myself. But I wasn't there yet.

———————

I was doing something weird with my hands. Seven months after my husband's departure, not a day went by where my clenched fists didn't leave indentations in my palms from my fingernails. Apparently stress, fear and sadness accumulated in my hands as if they were trying to hang on to something that wasn't there. Fist clenching is a major sign of an anxiety disorder, but I didn't know that at the time. All I knew was when I attempted to open my hand in the inverse direction—palms out and open, fingers widened to their fullest reach—I broke down in tears. Physically, it was only a tiny bit uncomfortable to open my hands, but something else emotionally was going on. It was as though the physical openness of my palms connected to some sort of emotional openness. As if stretching my palms into the position of offering and receiving was a platform for direct vulnerability. *This is nuts*, I told myself. *Get over yourself. For chrissakes, open your fucking hands and try not to cry. This is not that hard.*

Weirdly, it was hard. Nine out of ten times, I'd open my palms and cry. It was like opening Pandora's box, releasing all the buzzy mental insects. But maybe if I kept letting them out, they would fly away. Opening my hands was hard, but keeping them open was harder. I went into the desert and found two, palm-sized rocks.

Before going to bed each night, I spent five minutes with my hands open, outstretched by my side with a stone on each palm to keep them from reverting into clenched fists. After doing this for weeks, eventually the tears stopped. In addition to the therapy sessions, distraction tactics, and the physical release of riding my bike, this weird rocks-on-palms thing was my private therapy. Or meditation. Or whatever. I never gave it a name. But I did it for the next year, and I still keep the rocks in my bedside drawer. To this day I use them when life starts getting clench-y. There is a deep connection between emotional and physical openness. While I may never be able to articulate the healing powers of widespread thumbs and skyward palms, I do know fists are not the answer.

———————

Rocks helped. Therapy helped. Depression and anxiety lessened. (No one nefarious showed up at my door again). But I also needed to use humor, or something like it, to keep a record and mark my progress. Lists were fun. Since I already had a list of names called on social media, I decided to keep a list of Places Where I Lost My Shit in Public During Divorce documenting anywhere I publicly erupted into tears during 2014 and 2015. After perusing all journal entries, the list yielded:

Places Where I Lost My Shit in Public During the Divorce

Three local bike shops	Every coffee shop in Tucson	Every other gas station in town	Every other parking lot
Cold Stone Creamery	Every group bicycle ride	State Champs mid-race	Table at sushi restaurant
Jamba Juice	Chase Bank	Wells Fargo	Sushi bar, too
Southwest Air (middle seat)	United Airlines (check-in)	Trader Joe's (cereal aisle)	Safeway (egg section, now only needing the half-dozen size)

The list was long. The list was sad. But also strangely healing through its colorful prism of vulnerability. By acknowledging the thunderstorms of my meltdowns, it felt more like a weather report than psychoanalysis. As comedian Dane Cook tweeted a few months prior, "You can't rain on my parade because I designed it to be aquatic themed." Exactly. I was a crying mess, yes. But so too is the aquatic theme of divorce. The list didn't eliminate the Empties, but anything that kept them at bay was a much-needed step forward.

———————————

I also knew the only way to stave off the Empties was to counterbalance it with the Fulls. Maybe if I focused on something that made me feel full of hope and purpose, I could fill the hole of Emptiness. Racing my bike was great, but that was a self-focused endeavor. What gave me greater joy and fulfillment was fixing broken things. Or, at the very least, parts of broken things. Moving the dial one inch forward toward unbrokenness. *Half the Road* exposed corruption and fixed some stuff for women's cycling. The petition and La Course fixed the gaping hole of opportunity at Tour de France. Standing on the start line proved that we "no ones" are capable of standing up and creating change. Advocacy, disruption, organization and writing fixed some broken parts. If I were going to keep the Empties at bay, I knew what I needed to do. Solve problems. Activism made me feel full.

Determined not to amble back toward the cliffs of depression, I knew I needed to draw a metaphorical map moving forward. Start a project that would bring progress for others and peace for me. Maybe even a garden and a cat. Whatever it took to feel both momentum and balance. Necessity was indeed the mother of invention, and she'd been quietly stirring an idea on the backburner of my thoughts for many months. *Dinner time!* On the floor of my father's den, I grabbed a notebook and started sketching out the business plan for Homestretch Foundation.

42

BEGINNING OF THE HOMESTRETCH

Even in 2014, zero progress occurred from Jim-Pat McQuaid's 2011 comment that women "did not deserve a base salary." Brian Cookson, who cited this need for change during his UCI presidential campaign, didn't deliver upon his win.

"It's just not that easy to pass a rule," he speculated.[106] This ideology was wrong, of course, but on a personal level it went deeper. I would not be living in my father's den had I earned the same base salary as a World Tour male racer. I would probably have to give up racing altogether in 2015. During my training rides, I mused, *what if we could fix this rule? What if some of the pro women had a place to live for free... while we fixed the base salary corruption behind the scenes?* We could call it the Homestretch Foundation, in reference to the fact we we're in the homestretch of equality, but more work needs to be done till we're there.

The blueprint for Homestretch was simple: a) Fix the gender pay gap in pro cycling so women would finally receive an equal base salary as men at the World Tour level. b) While fighting for pay gap resolution, create a nonprofit residence where female pro athletes suffering financially could live and train for free. c) Take all of my personal angst, pain, wants and needs and turn that shit into something that will help other people.

Constructing the business proposal, of course, took longer. There was much research to be done on the demographics, data and numbers of how such a nonprofit and residence would run successfully. The data was vital, but so too was the mental picture. I envisioned a residence that would sleep eight to ten athletes. Behind this residence, there would be a small guest house. I could live there and manage the

---

[106] Interactive Reader Guide: No base salary for UCI World Tour Women

property while lobbying for base salary equity. Having a private place to emotionally heal, hope and rebuild soothed my personal demons. Finding the actual residence and financial investors, though, might take decades. Didn't matter. Creating a business to help others gave me great joy and inner peace. However long it might take. *Try, try, try.*

Making a business plan was a fantastic coping tool to fill the Empties, but it did not fill my bank account. I still needed a job. One that would work around racing with Wiggle-Honda in 2015. They wanted to keep me on the roster for another year. Which I really needed to check in on... it was December and I had yet to receive my contract's countersigned copy from Rochelle.

"You need to keep this quiet until we make the announcement," she said. "We're publicizing our signed riders on a schedule, and we're not announcing you until New Year's Eve." Laughed out loud at that one, as all things cycling and secrecy seemed to go hand in hand. But some secrets seemed okay. More than happy to keep this one.

Still, 7,000 Euro from my Wiggle-Honda contract wasn't going to be enough to live on. Royalties from *Half the Road* and *The Road Less Taken* were years away, and if they ever did appear it would maybe cover groceries for a week. The business plan for Homestretch Foundation was just that, still a plan, not a reality. While Wiggle-Honda was a World Tour team, without a base salary it was just another casualty of the gender pay gap.

I began searching career options. Nothing sustainable was panning out in Tucson, but I secured a few interviews with publishing companies and print journalism in New York City. While there, I received an email from the folks at Change.org who'd followed my Le Tour quest.

"Can you stop by our office?" Matthew Slutsky asked. "We're not hiring at the moment, but there's someone we want you to meet." On a cold December day in Manhattan I walked into the Change.org offices on West 17th Street. It looked exactly like I imagined; a collaborative workspace of desks brewing with activity and positive energy. Employees of Change.org clearly understood change-making was driven by passion and connection.

"Kathryn, this is Morgan Fletcher," Matt said, smiling, introducing me to a young woman in her early twenties. "Morgan, please tell Kathryn why you're working here."

In the summer of 2013, Morgan read a petition on Change.org that lobbied for women's inclusion at the Tour de France. She didn't own a bike. She'd never been to France. But the situation stirred her. The fact women were being kept out of the Tour de France was an inequity that spoke to her soul. What moved Morgan most was the number of people who signed our petition and the triumphant victory of La Course. A few months later, Morgan applied to work at Change.org. They hired her.

"I got this job because of your petition," she said.

Blown away, I stammered my gratitude to Morgan. What moved me most in that moment was the power of reach. Never did it occur to me the varied ripple effects from a petition about a bike race in Europe might reach a non-cyclist in New York City searching for a career path. What Morgan didn't know in that moment was how much she helped me. Still unemployed and in the seemingly endless throes of divorce, I grappled with the internal question of activism, *Was the journey worth the struggle?* There in the office of Change.org, Morgan unknowingly picked up the sledgehammer of *Hell Yes* and brought it down hard on my chains of doubt.

There was something else that gave me great satisfaction. Morgan is Black. Cycling is a lily-white sport with very little ethnic and racial diversity. Knowing a young, Black woman benefitted from our petition against old, white Frenchmen will always give me inherent joy. Joy and humor. The irony of the immediate situation wasn't lost on me: Morgan had a job because of our petition and I did not. As I left the Change.org office, I told her, "Maybe someday you can hire me." We laughed and parted ways, and I headed back to Arizona to see what the next few months would unveil.

———————

In the final days in 2014, I gained confidence knowing another year of professional cycling was in the works and that Wiggle-Honda; a team who stood behind me, finding my outspokenness was worth something. My self-assurance was rebuilding. Until December 29.

Rochelle hired a new director for 2015, Egon van Kessel. In the final days of December, Egon decided he found a better, stronger and younger rider. My countersigned contract never arrived and New Year's Eve passed with fizzle instead of fireworks. There would be no Wiggle-Honda for me. Pro cycling is as cruel as it is compassionate. Just like 2014, 2015 began teamless and jobless. But this time, something took root in the void. *I've been here before. I've walked these roads.* Rather than opening the floodgates for the Empties, I focused on the things within my control: Work on the Homestretch proposal. Find a non-cycling job. Race independently and show those World Tour teams that not signing a woman with an engine comprised of Zero Fucks Given would be their biggest mistake ever.

In my father's den, I hung up a mirror that I dug out from storage. While mirrors seem a common thing to hang in most bedrooms, for the last seven months I had no desire to look at myself. My confidence so low, I couldn't even stand my own reflection. In an effort to confront my self-esteem, I put up the mirror. Along each side of the tin-plated, embossed Mexican frame, I attached my race numbers from La Course. Wilted and washed (after forgetting to remove them from my jersey, pre-laundry), I pasted the crimped, cotton numbers *193* to the mirror. Slowly I began tolerating the reflection, my strength growing from the faded, weathered numbers with corners that flitted to life when the fan was on. Like two flags waving to remind me of what's possible. To remind me to hang on. To remind me that I mattered.

Good riddance, 2014. Game on, 2015.

43

El Grupo and Moving Forward

Between the University of Arizona campus and the downtown hub of Tucson's city, the El Grupo Youth Cycling facility sits in a quiet, urban neighborhood where it's not uncommon to see college kids on scooters, business men and women on commuter bikes and coyotes and javelinas trot by with equally laid-back, southwestern demeanor. Tucson is a special place. Grabbed my heart in 1998 and never let go. El Grupo Youth Cycling did the same in 2015, when Daniela Diamente and Ignacio Rivera de Rosales hired me as their part-time assistant director.

This much-needed nonprofit organization founded in 2007 gives kids from all socioeconomic and ethnic backgrounds the opportunity to explore the world of bike riding, racing and touring. Kids are given all equipment necessary to be part of a sport that many families can't afford. But El Grupo goes far beyond sports. Some kids are in foster care. Some are from wealthy families. Most are in between. Some carry brokenness on the inside, others on the outside. Boys and girls between six and eighteen coexist and support one another. Training sessions are not divided by gender but ability and experience. Community, belonging, respect and responsibility are instilled at a young age. I loved everything about the program. My role was split between assisting Daniela with administrative duties in the morning and training with the kids after school.

"We want you to continue racing," Daniela said, giving me a 20-hour work week. "Having you on around these kids as a pro cyclist gives them a sense of what's possible. Especially as a woman." When away racing, I worked online. My salary was $20,000. In the quagmire of divorce, homelessness, joblessness and worthlessness, $20,000 was life-changing. The intangible wealth of a job rife with positive energy and giggling children turned me into a millionaire. Not to mention, it is scientifically proven that people can't hear their own demons screaming when helping kids. El Grupo was a godsend.

The El Grupo clubhouse was sixteen miles from my father's apartment. I started commuting by bicycle, but on top of my own training needs and the El Grupo kids' workouts, the daily 32-mile commute became a challenge. I needed a car. But getting tied into a monthly payment filled me with a fear. Should I lose my job, the car would be repossessed. *Again.* Still reeling from the Prius, I wanted to own a car outright. No payments. Something no one could ever take away. After research and calculations, it would take roughly 10 to 12 months for me save enough to buy a semi-decent, used car. But what to do in the meantime? I wondered if maybe I knew someone who had a spare car I could rent for a few months? The vulnerability, however, was a bit unnerving. To ask for assistance meant admitting financial struggle and not having my shit together. I armored up and leapt onto the tightrope of vulnerability, putting a post on Facebook inquiring about friend-to-friend car rental options.

Within 24 hours, numerous messages from people in the Tucson cycling community poured in, proving yet again that cycling communities aren't just a giant herd of athletes in Lycra, but wonderful, kind human beings. A beautiful soul named Anne Hoff saw the post. We'd never met, but she followed the journey. Anne's daughter away at college, and her 1998 Honda Accord was taking up space in the garage. Would I like to use that until June?

"It's old, has sun damage and needs a new transmission," Ann said. *Me too*! I thought. A car incarnate. Perfect! I'm not sure what hit me first; the relief and thankfulness, or the irony that Wiggle-Honda dropped me but a Honda Accord picked me up. Either way, both paled in comparison to the glorious decade-old bumper sticker on Anne's seventeen-year-old car: a red and blue banner stating *Gabby Giffords for Congress.*

"Anne, you have no idea how much this means to me," I said to her as tears welled up. I let her know I had only $100 a month to offer as a rental fee. Anne waived it away.

"No, I'm not taking your money and yes, I do know how much it means. I've been through difficult times, too," she said, referencing her own divorce. "I know how hard it is to rebuild."

Rolling out of Anne's driveway, I wasn't just overcome with emotion and gratitude but further bolstered by the power of asking. Asking, when done the right way, opens the doors of trust and progress. And healing. The tightrope of vulnerability sways a lot less when we ask with the intent of giving back more than we receive. Now that I had the Honda—powered by Giffords!—my daily commute to El Grupo was shortened. I could spend more time on the business plan for Homestretch Foundation. More energy toward giving back.

I sat in silence at the divorce pre-trial hearing, staring vacantly ahead as my lawyer and my husband's lawyer brought out calculators. He did not show up. The lawyers tallied my literal worth, clicking the keys of their adding machines—*tak! tak! tak!*—into a most unpleasant symphony reverberating off the white, sterile walls of the courthouse room. At the end of the meeting, all houses and cars would remain his. Without children, I was ineligible to stake any claim in the home. I was still accused of hiding money in off-shore accounts, his attorney still convinced that my author, filmmaker, professional athlete self was hiding undisclosed riches in St. Kitts and Nevis. Took every ounce of courage I had to refrain from fishing out the nickel in my pocket, sliding it across the table proclaiming, *Yeah, you got me. Here's your finder's fee, lady.*

With the meeting left unresolved, the divorce was headed to court. In July. Seven months away. Later that day, the emotional effects of the pre-trial trickled over into my physical training. Something about the calculators, numbers and the tallying of self-worth made me not want to stare at the power meter on my bicycle as it tallied the watts, threshold and speed of my physical worth. I was already too hard on myself when my watts dipped or heart rate spiked. I was tired of measuring myself and my workouts. After nine years of training with a power meter, I knew my data internally. I just didn't want to stare at numbers anymore. *This is the year of Zero Fucks Given*, my gut whispered. I took the monitor off the bike. Unplugging, literally and figuratively. Little did I know turning off the screen would lead to my best season ever. At 40 years old.

On the one-year anniversary of *Half the Road*'s debut at The Loft, I tallied up the numbers of worldwide screenings, reactions, adventures, hurdles and victories we had since our premiere:

- 70 Screenings
- 8 Countries
- 10 Film Festival Acceptances
- 3 Film Festival Awards
- 1 Best Picture
- 1,044 iTunes & Vimeo downloads
- 1 week on iTunes Top 20
- 600 DVDs sold
- 1 La Course by Tour de France.

We were still being booked for screenings. Occasionally, I was asked to speak. In February 2015, The College of William & Mary in Williamsburg, Virginia brought me out for a presentation and speaking engagement. This time, during the Q and A after the film, I experimented with letting a little bit of vulnerability seep out in a public setting. This time, when someone asked about what the hardest part was about making *Half the Road*, I answered honestly. I owned up to the reality of how hard the role of activism was, and how it took quite a hit on my personal life. How sometimes changing the world does not exclude our personal universe. I used words like *divorce*, *crushing*, and *rebuilding*. I stopped myself before offering details of physical loneliness, Prius repossession and welling up with tears about Grizzy the Cat. Not all of that was necessary live on stage, but it was just starting to dawn on me that presenting my authentic self could help me reclaim my broken confidence.

Just down the road from Williamsburg, the city of Richmond, Virginia was selected to host the 2015 Road Cycling World Championships. Since this would be my final Worlds—as long as I didn't hold signs overhead—I wanted to end my cycling career by giving back.

For the past seven years, homestays and helping hands made Worlds happen for me. Not just me, but almost every small nation and low-budget cycling federation. Now that World Champs were going to be in the US, I wanted to help. Together with wonderful souls of the Richmond area—Ann Hardy, Wayland Hundley, Lora Toothman and Josh Cooley—we founded RVA Hosts, an organization providing host housing and assistance to all struggling athletes, prioritizing women first. Over the next eight months we secured housing for over 70 athletes and damn, did that feel good.

This giving back thing was working. Helping others calmed the voices in my head that I wasn't enough, worthless or Empty. The Cerberus was still there, but rather than barking or biting, he let me saddle up and take him out for ride. Activism wasn't going to obliterate my neuroses, but rather than trying to slay my demons, advocacy became my way of building a barn for them. Maybe we're not supposed to fight our monsters. Maybe we're supposed to acknowledge their existence, build a shelter and take them out for exercise. Let 'em run, wander and frolic in their strange, spazzy ways, bring 'em back exhaustedly spent, then tuck them into the barns we choose to create. Activism is a fabulous stable.

———————

Turns out the steady calmness and mental balance I felt in helping others wasn't some hippy skippy mumbo jumbo. Science was on my side. There was a direct impact of gratitude/giving on mental and physical health. At UCLA's research center scientists discovered feelings of gratitude and giving can change the molecular structure of the brain.[107] Furthermore, scientists discovered the brain isn't the only one in charge of sending out signals. In some situations, the heart sends signals *to* the brain. When the brain feels peace and happiness, the central nervous system jumps on the signal-sending bandwagon. Practicing gratitude and helping others enables the body become more at ease, less reactive and less resistant.

In contrast, the disordered rhythm of a stressed, erratic heart inhibits the ability to think clearly and make effective decisions. Which made total sense as to why the past year felt like a fog of disconnect and my cognitive function was at an all-time low. In 2015, I didn't know anything about the biophysical communications of brains, hearts, giving and gratitude. All I knew was making progress and helping others were the calming salve that healed internal wounds. And I liked it, this giving thing.

———————

When I returned from Virginia, something weird happened. A call came in from a dear friend who runs a bike shop on Tucson's northwest side.

"We received a package for you at Bicycle Ranch," Steve Morganstern said.

Only I didn't order anything. And there was no return address. An uncomfortable feeling set in. My mind immediately drifted to all the negative

———————

[107] Interactive Reader Guide: Gratitude/Helping Others & The Brain

possibilities. Arsenic. Anthrax. Tangible hate mail. My address wasn't public, so I deduced one of my recent social media posts—which thanked Bicycle Ranch for carrying my book—was the possible connection for someone to send a package there. Making my way to the shop, I stared at the padded envelope for a long time.

"Do you want to open this in private?" Steve asked, quietly.

"No, but I think you should be here in case a cloud of poison poofs up and kills me. Do you mind?" I asked.

"Ok," Steve said, taking a step back.

I peeled the package open. Inside was cash. One thousand dollars. Ten one hundred dollar bills. And a letter:

> "Kathryn,
> Can't think of a better way to do this, so here goes. You're one of the most deserving badass cyclists I know! The fact that you haven't been signed by a team yet is an absolute shame. While I can't offer you a pro contract, offer you a job, or a new book/movie deal, I can offer you this deal. In exchange for the enclosed, all you have to do is promise to do the following:
> 1) Keep kicking ass
> 2) Keep burning watts
> 3) Stay positive
> 4) Be fucking awesome!
> This is from my cycling slush fund. I can't do Leadville or Kanza this year, so my loss is your gain."

There was nothing more. No signature. No email. No return address. Inferring this was most likely male handwriting, I was both weirded out and moved to tears. There is no greater feeling than being believed in by others when we struggle to believe in ourselves. *One thousand dollars.* With one-third of my $20,000 salary going to my divorce lawyer, this extra thousand dollars was immense. As if it had a whole string of fat zeroes and multiple commas trailing behind like a comet of hope, help and wonder. I was still struggling with the internal concept of worth and value. Still haunted by my husband's words, *You don't need...* Yes I do! See? It says so right here in my new, anonymous, mystery contract. I need to keep being fucking awesome.

Soon after, an email came in through my website. The secretive donor wanted to make sure I received the package. The sender's email address was a string of numbers and the letter B. He wished to remain anonymous. I wrote back to B and thanked him for such unexpected generosity. With the unsettledness of a year filled with unanticipated abandonment, repo henchmen, strange vultures and

WannaTalkers, I was ill at ease with an anonymous man sending me money. Ungrateful, no. Weirded out, yes, a little bit. I had a decision to make: either I could believe humanity actually had people who did good things, or I could shut this down and not respond. I went with the former but kept my guard up. This would not be the last installment from B.

———————

In April, after coming in second place in the women's pro/elite field at Tucson Bicycle Classic, I landed a guest ride opportunity with an elite team in California called Zoca-Halo Sports. They brought me on to race Redlands Bicycle Classic. My Zero Fucks Given attitude was working and I was riding stronger than ever. I knew Redlands well. (It was the first race Wynona barred me from, too). Raced it many times and was excited to go back. But this time, two unimaginable life experiences were awaiting me in California. Neither of which I would wish on my worst enemy.

Before heading to Redlands in late April, I did what all American's love most: taxes. I went to see my accountant Cyndi Dain, as I had done for the past five years. Only this time, without my husband, which put *Accountant's Lobby* on my List of Places Where I Lost My Shit. Cyndi was kind, courteous and knowledgeable. She was also Wonder Woman in disguise. Sifting through the doldrums of paperwork, we eventually landed on the topic of health insurance.

"Any changes to your health care coverage?" she asked.

"Not yet," I answered. "Until the divorce finalizes, I'm on my husband's coverage." Cyndi stopped leafing the paperwork, raised her head and locked eyes with me.

"I need you to check," she said. The tone of her voice, the slow nod and strong, steady gaze made it clear she was to be taken seriously. My gut heard her loud and clear. But my brain didn't get it.

"Thanks Cyndi, I'm sure everything is fine. My lawyer explained it's illegal for him to remove me from our health care policy until the divorce is final. That's four months from now. There aren't any chang—" I explained.

"Kathryn, I need you to check," she repeated. "Today."

I called Blue Cross Blue Shield the minute I got home. My husband had removed me from the policy four months ago. *That's impossible*, I argued. We weren't divorced yet. Besides, I never received any mail. Or email. Or phone call. There must be some mistake.

"As the primary account holder, he can take off anyone he wishes," Blue Cross said. "We don't have to inform anyone. That's not our position."

"Your position is *wrong!*" I bellowed into the phone, launching a diatribe on how unethical it is to *not* inform people removed from their health policy. With a divorce rate of 50 percent in the United States, it became immediately clear to me I was not a unicorn in this situation. Despite one spouse removing another from health insurance during divorce proceedings is illegal, some take the risk and ditch their spouse's policy to save money. I called Cyndi.

"How did you *know*?!" I asked her.

"Because I've been in your position," she said. "And I've seen it in other divorces."

Cyndi then explained I missed the March deadline for health insurance enrollment. But with an emergency status request, I might be able to apply for local welfare insurance citing the divorce and unexpected health care removal. As I applied for AHCCCS, [108] I wept tears of anger. For the last four months, I unknowingly trained and raced in a high-risk sport without insurance. Then I wept tears of sadness and disbelief that my husband would secretly do that. The Empties had a field day with that one. Even my health didn't matter to him. I sank to a low, low place on the scale of worthless. Three days before the start of Redlands Bicycle Classic, my emergency status was approved. Welfare health insurance came through. Just in time for my first major crash.

---

[108] Arizona's low-income health care under the Affordable Care Act. Also known as Obamacare. Thank you, Mr. President, for saving my ass.

44

CRASHES, CRATERS AND SILENCE

On April 7, I flew to Redlands, California for the gut-punching sufferfest of bike racing awesomeness and perhaps my chance to prove to the pro teams that I still had it. Since removing my power meter, my training and recent results were the best they'd ever been. Adapting my Zero Fucks Given mentality from the personal state to the physical realm was working. Off the bike my confidence still waned, but when I raced a new persona took the helm. Channeling the struggle from the brain to the heart to the cranks to the chain, the wheels now turned with the newfound power of Unfuckwithable and turned my aggression up a notch. I couldn't wait to saddle my demons at Redlands.

Most of my Zoca-Halo teammates were collegiate athletes or recently-graduated racers, looking to make their way to the pro ranks, and I looked forward to meeting them. My roommate would be Erica Greif from Reno, NV, whose brother David was a student at University of Arizona. David was one of my talented training partners in the Tucson peloton of awesome guys on the Shootout.

"You'll get along great with my sister!" David told me, citing Erica's love of women's rights and artistic energy. She was 24, finishing up her college degree, newly engaged and working toward pro cycling aspirations. She was also an artist. Over coffee at El Mercado after a Shootout, David showed me Erica's artwork. Paintings, lithograph and sketches. Didn't surprise me such a talented artist was also a talented bike racer. Nor did it surprise me that Erica's plan was to drive from Reno to Redlands—an eight-hour drive—the night before the race, as college kids tend to possess this kind of energy. Erica had to take an exam the day before Stage 1. Then she'd hop in the car and arrive in Redlands by 2 am.

With our race starting at 8am and being 40 years old, I did not wait up late for Erica. I left her a note, explaining the layout of the room we were sharing. Like most small-budget teams, Zoca-Halo used Redland's homestay program. A local family took us in. Our shared bedroom had two mattresses partitioned by a half-wall to give us each some privacy. I took the bed in the back and left a note on her pillow.

> *Hi Erica! Glad you made it! Your bed is right inside the door, I'm in the back part of the room. Might be best to keep the door shut tonight b/c cats will try to get in. We should leave here by 6:45a. I'll get up at 6:15. Sleep well and see you in the morning! -Kathryn*

When the alarm went off, I stumbled toward the bathroom and peeked over to see if Erica was stirring. Her bed was empty. My note still on the pillow. I called our team director, Martin, confident that Erica probably grew tired and pulled over along the way to get some sleep. When Martin said he hadn't heard anything from her, my stomach somersaulted. He called her parents. I called her brother, David. No one had heard anything.

Clinging to the hope that no news was good news, our team started the race without Erica. Martin was stationed in the feed zone, midrace, when he got the call. Erica was killed in a head-on collision around midnight, two hours from Redlands. Two young women in the oncoming car also lost their lives. Distraction? Drowsiness? No one had answers. Only shock and loss. We were given the news at the finish line. The devastation set in when David's voice sobbed in confirmation over the phone. *She's gone, she's... gone.*

Trying to juggle grief, bike racing and the unthinkable death of a young teammate was like juggling knives without handles. As we wept, absorbed and wondered what to do, the team—Julie Emmerman, Bethany Allen, Megan Aldrete, Kaytie Scott, Martin Santos and I—decided together we'd continue racing because Erica would be pissed if we didn't. David confirmed our decision. So we kept going.

The next two days were a blur. Since I was Erica's roommate and teammate at Redlands, I fielded questions from the media. Tragedy was the last thing I wanted to be a spokesperson for in women's cycling. There were three more nights at our homestay, and the sight of Erica's unslept-in bed brought me to tears. The couple we were staying with, Steve and Jeannie, were sensitive and kind.

"Do you want us to remove her cot?" they asked.

"No, let's leave it," I said, thanking them.

For the next three nights, I left the nightlight on and kept the note on her pillow. I turned down her sheets every night, and pulled them back up in the morning, wanting to feel she was still here with us in some small way. Maybe she was.

Heaven, Eternity, Afterlife, Universe, whatever. I believed in energy, unknowns, maybes and wonder. If there were any energy out there trying to make sense of what just happened and where to go next, I needed Erica to know there was a light on and a bed nearby. Didn't tell my teammates about the bedroom ritual. I liked keeping that one just between Erica and me. Roommate solidarity.

Eight years of race homestays and team camps, where it's normal to herd as many women as possible into tight quarters where we griped about the loud snoring, nervous twitching, the night owls and the early risers… I now cherished the chaos of closeness. I never imagined a room with two beds and one rider could feel way too big and far too sad.

The night after Erica's death, JET Cycling—a junior elite team at Redlands—had our team over for dinner. Among this sweet, kindhearted group of talented young women was a nineteen-year-old up-and-coming rider making quite a name for herself; Kelly Catlin. *Wait, I know that name. That's the kid who so eloquently signed our petition,* I thought to myself, and went over to say hello.

"Thanks for signing the petition, Kelly," I smiled.

"Thanks for writing it," she responded. We chatted for a bit, neither of us knowing an Olympic medal was in Kelly's near future. While there wasn't much brightness at Redlands that week, meeting Kelly remains a beautiful memory. Her story was just beginning.

The next day, the race officials brought our team to front of the start line and held a moment of silence for Erica. We Sharpied black hearts onto our arms with an "E" in the middle. Our teammate, Bethany, went on to claim the Best Young Rider jersey. On the final day, the emergency room claimed my own jersey.

———

The weather was perfect. Sun shone brightly and visibility was crystal clear during the Sunset Loop stage, set high in the hills above Redlands. There was no excuse for me not to see the edge of the road. The peloton had whittled down to less than thirty racers on the last lap, and I was among them. Feeling strong, confident. Just past the feed zone, my front tire blew. Calm and collected, I drifted to the back of the peloton. *No problem, I got this.* Then, all of a sudden, I didn't got anything. I rode right off the road and crashed into the soft dirt shoulder alongside the pavement. On the way down, my right elbow caught the lip of the jagged asphalt and kept a sizeable chunk of my flesh as a souvenir.

Adrenaline took over. I quickly rose, raising my hand toward the caravan to signal for a wheel change. I didn't need a wheel change. I needed an ambulance. The giant red crater at the base of my right forearm was filled with chunks of pink flesh, gray gravel and the flash of white bone at its center. What used to be my elbow now looked like corporeal gazpacho. Something between a scream and a barf belched from my vocal chords as the medic car approached. There would be no return to the peloton. The doctor approached, quickly assessing the situation.

"You need to get to the Emergency Room," he stated. I nodded and started making my way to the car. "No, no," he stopped me. "We can't take you."

"What do you mean?" I stammered, now dazed. "You're the medical van!"

We have to stay with the race in case something happens," he said.

"*Something happened*!" I squeal-squawked, holding up my bloody crevice with protruding bone and the stream of blood cascading from my limb.

"Yes, but you're conscious," he theorized. "We need to stay with the peloton in case anyone gets seriously hurt." Only four miles remained in the race.

"But... how am I supposed to get to the hospital?" Now I was holding back tears. The Zoca-Halo team car stayed with the race, confident the medical van would take care of me. Now the medical van was pulling away. My adrenaline was depleted. The pain set in and the blood kept running.

"I'll take you," a spectator said, lifting my bike in the back of her truck. As bizarre luck would have it, this woman happened to be the mother of my teammate. Teri Alderete parked near the feed zone to cheer for her daughter, Megan. She was mere feet from where I crashed. Not a native of Redlands, Teri had no idea where the hospital was and her phone did not have an audible Mapquest, so she typed in *hospital* and I held the phone in my unscarred left hand and the next twenty minutes went something like this:

> Holy-shit-this-really-fucking-hurts-HEADWESTONSUNSET LOOP-I'm-going-to-throw-up-IN200YARDSTURNRIGHT-I-can-see-the-bone-I'm-in-a-lot-of-pain-I-was-doing-so-well-in-the-race-CONTINUESTRAIGHT-my-husband-left-divorce-is-awful-INTHREEMILES-your-daughter-is-really-nice-THEDESTINATION ISONYOURRIGHT-I'm-pretty-messed-up-and-I-don't-think-I-will-ever-be-okay-ARRIVED!

Making way to the emergency room, relief and wooziness caught up with me. An orderly rushed toward me with a wheelchair. In an effort to assist me into seated position, he grabbed my elbow. To this day, I'm not sure I'm capable of recreating the sound that emanated forth, but I'm quite certain the noise that came out of me would've made an exorcism sound like a lullaby.

My lovely Zoca-Halo team jersey was cut off, morphine doled out and the gaping wound scrubbed, stitched and stitched and stitched again, three layers deep of sutures and grossness. At some point during my five-hour stay in the trauma unit, reality seeped into the big picture. My new health insurance went into effect three days ago. Had Cyndi, my angelic tax accountant, not shared her wisdom with me to check on my insurance status during the divorce, this emergency room trip would have technically bankrupted me. Thanks to Obamacare for low-income earners, I was fully covered. Thanks to my I've-seen-weird-shit-happen-with-health-care-droppage-during-divorce tax accountant, I would be okay.[109]

I broke down in both gratitude and sadness. To be left without health care was wrong. To be educated on the solution was lucky. I was overwhelmed with thankfulness for Cyndi. This was a year of finding out just how much pain I could take, and elbows ranked relatively low in the grand scheme of things. On the way home from California, a call came in.

"You rode strong at Redlands," said Jono Coulter, director of UCI team BMW-HappyTooth Dental. "Till the crash, anyway. How long will it take to heal?" I told him I'd probably be back on the bike in less than three weeks.

"Tour of the Gila is in four weeks," he said. "We need an extra rider. Can you commit?" *Absofreakinglutely.*

With my arm in a soft-cast for ten days, the doctors decreed no riding. Let thy body heal. My dad suggested we drive to the Grand Canyon. He'd never been.

"Let's go see the only hole larger than the one in your elbow," Dad reasoned. "That'll cheer you up!" Good point. We embarked on the five-hour road trip to northern Arizona. Even better than the gaping hole in our earth was the fullness of bonding with my dad. Steering clear of divorce negativity, I told him all about the Homestretch Foundation plans I was working on. After babbling incessantly for days about all things progress and activism, my father noted I was most happy and alive when creating change. The conversation continued long after we returned from the Grand Canyon, as I puttered about the apartment babbling about advocacy.

---

[109] I have never felt such gratitude for paying taxes as I did in 2015. Long live fabulous female tax accountants. While the gender data gap offers no stats on this claim, I'm not sure a typical male accountant would have caught this/warned me as Cyndi did.

"Was I always like this, dad?" I asked, seeking insight on where and why this this inner pull toward fairness, justice and change-making started.

"Yes," my father said, exhuming a well-worn, wrinkled folder marked *Kathryn Files* from the depths of a cabinet in his office. From elementary school journals to ESPN journalism, my father saved the entire paper trail of my existence. *Every* scholastic report card. Every grade, every teacher note, every quarter of the school year.

"I think it started here," he said, handing me an old document from the folder. "You might find this interesting."

"Dad, why would you save—"

"It's what I do. I'm a professional filer."

The report card he handed me was two pages long, written on a typewriter, complete with two misspellings meticulously whited-out and typed over. The date read March 1983. My second-grade teacher, the soft-spoken and lovely Mrs. Abbott, clearly put some serious time and effort into the report card of a seven-year-old. How could there possibly be anything interesting to say about a child this age, when we barely remember our own self at that age?

This is what I knew of myself at age seven: I love playgrounds. Being outside is awesome. My best friend is Emi, the new girl from Japan. I love ice skating on Monday afternoons from 3-5pm. Is it Monday yet?! I also love *Good News*, Mrs. Abbott's class newspaper. I want to write for a real paper someday. I also like making stories in my head. I like writing down words that rhyme. Sometimes two words sound the same but they're spelled differently and mean different things. That's a homonym! Did you know that? That's magic. I want to learn every word on the planet. *The Secret Garden* is my favorite book because it has a lot of pages and I can read them all by myself. Boys and girls look different but we're the same. We all like recess and snacks. Dinosaurs are so cool. Everyone loves the T-Rex and the Stegosaurus, but the Brontosaurus is my favorite because no one else thinks they're interesting because they just hang out and eat leaves and they're not fast. Every dinosaur needs love. Also, if you want to ride a dinosaur, the Brontosaurus is probably the only one who would let you put a saddle on and not eat you, so duh, Brontosaurus are the best. I hate skirts and dresses. I can't climb trees very well in those. I wanted to be in Brownies like the other girls in my class. But when I joined, some of the girls laughed at me because I wore the Brownie pants instead of the Brownie skirt. I'm not going to be a Brownie anymore. It feels bad when people are mean because I wear pants. Clothes are dumb. Unicorns are real. They're just hiding.

My teacher, Mrs. Abbott, must've seen something else unfolding beneath the depths of my mullet. Something I wouldn't see or understand for many years. From the Brownie incident to the *Good News* journalism to the lobbying for Brontosaurus (long before these beautiful creatures became a metaphor for antiquity), Mrs. Abbott uncovered a personal truth: I was hardwired to an internal control panel of judgment, justice and equality.

> Name of Child: Katie Bertine[110]
> Date: March 1983
> Class: 2nd grade
> Teacher: Mrs. Linda Abbott
>
> This report reflects the overall development of your child.
> Katie is a remarkably even-tempered child who is reliable, sensitive and understanding. Her constancy is a large asset: children feel comfortable and secure in her presence and she has a calming, settling effect on all those around her. She finds great satisfaction in patiently assisting others.
> ...Although she is only seven, Katie has already developed a sophisticated sense of justice. When situations with classmates arise which she considers to be unfair, Katie articulates the problem and often serves as an arbitrator and mediator. She appreciates the value of compromise."

Whoa. All my other report cards used generic terms like *plays well with others*, but the astounding Mrs. Abbott saw a seven-year-old as an Arbitrator of Justice, a Mediator of Fairness, Appreciator of Compromise. I didn't know any of those big words at seven, but I did know unfairness was wrong, compromise was right and everyone should be able to wear pants if they want. I couldn't see the parallels of unicorns and justice, but even as a child I knew this: Equality is real. It's just hiding.

Neither Mrs. Abbott nor I knew these traits would manifest thirty years later. But perhaps I knew back then that inequity unlocked something within me. Perhaps I knew about the sensitivity back then, too. When my fellow Brownie troopers laughed at me for wearing the pants, it didn't just anger me that skirts and pants weren't considered equal. It crushed my soul to be judged. I burst into tears that day, in the middle of Mrs. Abbott's classroom. (She scolded the girls who teased me and they actually wrote a heartfelt note of apology.) In time, I learned to channel sadness into fuel for the fire. But it also took me seven *more* years to wear a skirt after

---

[110] No, you may not call me Katie. There were six Katies in my class of 35 girls, kindergarten through 12th grade. A dizzying experience. Switched to my given name, Kathryn, shortly after graduation.

Browniegate. My sensitivity and stubbornness weren't polar opposites. They were twins.

My father's file folder brought me a lot of joy. Understanding, too. Rather than question why I was so drawn to activism and where it all came from, now I could just go ahead and accept my hardwiring: I was a Unicorn seeker, Brontosaurus saddler, Good News writer, Sensitive Stubbornist, Arbitrator of Justice and Creator of Change. End of story. Sort of.

Three weeks later, I drove to the infamously grueling UCI Tour of the Gila stage race in Silver City, New Mexico. My elbow crater closed up just enough to keep going. After adjusting my aerodynamic position so I didn't have to lean on the wounded elbow, I threw down my fastest time trial, finishing 11th overall and first among my teammates. A year to the date my husband left, Jono signed me to BMW-HappyTooth Dental Pro Cycling for the rest of the season.

Even a year out from my husband's departure, I could still feel the living room carpet against my cheek where I collapsed in a pile of destruction. The scent of the backyard in bloom. The touch of Grizzy's paw on my face—each tiny, rounded, padded toe. Biology gifted me with XXXL Feelings and no receipt for return. It would take some time to understand this was a beautiful gift in the perfect size, but that realization was years away. In May 2015, memory was a stone-cold bitch. The divorce hearing was still two months away and the anniversary of his departure was a tough one. Took everything I had to focus on the positives. The new team. El Grupo. RVA Hosts. Homestretch proposal. Distraction was working. I even started experimenting with something I never thought I'd be ready for: Dating.

45

"MAJOR" CHANGES

The loneliness was in full swing, but my skills in steering clear of WannaTalkers, vultures and bears grew stronger. *Maybe I should try putting myself out there?* Occasionally, a fellow cyclist would ask if perhaps I might like to go for a ride sometime. I almost always declined. Asking a female pro cyclist out for a ride was like asking most working women if they wanted to hang out at OfficeMax. I had no interest in mixing love and work. After my marriage to a fellow cyclist didn't survive, I usually ran the other way when asked out for a bike ride.

One day, I ran into an old friend in downtown Tucson. Clegg was a major in the United States Air Force, not to mention strong, smart, athletic and handsome.[111] Also, he was divorced. Something about this mutual experience comforted me, as though members of the D Club shared an unspoken bond of Difficult Pasts. Different pasts, yes. But at least we knew to tread carefully approaching such topics.

Clegg and I began spending more and more time with each other. (Mostly at his house, as I still lived with my father). We went on trips together. Sometimes we rode bikes. Mostly we made dinner, watched movies and spent weekends together doing things normal couples do. I posted none of our relationship on social media and neither did he. The privacy felt wonderful. Safe. When he tenderly helped dress my elbow wound each night, I might have even felt love.

By June, the elbow scar morphed into a purplish keloid of spongy weirdness. In a fascinating feat of biology, the internal stitches buried closest to the bone began

---

[111] Clegg's real name is Major Kevin Clegg, USAF. Since Kevin is also the name of my filmmaking partner for *Half the Road*, I'm using "Clegg" to keep authenticity but avoid confusion. (I almost used "The Major" but he'd surely cringe.) There were Kevins in the Tucson peloton, Kevins who donated to *Half the Road*, Kevins at ESPN. Here's to all the great Kevins who've been part of my journey. I love them all in different ways.

to rise up and work their way out of my skin. I often ran my hand gently over the closed wound and came away with a piece of black medical thread. That crazy crater was so deep I wondered if an arrowhead might surface. Maybe a doubloon. All I knew was that I loved this bizarre scar. Felt like a tangible reminder of what I needed to remember most: We all fall down. There will be pain. If we can rise, we can heal. Wounds will close. Buried things will surface. Pull them out. Inspect closely. Set them down. Keep going. Scars are beautiful. Visible dents and divots are not bodily imperfections but brilliant stars that will shine on as constellations of our past.

On a sweltering Tucson morning in July, I made my way to the county courthouse. In front of a judge, my lawyer and I sat on one side of the courtroom. On the other, my husband's lawyer and an audio speaker. Refusing to show up, he called in. Monosyllabic responses of *yes* and *no* came through the speaker and I came undone by the sound of his voice. Tone, timbre and the vocal inflection of those we love are a direct umbilical cord to our heart. To our past. I wasn't prepared for that lesson. Somewhere between the fog of sadness, tears and disconnect, the judge decreed I had no stake in the house and car. Then gave my husband half my savings. I kept thinking there was nothing left to lose and I kept being wrong.

Half the road, half the heart, half the bank. For the first time in my life, I wanted to kick equality square in the nuts. Strange are the loopholes of marital "equity" and stranger still the depths of divorce. Leaving the courthouse, my father drove me to Chase Bank. Better him at the wheel with all my brain cells lost. At the counter, Linda, a sweet, gray-haired woman in her late fifties assisted me in writing the cashier's check to my husband. By the comma, I completely lost it. The pen shook. The sobs set in. Down came the rain. All over the check. Linda quietly printed another one. Before I picked up the pen to try again, she grabbed my hand and looked me in the eye.

"I'll be 60 next week," Linda said, her voice welling up and eyes brimming in solidarity, holding my hand in both of hers. "I've seen it all. I know what kind of check you're writing."

Linda then told me of her divorce, her abusive husband. That she got out, got her kids to a safe place and started over. That it took a long time, but she was happy now. She was alright and someday I would be, too.

"You're going to be okay," she said, fully understanding that I was not. She intoned my silence and said it again, twice. *You're going to be okay.* I gripped her hands and thanked Linda from the bottom of my fractured, flummoxed, not-yet-okay heart and left the bank poorer in money, richer in sisterhood, a millionaire in life lessons and deposited *Chase Bank* to my list of Places I've Lost My Shit in Public.

———————

The tears dried in time for *Bicycling Magazine* to show up for a photo shoot the next day. Their September 2015 issue would feature change-makers in cycling and they kindly wanted to include my seemingly-strong-woman persona not knowing I was a raging mess within. *Bicycling* emailed the photographer's contact details. *Chris Mooney, Chris Mooney.... How do I know this name?*

"Have we met, Chris?" I asked, when he showed up at my dad's apartment.

"Sort of," Chris answered. Treading carefully, Chris explained he was the photographer who covered my wedding for *The New York Times*. We didn't technically meet because his role was to be as inauspicious as possible. Show up, take pictures, leave quietly. An awkward pause ensued. Chris had seen the Just for One Day video clip and knew the marriage was over. I had two choices in that moment; crumble or deflect. My instincts chose the latter, especially since I just caked on makeup for the shoot.

"Well, Chris, thank you. The photos were truly beautiful," I said, while the Cerberus wandered out of its stable and barked, Burn-the-negatives-delete-the-files-and-stomp-on-the-hard-drive-until-the-plastic-shatters-and-melts-like-the-cesspool-of-my-splintered-confidence-and-broken-soul. Ok, sit, Cerbie. Sometimes I loved my demons as much as I loathed them.

I donned the equality kit jersey for the photo shoot and channeled my *Zero Fucks Given* gaze into the camera held not by my former wedding photographer, but a talented photojournalist on an assignment of change, activism and justice. For that, I could stand strong.

Looking strong and being strong were two different concepts. Although taking baby steps forward, I was still in a mode of self-preservation. Confidence was better, but far from high. To the public I was rabble-rouser of justice. But I still saw myself as a fragile, crock-pot of hot mess. So when a young cyclist named Phoebe Wang reached out to ask what life advice I had for her as a 22-year-old woman, I asked her if she really wanted advice from a 40-year-old divorced woman on welfare insurance who lived with her dad. Apparently she did. I made Phoebe a deal. I would give her my insights on things I wish I knew at 22, but only if she would write a letter doling advice to her future 40-year-old self. Phoebe agreed. I went first.

Dear Phoebe,
At 22, I thought I knew the Order of Things. That life would be college-job-marriage-kids-security-normalcy. I didn't know shit, Phoebe. But sometimes that's a good thing. The decade between 22 and 32 is so formative; you will evolve so much and your teachers will be the most unexpected people and situations. Every time something weird, terrible or wonderful happens, make it your job to ask yourself, *"What did I learn from that?"* If you can do that, there will never be a wrong path or a wasted minute in the entire course of your life. Also, trust your gut. We get lost sometimes because we try to ask our gut *Why?* But guts don't do dialogue. They just know *Yes* and *No*. So listen to the gut and let the brain uncover the *Why* on its own timeline. Trust the gut. The heart lives in the gut.
Also this: Be happy, Phoebe. Happiness should be a given, but our society likes to smack down The Happy. Screw that. Prioritize happy (it may come with struggle, but happy and struggle can strangely coexist). I have seen too many 22-year-olds do what they're "supposed to do" and then when they get to their 30s and 40s they look around and wonder what and where the hell they are. They didn't listen to their gut. And finally, this: Be nice to people. Surround yourself with others who share your moral fibers. Ten, twenty years from now some of the people you know will be doing some pretty interesting, incredible things. Celebrate their awesomeness. Especially the women... Be extra kind and supportive of women, publicly too, whenever possible.
I'm honored you asked, Phoebe. You're a great young woman. Ok, your turn. I'd love to know, looking down the road... What advice do you have for your 40-year-old self? -Kathryn

Phoebe responded not via email, but by sending a photo of her handwritten journal entry. With artistic penmanship and green ink, the 22-year-old shared her insights and guidance for her future self. Which I immediately typed out and saved in a file, just like dad.

Dear Future Phoebe,
Quit being ashamed of your past and ruminating over regrets. Give yourself some grace. Remember the scariness of 22. Don't forget the people who did little things for you. Listen to them. Learn from them so they can learn from you. If they don't listen, don't be offended, because you didn't listen either and that's how you learned. If you're rich, tip well. If you're poor, tip well. Remember that tips don't equal money. Quit looking back. Look forward. Open your eyes. Remember how it feels to discover. You haven't seen it all. Growing doesn't always equal taking root. Question things. Hold your "truths" under light. Yesterday's "truths" may not be true today. I hope you're doing okay and happy, 40-year-old self. If you're not, this doesn't need to be the

rest of your life. You better not be boring as fuck. If so, live recklessly. Dye your hair purple. Sit on your fire escape. Buy velvet drop-crotch pants. Look up.
Love,
Your 22-year-old self.

I read Phoebe's words often, smiling every time. She had no idea the strength it gave me to feel that in some small way perhaps I mattered. At least to her. Someday, if the Homestretch Foundation got off the ground, there would be lots of young women in their early twenties struggling with pay gaps and life questions. Maybe I could build a roost for a flock of Phoebes. They'd bring the purple hair and velvet chamois. I'd provide the fire escapes.

––––––––––

As the second edition of La Course by Tour de France loomed near, my UCI team BMW/HappyTooth was not ranked in the top 17. No invitation was received and that was okay. We were a second-tier pro team with a limited budget and a roster of rookie pros. I stood on the start line of my dreams last year. The fact that other women could stand on the line this year gave me plenty of joy. Less joyous of course; ASO failed their promise to Le Tour Entier. Prudhomme and Le Moenner did not add two to three days, incrementally. Rather than fire off another petition, Le Tour Entier released a statement. We were willing to work with ASO to continue to grow La Course, but it was ASO's move to make things happen. We drove the progress bus, parked it at the proper spot and handed the keys to ASO. We would keep the pressure on, but we would not do ASO's work for free.

Time had flown by, and it was hard to believe a year had passed since the race and two years since the petition took root. Marianne Vos would be back at La Course in 2015. Emma Pooley retired from pro cycling and was putting her two PhDs to use in geotechnical engineering and civil law. Chrissie Wellington gave birth to a daughter, Esme, and started work with Park Run UK inspiring sedentary people to get up and get moving. We were all busy doing what time requires: moving forward.

Activism is a tricky thing when it comes to finish lines. When to hang on, when to let go... and answering the question that tangos back and forth over the borders of business and personal: *Did I do enough?* Yes, we officially got the Tour de France to allow women to race. No, the women's race is not yet equal. *Must I keep fighting? What if I don't, and the Cerberus gets out and the Empties get in?* Tuning into my gut I listened to what the probiotics of progress had to say. They agreed sometimes letting go is the best way to let something grow. Or, at least get hired to tend the garden.

I reached out to ASO. Since 2015 would likely be my last year racing professionally, this was the perfect opportunity to start seeking full-time employment. It was the right time for ASO to hire me to seek investors to grow La Course by Tour de France into a full stage race. Armed once again with stats and data, I met Thibaud Coudriou in Los Angeles where ASO set up a US office to run the AMGEN Tour of California. Now we had more data and the stats were on our side.

The seven-day Tour of Utah had just reported a $20M economic impact for their 2015 men's race. The U.S. Pro Challenge of Colorado claimed $105M. Only a fraction of those days featured women. Imagine the return of investment if they included women? To get an investment plan off the ground for the Tour de France, I asked Thibaud what exact numbers ASO needed to make La Course at *least* a five-day event by 2016.

"Two to four million dollars," Thibaud said. Considering this is what most corporate investors pay for a 30 second SuperBowl advertisement, a five-day stage race was a drop in the bucket. Not to mention, far more exposure.

"Hire me to find these investors and I'll make it happen," I told Thibaud.

"We're not hiring for that position," he said. "But if you find investors for a women's race, please send me their contact information." Same as before. They wanted me to dump multi-million investors in their lap without a contract, where they could take the money and invest it in the men's Tour de France and/or their own pockets. Yeah, I don't think so.

It was now clear that something else was at play behind the scenes at ASO. If the data, stats, fans and media already proved it was financially lucrative for ASO to invest in women at the 2014 Tour de France, why weren't they growing it?

On ASO's scales of justice, one side held data. On the other sat apathy, sexism and laziness. Unfortunately, the latter was heavier. (Dinosaurs weigh a lot). I had done my part. It was time to let ASO go and watch its future unfold. Best case scenario, ASO would continue to add more days and UCI would step up to mandate equal inclusion of women at World Tour events. Worst case scenario, they both end up in a book that highlights their antiquated, sexist, dinosaur ways... instigating a new generation of activists. Either way, change is coming. No fight is over until the scales of justice are equally weighted.

Speaking of weight, my twelve-pound divorce deficit finally stabilized and my body dipped no lower in 2015. I was lean but healthy, starting to put some pounds back in place. I didn't see just how lean life whittled me until I traveled to the New York State Road Race in Albany with my friend, Myles, snacking on a sleeve of crackers in the car.

"Dude," he said, waving the long, empty, single-column watercress cracker box at me. "I bet you could fit your upper arm in this." Cyclists are not known for their upper body mass, but still. A cracker box? C'mon.

"That's ridic—" I said, confidently grabbing the box and sliding it over my forearm, where I was sure it would stop. It did not. The box proceeded past my non-injured elbow and encompassed my entire upper arm. "—ulous," I whispered, defeated and laughing. The laugher turned this silly moment from ridiculous to poignant. The past year rendered me so fragile there were few instances of laughing. This bout of silly giggling was much needed. Better still, this comic crackergate was symbolic.

There was a time in my past when body weight was a difficult subject. Twenty years before, during my early twenties, I struggled with an eating disorder. Those demons were successfully put in proper stables a long time ago and stayed quiet, even throughout the divorce. This time, weight was lost due to stress, not starvation. In the past, something as jovial and trivial as this cracker box charade would have wreaked havoc on my psychological state, but today it brought laughter, lightness and growth. Far too often, there is a negative belief thrown around the eating disorder community that people who suffer will *never truly* get over anorexia or bulimia. I refute this wholeheartedly. It *is indeed* possible to recover. I've done it. Lived it. It is my greatest hope that anyone struggling with the demons of food and body image will stop listening to the Never Trulys and start believing in the Yes Indeedies. I promise. Eating disorders are surmountable. There is a time and place when our proverbial biceps, cracker boxes and laughter can and will coexist in peace. Believe, believe.

To this day, Myles still calls me Crackers. Makes me smile every time.

At the Albany road race, I placed 7th. Later that day $40 appeared in my PayPal account, with a message from a stranger following the event.

"If you were a man who finished 7th you would've received $40 in prize money," he wrote. "But they didn't pay the women's field. So here you go." I took Myles to dinner, splurging on more than a sleeve of crackers.

The Empties and the Cerberus were doing well in their stables, mostly staying put as my inner balance grew stronger with my new team, El Grupo work and spending time on my proposal for Homestretch Foundation. But the latch on my mental stables jiggled with a sudden U-turn from Clegg.

After dating for four months, we were growing closer. Being careful to let the relationship grow at its own pace, we steered clear of labels, definitions and social media. My sense of trust and peace were tiptoeing forward in sync. I felt safe and confident in Clegg's presence. Then, one night, he left. Abruptly. Weirdly abruptly. We were lying there. Just being. Then, poof. Gone.

"I have to go, I can't be here right now," he said, bolting out the door. My stomach turned. Memories of my husband leaving in such an unpredictable manner rushed in, bowling me over. Hurting and hollowness came charging forth and I feared the latter more than the former. The *What Have I Dones?* battled it out with the *What Didn't You Dos?* while ambushed by the *Oh No Not Agains* and ultimately defeated by the *I Am Still Not Enoughs*.

We spoke the next day. Clegg acknowledged his odd behavior had nothing to do with me, but he wasn't sure what was going on with him. I suggested perhaps he was freaked out by our growing closer. We both knew the depths of divorce. Perhaps the vulnerability of closeness brought up memories from his past. I was expecting the conversation to be brief, but Clegg kept going. We talked about his childhood. We talked about his job. We talked and talked and talked until he decided he really needed to sort some stuff out. Indeed, there was definitely something within him searching for answers I could not provide. Despite my rattled confidence and sadness, I understood. *Let him go.* Strangely, another feeling arose. Something I couldn't articulate. *This man will circle back in my life. Somewhere, somehow, some way. Just wait. This isn't over yet.*

In September, a letter showed up from the accounting firm where my divorce proceedings were filed. I froze in terror. *No, no no. This is supposed to be over.* Picking at the cellophane window on the envelope, I was too terrified to open what appeared to be a bill. Or a lawsuit. Maybe both. For three days, I left the envelope on the counter. By the end of the week, the anxiety was so overwhelming I had to ask my dad to open it. He obliged, smiling as he placed the check on the counter. I had overpaid the divorce accountant by fifty dollars. They were refunding me. Moral of the story: Sometimes the greatest thing we can do in life is get out of our own fucking way.

———————

I packed for Richmond, Virginia, and headed to the 2015 UCI Road World Championships. Our RVA Hosts initiative resulted in free accommodations for 70 athletes from 17 nations, thanks to 200 volunteers who made it happen. I happened to be one of the homestay recipients and lucked out with being assigned to the Goldberg family on Monument Avenue, right on the race course. The Goldbergs not only housed me, but also had enough room for my father to stay, who was now able to watch me race Worlds for the first time. This would be my final Worlds, the eighth time representing St. Kitts and Nevis and my first time racing in the Team Time Trial with my professional team. After starting the season unsigned and unemployed, then six months of guest riding, elbow-gouging, sanity-wavering, therapy-helping, claw-my-way-backing and demon-saddling… here I was with BMW-HappyTooth Pro Cycling, flying my St. Kitts and Nevis stripes on my jersey, toeing the line in all three events at the age of 40. Funny how things work out when we just hold on, keep going and get out of our own way. I wanted to scream from the rooftops, *"Hey, all you people going through hard shit, hold on! Don't crack yet! Your 'worlds' is coming! Wheee!"*

On the day of the Individual Time Trial, I finished 34th. In the world. After eight years, this was my fastest and best result Worlds. Since taking the power meter off my bike and switching my training protocol from FTP (functional threshold power) to GZF (giving zero fucks), I had my best season in 2015. Not just physically but mentally. I still struggled with confidence and heartache, but rather than the bike being the coping mechanism, this year it felt more like a chariot to take me to better places. I was the second oldest athlete at Worlds, surpassed only by Kristin Armstrong, who finished fifth but would go on to claim Olympic gold eleven months after Worlds. While 34th is a far cry from the podium, I won the battle of ageism that day. Stronger, better, faster, older. That was enough. I was enough. *Finally.*[112]

———————

[112] Around this time, the impulse to write returned. Two years passed since I had any courage to put pen to paper. While I wasn't ready to write a book, I wanted to test the waters of truth and vulnerability. Taking off my power meter, then having my fastest year on the bike at age 40 was the inspiration to write an essay on turning technology off and looking inward. *Bicycling Magazine* published it a few months later. Interactive Reader Guide: My Year Without Power.

My season wasn't quite done. My final Caribbean Championships were in Barbados. I had a plan. I would retire from the sport directly afterward… with one caveat. If a UCI World Tour team offered me a contract with a livable wage above the poverty line, I'd stick around for 2016. That was one hell of a unicorn longshot, though. I'd be 41. While the age minimum was gone, stigmas were still in place.

Three wonderful things happened in the Caribbean. I repeated as the Time Trial champion for the third year in a row and I captured the silver medal in the road race. But the biggest victory came at the medal presentation. UCI President Brian Cookson hung the medals around my neck and did not strangle me.

Three years passed since I interviewed Cookson for *Half the Road*. Our last interaction over email was extreme displeasure for how he was portrayed. When I saw him at La Course, we did not engage. Now here we were, face to face in Barbados. Cookson had every opportunity to refuse interacting with me. But he didn't. After the medal ceremony, we sat down in the lobby of our small Caribbean hotel and talked.

I asked him how things were going with the UCI presidency. He asked me how racing was going. We talked about the growth of women's cycling. I thanked him for appointing a female vice president—Tracey Gaudry—to the UCI. Cookson was still just one year into his presidency. The jury was out on whether he (and she) would deliver progress for women's pro cycling, but there in Barbados we made peace with each other. Remaining open to discussion and possibility is the only way we will ever move this weird world forward.

We must remember something about the Cooksons of our quests. Difference is vital. Cookson not believing women are able to race the Tour de France motivated me just as much, if not more, than those who did. When we fight for what we believe, there will always be Brian Cooksons of Disbelief and Emma Pooleys of Hope. If we become disheartened by those who differ in opinion, we will succumb to the weight of disappointment. We must see the Cooksons as a life-preserver, buoying us with the exact necessity of *why* we need to stay afloat; to educate, enlighten and change minds. We may not have changed Cookson's mind about the Tour de France, but we did open his eyes to the importance of women's professional racing. He confided in me he hoped to start a women's professional team someday. I wished—and *still* wish—him all the best with this goal, and that he can count on me for support.

As I flew home from Caribbean Championships my inbox chimed forth a new email. BMW-HappyTooth Pro Cycling would fold at the end of 2015. But a new sponsor was stepping up and the new team would race at the World Tour level. The manager sent a contract and asked if I would be part of the squad. My salary started at $25,000. At 41, signed to race with Cylance Pro Cycling for 2016.

I decided immediately: 2016 would be my last season of professional racing. For real, this time. No exceptions. I wanted to go out on top – racing for a salary above the poverty line on a World Tour team at the age of 41. I announced my upcoming retirement at the *start* of the season, rather than the end. Proactively going into each race knowing it was my last go 'round on the pro circuit brought a tailwind of *nothing left to lose*. Yes, yes. 2016 would be perfect! We weren't in 2016 yet, though. Between divorce bills and life bills, money was tight that November. So when Bicycle Ranch informed me a second anonymous package arrived, I was curious, skeptical and a little bit weirded out. *If there's another $1,000, I will quite frankly shit.*

Anonymous B struck again, but this time it wasn't an envelope containing $1,000. It was five times that amount. Cash. Same circumstances applied. He wanted nothing in return, only to help someone who was standing up for something but struggling to get by. He also knew, from my social media posts, that someday I wanted to write a book about it all.

> "So basically what you are getting looks shady as f*ck. But I can assure you the money is legit and was not acquired through nefarious means. No mob guys are going to be coming to track you down and if they do it had nothing to do with me. Sometimes we need something to help us let out the breath we have been holding on for too long. I can't imagine the heartache you've been through over the last year or so. To lose your marriage, house, job and cats and then have to start over again is massive. I am glad you are making your way through, but I know those pains won't go away easy... I hope that by giving you this you don't feel any pressure. It was not meant to change in any way what you are already doing. Go write some shit. You mentioned you had outlines and journals ready to go. I know you have a definite story that you want to tell. I know you have a story that we are all waiting to hear. With that said, please write whatever feels like the story you need to tell. Keep doing what you're doing. -B"

I responded, thanking this unconventional stranger-supporter for such incredible generosity. Told him I had started writing a few chapters about activism and all it took to get La Course off the ground. What I didn't tell B was how dry, dull and uninspiring those chapters were. Or how I wasn't ready to write about the personal side of the journey. While my confidence on the bike soared, my private conviction and self-assurance was nowhere near ready to discuss all that went on behind the scenes. How could I tell people to go stand up for change…and oh, by the way, it might leave you divorced, depressed and suicidal? Couldn't imagine anyone would want to read that stuff. Or hear the musings of a strong, powerful changemaker… who still lived in her dad's den at 40, sad and lonely as hell? That didn't quite scream bestseller. No way was I ready to write those truths in 2015. *Maybe someday.* I thought, throwing the first few attempted drafts into the cybertrash, hearing it land with a rewarding, crumpled *Thwick*!

Valuing B's request for anonymity, I asked only once if he would tell me who he is. When he cited he preferred to remain anonymous—and that if I did figure who he was, not to tell him—I obliged. Occasionally, I wondered if B might be Clegg, but I was quite certain this method of communication was not his style. While we hadn't spoken in months, we sometimes texted or commented on one another's social media posts. My gut twanged the iron string that Clegg would circle into my life again, so I let it go. And with the new money from B, I started shopping for a car.

———————

With B's generous installments totaling $6,000 and my Car Fund Savings Account adding a few more, I could finally do it: purchase a better-than-decent used car for cash that no one could ever take away. I knew exactly what I wanted. Another Prius. There was something incredibly confidence-restoring about buying the same car that was taken away. To reclaim what was lost, but an even better, newer model. Made my soul feel strong. The hybrid engine was a huge factor for gas savings, too, but the biggest draw was livability. Whereas most women my age were in the market for family-sized SUVs, I wanted something that could double as a shelter. I knew I could sleep in a Prius diagonally with the backseats down should I face homelessness again in the future.

Researching online, I found an old Prius with 40K miles in Oklahoma City, and used the remainder of my Southwest Airlines miles to book a one-way trip so I could drive my golden chariot back to Tucson. This was not a hyperbole. The car color was actually golden-hued, and I loved that too. The old Prius was silver. There was something metaphorically rewarding about upgrading to gold.

On the fourteen hour drive back to Arizona, somewhere in rural New Mexico, I engaged in a business call. A reader who followed my quest since the ESPN Olympian days emailed through my website, asking if I might consult with him on a cycling business he was starting. He wanted to make sure his business would be marketed equally toward women and men. More than happy to oblige in gender equity consulting, I took the call. Neither of us had any idea it would be life-changing. A reminder, at least, there will always be people who don't understand our activism plans for equal opportunity… and others who see the vision clearly and want to join forces. *Always, always take the call.*

As 2015 wound down, I was named to the Rodale Top 100; people making a positive impact in society. The list including Geena Davis for gender equity in film, Matt Damon for his water.org project and Pope Francis for religion and climate change.[113] Truly honored to keep such company, I began receiving invitations to speak. Accepting the keynote speaker role at the Women's Salon Series in Tucson, I figured this might be a perfect opportunity to test the boundaries of vulnerability. I shared the story of how *Half the Road* and La Course came to be, tailoring the speech to include stats, data and some personal details. I wasn't ready to go full commando and drop my vulnerability trousers, showing all scars of suicidal idealization, but I definitely stepped outside my comfort zone. When I spoke of my husband leaving and the subsequent effect of wearing two masks, I looked directly into the audience. Heads nodded. Among some of the 200 women, there appeared to be mutual understanding. Afterward, three women approached. They'd come to the series for years.

"This is the most impactful lecture we've seen so far," one woman said. When I asked how this differed from the others, she replied, *Because you let us see what really happened.* I thanked them profusely. If scars, truth and honesty were the trilogy of impact, maybe there really could be a book someday. Perhaps deep inside, part of me knew the story wasn't over just yet.

---

[113] When Rodale was acquired by Crown Publishing in 2018, many sites like the Top 100 disappeared. But here's a partial one. Interactive Reader Guide: Rodale Top 100

46

LEARNING TO TRUST, LEARNING TO LOSE

Years ago, I learned a valuable life lesson. Open random emails, respond with kindness, engage with strangers. Had I not done those things, this journey would not exist. Sure, terrible things can happen when too trusting of strangers, but it helps to remember there is good in the world, too. I went with the latter belief when Tom Bailey of Seattle first reached out via email.

Tom worked in biotech but was passionate about cycling. Approaching 50, he wanted to switch gears and start a direct-to-consumer bicycle company. He followed my career since the ESPN days. Would I be interested in collaborating on gender equity marketing strategies? I did a quick background check. With multiple Harvard degrees and numerous CFO positions, I rendered Tom was likely not a serial killer or woman hater. (Then again, Ted Kaczinsky went to Harvard. So did Bill O'Reilly.) I met him for coffee in Tucson. Driven, smart and motivated, I agreed to do some consulting work for Tom. Data collection, market research and whiteboarding ideas were simple to do from home and flexible enough to fit in around my El Grupo job and training schedule. One day, as we brainstormed plans for his bike business endeavor, Tom asked,

"By the way, I've followed your activism career. What advocacy are you working on now?"

I told him all about the business plan for Homestretch Foundation. How there was still no base salary for the World Tour women and no training facility in place to assist female professional cyclists earning below the poverty line. How those things needed to change.

"We need a place where women can live and train properly, so they don't have to quit pro cycling because they can't afford to eat and pay rent," I summarized. "And we need to change the base salary rules."

"Great," Tom said. "Let's make it happen."

At first, I took his response as moral support. As in, *I stand behind you! Go get 'em, KB! Let's make it happen!* So, a few weeks later when Tom asked if I started looking at houses for the proposed Homestretch residence, I assumed he misunderstood. I explained house hunting was a long way off. I had not yet shopped the proposal. There was no investor yet for Homestretch.

"Start looking for houses," Tom said. "I'm in."

I remember time slowing down and my pulse speeding up. My hopeful side loves believing anything is possible. But my wounded side was far too scared to believe this guy was for real. Besides, what was in this for Tom? Why would *he* want to create a nonprofit to combat salary inequity?

"Because I have a daughter and a son," Tom said. "I can't live in a world where they're valued differently." His teenagers weren't cyclists, but the bigger picture of Homestretch was not lost on him. If we created a platform to assist women and lobby for salary equity, then other parts of society could follow our format and do the same.

Still in disbelief, I began scouring the Tucson housing market. My original business plan laid out the most ideal situation; a residence that could comfortably sleep eight to ten athletes; two per room. This wasn't some youth hostel or summer camp for teens. This was a residence for grown-up women who worked two jobs. One roommate was ok, but Homestretch was not to be reminiscent of squish-them-in-like-sardines host housing. Ideally, also a guesthouse for the manager. *Perhaps that could be my job after retiring from pro cycling.*

Reality, however, reared its logical head. A five-to-six-bedroom residence would be astronomically expensive. Especially to someone who thought earning $25,000 a year rendered her among the wealthy elite. In 2016, the going rate for such a residence in Tucson would be in the $500,000 ballpark, minimum. Ooof. After almost two years of living in my dad's den, I told Tom a small, two-bedroom home would be enough to get Homestretch started. Even if we could help just one athlete, that would be enough. I let Tom know the details, to which he laughed heartily into the phone.

"Since it costs about a million dollars to own a tiny apartment in Seattle, $500K for a large house sounds like a terrific bargain," he said. "Look at the properties you envisioned in your plan."

"Seriously?" I breathed.

"Yes," he instructed. "Always go after what you want." In the meantime, Tom began drawing up the forms and contracts that go along with the tedious behind-the-scenes work of creating a nonprofit. When I saw the actual paperwork and his commitment to not half-assing around, I started to believe the Homestretch Foundation could really, truly happen. Sooner than later.

––––––––––

Tom wasn't the only unexpected email in my inbox. The next one came from *Bicycling Magazine* asking for an interview. They wanted to know the real story about making *Half the Road*, petitioning ASO and creating/racing La Course by Tour de France. I hesitated before responding. If I were going to publicly talk about life as an activist and all that really happened over the last two years, then I'd have to go deep into the caves and stables. Masks were not an option. No more half-truths. Standing up for what we believe is not a journey of kittens and rainbows. We needed to talk about the trolls and the demons. The support and abandonment. Not just the ups and downs, but all the multidimensional zigzags, cliffs and trampolines that don't make sense, but there they are. Divorce. Devastation. Exit plans. Robin Williams. Getting help. I would have to talk about it all… because if I didn't, the authenticity of activism would be compromised. But was I ready? That would mean saddling the biggest beast in the stable. Not the Cerberus of self-worth, but the Vulnerability of truth.

I thought about it for quite some time, then answered Leah Flickinger of *Bicycling Magazine*. "Ok, I'm ready," I said. She sent freelance journalist Steve Friedman to Tucson in January 2016. In truth, trust and fear I put it all out there. Rode every beast in the stable. The interview took three days. Publishing date was slated for September. I doubted any major life event would happen between now and then.

––––––––––

Our Cylance Pro Cycling team camp took place in Irvine, California in January. Some of the best national champions, Olympians and experienced veterans of the sport were on the squad—Valentina Scandolara (ITA), Shelly Olds (USA), Rossella Ratto (ITA), Carmen Small (USA), Doris Schweizer (SUI), Alison Tetrick (USA), Sheyla Gutierrez Ruiz (ESP), Krista Doebel-Hickok (USA), Rachele Barbieri

(ITA), Erica Zaveta (USA)—and I (SKN) pinched myself to be among them. What a year this would be.

In 2012, I raced to prove a 36-year-old could in fact land a pro contract. In 2013, I raced to prove that it wasn't a fluke. In 2014, I raced for a Tour de France for women. In 2015, I raced to keep myself from coming unglued. In 2016, I would race for the pure joy of the entire journey. That was enough. I was finally ready to embrace everything that lead me here.

Everything was wonderful at team camp. Except for the peanut butter incident and race schedule vagueness. One morning, I noticed our team breakfast spread did not look the same as it did the first day. All the nut butters were missing. Strange. These healthy fats are an essential ingredient for most endurance athletes. A dollop of peanut or almond butter at breakfast was the norm. Also strange; we had two large jars the day before. No way they were finished. I asked our soigneur where the peanut butter was hiding. She took me aside and explained it had literally been hidden. By our team director, Manel Lacambra. He believed nut butters would make athletes fat.

"You're joking!" I laughed. She wasn't. She opened the cabinet just a crack, and there they were. Two jars of nut butters obscured behind ketchup and mustard and just about every other condiment commandeered into Operation Cover Your Nuts. I snorted a quick laugh and shook my head, questioning which was more stupid, the ignorance of Manel thinking peanut butter made athletes fat, or the idiocy of hiding portly peanut butter jars behind the slender salt shakers. *Stealth move, Houdini. We can see it, you know.*

The ridiculously ignorant act of hiding food wasn't just silly and passive-aggressive, but also a method of control. My gut took note of it before my brain did, and a red flag went up. Monitoring the caloric intake of adult female pro athletes isn't normal. If Manel hid peanut butter, what else was he hiding? Such answers would unfold in time, but for now, I waited until Manel left the breakfast area. Then I put the nut butters back on the table.

When the time came for our first massage with the team soigneurs, the memories of water buffalo horns and bleeding backs burbled to the forefront of my thoughts. I quickly pushed them away. That couldn't possibly happen again. It didn't. But another message was communicated. It's no secret in the sport that team staff talk about team riders. One of the soigneurs acted a bit cold during the massage. She was aware I was a writer and when I tried making pleasantries with her, she let it be known that she "never trusts journalists." The comment stuck with me for a long time. Wouldn't it be much easier to live an honest life rather than worry about what journalists might uncover? I left the massage without physical or mental bruising, but what lingered was a sense that perhaps Manel spoke of me in a less than positive way. Apparently I had a reputation for telling the truth. Despite the progress we were making in women's pro cycling, not everyone was comfortable with that.

When it came time to discuss individual race schedules, my gut somersaulted when Manel said he would "call to let me know my schedule." Other athletes already knew their upcoming races. Flashbacks to Wynona raced into my head and heart. *We're not going to race you, Kathryn.* No no no. That wasn't going to happen again. That experience was a fluke. Wasn't it? *Of course* I was going to race. Cylance Pro Cycling is a World Tour team! All UCI teams must race their athletes a minimum of once a month, unless sick or injured. The problem was, I *still* didn't know that rule. Not yet, anyway.

When Manel asked for my passport info leading into Tour of Qatar, I felt better. When he said I was the "reserve athlete" I cringed. When he didn't race me in January, February or March my heart sank. I knew something was very wrong when Manel would not return my emails requests to talk. Reaching out to our team manager, Omer Kem, I explained the situation. Omer suggested I go do a bunch of races somewhere and "prove myself." *Hold up, mister. I already proved myself... That's why you signed me to the team, Omer!* He believed it was Manel's decision whom to race, just as Profaci gave his power to Wynona. So when a Mexican elite team called to ask if I would guest-ride at the UCI Vuelta Feminil in La Paz, Mexico in April, all expenses paid, I agreed. If that's what Cylance wanted, fine. Besides, I loved racing. Staying sharp, focused and race-ready was a necessity. The next month would be anything but sharp, focused or ready for what came next.

On Tuesday, March 6, 2016, I went to an evening yoga class, as I did every Tuesday. Yoga is one of the best things a pro athlete can do for their physical and mental well-being. When dating, Clegg and I often went to the Tuesday class together. After we broke up, I steered clear for a while. Then I went back for two reasons. First, the instructor was terrific. Second, maybe I would run into Clegg. Months had passed since his abrupt exit, but I still couldn't shake the feeling he'd come back into my life. Someday, somehow. Regardless, I moved forward. Dating, even. All was well. Returning to Tuesday night yoga for many weeks, Clegg never showed and the hope he might eventually subsided. Tuesdays were no longer our yoga night, but *my* yoga night. Except that particular Tuesday in early March.

That night at yoga, during the final pose of savasana as the lights went down, the instrumental music swirled and we rested on our backs on our mats, something happened. I was overwhelmed with thoughts of Clegg. Not memories. Not reminiscence. Not sadness or foreboding. Just fervent, powerful thoughts. Very, very intense ones. Which is odd because rarely does *overwhelming* and *savasana* coexist. Thoughts of Clegg barreled through the stillness with such force, my eyes flicked open. *Huh. Weird. Need to reach out to him*, I thought, closing my eyes again.

The text message came the next morning from my former coach and close friend, Gord Fraser. *Did you hear about Clegg?* Gord knew Clegg and I dated. In the split second it took to dial Gord, my subconscious already calculated the probability of possibilities: Car versus bike? Sporting mishap? Possibly. Shit, shit, shit. Military accident? Unlikely. He worked in an office on base. Car accident? Maybe. No one is immune. Steering clear of Worst-Case Scenarios, I set my sights on the hope he was possibly hospitalized but okay. Gord answered immediately.

"Clegg is dead," Gord began. Nothing prepared me for the next sentence. "He was found this morning. Suicide."

Tears, disbelief. The time warp of unforeseen loss sucked away my breath, logic and coherence. Scenes of our togetherness began their scroll on memory's reel of non-sequiturs. *Watching Game of Thrones. Barbequing portobellas. Industrial size gallon of honey in the pantry. Lots and lots of tea. Peach pie. Primo, his favorite exclamation. Slacklining in the park. Sheldon the turtle and the chickens in the backyard. So many omelets. Salads with grapes. Descending Mt. Lemmon on road bikes. Shredding Redington Pass and Fantasy Island on mountain bikes. The plastic unicorn ring for my birthday. Watching documentaries. Guitar lessons with teenage Leroy across the street. Two lost souls swimming in a fishbowl... wish you were here.*

Is that what happened last night at yoga, I wondered. Did the powerful tide of Clegg swim in for a fleeting, palpable moment as if to say goodbye? Can souls do that? Say goodbye? I don't know. I loved not having the answer. Wonder is enough.

I called our close friends. A small group of us met to grieve, question, wonder and simply be together, sorting through the If Onlys and What Ifs that rain down so inextricably hard on those left behind by suicide. Dan Taylor held the get-together. I arrived like the others, an undone mess of puffiness, tears and free-flowing snot.

Dan had a house guest staying with him when the tragedy unfurled. Three weeks later, Joseph Lauricella asked for my number. Any man who is attracted to a woman when she looks her worst is definitely worth one date.

We went on three. Still too shaken and raw by Clegg's passing, I wasn't ready to go much faster or further. But I did find comfort in Joseph's openness and willingness to talk and listen about Clegg. About suicide. About reality. I didn't open up about my near miss with death and exit strategies. That wasn't third date material. Besides, I was about to leave for Mexico to race UCI Vuelta Feminil as a guest rider for Speedbikes La Paz. *Focus, focus*. Casual dinner dates were my emotional limit.

Before heading to La Paz, I was booked for a lecture and screening of *Half the Road* in Boulder. I went, retracing some of the steps Clegg and I took just months ago during our vacation together. Lunch at the Dushanbe Tea House, a walk down Pearl Street, a hike in Nederland hoping the catharsis would clear my brain for the speaking event a few hours later. I was a bit worried I might fall off the vulnerability tightrope during the audience Q & A. *So, Kathryn, what are you working on now? Oh, you know, trying to keep my shit together as my former boyfriend just died, my team isn't racing me and I'm horribly lonely*. Luckily, most of the questions stayed on cycling, equality and UCI issues. I was in the clear, until a woman asked directly about vulnerability.

"How do you deal with putting yourself & your goals out there?" she inquired. "Would you be willing to share an example of your own vulnerability?" Oof. She actually used the V word. Now I had to share something. Tossing out clichés like, "Well, golly, you just have to be strong and fight for what you believe!" wasn't gonna help anyone decipher the truth of activism, either.

Very rarely are we taught this truth: Vulnerability *is* strength. Not weakness. The strongest thing we can do is share bits of our flailing humanness with others. When we open up, so too do others. Rarely are we taught that No One Truly Has 100% Of Their Shit Together So Let's All Hang Out And Flap Around. (I envision tiny humans skittering around a dilapidated chicken coop and a giant Kurt Vonnegut comes out, feeding us nuggets of humor-truth.)

That night at the film screening, I let people into a few of my flailing moments. I wasn't ready to talk about Clegg, but I spoke about the divorce, the mask-wearing and how it knocked me to the ground during the release of *Half the Road* and racing La Course. As with my previous lecture, I looked directly into my audience and made eye contact with people as I spoke. That was scary. *Flap, flap!* But people looked directly back. Some nodded in solidarity. Others smiled. A few even cried, perhaps moved by personal understanding, honesty or boredom. Hard to say. But together we flailed. And at the very least, one of us moved forward.

Strength. Connection. Paprika. Not always the easiest ingredients to work with, but maybe it's all we need to get by in this world till our giant Kurt Vonnegut calls us back to the coop. Till then, we're all here to putter around, ask one another questions, seek our own truths and flap on, little chickens. Flap on.

47

THE CRASH

La Paz, Mexico sits two hours north of Cabo San Lucas in the middle of the Baja Peninsula. I arrived in this charming, colonial city for La Vuelta Feminil, a UCI two-day stage race that carried the prestige of Olympic qualifying points—which pro cyclists were hungry to find leading up to the 2016 Rio Games. While my Olympic chances of qualifying were slim, a win in Mexico would rank me in the top 100, which would bring SKN a berth to the Games. The upside: a chance existed! The downside, both stages were built for sprinters. Which I wasn't. While the courses didn't suit my less-than-impressive sprint abilities, the chance for a time-trial breakaway did. So that was the plan. I would try to breakaway. Trying is my favorite.

When I stood on the start line that morning, there were no thoughts of "proving myself" or racing to demonstrate my worth to Cylance Pro Cycling's management. I flipped my thinking: *From now on, let them prove they're worthy of me.* Ooooh! How badass it felt to think this way! As luck would have it, this would be one of my last thoughts for a very long, long time.

April 3, 2016. I remember the beautiful, warm weather. The spray from the Sea of Cortez as the wind lightly carried it from the Gulf of California into our peloton racing alongside the roads of its shore. The many fans who gathered along the boardwalks and medians, cheering. I remember the eight laps of eight miles comprising the 64-mile circuit race, and the short but treacherous stretch of unsafe grates and gangly rebar. I remember nò one crashed there, and I sighed in relief when we passed it for the last time. I remember heading into the final mile of the race. Then a curtain dropped in the theater of time. I remember nothing more.

Three days after the crash I opened my eyes. I did not know it was three days later, nor that there was a crash. Four men stood at the foot of my bed, wearing white jackets. *Hospital,* my brain whispered. My eyes took inventory from the left. Doctor…doctor…doctor…bike mechanic from our team…

Trying to remember the mechanic's name,[114] something squeezed my hand. Swiveling my gaze to the left, there was someone sitting next to me whose name I thought was Joseph, but now nothing made sense. Joseph was the man I went to dinner with in Tucson. But he did not come with me to Mexico. *Where am I? What is this?* Memory latched onto my previous hospital knowledge; the elbow crater in Redlands, the dog collision in Tucson. Glancing at my limbs, there were no bandages or casts. As my head tried to piece together where I was, I passed out.

I remember very little about the first five days at Juan Maria de Salvatierra Hospital before being airlifted to University Medical Center in Tucson. Less than ten short, fleeting slivers of recollection remain in my memory. The observant doctors at the foot of my bed. A small plate of green Jell-O cubes stacked into a tiny pyramid jiggling on the tray next to my bed, dancing to the beat of nurses' footsteps. The shock of cold metal on my thighs and buttocks where they placed the bedpan. Joseph, beside me. And beside him, a window. I remember the sunlight on the wall. Below the window, Joseph's sleeping bag. A fleece blanket of brightly colored geometric shapes covered my bed and felt so very, very soft. I remember someone giving me a cell phone, and my father's voice on the other end. The conversation escapes me but I could hear tears in his words. I vaguely remember being wheeled into a small airplane.

Here is what I don't remember. Falling on my head in a bicycle race, breaking my skull twice and nearly dying in the middle of the road. But my teammates, the race director, the team mechanic and the doctor on duty at the race; they remembered. Eventually telling me exactly what happened that morning, less than a mile and a quarter from the finish line. To write of ourselves as a character we don't remember is indeed a bizarre vortex of nonfiction. Here's what I was told.

As the peloton wound through the lovely streets of La Paz, along the eastern coast of the Sea of Cortez, through the streets of the commercial district, up the beautiful costal hills, and down to the promenade of the main boulevard, with the sea on the right, *hoteles, bodegas y restaurantes* on the left, and crowds of spectators interspersed on both sides, there was nothing dangerous or treacherous in the road. Human error was at fault.

---

[114] Lenin Verdugo. Thank you for all you did to help me, Leni.

The narrow, two-lane road was separated by a median typical of many Latin American and European countries; a raised platform with a paved sidewalk in the middle, roughly six feet wide. These medians stopped and started every hundred meters or so, with a ramp for bicycles, pedestrians, etc to use easily. During our race, the medians were filled with cheering spectators and recreational cyclists.

In the tactics of professional racing, it is not uncommon to see a cyclist deviate from the peloton and seek a median or a sidewalk to hop upon and escape. Most members of the peloton find this maneuver a bit of a showboat move. Not to mention, dangerous. If a cyclist leaves the road for a short jaunt, they'll eventually have to rejoin the group. To cut back into the peloton from a risky angle is treacherous to all involved.

As we barreled down toward the finish line at full speed the median reappeared just as it had on the previous seven laps, sitting idly in the middle of the road, as medians do. Still on the outskirts of town only a handful of spectators dotted the sidewalk of this particular median. The rider directly in front of me decided this median was her chance for a possible escape. She cut left, veering toward the ramp. Then she changed her mind.

Angling sharply, the rider swerved back into the peloton, attempting to reclaim space that was no longer there. Her impulsive move took six riders down with her. I was the lucky recipient of being on the bottom of the pile. Launched from my bicycle, I flew over my handlebars and landed on the right side of my skull, becoming the human landing pad for others.

My fellow competitors who tangled up in the crash slowly rose to their feet. Collecting their undamaged bicycles and bruised bodies, they slowly pedaled toward the finish line with vibrant road-rash, dazed confusion and muttering profanities to which every professional cyclist is well-versed in the aftermath of a crash. The majority of bike crashes are grounds for minor physical pain and internal questioning of why we do this sport. Some crashes bring broken collarbones and painful-yet-healable injuries. On rare occasion, crashes bring career-ending injuries. Rarer still, a crash that brings skull fractures and possible death.

On the bottom of the pile, my body convulsed in spasms of seizure from the twice broken skull, bleeding brain, fractured clavicle, hip hematoma, facial lacerations and purpling eye; all on my right side. Within minutes, the official medical car following the race pulled up to the scene and Dr. Carlos Argueta assessed the situation, calling immediately for an ambulance. Kneeling next to me and checking my pulse, he started his watch. Seizures, time and oxygen to the brain are a delicate balance. Eight minutes ticked by. Then nine. Ten. The seizure was not subsiding.

"*Ella nos está dejando,*" Argueta said. "*...está muriendo.*" *She's leaving us... she's dying.* The ambulance was too far away. Argueta rose, ran back to the medic car, grabbed a syringe of Ativan[115] and plunged the needle into a vein. The tremors slowed just enough so pulse, breath and oxygen fell back into rhythm and balance. The wail of the ambulance neared. Argueta calculated the drive time to the hospital. Less than twenty minutes, not too much traffic on a Sunday morning. There could be enough time.

As I lay in the middle of the road unaware to everything in the universe, our bike mechanic, Leni, gathered my bicycle, helmet and the plastic remains of shattered sunglasses. Sports medicine specialist Dr. Emilio Estrada and neurosurgeon Dr. Eduardo de la Vega awaited my arrival at Salvatierra Hospital.

Perhaps the crash remains embedded somewhere beneath the shell of my skull, a pearl of memory in a forgotten oyster. Apparently my brain does not care to dive for such treasures. But there is one strange thing that swims in the chasm between memory and mystery.

When I recall the day of the crash, I have two literal perspectives. Heading into the last mile of the race, my view is that of a cyclist: eyes forward, looking straight ahead, amidst my tribe of bike racers. But I have another image, too. Another perspective. An entirely different angle where I can see the curve in the road where the crash took place, and the peloton moving forward... this time, though, from above. There were no celestial beams nor wings and haloes nor Hollywood clichés. But there exists a perspective in my memory where I see the mountains to my left, the sea to my right, the finish line up ahead and the streets of La Paz unfolding from higher than my human height.

A hundred feet, half a mile above? Hard to say. Neither memories nor near-death experiences have a built-in altimeter. Higher than a birthday balloon released, yes. Lower than an airplane, yes. Maybe closer to a bird at the height of its flight. My view is wide, without a focus point beyond the geography of what I last

---

[115] Ativan, Lorazepam, benzodiazepine sedations & generic equivalents are used to diminish seizure severity usually related to epilepsy. Clearly helps seizures caused by external brain injuries, too. Interactive Reader Guide: How Ativan Works

remember below. There was no emotion or feeling accompanying this perception. No pain nor peace nor fear nor anything. Just view.

I don't know how this perspective got there. Was it created the day of the accident? Did it burble forth later, from the healing depths of pain management medications? Did I dream it? I don't know. What I love most about this memory is the beauty of wonder. Whatever the reason, whatever the whys, whos and hows… all I know for certain is that I was so fully immersed in the present during this perspective. Apparently it was not my time to go anywhere else. Just to be right there. Having that view.

I sometimes like to wonder if there was another energy out there, hanging out with me in that moment, hovering above the day. That's when I think of Clegg. If anyone could have caught the flyball of my fate cruising through the centerfield of sky, then hurled it back to earth with a quick hug and a whisper, "*Not today, Kathryn,*" it would've been Clegg. I missed him so much. Memory is the wormhole of nonfiction and I believe Clegg was there that day. Circling into my life just like I always believed he might. So be it, then. He was. He did. *Primo!*

Regardless of the unprovable stuff, there was a tangible element of Clegg's link to what was happening in Mexico. Joseph came into my life because of Clegg's vigil. Now he was in my hospital room figuring how to get me home. Chance, luck, fate, guidance? Doesn't matter. Human connection is a real and powerful thing.

On my fifth day in the hospital of La Paz the neurosurgeons decided they no longer needed to induce a coma nor go into my skull with a drill. The two broken bones in my cranium—the sphenoid ridge and the temporal lobe—expanded just enough to let my brain swell. While the swelling was still dangerous, my stabilization was safe enough to be airlifted back to Arizona. The doctors discussed the options with Joseph. Commercial jetliners were out; their altitude unsafe for a healing brain. But a medevac plane flying at less than ten thousand feet was okay. Paying for such a plane, however, was another story.

As I lay semi-vegetablish in the intensive care unit at Salvatierra, drifting in an out of coherence, Joseph sat by my side coordinating plans on how to get me back to Tucson. As I had only known Joseph for a few weeks, he knew *a little bit* about my pro cycling life, but had no idea how underfunded and downright shady the sport could be. Especially with team management and injured athletes. Basing his knowledge on men's professional sports, Joseph was confident my team would get me back to the States. After all, what pro sports team leaves their injured athlete down on the field? So when Joseph called the manager of Cylance Pro Cycling to help him arrange my transportation back to Arizona, he was shocked to hear the reply.

"Technically, Kathryn wasn't racing for Cylance in Mexico," Omer said. She was guest-riding for a different team."

Luckily, before the accident, I mentioned to Joseph how Cylance had not raced me for the three months. How they asked me to prove myself by racing in Mexico. And with that, Joseph got a first-hand look at the disturbing side of women's professional cycling. Corruption was afoot. Omer's shirking responsibility didn't sit well with Joseph.

"Are you fucking kidding me?!" Joseph bellowed. "You're gonna leave your athlete hospitalized in a foreign country because she wore a different jersey that day? After you and Manel suggested she race here? No! What kind of team does this?! I'm onto you, Omer. This won't look good."

Of course, bellowing phone calls, team politics and airplane charters had zero impact on my state of mind. All I knew was that green Jell-O jiggled, fuzzy blankets felt warm and apparently I fell down in a bike race. *Geez, I must have broken my arm again.* For the first two weeks, that's why I believed I was in the hospital.

Joseph kept making calls. At the very minimum, chartering a medevac plane to cover the ninety-minute flight time between La Paz and Tucson cost $18,000. My welfare insurance definitely didn't cover international charters. Driving was not an option with my need for drip medications. The next day, Omer called Joseph back. Perhaps the risk of Cylance looking bad in the media for leaving a teammate stranded made an impact. Omer spoke with Stu McClure, the owner of the billion-dollar cyber security company and Cylance, Inc. footed the bill for the medevac flight.

Five days after the crash, I was airlifted to University Medical Center in Tucson. Swaddled in the fuzzy blanket donated by Annet Rios, sister of my Mexican teammate, Jenny Rios, I remember very little of the flight from La Paz except feeling safe, warm and cared for by saintly people I barely knew.

It would be months—no, years—until I could properly articulate my gratitude for those who looked after me in Mexico. April 8, 2016 marked the start of my second stay at three hospitals during the recovery journey. But even more remarkable is what happened on April 7.

Two months before smacking my skull on foreign pavement, the Homestretch Foundation plans were in the midst of solidifying. My business partner, Tom, and I submitted the official nonprofit paperwork, registered all necessary domains, trademarks, rights and the tedious tasks of general business set-up. In early March, I found the perfect residence for our facility. Scouring the northeast neighborhoods of Tucson, largely considered the best training grounds for road cycling, I found a property for sale that had one main residence and two guesthouses. In fact, I'd ridden by it for years, the *For Sale* sign swinging near the bike lane on Tanque Verde just down the street from my father's apartment. I loved that this place was within walking distance of Dad. What the sign didn't show was that this place was a venerable compound, in the non-creepiest way! The home was original, lovely and also within walking distance to grocery stores. An important logistic of Homestretch, as we knew our foreign residents would not have cars.

The owner of the house was in her eighties, and so too was the décor. Giant chandeliers, shag carpeting, decorative columns and evidence of hoarding greeted us when we first visited the property.

"Oh, hell no," Tom decreed, condemning the aesthetics.

"Oh, hell yes," I dissented, envisioning the potential.

Eventually, Tom saw what I did. Four bedrooms in the main house could sleep between six to eight athletes. One guest house for two pro cyclists. One guesthouse for the manager. All of it—3,000 square feet, two acres, five miles from Mt. Lemmon—for half a million. Tucson's extraordinarily inexpensive housing market was our wonderful ally. We put an offer in on the house and it was accepted. The Homestretch Foundation became a reality in the making. We were set to close on April 7, 2016.

Dates, calendars and time were not concepts I could comprehend on April 7. The swelling in my brain was still severe. Enough to prohibit predictions of recovery. Would I live? That seemed mostly possible. Would I be the same person? Completely unanswerable on that date. Which is why it remains both astonishing if not mind-boggling that Tom went ahead and signed the closing papers on the Homestretch Foundation house anyway. Had the situation been reversed and I were the one with a business partner besieged by a severe brain injury where the outcome was yet unknown, I would not sign legal paperwork to continue such a project. *Oh hell no*, would be my first thought. Tom dissented this time, and chose the *Oh hell yes*. When I asked him many months later why he committed to investing in the property, his answer made my eyes well.

"I had to believe that you and your brain were going to be okay in the long run. I knew how much you wanted this," Tom said, in a matter-of-fact tone, adding, "If things went the wrong way and you didn't survive, then we would have named the Homestretch after you." *Gaaaahhhhh!* I was moved to tears. Also, laughter. Tom's factual tone struck me as wonderfully humorous. He is an All Business All The Time kind of guy, scoring very high on the get-shit-done spectrum but very low on the emotive scale. To him, it was business-as-usual to proceed regardless of his partner's brain status. To me, it ran deeper. The thought *anything* might be named after me if I died... that struck me to my core. The last two years were so rife with feeling worthless, difficult, unlovable and just about every other negative adjective on The List, that I was certain most people would sigh *good riddance!* rather than name something after me. April 7 wasn't just the date we secured the Homestretch. It marked the date of an awareness that perhaps people actually did care about me. I wouldn't know how many others cared for a few more months, but I did learn this that day: There are people in our corner supporting us, even if we don't know it or believe it.

May we all have our own April 7. May all of us who struggle with demons and self-worth someday realize there are others who believe in us even when we don't believe in ourselves. Find them, seek them, thank them. Preferably before falling upon your head.

48

RAGE AND REMEMBERING

A t University Medical Center in Tucson, April 7, 2016 came and went without distinction. What I was very aware of, so I'm told, were the nurses coming and going through my ICU room every thirty minutes. [116] Apparently I did not like this one bit. As the nurses checked my vitals and monitored the various drips of morphine and medicines, I screamed insults and questions clearly steeped in fear, confusion and the strange labyrinth of brain distortion. *Fuck you, nurse! What are you doing to me? Why am I here!? You're hurting me!* After my numerous attempts of pulling the IVs from my arms and electrodes from my head—which caught on my hair, leading to more foul streams of screaming—I was restrained, eventually passing out, ceasing all horrible diatribes on the angelic nurses and doctors of brain trauma. Bless those souls. May there be a special place in the Universe for all caregivers to the mentally infirm. You are deities and deserve to be treated so.

In my muddled cosmos, however, nurses remained scary entities. Despite the fact they answered me every millionth time I asked why or where I was, none of the answers stuck in my memory. Here's what did stick. Collarbones. Voice recordings. Friends. Periods. Wandering.

My right collarbone fractured in the crash and likely helped save my life. The blunt force of impact was so intense it broke my skull twice, but that could have resulted in a more severe head injury had my collarbone not absorbed the shock first. While in Mexico, the brain swelling was too intense for collarbone surgery. During my second week of residency at UMC, I was wheeled away for collarbone

---

[116] All pages about my hospital days were made possible by the journals and stories relayed by my father, friends and Joseph. I am forever thankful for their notes and memories. Lifelong apologies if I ever yelled nonsense at my loved ones during that time.

reconstruction. Apparently, I serenaded the surgeon on the gurney to the operating room. *I know you... I knooww yoooou! La la la.* I did not know him, nor do I remember singing, but I do remember being fascinated by the x-ray of a titanium plate in my clavicle. Eight screws, seven of which bore straight down. One set at an angle, which my confused state did not appreciate. I was quite certain the doctor made a mistake and dropped one screw into the abyss of my shoulder cavity. The nurses assured me the crooked screw was supposed to be that way; the angle held the bone exactly where it needed to be, it just looked funny on the two-dimensional x-ray. I didn't understand and simply added it to my list of things to yell at the nurses. I would later come to see this collarbone plate with the errant screw as the perfect mirror of my life: On the straightforward path of stability, sometimes it's important to take a left turn.

On my ninth day in the hospital, a psychologist specializing in brain injuries came to see how my mind was recuperating. I do not recall this visit, but I do have a transcript of our rather informative chat. Joseph decided to audio record our meeting. Whether the doctor timed her visit directly after an influx of daily medications hit my system, I will never know. What I do know is some deep-seated, pent-up anger, hostility and vocabulary remained buried within and decided to come out to play that day.

First the doctor asked my name, date, and a few basic math equations like two plus two and my ability to count backward. Despite the fact I took remedial math from fourth grade through high school, I sailed through that part of her exam. Even nailed *one hundred minus seven is? 93!* on my very first try. When she asked me to solve ninety-three minus seven, I gave a very solid answer of "Eightywhatever." The confidence in my voice was both impressive and worrisome. When we switched from numbers to letters, things got interesting.

"Repeat after me," the doctor said, annunciating clearly and slowly. "*The cat always hid under the couch when the dogs ran around.*"

"The cat always hit the couch where under the dog in the room!" I repeated with self-assurance.

"Kathryn, in sixty seconds, I want you to name as many words as you can think of that begin with the letter F," she instructed, "Ok, beg—" I cut her off and dove right in.

Fox, fish, fork, friend... were not on my list. In my dazed, semi-coherence my steam train of broken thoughts gathered speed and barreled straight into the tunnel of F-bombs. *Fucking, Fuck this, fuck that* went into repeat mode and the tone of my voice grew with agitation as my head pieced together bits of apolitically correct creations—*Fucktard! Flaming fuckity! Fuck, fuck, fuck!*—then I deviated on a rant of my aching collarbone. Joseph jumped in, steering back to the F focus.

"Any other F words you can think of?" he asked, assisting the doctor. Thinking hard for a moment, I finalized my F soliloquy with a nod toward my senior editor days at ESPN.

"*Fact-check*!" I snarled.

We weren't quite done with brain games. Moving on to reasoning and categorization, the doctor asked how a banana and an orange are similar. I swiftly solved they're both fruit. When she asked how a train and bicycle are similar, I quickly explained they're *not* similar at all, trains and bicycles are very, very different, lady. What's funny now but worrisome then was the tone of utter condescension in my voice. Like the doctor was stupid for thinking trains and bicycles were similar. (She wanted me to say they were modes of transportation.) When she asked how watches and rulers are similar, I assured her "those tools are for people who don't know how things work." When she asked me if I recalled the three words she told me to remember in the beginning of our session—a color, a flower and a body part—I could not remember *red* or *daisy*, but the body part I definitely knew.

"Somebody's head fell off!" I declared with certainty. No. The correct answer was *hand*. Whatever. Fuck that, fucktard. I felt pretty good about the quiz. For every reply, the doctor never laughed nor broke character. She simply affirmed, "Okay!" to all my responses, with a positive intonation like I'd taught her something. God bless the research staff of brain injuries.

Months later, Joseph replayed the recording for me and I wept with tears of cringe-worthy merriment. How strange and surreal to listen to an unfamiliar version yourself. Damn, there was a lot of anger swimming around in that brain of mine and I both loved and hated listening the recording. Hearing my father and Joseph snickering in the background makes me laugh to this day, but it also reminds me how horrifying it was for my loved ones at the time. I can only imagine my eighty-year old dad sitting there envisioning his foul-mouthed, angry, invalid daughter living on his couch for the rest of his life, rendering him to a caretaking role. I bet he had some F-bombs of his own.

While I have slight recollection of visitors who came to see me, my longtime confidant, Marilyn Chychota, won the gold medal of Kindness, Patience & Gross Bravery. She was there the moment my medevac plane landed in Tucson. After fifteen years of close friendship, Marilyn knew the passcode on my phone, often chiding me for its unsafe simplicity. The nurses and my father wisely kept my phone away from me in the hospital. It was Marilyn who logged into my Facebook account to let people know I was alive and recovering. It was Marilyn who held my hand and answered the same questions over and over again about where I was and what happened. Marilyn was also present the day I put my hand between my legs, retracted it with blood and screamed at bloody-murder-decibel-level that I was hemorrhaging to death.

I cannot imagine what it was like to explain the menstrual cycle to a 40-year-old woman with a brain injury, but Marilyn did so gently and calmly, promising that I wasn't dying. But, just like cats hitting the couch when a dog is under room, I didn't really understand what Marilyn was saying. When she returned with granny panties from Walgreens and helped change my maxi-pads for five days, I felt safe enough in Marilyn's presence to understand that whatever the fuckity fuck was happening between my legs, at least I would not die alone. Friends like this deserve bronze statues. Someday I will commission one for Marilyn.

After ten days at UMC, I was transferred to St. Joseph's Hospital on the east side of Tucson to begin my third residency of brain recovery. No more IVs, restraints or ICU units. Still on anti-seizure drugs and other stabilizers, I was finally able to walk to the bathroom. With guidance. This seemed a huge step forward. The focus at St. Joe's revolved around charting my mental acuity. I filled out multiple choice tests and baked brownies in a special kitchen built for patients recovering from brain injuries, where doctors observe whether patients are able to follow basic instructions and do simple tasks. After acing the brownies test, I was sure I was ready to go home. My awareness and memory seemed perfect. Nearly three weeks passed since the accident, and I wanted desperately to be out of the hospital. I wanted to go home. I began to get surly about it. *I am fine, fine, fine. See? Look! I can walk, eat, sleep, think and bake desserts all by myself. Let me go home!* After a week at St. Joe's I was released to my father's care.

Under doctor's orders, anti-seizure medication (Keppra) continued for the next two months. I slept eleven hours a night and took lengthy afternoon naps as my brain undertook the arduous journey of rebuilding. Screen-time was limited to an hour a day, which was fine with me. My brain did not enjoy rapidly moving screens filled with pixels and brightness. Other than walking, no physical activity yet. Certainly not bike riding. Balance was an issue and my head, hip, face and collarbone were still healing from impact. While my heart desperately wanted to ride, my brain luckily replaced this impulse with a penchant for sleeping.

Days drifted by. Dozing on my dad's couch my body settled into rest and recovery. I was now aware I'd endured a serious crash and sustained a traumatic brain injury. When friends visited I noticed they studied me very, very closely. Looking deep into my eyes, enunciating slowly, asking *how…are…you…doing?* then bracing for a Very Different Kathryn to respond. But I didn't want to be different or strange. I wanted to be the Same Weird Kathryn I was before the crash. Life experiences change us of all, though. Sometimes, as I eventually learned, we even become two "Catherines."

One day in mid-May, my father and Joseph sat down with me to explain exactly what happened after the crash in Mexico. My eyes widened as I peppered them with questions. *Tell me everything! How did Joseph get down to La Paz? How did you even learn about what happened?*

Joseph explained. After two weeks of our voracious texting habit, he thought it was odd not to hear from me after the race. After many hours passed, he checked Facebook and saw the ominous post from my teammate, Dani, on my cyber-wall: "*We are praying for you.*" Joseph tracked down my teammate. After connecting with the race director, hospitals and doctors he bought a plane ticket that night. Two flights and a shuttle bus, Joseph was in La Paz the next morning. With a sleeping bag and mattress pad, he camped at the foot of my bed. The hospital was understaffed, so neurosurgeon Dr. Eduardo de la Vega asked Joseph to keep an eye on all my movements and report to him if and when anything happened.

"Here," Joseph said, opening his notebook and giving me a handwritten hospital form. "They had you listed as a Jane Doe until someone identified your race number and called in your name. Here's what they hung above your bed."

In green Sharpie, I was christened *Catherine Varziny* born on March 4, 1981. Catherine has a thousand spellings and Bertine/Varziny made sense to me, especially when hurriedly verbalized over a hospital phone. *B* and *V* sound similar in Spanish. Vowels at the end of words like *e* and *y* are often elongated.[117] But the birthday guess blew me away. I had a good laugh at the fact I appeared six years younger in the middle of a seizure. March 4 however, made a direct impact. That was the exact date St. Kitts and Nevis gave me citizenship in 2008. A date I held

---

[117] For clarity's sake, Bertine is pronounced ber-TEEN. Rhymes with Queen. Varziny is pronounced bar-ZEE-NEE. Rhymes with Thank You For Not Letting Me Die, Glorious Doctors of Salvatierra Hospital, Call Me Anything You Want.

very close to my heart. Wrote about it in *As Good As Gold*. *Always march forth in the direction of your dreams*. For the hospital to randomly assign March 4 as my birthday was pure luck and personal awesomeness.

My father then mentioned what a gift it was to have Joseph there to bring me home. At 80, things like last-minute plane tickets and countries where he didn't speak the language were not something he could have done alone. Telling me this, dad's voice broke. Hadn't yet occurred to me how frightening and difficult it was to watch this injury unfold from the perspective of a parent.

"You really fucking scared us," Dad said, smiling. "Please don't fall on your head again."

Slowly it sank in just how close to death I was. Overcome with gratitude, I dove into social media and searched for all the doctors and people who helped me in La Paz, hoping to thank each of them personally. Instead, I found something else: an awakening.

Looking back through social media timelines, there were posts everywhere. All over Twitter and Facebook and Google. Comments, questions, answers bouncing back and forth from friends and strangers across the world expressing concern, sending love and healing wishes. There were articles about the crash from VeloNews, Cyclingnews, local news and even BBC. My inboxes were full. From people I didn't even know. Something deep inside me unlocked and the tears came streaming down. Not misty, feel-good tears. A deluge of reckoning. A river of awareness. There were people in this world who actually *cared* about me.

They cared whether I lived or died. For the past two years, all the pain I shoved into my brain about worthlessness and emptiness swirled into such a tornado that it never even dawned on me that someone—or maybe even more than one person— would miss me if I weren't here. Depression is crafty that way. While I'd made baby steps of emotional progress since the divorce, the concept of being loved and missed by others was beyond my grasp. Until that moment.

"Dad," I sobbed. "*People care!*"

"No shit, honey," Dad said, bewildered. "Of course they do."

"Yeah, well, this is new shit to me," I blubbered.

Hot damn. It took breaking my head on the pavement and scrolling through the internet to lift the curtain of my near-demise and get a glimpse what lay behind: I affected people. They actually cared. It took almost dying to see I was loved. Under my shroud of depression, I got used to the darkness. Since my spouse didn't see much worth in me, how could anyone else? But there it was, in the posts, tweets, articles, emails, messages and comment sections of social media… people cared. I read all their words, every single comment. Sifting through the kindness, I could finally see I was loved despite my many broken parts.

From that moment on, the two cracks in my brain became metaphoric windows. One let the darkness out, one let the light in. Just like Leonard Cohen promised.[118] Now I had skylights in the stables of the Empties, sunlight on all my tempestuous beasts. They looked a lot less frightening now.

After the light rushed in that day, I put on my Big Girl Bravery Pants and wrote a public post about the crash being such a gift.

> "For two years, my Old Brain often wondered if anything it ever did truly mattered at all. Old Brain was hurting and couldn't see the beautiful support system of friends, strangers and loved ones. Then something crazy happened: I knocked my head so hard on the ground that everything emotionally painful in my head… changed. Apparently I left the Sad Pain of Old Brain on the Mexican road where I crashed. Or maybe in the emergency room? Wherever. I dunno. But it's gone! In the last two weeks of healing at home, New Brain grew in (or grew up) and said: *Kathryn, your friends were scared, sad and thought you had died or were dying. They sent you messages, texts, cards, emails and calls. They love you and/or care about you. They think your Old Brain and heart are worth it, even during all those years you didn't.* I read all your emails, comments and kindness over the past month and I am just so damn moved. Your kindness helped build me a New Brain. Thank you. I love you guys."

One day, a message came through Facebook from the man I was engaged to in my late-twenties. Our relationship sadly ended when his alcoholism did not. I mourned deeply for him and for us. While I eventually moved forward, the weight of silence remained. Definitely built its own stall in my demon stables. Eleven years passed and I never heard from him. But after the crash, he reached out. *Kathryn, I heard what happened, I've been meaning to contact you for years…* The beautiful closure of What Ifs and If Onlys finally came to rest. We wrote a few times and saw each other a year later at our college reunion. Kindness and compassion superseded all other emotion. Cracks and light, cracks and light. To this day we keep in touch. The stable stall, empty.

---

[118] Leonard Cohen's lyrics in "Anthem" proves true for all broken souls and cracked craniums: *There is a crack in everything / that's how the light gets in.* Interactive Reader Guide: Leonard Cohen's "Anthem"

Lying on the couch one day during the brain healing months, I gathered the courage to ask my dad if George ever got in touch while I was hospitalized. My father shook his head. George knew about the crash, as people who didn't know about our divorce reached out to him. Still, no call nor message came through the wires. Into this crack, I poured the light of all those who did reach out. Into this stable, I went and saddled up the beast of sadness and took it out for a quick trot, then put him back. I was getting the hang of this stable thing: Be sad, be hurt, be lonely. Take the beast out for a ride. Then put it back in the stable before darkness sets in.

Six weeks after the crash, I turned 41. Birthdays would forever become a celebration of Still Being Here as I reveled in the simple joy of having one at all. Still on Keppra, I was unable to drive so my dad and Joseph shuttled me around. I felt like a child, invalid and celebrity all at once. Most of my dates with Joseph were spent going for walks around parks with his dogs, and lying on a picnic blankets in the grass. Sunshine, walking and lounging. My brain liked that a lot.

My mind still struggled with loud volumes, competing noises (multiple discussions, indoor acoustics, etc), rapidly moving screens and fast-paced conversations. Meds made food taste like cardboard. My collarbone ached but not horribly. The scars on my face still looked like Harry Potter headbutted my right eye socket with his lightning-bolt forehead. Sleep was so abundant I proclaimed myself victor of the 2016 Napping World Championships. Emotions ran a bit willy-nilly, as was normal for TBI patients as brains found their way back together. Sometimes when typing, my brain came up with words and spellings that made no sense. But I understood these side effects were minor in the grand scheme of brain injuries.

By eight weeks, there were roughly four different trains of thought traversing the tracks in my head: *1) I Am Totally Fine And Everything's Great And I Want To Race Bikes NOW. 2) You Have Three Broken Bones and a TBI. Let's Calm The F#$% Down. 3) Breathe, Hug People, Be Patient. 4) Imma Take a Nap.* For the most part, things were settling into place.

When Joseph brought out a birthday cake with forty-one candles, memory brought me back one year before, when Clegg brought out an ice cream cake in my favorite flavor, mint chocolate chip. I smiled, wept and said thank you loud enough so both of them could hear.

49

Back in the Saddle

Two months after impact and finally weaned off the anti-seizure meds, I grew twitchy. My neurologists gave me permission to start moderate exercise, by which they meant fifteen minutes on a stationary trainer or spin bike. I was ecstatic. My father accompanied me to L.A. Fitness, casually walking by the spin bike studio every five minutes to make sure I didn't seizure and fall off. I survived and remained upright. As I turned the pedals a few minutes more each day, so too did motivation turn the cranks in my mind. I wanted to race again. But not to win. To say goodbye.

I already announced 2016 would be my last year of racing professionally, *before* I fell on my head, which gave me a lot of inner peace knowing the crash was not my reason for retiring. However, the fact my last race almost killed me didn't sit very well. I developed a plan. If my brain healed properly and my neurologists agreed, I wanted to race one more time. Not for victory. Not for ego. For closure. To end my career with something other than a brain injury.

The 2016 La Course by Tour de France was slated four months after my crash. Cylance Pro Cycling had qualified. My neurologist, Dr. Ryan Kretzer, was a cyclist himself and understood my desire to be there physically and emotionally. He said we needed to wait until the very end of June to see how the brain was doing. He called me into the office to see my MRI images. I had not yet seen a photo of the fractured temporal lobe and the sphenoid ridge, and was immediately mesmerized by the pizza slices.

There on the screen beneath the temporal fractures were two triangular images of impact. While I fell on my right side, the trauma sent my brain flying into the left side of my skull, then back again to hit the right wall. These triangles of trauma showed the damage of the impact.[119] Dr. Kretzer explained there are three levels of concussion. One being the least damage, three being the most severe.

"You were a four," Dr. Kretzer said, noting the term "concussion" didn't quite apply to this level of injury. "Because your skull broke twice, it allowed the brain to swell and expand. Technically, those breaks were helpful." Cracks and light! Cracks and light!

"If I were going to permit you to race again," Dr. Kretzer said, "The best option would be a single-day event where you already know the course and can safely remove yourself from the chaos of the final sprint. No short criteriums, no dangerous corners." I fully agreed. No need to go for the win. Being there was enough. Without being revived in the middle of the road.

"You cannot hit your head again, or…" his voice trailed off. I nodded solemnly, promising to do everything in my power to remain safe. The doctor gave me medical clearance to race one final event at the end of July.

With a surge of emotion, visions of La Course danced in my mind. To end my career at the race I/we created would bring consummate joy and closure. Not to mention, quite a bit of media exposure for Cylance Pro Cycling. With news sites following my recovery from the crash, many began asking if I would be at La Course. Surely Omer and Manel would find it favorable to send me there. So I asked. Only to receive an angry response from Omer that asking Manel to race La Course was disrespectful. That I was being difficult and aggressive. How dare I ask to race La Course after all Cylance did to fly me back from Mexico. Did I have any idea how expensive that was? Omer's tone inferred I was lucky to be on the team at all.

There would be no La Course by Tour de France for me. I had two choices: self-combust or let it go. My brain chose the latter. In late July, half the Cylance team was slated for La Course, half the team would be sent to Cascade Cycling Classic. In early July, I was sent a plane ticket for Bend, Oregon. Cascade would be my last race as a pro cyclist.

———

Despite being couch-ridden for nearly three months, my fitness came back very quickly in mid-July. After being an endurance athlete for nearly 30 years, the three-month rest was exactly what my body needed. Between physical therapy sessions at St. Joe's, gentle yoga with modified poses for broken bones, and massage therapy

---

[119] For scale of reference, if the human skull were an oblong pizza pie divided into eight slices, two of my slices were dropped on the floor.

for victims of sustained trauma, the doctors noted my accelerated physical/neurological progression. I was given permission to race.

As the chapter of closing my racing career neared, a new one was being written. Three months after the crash, I moved into the guesthouse of the future Homestretch Foundation—the property Tom closed on in Tucson while I drifted in and out of consciousness in Mexico. The business would launch in autumn, and I settled into my new living quarters in July 2016. A bedroom, bathroom, kitchen and living room. The casita seemed like a colossal palace after sharing my father's small apartment for two years. As I unpacked my storage unit an overwhelming sensation rushed forth. *Too much stuff.* In the haze of divorce, I saved everything I possibly could. But after two years of living with just the basics, I now understood possessions were anchors. At the end of the day, I moved everything that mattered into a 6ft x 4ft closet that would have made Marie Kondo jealous. I saved four empty suitcases and two plastic storage containers. Should there ever come a day my life unhinges again, I would be able to pack my life into these six things and happily live out of the trunk of my Prius.[120] But for now, I had a roof, a race and a path.

With an enormous box of team gear from my five years on the pro circuit, I drove down to El Grupo Youth Cycling and gave one kit to each of the girls. On the outside, cycling outfits were just a bunch of fabric and seams. But woven in, a quiet truth: *Go after your dreams, girls.* Each one of those kits represented a slap in the face to anyone who laughed/doubted a woman in her mid-thirties could ever turn professional in cycling. Watching teenage girls wear these kits was like watching an army of possibility storm the castle of inequity. Sometimes Lycra is the best armor. I smiled as the girls suited up. They didn't know the whole backstory of the pro team kits. They just knew I was really happy. We took a photo and it continues to give me greater joy than they will ever know.

The last item in my storage unit was the Jamis Xenith. My bicycle from Colavita. The one I wasn't prepared to part ways with when everything else was being taken away. Now I knew exactly where the bike had to go. But first, settling in.

---

[120] To this day, I show friends my closet and express gleefully, *"My closet fits in my car and so can I! I'll never be shelterless again isn't that awesome?!"* Most friends nod and say *uh-huh* politely, slightly concerned I'm fully prepared to live in a Prius.

50

The Importance of Turning Left

L eaving my father's apartment was equal parts emotional and humorous. Emotional, as the gift of spending two years with my dad was not lost on me. How lucky for any child to get to know a parent as an adult, to call them a friend and mentor. My dad was there through every nook and cranny of joy, devastation, depression and physical injury, weathering every unpredictable storm along with me. In dad's apartment, I crumbled, cried, rose, faltered, fell and rose again. On the couch, I slept, wept, hurt, healed, again and again and again. On the floor, I crunched, push-uped, stretched and drew plans for the Homestretch Foundation. Through the front door, I left for races, work, therapy and finally understood how lucky I was to come back through it every time. In that apartment with my dad, I was able to rebuild. To reflect. To regain. To heal. To grow. To find purpose. To finally believe I'd be ok. My father's kindness reminded me what truly matters in life: Help others. Especially when they fall down. Be the change that helps them rise.

I bawled like a child trying to thank my father for the present of who he is and all he did for me and how leaving the apartment was such a colossal step forward in a new dir—

"Hey, hey, hey," he soothed. "You're only moving a half-mile away. Remember?"

True. A mere walk away. Still, wanting to make sure we stayed in contact at least once a week, Dad and I began a tradition in 2016: Spin n' Din on Wednesday nights. For the next four years, we would meet at LA Fitness for spin class then go to out dinner. The presence of an active octogenarian spinning along right beside them was inspiring to the class, but my father's nature is far too humble to see it.

"But I'm so much slower than they are!" he lamented.

"Dad, no one cares about your speed," I argued. "Don't you see that?"

"I see an old fart," he quipped.

"Well, we don't!" I corrected. "Now, who's the vice president?"

"Aaron Burr!" Close enough. Fist-bumps, laughter, cycling together. Wednesdays were my favorite day.

On a sweltering July afternoon in Tucson, Tom visited the Homestretch from Seattle. Going over the paperwork, planning and renovations before our grand opening in the fall, we had worked together for about eight months by this point. Now that I had a brain functioning at 98 percent capacity, I finally had the courage to ask Tom a question left simmering on the backburner for quite some time.

"Tom, I have to ask you something," I said. "What makes a person reach out to an ESPN writer who *didn't* make the Olympics, then went into an unglamorous life of pro cycling, poverty and poking fingers at the patriarchy? Makes no sense to me. How could that possibly be someone you envision as a business partner?"

"Because you turned left," he said, as if that made perfect sense. It didn't. I asked for more information. Tom obliged. He explained he'd taken a very typical path in the American life; college, career, marriage, kids. Work, provide, save, insurance, 401k, investments. He'd taken all the right steps toward success. All the metaphorical right turns.

"Turning right is easy," he said, "but turning left is hard. No one knows what's out there. You turned left and took us all with you. I wanted to see what happened." I tried stifling a giggle, but failed. A full-blown laugh echoed forth. I told Tom it was rather amusing to me that a multimillionaire in high finance was sitting here telling a 41-year-old divorced woman making $25,000, eating a sandwich made from three-day-old Safeway precooked chicken, that her life was somehow worth following. *Left turn, indeed, buddy! Welcome to the gong show*!

At that point, Tom knew nothing of my personal life. Only what was published in books, articles and social media. He knew nothing of the Cerberus, stables, close calls with suicide or the devastation of divorce. But he was about to. The *Bicycling Magazine* article featuring all my vulnerabilities would be released in two weeks. Part of me wondered if too much personal information and the realities of my left-turn-life might cause Tom to turn right around and un-invest in Homestretch.

Shortly after settling into my new digs, *Bicycling Magazine* called. They were ready to publish the piece about my life in activism and wanted to shoot me for the cover in Tucson. I nearly fell over. *Me? On the cover?* I was certainly no fashion/fitness model, but was utterly honored they believed my journey worth telling. Let alone put my mug on the front. My mind had a blast envisioning the caption:

> *"Kathryn Bertine is a non-Olympian, non-model, non-millionaire, non-famous, 41-year-old woman with an asymmetrical face and a brain injury. But we put her on the cover anyway, because she did stuff, tried hard things and somehow survived. Hopefully others will see this and know they too can do hard, important stuff with their lives. Except the falling-on-your-head part. Don't do that."*

Photographers love early morning light so at five o' clock I rode between milepost 12 and 13 on Mt. Lemmon, with the stunning peaks of the Catalina Mountains on my right and the Tanque Verde valley below, as Jose Mandojana's camera clicked and whirred among the beautiful peaks. Two days beforehand, my bicycle arrived from customs in Mexico. Anticipating carbon fiber damage beyond repair, my hopes were low. Pulling the Cannondale frame from the box hope turned to amazement. This couldn't *possibly* be my bike… it was completely intact. A tiny scuff of the rubber hood of the right handlebar. A barely noticeable paint scratch the size of an ice cream sprinkle on the first "a" of Cannondale. That's it. The bicycle— and wheels—had zero structural damage! My skull had literally taken the brunt of the impact.

In the bottom of the bag was my yellow Mavic helmet. That too, unshattered. Just a small, shallow dent and cosmetic scratches as if the helmet maybe fell off a garage shelf. What was completely crushed were the sunglasses, which splintered into my face upon impact causing the bloody gash, facial lacerations and black eye.

Gone, however, were the shoes and pedals. To which I enquired about with Leni. Puzzled, told me he packed them. After some investigative work, Leni discovered "new shoes" on a local rider who helped pack the bike. *Keep 'em,* I thought. That's the very least I can give back to the all the people who helped me in La Paz. Besides, if my ginormous size ten women's feet fit some men, then hooray. Equality!

Back in the saddle of the unharmed Cannondale, a sense of steadiness and conviction rose with each pedal stroke. Something about this unbreakable bike levied courage within me. People began asking if riding outside brought flashbacks to the crash. Nope. Had I been hit by a car while racing, yes perhaps that would induce fear. But my accident was rider-error. Climbing up mountains on my beloved roads of Tucson brought only peace and joy. And a hunger to race once more. I couldn't wait to get to Bend.

Letting go of racing La Course finally settled in. Sometimes learning to unplan, unwant and unwish is a vital skill to our emotional wellbeing. All that mattered was the Big Picture: Where I raced didn't matter. Team director politics didn't matter. Being alive mattered. Moving forward mattered. Being able to close a chapter in this weird, wild journey of pro cycling, equality fighting, head crashing, life-or-death expedition mattered most. Standing on the start line of Cascade Cycling Classic was pure. Finally, it wasn't about winning, wanting or proving myself. It was about inner peace, acceptance, saying goodbye to racing. Sometimes in life, the start line is the win. I won big at Cascade.

Technically, my Cylance teammate Carmen Small won big, capturing the first stage victory.[121] My job as a domestique, along with Krista Doebel-Hickok and Erica Zaveta, was to help secure Carmen's place on the podium. What a gift it was to domestique one last time. What a gift it was to use my brain and body again. During the first three days, I rode at the front of the peloton. Rode at the back. Pacelined, attacked, drafted, went fast, went slow, shoved countless waterbottles down my jersey for Carmen. I watched amazing northwestern views of the Pacific Crest for miles upon miles. Exhaustion was there, too, but after brain injuries and broken bones, fatigue just tickles.

Tickles and tactics aside, the best part of Cascade was neither the start nor the finish. It was the people. The cracks and the light. Each day, riders from different teams—friends, competitors and women I've never met—sought me out and spoke kind words as we rolled along together: *Welcome back. Nice to see you. Happy you've healed. Glad you're still here.* Kristin Armstrong, too, even drifted through the peloton to find me. She shared stories about how she helped connect people to my father while everyone was trying to figure out how to help while I was in Mexico. Such conversations meant the world to me. While the awakening of comments on social media helped lift me to a higher place, the light through the cracks poured in much stronger now. With face to face communication, hands on

---

[121] Carmen would finish second overall to Olympic gold medalist Kristin Armstrong by the end of the five-day event.

my back, hugs coming in... to see support is one thing, to physically feel it is another.

Originally, my doctors cleared me to race *one* day. The five-day race of Cascade challenged this. No high-risk criteriums and dangerous corners, they warned. The first three days were long, endurance courses with little technical difficulty. On the fourth day, however, was the criterium. I stuck to my doctor's request to not race dangerous corners and bowed out of the race with my teammates' full permission and support. Carmen, Erica and Krista graciously looked me in the eye and said, "Good. Smart decision." I didn't care what Manel or Omer thought anymore. Fuck 'em. Listening to smart doctors, good-judgment teammates, and one's own brain must always be prioritized over team management. Rather than prove myself to those guys, I proved myself to me. *Ego roga, ego ingruat, iterum ego ruga.* I raced, I crashed, I raced again. That was enough. Comeback, closure, check.

The *Bicycling Magazine* article, originally slated for September, got pushed to July when the editors released it online before print. Lying in my futon bed at host housing in Cascade, my pulse skyrocketed with vulnerability as I read the piece Steve Friedman wrote. Terrified at the start, calmed by the middle, stable by the conclusion... The story was true and Friedman's creative license was kind. My background was accurate, my quotes correct and it was all out there in black and white. The activism. La Course. The divorce. The struggle. The near brush with suicide. It was all out there.[122] Nerves zipped and zinged through my psyche, soul and inbox. Messages began rolling in through social media and email, and it took a few days to gain the strength to I open them. Would I need to start a new List of Names Called? Would the Trolls outweigh the Kind? What, exactly, happens when we talk about the truth of standing up and speaking out? When we take off our masks and strip down to full authenticity?

---

[122] Interactive Reader Guide: *Bicycling Magazine*; Kathryn Bertine had it all figured out. Some people asked if I would change anything in the article. Only two small points. In the print piece, Steve Friedman uses the word "depression" liberally, and this would've been a perfect opportunity to highlight the many different branches. Situational, chronic, etc. Also, the final paragraph suggested "the future was hazy." This made me giggle. a) He knew about Homestretch Foundation. b) Everyone's future is hazy. The rest he got right and I'm incredibly thankful for Friedman's accurate portrayal and candidness.

Kindness happens. Humanity happens. Connection happens. When I finally mustered the courage to open emails and read comments, the good outweighed the bad by 99.9 percent. What struck me most were these six words so many readers used: Now I don't feel so alone. They wrote to me about their hopelessness, depression, despair, contemplations of death and how they felt like no one could possibly understand the level of hurt to which they sank... especially on the heels of divorce or loss of loved ones. That this article helped them. That if someone who appeared so strong, accomplished and as though they had their shit together also had the same demons and issues... then maybe they weren't so alone in this world.

All fear and regret I once had about doing the interview for this article flew straight out the window. If making others feel Not Alone is the end result, then vulnerability is truly worth the risk. Cracks and light!

When the print issue of *Bicycling Magazine* arrived in the mail, I nearly dropped it. Only one word ran across the front page; *Unstoppable*.[123] Four months ago, the more accurate title was *Unresponsive*. Time is crazy passage of luck, hope and healing. Better still was the image they selected. Rather than a posed headshot where women are often airbrushed, blow-dried and smiling, I rode my bike with a helmet and sunglasses. Well, smiling, too... because that's what I do. But rather than portray me in an outdated stereotype of femininity, *Bicycling Magazine* portrayed me climbing up a mountain as a pro athlete who just happened to be female. Bravo, editors. My heart soared. Maybe somewhere some little girl would see that not all cover models sit around looking pretty. Some of them stand and climb toward what they believe.

A few weeks later, I received a letter from Iraq. U.S. Army Chaplin CPT Owen Chandler received the magazine in a care package from his family. Not not knowing my address, Owen sent a beautiful, handwritten letter to El Grupo, hoping it would eventually reach me. It did. The tailwinds of Tucson are a powerful thing.

---

[123] Those who had a *Bicycling Magazine* subscription received a different cover than the one than the magazine on news racks. Same photo, but the store copy read *Strong! Bold! Fearless!* Fine by me, *Bicycling*. Thank you from the bottom of my heart.

14 Sep 2016 / Camp Taji, Iraq

Dear Ms. Bertine,

I am currently serving with the Army in Iraq and my wife sent me some of my *Bicycling* magazines. We live in Tucson and she told me there was a beautiful story about a rider from the area. I read the article; it was as my wife said: honestly beautiful. As the father of two beautiful, red-haired daughters, I cannot thank you enough for your strength, candidness and desire for life with meaning and equity. I am always looking for stories and people that I can point to in order to show my daughters deeper understandings of the power that exists within them. I hope one day their paths will be able to cross with yours. They have the opportunity for special futures because souls like yours created powerful tailwinds for them. I know that it did not come without great consequence to you. For that, I'm sorry, but know your story has inspired many.

Peace,

Owen R. Chandler

The light that poured through the cracks in receiving such a letter was immeasurable. Dawned on me, too, that little girls weren't the only ones who needed to see women on the cover of male-dominated sports magazines. Fathers, brothers, uncles and grandparents did as well. From documentaries to petitions, dads of daughters were the most powerful troops in my army of activism. They were the ones who best grasped the consequence of a future without equal opportunity. I wrote back to Owen, and asked if I could meet his girls someday when he returned from Iraq. Four years later we did. Rule of activism: whenever possible, meet some of your three billion daughters.

After the *Bicycling Magazine* issue circulated and the data was compiled on Steve Friedman's article, the statistics proved true: when we invest in women's visibility the return of investment doubles. The September 2016 issue was the best-selling issue of *Bicycling* that year, selling 20 percent more copies.

"It was clear that readers responded to a strong woman and inspiring message on the cover," said Leah Flickinger, executive editor. Unstoppable proof, indeed. Including women matters. Honesty matters. Vulnerability matters. Regardless of gender, when we share our authenticity, humans connect. Readers *want* truth. People *want* to know what really happens when we take left turns in life. No matter the subject, no matter the journey, we all want to know we're not the only broken ones out there.

51

Together We All Move Forward

In December of 2016, I officially retired from professional cycling and opened the doors of Homestretch Foundation, providing free housing to female professional athletes (and rising elites) struggling with the gender pay gap.[124] While the athletes live here for free, they must give back two hours of community/volunteer service each week. It's a beautiful thing to watch them absorb the reward of helping others.

This wasn't just about salary equity in professional sports. It was about creating a safe, tangible place to help others move forward. This house was a concrete reminder that standing up for women truly mattered. Figuratively and literally, no one could take this one away from me.

Eight athletes, selected through an application process, live at the house from one to seven months depending on their needs. In addition to rent-free accommodations, we supply our residents with connections and opportunities for their careers both on and off the bike. The mission is neat, tidy and succinct: Together we all move forward. And it's working. After years of lobbying the UCI on the gender pay gap, we won. As of 2020, all UCI Women's World Tour women's teams now have a base salary.

After five years, 70 athletes from 17 countries have come through our program.[125] Road racers, mountain bikers, track cyclists, cyclocross athletes and two Olympians so far, with an average age of 27. Donors cover the costs of our residence. The foundation is thriving. Our website has all the info. Well, not all of

---

[124] Interactive Reader Guide: Homestretch Foundation
[125] Afghanistan, Austria, Australia, Brazil, Canada, Denmark, England, Germany, Guatemala, Ireland, Kenya, Mexico, Netherlands, Scotland, South Africa, Sweden, United States.

it. There is no tab that says *Click here to learn how Homestretch built a beautiful stable for Kathryn's demons by helping other people thrive*!

I don't think I understood just how much peace activism and advocacy brought me until Homestretch was well underway. Nor did I truly understand the ripples of reach in creating change. Until 2019, when a Homestretch resident Daphne Karagianis told me a story.

"I was looking through some old photos and I found this," Daphne said, handing me a photo of the two of us from the sidelines of La Course by Tour de France in 2014. "I remember being at La Course and trying to find you like a crazy fan girl," she continued. "I found you, then I asked you for a photo. I'm sure you got a lot of this that day, so you might not remember. But it was a big moment for me. Crazy to stumble upon this now, and I get to pinch myself and know that you're now my friend."

My eyes welled up immediately. Wait. The woman from Chicago who flew all the way to Paris for La Course. The one who asked if I was nervous. We took a selfie. Yes, yes! My demons were at their growliest in 2014 and it never dawned on me a young woman just starting her quest toward pro cycling would consider me someone worthy of tracking down and taking a selfie. (Nor did she write this in her Homestretch application.) Four years later Daphne was selected as one of our first residents at Homestretch Foundation. A year after that, she signed her first professional contract. Five years after our photo on the Champs-Élysées, I understood the power of reach. With tears and joy, I told Daphne she couldn't possibly know how much her story meant to me, and if my demons of Self-Worth ever get antsy in the stables, I will show them our photo, shining its glorious light through the cracks till they shut the fuck up.

The ripple of reach is real. Happening all around us, even when we can't see its rings. Perhaps we're aware of people who motivate *us*, but rarely do we notice that perhaps *our* ripples reach others, too. Pause. Look around. Reach is as strong as it is silent. Accept incoming ripples, and be the rock to cause new ones. Make those ripples count for something. We don't have to be the one making films, petitions, races or foundations. Supporting those who do makes the biggest ripples of all.

Ripples, reach, current. In my mid-40s, I see clearly now how much connection matters. Society loves dismissing individuals. But they can't ignore the masses. To stand up and fight for what we believe is important, but the most vital ingredient of progress is human connection and working with others. When we bring others along on the journey, incredible things happen. The truth is plain as day: *Together* we all move forward.

In the end, connection, togetherness, authenticity, vulnerability and standing up for what we believe will always, always win. Seven years of demons, stables, cracks and light, I finally know the answer to the question every activist endures. Everything we endure to stand up and fight for what we believe... is it worth it? Yes. The struggle is worth the journey. I'd do it again if I had to. All of it, all of it. Peace comes when we can say the same thing to our past and future; *I am ready for everything you bring*.

Epilogue/Spillogy

Ok, maybe one more list. After seven years in activism, each of these sections could have been their own book. There are there are a few loose ends to tie up in this epilogue. Or rather, spillogy. A term my brain created after the crash. With squeamish delight, I kept a new list during brain recovery: Words That Made Perfect Sense In My Brain But My Hands Typed Them Differently. My brain would think one thing, but my hands typed something else. Neuroscientists say these short-wirings are normal after a TBI, not to worry. The misspellings happen less frequently now five years post-crash but these are my Top Four favorites.

My brain thought Chicken and Egg. My fingers typed Cocken.

My brain wanted Form-fitting. My fingers decreed Morfina.

My brain said Anonymous. My fingers announced MomEnough.

My brain requested Epilogue. My fingers negotiated Spillogy.

Welcome to the Spillogy. Life does indeed spill over from one phase to the next. Here are a few things that happened between 2017 and 2020 after the journey of activism…

On a warm winter Saturday in 2016, I pedaled up to a red light at the intersection of Broadway and Randolph in Tucson. That particular Saturday was a personal milestone, my last official day as a professional cyclist. But the symbolism skyrocketed into the stratosphere when I looked to my right as a cyclist rolled up. On the recumbent bicycle next to me was Gabby Giffords.

Seven years passed since the assassination attempt that lodged a bullet in her brain and took the lives of six other Tucsonans who had gathered at Gabby's beloved community meetings; Congresswoman on Your Corner. Not only did she miraculously survive, but she persisted. From women's rights to gun control, Gabby continues to speak out. Despite the physical and neurological hurdles of recovering from a brain injury, she rides her bike and trains every year for the El Tour de Tucson community ride. Now here she was, once again, my congresswoman on my corner.

I went into total fangirl mode, asking if I could shake her hand. Gabby kindly obliged. I mumbled some quick words about how inspiring she is to me but I didn't want to take up her time, so I said goodbye and thanked her. But if I'd had my thoughts composed, I would have told her this:

Gabby, you are far more than an inspiration. You're a game-changer and a life-changer, and you had a direct impact on me. On January 8, 2011, I was an out-of-work journalist holding down two part time jobs and a dream of professional cycling. I wrote a piece about the fateful shooting, Christina-Taylor Green's untimely passing and your unbelievable survival. That piece got me hired as a senior editor for ESPN. Which opened the doors for me to write about strong women. Which led to making a film about strong women. Which led to successfully lobbying for women to race at Tour de France. Which led to a public uprising, a personal downfall and physical devastation with my own brain. Oh, and the borrowed '98 Accord with a Gabby Giffords for Congress bumper sticker got me through the toughest stretch. Luck and time were in my favor. Gabby, I rose again, too. And like you, kept lobbying for what I believe. Who knew such doors of change and progress would open from a day marred by violence and loss? Not I, then. But now, yes. Hope hides in tragedy. Thank you for helping me find it.

To see Gabby and physically hold her hand... now I understood the most rewarding journeys are not the ones that travel right, left or straight, but the ones that come full circle. Gabby's ripple effect created my ripple effect. As she pedaled off, I wanted to yell, *Let's keep throwing stones!* Kept that one to myself, for general sanity reasons.

I still drive the used Prius I bought in 2015. In 2020, I affixed a bumper sticker. Not Gabby Giffords for Congress, but the next best thing. Her husband, Mark Kelly for U.S. Senate. Navy commander, NASA pilot, visionary leader.... Damn straight I donated, cheered and voted. Better still was fundraiser drive for Mark, where I met Roxanna and John Green, the parents of Christina-Taylor Green. I told them how their little girl played a significant role in my journey and that she was with me that day on the Champs-Élysées, swinging for the fences. Always will be.

Ah, the bike in storage. My beloved Team Colavita Jamis Xenith with the custom carbon paint and my name emblazoned on the top tube… the metaphorical diamond-encrusted golden Ferrari that trumpeted an angelic chorus of *Ahhhh!* when gazed upon. The fact I landed pro contract at all, let alone at 37, was an impossible anomaly in 2012. This bicycle was the crown jewel of a dream achieved. *I'm keeping you forever*, I whispered to the handlebars, which seemed a logical place for its ears.

When life unraveled, I slid my Jamis/Ferrari into the cracks of my storage unit. I wasn't ready to let her go. But something didn't feel right. Bikes are supposed to be honored, mounted and ridden. Not shelved, disassembled and hidden. Simultaneously, my dear friend and college rowing teammate, Jenna, was busy conquering breast cancer. She also loved cycling, and we found her the terrific, donated Serotta in 2015… unfortunately, the bicycle happened to be extremely heavy. Lead-dipped-in-lead heavy. The idea of Jenna riding something that weighed her down when she was fighting the weight of cancer just wasn't ok. I sent her the Jamis/Ferrari. She earned it far more than I. *Keep her safe*, I whispered. Swear I heard the derailleur click an affirmative. Jenna and her beautiful family came to visit me a few years afterward. Nothing gave me greater joy than seeing her ride the bike that gave me my pro cycling dreams. Jenna was celebrating a much greater achievement: Five years in remission.

Moral: Impossible things happen. Hold your dreams close. Hold your friends closer. Keep memories forever. Let tangibles go. Give, give, give. Joy, peace and love will come barreling back with more power than a Ferrari will ever know.

———————

I still buy Colavita olive oil and pasta. Always will. Despite the managerial angst of others, Profaci gave me my pro cycling dream. For all the behind-the-scenes woes of ESPNW, I am thankful for ESPN. Without the original Olympic assignment, this journey of activism wouldn't have happened, nor the bond with my beloved St. Kitts and Nevis. I regret nothing from the lessons learned and opportunities created during these ESPN and Colavita years. ASO and UCI have made a few progressive steps but are still in desperate need of change. I will continue to call out their inequity, flaws and issues. Join me.

———————

Joseph and I remain close, connected friends. While our couplehood did not sustain, I am eternally thankful for all he did for me in Mexico. May everyone experience a relationship that, despite romantic end, results in lifelong love, peace and friendship. Namaste, dear Joseph.

I no longer post my relationship status online. Perhaps someday if I marry. Right now, it remains my personal boundary between vulnerability and privacy. May we all create the boundaries we need for our own authentic journeys.

Six months after falling on my head, I walked Marilyn down the aisle to her groom on the sandy beaches of Maui. Rule of life: surround yourself with friends who have your back, no matter what. Especially those who will change your maxi pads in the intensive care unit.

Tom and I still run the Homestretch Foundation. Like most activists, my greatest hope is to get a project up and running successfully, then step away. My ultimate dream is for all my activism projects to someday become irrelevant. To have "equal opportunity" become an outdated term. To hear someone say, *Remember when there was a house for women pro athletes because they were paid less?* It will happen someday. Sooner than later. We're in the homestretch.

Mystery B occasionally sends emails and donates to Homestretch Foundation. Nothing creepy ever happened. And no, B is not Tom. I checked.

On the first anniversary of my brain injury, I flew to La Paz, Mexico to thank the doctors who saved me and everyone who helped me. Dr. Argueta, Dr. De la Vega, the Salvatierra hospital staff and wonderful Leni... who took me to the site of the crash. Indeed, it matched perfectly where my memory dropped its curtain. Since I never got to finish the race that day in 2016, I brought running shoes with me in 2017. Gratitude and I ran the last mile and a quarter together, soaking up the sunshine, sea breeze and beauty of La Paz. Life doesn't always bring the finish lines we expect but we can all create our own closure.

In 2018, I pledged my brain to the Concussion Legacy Foundation.[126] Their incredible work studying brain trauma of athletes with will yield imperative data in

---

[126] Interactive Reader Guide: Concussion Legacy Foundation

the future. When my time is up on this planet, I'm certainly not gonna need that thing. If my weird squishy blob of fissures, cracks and fancy pizza helps unlock medical mysteries of the mind, please have at it, you awesome neurologists you.

Kelly Catlin, the teenage cyclist who signed our Tour de France petition then went on to win a silver medal in track cycling the 2016 Olympics, died by suicide in 2019 at age 23. She sustained a concussion beforehand. Other signs were there, too. Whether or not brain trauma was the reason, what matters most is this: We need to talk about suicide. There are far more people teetering on the edge than we realize. While it's not our role to be a net to catch the falling, we can do our part by checking in with friends and family. To ask, ask, ask… *How are you* really *doing*? Remember the pendulum effect. Sometimes the strongest struggle the most. Hug the strongest person you know. Ask your funniest friend how they're really doing. Tell those who've Got Their Shit Together, it's ok to come undone. Check in on the Happiest, their demons are often the deepest. Remind people you love them. Tell them they matter. Stay, stay, stay. We miss you, Kelly.

I still talk to Clegg sometimes. At yoga. Or hiking. Sitting around the house. Just to let him know I'm thinking of him. The year we opened Homestretch, his mother sent a donation check. It was not the amount but the memo that brought me to tears: *Kevin would want you to have this*. Staying connected with friends and family, our ripples of existence continue. I miss you, Major.

As for my demon stable, it's still there and always will be. But my Cerberai are smaller because I choose not to feed the ones that bark the loudest. It's working. When they growl, I saddle up and let wonder take the reins.

When I moved into the guesthouse at Homestretch Foundation, a cat kept showing up on the porch. A Tortoiseshell breed. Just like Grizzy. Every day she sat on the porch, stared me down and meowed persistently, as if to say, *"I live here!"* Neighbors clued me in. She was abandoned by the previous renter. Omg, my spirit animal. I took her in and named her Persistence. The best things happen when we keep showing up. Percy and I are forever in love.

Sure enough, six years after Pascal and I sat down to a meeting with the Dubai Sports Council in 2014, the Ladies Tour of Dubai debuted in 2020.[127] Four days of racing, just like the men's Tour of Dubai. Better still, our Homestretch resident Callie Swan raced the event with her Canadian pro team. While there, Callie and Pascale became good friends. My inner activist and retired pro racer vicariously lived happily ever after.

Marianne Vos continues to race professionally and use her voice for change. Chrissie Wellington advocates for grassroots sports with Park Run. Emma Pooley races multisport events for fun, but only events where men and women get to race the same course. Her feisty spirit still remains, so too does her positivity.

"It delights me to see so many more women and girls out on bikes. As 51 percent of the world's population, women's purchasing power is growing, so the cycling world will have to recognize us," Emma said. "The demand is there." As for the ripples created, Le Tour Entier is thrilled to see others take up the torch and continue to improve the sport of cycling. The Cyclists' Alliance,[128] which focuses on women's rights in the pro peloton, is making a fantastic difference.

On May 18, 2020 my father passed away unexpectedly and my world shattered. My best friend, my lifelong rock, my favorite editor. I still don't have the words, but someday there will be many, many words. Perhaps a whole book of words. (This particular one wouldn't exist without him). We did get one last spin class in before his funeral.[129] I love and miss you so much, Dad. You are always there for me, still. Every day. Oh, and say hi to Burr and Fillmore. You're gonna love our new Vice President. Please keep watch over Harris.

---

[127] Interactive Reader Guide: Women's Tour of Dubai 2020
[128] Interactive Reader Guide: The Cyclists' Alliance
[129] Interactive Reader Guide: One Last Spin with Dad.

Appendix

An Activist's Manual

I would be remiss to leave readers without one more list: The 22 Golden Rules of Activism Learned Along the Way. For anyone heeding the call of standing up, speaking out, blazing trails and driving buses... here's a checklist. Go get 'em.

Accepting the Call. When we listen to our gut and decide to jump into the role of creating change, we must be prepared for a long journey. Not everyone will understand your mission. Change scares the pants off people. Especially traditionalists. Be prepared for how many people won't be on your side. Activism isn't all battle cries and frontlines. There's a ton of work behind the scenes. Never be so naive as to believe changing the world won't alter your personal universe. Heeding the call to do what's right is equal parts terrifying and exhilarating. Falling and rising. Resting and weeping. Leaping and lifting. There is no half-assing the call of activism. Either you're all in or not in at all. Once you're all in... hit the damn *send* button.

Know Your Why. Acknowledge the source of your drive. Why is it so important to you to see something change? Where does this drive come from? Dig really, really deep. Then really, really listen. This thing you are fighting for... why does it matter to you? Why should people trust *your* vision? Authenticity matters. If we don't know our *why*, we won't know our *how*.

Assemble a Team. ASO and UCI didn't acknowledge me when I reached out alone. *Half the Road* and *La Course by Tour de France* would not have happened without a team. Build a team. Keep it small. Divide the work. Conquer the mission. When it's *your* mission, be prepared to do the most work. The smartest leaders are not those with all the answers, but those who ask the right questions. To lead is to listen. Assemble people who will listen as much as they speak. We don't need fame and fortune to surround themselves with the right people. Remember the wise words of Margaret Meade: "A small group of thoughtful citizens can change the world."

Ask. Listen. Think. Plan. Act. Before taking public action (petitions, campaigns, etc) first ask the opposition for an opportunity to discuss plans *together*. Call. Email. Snail mail. Repeatedly ask for a private meeting first. Pro tip: Do not use "tagging" in social media as a way of asking. This is unprofessional and passive-aggressive. You want change? Call and write the opposition directly. If they don't respond after multiple attempts, *then* use their silence to your advantage on social media and petition platforms. But first ask, ask, ask. More than once. Some say, *Activists act!* No. Activists *ask*. Then listen. Then think. Then plan. Then act. Choosing the reverse order makes one a reactionist, not an activist.

Create a Plan. With Solutions. Perhaps the wisest slogan ever created is *Talk minus action equals shit*. Words are nothing without a plan of action. Plans show intent. Plans hold one accountable. Our Le Tour Entier website and manifesto were written before and during the launch of our petition. A storyboard of post-it notes preceded *Half the Road*. People might listen when you talk about the world's problems. But they won't stand up, fight or follow until we create plans and solutions to conquer the problems at hand. Do not ask for change until you have solutions planned in advance. When in doubt, grab kinesio tape, a poster and a stage. Stand.

Check Thy Ego. Plans that help the masses = activism. Plans that help you = egotism. Occasionally, people reach out to ask me, for example, how to raise $50,000 so they can bike across Europe "to inspire others." Whoa, hold up. Unless there's a direct mission connected, that's not activism. That's a vacation. Dubbing oneself "inspirational" should not be used as a marketing strategy. Asking and giving back must be equally weighted and mutually beneficial to one another. Yes, I wanted to race the Tour de France, but getting a race for women wasn't about me. In fact, I almost *didn't* race and was incredibly lucky to be added at the last minute! True activism is about what's best for all, not for one.

Bakeries, Pie and The Breadcrumb Conundrum. For all women and fellow minorities who embrace the call to activism, always leverage *full* equity. Had we launched a Tour de France petition calling for women to receive only part of the distance, the world would not have paid attention. Equal access means equal access. Build a bakery where everyone will get the same pie. Never settle—nor negotiate—for breadcrumbs. One day matters, but ask for *every day*. Acknowledge small gains, but never settle for breadcrumbs. Always fight for the whole pie. Equal opportunity is not served in slices.

Don't Break Ceilings. Remove Walls. "Breaking the glass ceiling" is the most used analogy of women making headway. Intended as a compliment, it's also a flawed analogy. To break a glass ceiling means we must walk amongst the shards. Instead of shards and brokenness, a far better way to eliminate the glass ceiling is to remove the walls. No walls, no ceiling. UCI, ASO, sexism, patriarchy, traditionalism... these were/are the walls. May the first goal of every activist be to identify the walls holding up each ceiling of injustice. Only then can we raze the walls of ignorance, irrelevance and outdatedness and replace them with pillars of progress. Pergolas are the perfect architecture for Progress; where ceilings are shelter, not cages, and ideas roam free. Repeat after me, dear activist: *I am not here to break glass ceilings. I am here to remove the walls. I am an architect of pergolas built with columns of justice, teamwork, opportunity and inclusion.*

Connect with Journalists, Media, Scientists and Statisticians. Once a plan for change is established and the mission mapped, get the media involved. Seek out and make friends with smart journalists and politicians. Local, national and international. Let the media and government know what you're doing and why it matters. Write well. Be professional. Keep the Big Picture front and center. In *Half the Road*, Cookson believed, "Women are slower." So we found an exercise physiologist to prove him wrong. Stats and data are imperative. Economic researcher Daam van Reeth of the Netherlands publishes stats on how women's cycling is watched more than men's in Europe. Now journalists are covering more women's races. All hail the vital trilogy of journalism, data and stats. Connect with these makers, movers and shakers.

Eliminate Should, Just and Sacrifice. How we portray campaigns for change is imperative. *Should* is one of the most passive-aggressive words in the dictionary. It hints at the idea of change, but places no action or initiative. Which campaign would you support? a) *ASO Should Allow Women to Race* or b) *ASO Must Provide Equal Opportunity.* Stop should-ing and start must-ing. Another word on the Least Persuasive list; *Just.* Women use it far too often. "I just think that..." "We just want equity..." When we eliminate *should* and *just*, we're stronger. *Do something, UCI* is a hell of a lot better than *UCI should just do something.* As for sacrifice, I urge activists (and pretty much all humans) to understand the difference between sacrifice and choice. When we step in front of a train to save someone else, that's sacrifice. When we decide to turn left when everyone else turns right, that's choice. As activists, we make a *choice* to stand for what we believe. Not a sacrifice. If you're gonna walk the walk of activism, own it. Eliminating should, just and sacrifice will make it a little clearer.

Goliath is a Person. Taking on dinosaurs, traditionalism and conglomerates isn't easy. But it *is* doable. In the story of David and Goliath, a young boy uses his slingshot to take down a towering beast. Case in point for creating change. We often look at giant corporations, laws and regulations as goliath entities. Out of reach. Inaccessible. But they're not. *People* run companies. *People* create laws. *People* are at the heart of every organization we wish to change. Where there's a pulse, there's possibility. Remember, nature didn't create inequity... people did. Which means we can change it. As long as we have voice and vision, we can get to any goliath. Mutually beneficial plans make the best slingshots.

Anticipate Ignorance and Embrace Opposition. At the start of my mission for gender equity in cycling, I naively believed everyone would think women racing the Tour de France is a great idea. Ignorance kicked my ass. Many people believed we were lobbying for women to race *against* men, rather than a separate field. Despite adding such clarifications into our manifesto, better still would've been anticipating such ignorance at the start. No matter how clear your mission might seem, ask yourself: *Would a kindergartener understand?* Then educate the masses as so. Educate with clarity and kindness, not condescension and anger. Even with education, there will still be opposition, largely from traditionalists who struggle to envision change. When opposition comes, use data, facts and science to back your point. If opposition turns to Trolldom, let it go. In a world where the majority believes only what they see, rather than what is possible, change is a hard path to carve. Activism is the relentless journey of bushwhacking through ignorance. Bring a machete, persistence and hope.

Responding to Critics, Rivals and Trolls. Always welcome criticism as a checkpoint. Critics provide opportunity for activists to evaluate their mission. Critics are an incredibly helpful tool to create a solid foundation. Let their doubt show an activist where to build reinforcements.

For example, when lobbying for an equal base salary in pro cycling, many critics said: *You can't have a base salary until the media promotes women.* Ah, the You-can't-achieve-X-until-Y argument. An activist, however, must prove how we can put Y before X if A, B and C are involved. The beauty of critics is that they remind us why activism is necessary. Every movement has critics. *Women playing tennis for money? Ridiculous! Women running a marathon? Their uteruses will fall out! Pro cyclists with base salaries? Every team will fold!* Having a well-mapped strategy will help counteract critics. Won't eliminate them, but establishing a website and manifesto can help redirect and educate critics.

Rivalry is an asset. Rivals are often those who strive for the same result but take a different form or path. Consider Lucy Stone. In 1866, Stone helped the American Equal Rights Association along with Susan B. Anthony and Elizabeth Cady Stanton. They all wanted the same thing; for women to vote. But they took different paths. Yet they formed an *alliance* as adversaries, because equality was on the line for all of them. Case in point, respect and embrace rivals. Build bridges to work toward the same goal, no matter who's on which path.

As for trolls, here's the golden rule: Don't respond. Nothing upsets a troll more than seeing they have zero effect on you. Critics and rivals are vital assets. Trolls are inconsequential nonsense. They all share one thing in common: internal fuel for an activist's fire. Onward!

Laugh. As much as possible. As my List of Names proved all too well, the public will sink their fangs into activists. When it comes to ignorance and fear, laugh as much as possible. I often joke that UCI and ASO don't allow women to race the same distances as men because *the women would never get back to the kitchen in time to cook dinner.* (Not everyone thinks that's funny. That's okay. I do.) Always keep a sense of humor. If we can't laugh at our targets for change, then the march toward equal opportunity becomes dangerously exhausting. Laughter is the unsung soldier in the ongoing battle for progress. Whenever possible, follow the wisdom of Oscar Wilde: "If you're going to tell people the truth, be funny or they'll kill you."

Identify Demons and Vulnerability. Laughter is one thing, but demons and vulnerability are something else. Within me, there is a pendulum between strength and sensitivity. Both run equally deep. Many activists will share these traits. Don't mask either. Don't slay your demons. Build a stable. Grab a saddle. Let them roam free and teach lessons. Stumbling will occur. It's okay to fall. Embrace vulnerability. Sprinkle it into your soul like emotional paprika. Activism isn't sexy. But truth is. Truth, hope and knowledge are the greatest tools we have to build just about anything. Yet wielding our power of vulnerability may be the greatest weapon of activism. You'll know it's working when you start defining vulnerability as strength instead of weakness.

Rest and Recover. For activists, rest is critical. As breathing has an inhale and an exhale, so too must the breath of every activist: Inhale doubt, exhale courage. Inhale rest, exhale action. Inhale vulnerability, exhale strength. Fight, fight. Rest, rest. Boundaries, boundaries. Be aware of compassion fatigue. This is a real thing. An extreme state of tension and preoccupation often associated with doing things that move the world forward. Caregivers, veterinarians, activists and others can all suffer compassion fatigue. When we won the victory of La Course by Tour de France, my mind spiraled when people said "just one day isn't enough." When activism and divorce coincided, oof. The dark shadows of self-worth and depression crept in. Had I rested, recovered, identified my demons and explored vulnerability sooner, that chapter of activism would be very, very different. Please rest, dear activists. Rest and recovery will only make you stronger.

Ask for help. Eventually I did. But not soon enough. I came far too close to the Exit Plan. I didn't know activism had a rock bottom. It does, if we're not careful. The best thing we can do when we hit rock bottom is not rise up, but dig down. Rise eventually, yes, but not upon impact. First dig. Scrape. Claw. Before we rise from the depths of our fall, we must sink our hands deep down and explore knotted roots of who we are. It can be a dark and tricky maze. When you get lost, asking for help is the best way out. If you stop feeling anything, ask immediately.

Everything Happens. Deal with it. Not everything will go smoothly on the journey of creating change. Some of it will just plain suck. Not everything happens for a reason. Sometimes things just plain happen. Shitty things, great things, weird things, right things, wrong things. Reasons and lessons are very different things. Things happening *to* us and things happening *for* us offer very different paths. Choose the latter. Learn the lessons. In the midst of tough times, instead of asking *Why me?* have the courage to ask *What's next?* Also, carry some proverbial Trident gum. When things don't measure up, tape it to the handlebars. Sometimes that's enough to keep going.

Support Other Women. An unfortunate truth presented itself when I stood up for women's rights. Not all women support women. Watch out for She-rannosaurus Wrex of the outdated dinosaur traditionalists. They are mean beasts. Luckily they have tiny arms. In the end, the tribe of women who *do* support women have the greatest reach. Women, whatever your mission, whatever your plan… support one another. Progress will be achieved faster and easier together.

Channel Your Katherines. Research and seek inspiration in those who came before you. In my research, I coincidentally found four Katherines and used them as the four pillars of my Progress pergola. Katharine Graham, Kathrine Switzer, Katie Hnida and Kathryn 'Tubby' Johnston. *Tonight we publish. Today we run. Tomorrow we play.* Whether we choose to be the rock or the ripples of creating change, each is as vital as the other. Every one of us can effect change by using our voice as a metaphorical newspaper. To speak is to publish, vote, run and play. All our ripples matter. When we meet traditionalists clinging so tightly to the comforts of the norm, let our brave, inner Katharine Graham look opposition in the eye and say, *tonight we publish.*

Redefine Victory. Rocky Balboa lost. No one really remembers that, though. We remember he won his dream of stepping into the ring. Rocky reminds us trying is what matters most. To become an activist, we must embrace our inner Rocky. We must remember that even if we don't get our proverbial 21 days at the Tour de France, all change begins with one day. That one day moves everyone forward. Stepping into the ring—and riding impermissible roads—defines true victory.

Embrace Fear and Wonder. Activism is one scary ride. When Rosa Parks sat down, she taught us we must "never be fearful about what you're doing when it's right." Putting ourselves on the frontlines of change is terrifying, but the greatest antidote to fear is action. Action begins with bold embrace of wonder. In our modern culture, we so often regard wonder with a hint of whimsy, childhood nostalgia. Ideas that float about in fantasy and make-believe. But rarely do we entwine reality and wonder into an instrument for change. Change happens when we start to wonder about our surroundings. Our patterns and traditions. When we question the way things are right now, we can unlock the doors of what may be. We are all untapped activists.

Gloria Steinem said, "If you find yourself drawn to an event against all logic, go. The universe is telling you something." Couldn't agree more. When you hear the call, go. Let your compass guide, your mind engage and your voice lead the way. Draw a damn good map, but prepare to bushwhack. Go. You got this. *There. Are. No. No ones.* The power to change this world is in no one's hands but our own.

Kathryn Bertine

There's no smiling while climbing! Except for team photo shoots. Especially when you're a 37-year-old who just signed her first pro contract. The early days of Colavita Pro Cycling 2012.

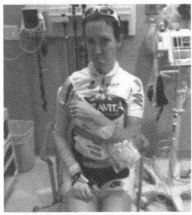

Snap goes the radius! Cyclist vs. stray dog. Kept it quiet from our director, so as not to endanger my chances of being cut from the team.

2007 U.S. National Championships in Seven Springs, PA. Left: clueless newbie rider with pro team aspirations. Right: Amy Dombroski kindly lets me share her tent.

© Courtesy of Amy D. Foundation

Amy Dombroski, always with us.

Left: Huub Harings, Dutch cyclocross champion and Tour de France rider of the 1960s. Right: SKN team mechanic.

Note: *Color photos at kathrynbertine.com/photos_stand*

On the bike for Colavita Pro Cycling in 2013. After being benched by Wynona, I often raced solo in men's events.

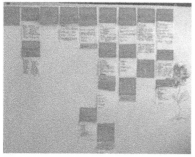

Half the Road as a fetus! Science might not tell you this, but Post-It Notes are the mitochondria of activism.

Behold, the Little Purple Bloggie! This $99 camera traveled in my pocket for two years as we made *Half the Road*. Because of LPB, I caught an interview with Patrick Dempsey.

This is how we edited *Half the Road* in Hood River, OR during 2013. No doubt cinematographer/editor Kevin Tokstad loved sharing an office with me barking sweaty orders from a turbo trainer.

Half the Road sold out premiere at The Loft Cinema, in Tucson, AZ in 2014. Seven pro cyclists, L to R: Nicky Wangsgard, Addy Albershardt, Alisha Welsh, Amber Pierce, me, Jade Wilcoxson, Robin Farina, Lauren Hall.

With Chrissie Wellington in Costa Rica. She gave one of the best interviews in *Half the Road*. We didn't always agree on everything during Le Tour Entier, but that's the strength of true friendship. It's healthy and normal to disagree and still love and respect one another.

Our official poster for *Half the Road*! Watching it hang in movie theaters gave me the best chills.

Much to the chagrin of outdated traditionalists who believe "women are slower," I garnered an overall win at the Fire Road 100 in 2013.

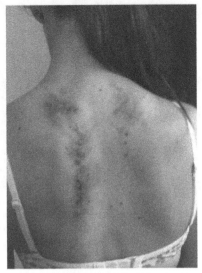

The massage from hell. Colavita Pro Cycling, 2013. My brain and heart still wince when I see this.

The 2013 UCI World Championships in Florence, Italy. When it comes to standing for equal opportunity, if you give me a stage, I will give you a show. The UCI fined me €50 for holding up an equal sign.

This is where we launched the ASO petition in 2013. I was in upstate New York. Didn't have wifi. Never underestimate the power of strong flowerbeds and kind neighbors.

Le Tour Entier founding members: me, Marianne Vos, Emma Pooley, Chrissie Wellington. Or, as the media often preferred, "Three world champions and that other lady." Here's to all the other space dust bus drivers out there... remember: We ALL have the power to create change. Never let anyone tell you different.

Le Tour Entier's secret meeting with ASO in 2013. L to R: Marianne Vos, Chrissie Wellington, me, Kristy Scrymgeour, Marion Clignet, Emma Pooley. Tracy Pinder is taking the photo.

@Anton Vos

Marianne Vos modeling our Equality Kit with Castelli. Our iconic kit now benefits the Homestretch Foundation. Want one? Let's be twins. Get it here: www.homestretchfoundation.org/store

The official logo of La Course by Tour de France... after we shot down their pink n' purple lipsticked version.

Day before La Course by Tour de France, Rochelle Gilmore surprised me with new jerseys. She added my St. Kitts and Nevis national champion stripes. A huge honor in cycling. I couldn't stop smile-crying.

The New York Times photo for their piece on La Couse by Tour de France. (The wrinkles on my jersey are a good indication of the stress-related weight deficit that summer). On the upside, NYT put a woman on the front page of Sports!

Storming down the Champs Elysees on July 27, 2014. An historic day as women race La Course by Tour de France. I am in there somewhere, equal parts healed and broken.

Rolling to the start line of La Course by Tour de France. The photo I hung on my laptop writing this book. All smiles and strength. All lies and heartache.

Always wave to your dreams. Sometimes they wave back. Rounding the Champs Elysees at La Course by Tour de France. Greatest flat tire of my life.

"Women's racing is boring," said no one in this century who isn't a dinosaur. Sprint finish at La Course by Tour de France. Vos takes the win, followed by Kirsten Wild and Leah Kirchmann.

With the indomitable Emma Pooley after La Course by Tour de France 2014. Racing in Paris is beautiful. And very, very dirty. A perfect metaphor for activism.

A stranger came up and asked for a selfie at La Course. Four years later, Daphne Karagianis became a pro cyclist and resident at Homestretch Foundation. Never underestimate the power of influence and reach.

Elbow Crater. Redlands, CA. 2015. Luckily my health care went into effect just days beforehand, thanks to Cyndi the Angel Accountant.

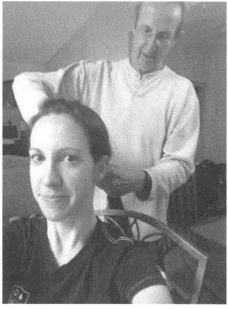

While my arm was in a cast healing from Elbow Crater, my dad made my ponytail every day. May every woman have a dad who helps her reach for the stars. And sometimes her hair. I totally won the dad lottery. Love you so much, PKB.

What? I'm just covering a sponsor logo. 2013 Caribbean Championships in Curacao. The race proved victorious, but perhaps this photo was an omen of more brokenness to come.

With the good folks of Change.org in NYC, 2015. Our petition was one of their most successful in 2013. Morgan Fletcher is third from left.

In 2015, I won the Caribbean Championships. What's far more impressive is that UCI President Brian Cookson did not strangle me when placing the medal around my neck. Thank you, Brian.

2015 Redlands teammate, Erica Greif. With us in spirit. Long may you ride.

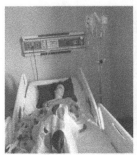

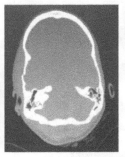

April 2016. La Paz, Mexico. I'll wake up three days later. Joseph is holding my hand. Pizza slices, collarbone screws, and cracks n' light from coup-contrecoup brain injury.

The sign on my hospital bed.
Catherine Varziny, March 4, 1981.

During recovery, I was allowed to ride inside. Dad and I started going to spin class together every Wednesday. We did it for four years. Sometimes we showed up wearing the same shirt. ♥

My last professional race, Cascade Classic 2016. L to R: me, Krista Doebel-Hickok, Erica Zaveta, Carmen Small. Cylance Pro Cycling.

At the end of the season, I gave away all my pro cycling kits to the girls of El Grupo Youth Cycling. This organization—and these kids— will always hold a special place in my heart.

As of 2021, Homestretch Foundation has helped 70 athletes from 16 countries. We also won our fight to have UCI create a base salary for Women's World Tour pro teams.

On the cover of *Bicycling Magazine*, September 2016. Honored and humbled.

The mirror with my La Course by Tour de France numbers and reminders of positive encouragement. I don't have such a hard time looking into it now.

Out for a ride one day in 2018, I met my Shero: The indefatigable Gabby Giffords. She didn't know then how much she played a role in my journey, but I told her in 2020. Now we're buddies. I'm forever her biggest fan.

Thank you for everything, Christina-Taylor Green and Robin Williams.

For this domestique, that day was July 27, 2014. There are no "no ones" in this world. We all have the power to create change. Go get your day. Let me know. I'll be cheering & waving. #TeamStand.

BIBLIOGRAPHY & REFERENCES

BOOKS

Best, Isabel. *Queens of Pain, Legends and Rebels of Cycling*. Rapha Press, 2018 p. 11-57.

Giles, Roger. *Women on the Move: The Forgotten Era of Women's Bicycle Racing*. University of Nebraska Press, 2018.

Graham, Katharine. Personal History. New York. Knopf, 1997.

Switzer, Kathrine. *Marathon Woman: Running the Race to Revolutionize Women's Sports*. De Capo Press, 2009.

WEBSITES & ONLINE RESOURCES

Associated Press. "Director Quiet on Women's Tour" *ESPN* July 16, 2013 http://www.espn.com/sports/endurance/tdf2013/story/_/id/9482341/ 2013-tour-de-france-director-say-female-riders

Aubrey, Jane. "Petition plans for women's Tour de France unrealistic, says Cookson." *Cyclingnews*. July 17, 2013 http://www.cyclingnews.com/news/petition-plans-for-womens-tour-de-france-unrealistic-says-cookson

Clemitson, Suze. "Celebrating Alfonsina Strada, the woman who cycled the Giro d'Italia." *The Guardian*. May 12, 2014 https://www.theguardian.com/sport/100-tours-100-tales/2014/may/12/alfonsina-strada-giro-italia-woman-grand-tour

Ferrie, Kevin. "How irascible, lovabie Glaswegian Jock Semple helped transform women's running at Boston Marathon." *The Herald Scotland*. April 14, 2017. https://www.heraldscotland.com/sport/other_sports/15226330.how-irascible-lovable-glaswegian-jock-semple-helped-transform-womens-running-at-boston-marathon/

Finley, Patrick. "Tucsonan Kathryn Bertine pushes for women's Tour de France." *Arizona Daily Star*. August 1, 2013. http://azstarnet.com/sports/patrick-finley-tucsonan-kathryn-bertine-pushes-for-women-s-tour/article_b2e65386-ede3-57e0-9813-a6f6daddb2d1.html

Jennings, Andrew. "Cycling boss JimPat McQuaid's Apartheid Secrets." *Sport & Politics*. Feb 28, 2013. https://www.jensweinreich.de/2013/02/28/cycling-boss-jimpat-mcquaids-apartheid-secrets/

Marshall, Ruth. "Women Cyclists Change Tour de France Forever. *The Washington Post.* July 22, 1984 https://www.washingtonpost.com/archive/sports/1984/07/22/women-cyclists-change-tour-de-france-forever/23b0e209-a4f3-47fd-8260-7d35a69fa189/

Masters, James. 'Half the Road': Are women cycling's second-class citizens?" CNN. July 25, 2013 https://www.cnn.com/2013/07/25/sport/cycling-women-tour-de-france/index.html

Nye, Peter Joffre. Doris Kopshy: America's First National Women's Champion. Bikeraceinfo.com https://www.bikeraceinfo.com/riderhistories/kopsky-doris.html

Schilken, Chuck. "Female cyclists start a petition to be included in the Tour de France." *Los Angeles Times.* July 13, 2013 http://www.latimes.com/sports/sportsnow/la-sp-sn-tour-de-france-women-20130712,0,6590493.story

Staff, BBC. "Cambridge University anti-women students 'confetti and rockets' digitized." *BBC News.* August 11, 2018. https://www.bbc.com/news/uk-england-cambridgeshire-45096690

Staff, Cyclingnews. "Hosking to apologize for remarks to McQuaid." *Cyclingnews.* Jan 2, 2012. https://www.cyclingnews.com/news/hosking-to-apologize-for-remarks-to-mcquaid/

Staff, The National UAE. "Dubai Sports Council budget rises to Dh442 Million." *The National UAE.* Jan 9, 2014 https://www.thenational.ae/uae/dubai-sports-council-budget-rises-to-dh442-million-1.326663

Staff, The Telegraph. "Eileen Gray, Cyclist – Obituary" *The Telegraph.* May 22, 2015. https://www.telegraph.co.uk/news/obituaries/11624291/Eileen-Gray-cyclist-obituary.html

Staff, VeloNews. "Top women pros say they deserve minimum-salary guarantee." *VeloNews.* 2011. https://www.velonews.com/2011/09/news/top-women-pros-say-they-deserve-minimum-salary-guarantee_193399

Stokes, Shane. "La Course is a stepping stone toward a women's Tour de France." *Velonation.* February 2, 2014. http://www.velonation.com/News/ID/16253/Bertine-New-La-Course-race-is-stepping-stone-towards-a-womens-Tour-de-France.aspx

Zellner, Xander. "Women want their own race at Tour de France." *USA Today.* July 17, 2013. http://www.usatoday.com/story/sports/cycling/2013/07/17/tour-de-france-women-petition-for-change/2530107/

ACKNOWLEDGEMENTS

When my agent first brought the book proposal for *Stand* to corporate publishers, they quickly shut it down. Over twenty responses from traditional publishing, every single one of them saying the same thing. *A book about women standing up and speaking out just won't sell. We'll pass.*

My gut wholeheartedly disagreed. After a year of trying to convince Traditional Corporate Publishers otherwise, I decided to self-publish and prove them wrong. Damn straight it matters when women—and all minorities—stand up, speak out and work together to move our world forward. If you're reading this, you either found it on Amazon, or I'm driving around the country and you bought it from the trunk of my decade-old Prius in a Safeway parking lot. Wherever you found *Stand,* thank you for proving advocacy, authenticity, patience, timing, memoirs, manuals and truth matter. Thank you for or being part of #TeamStand.

This book took three years to write and would not have happened without so many people mentioned in these chapters. My hero/father Peter K. Bertine, Tom Bailey, Marilyn Chychota, Lauren Hall, Amber Pierce, Dotsie Bausch, Eric Berman, Jo Roberts, Joseph Lauricella, Dr. Argueta, Dr. De la Vega, Dr. Ryan Kretzer, every member of The Shootout, every donor of *Half the Road*, every signer of the Tour de France petition, every spectator of La Course, every donor and resident of Homestretch Foundation. Shout out to the Tucson coffee shops where many chapters were written: Coffee X Change, Crave, Le Buzz, Cartel, Stella's, Brew'd. And of course, my father's den. Part of my soul lives in all of these places.

Going the route of self-publishing was, like everything else in this book, not a solo venture. #TeamStand made it happen together. Thank you, infinitum, to my incredible editor Emily Gindlesparger. Remember the terrific yoga instructor I mentioned? That was Emily. Yoga teacher by night, book editor by day. I like to think Clegg might've sent her my way. Namaste, dear Emily. My gifted copyeditor, Wendy E. Coulter, who brilliantly caught all the invisible errors an author's eye never sees. The amazing graphic designer Jennifer Vasko, who must be psychic, as she took the vision in my head (but made it better) and turned it into our striking cover. Gives me the best chills. Our vital tech guru, Thorsten Radde, who did all the nitty gritty of website work, book formatting, etc. Without his intelligence, this book would've remained a Word document. And to the indispensable Leslie Barrett and Marika Flatt of PR by the Book, who believed this book mattered even before reading it. You all made this book happen and my gratitude knows no bounds.

How do we thank history? There are not enough pages in the world to acknowledge and pay tribute to the women and men who blazed trails and drove Spacedust Buses so future generations could keep moving the equal opportunity dial forward. So many remain unknown, unnamed. Even though I don't know you, I see you. I feel you. You matter. Thank you.